News from Abroad

Eighteenth-Century Worlds

Series Editors:
Professor Eve Rosenhaft (Liverpool) and Dr Mark Towsey (Liverpool)

Eighteenth-Century Worlds promotes innovative new research in the political, social, economic, intellectual and cultural life of the 'long' eighteenth century (c.1650-c.1850), from a variety of historical, theoretical and critical perspectives. Monographs published in the series adopt international, comparative and/or interdisciplinary approaches to the global eighteenth century, in volumes that make the results of specialist research accessible to an informed, but not discipline-specific, audience.

News from Abroad

Letters Written by British Travellers
on the Grand Tour, 1728–71

Compiled and edited by
James T. Boulton and T. O. McLoughlin

LIVERPOOL UNIVERSITY PRESS

First published 2012 by
Liverpool University Press
4 Cambridge Street
Liverpool
L69 7ZU

Copyright © 2012 Liverpool University Press

The authors' rights have been asserted in accordance with the Copyright, Designs and Patents Act 1988.

All rights reserved. No part of this book may be reproduced, stored in a retrieval system, or transmitted, in any form or by any means, electronic, mechanical, photocopying, recording, or otherwise, without the prior written permission of the publisher.

British Library Cataloguing-in-Publication data
A British Library CIP record is available

ISBN 978-1-84631-850-4 *cased*

Typeset in Caslon by R. J. Footring Ltd, Derby
Printed and bound in the United States of America

Contents

Preface	vi
Illustrations	vii
Acknowledgements	viii
'Old Style' and 'New Style' Dating	ix
Map	x
Introduction: The Grand Tour	1
The Tourists and Their Letters	4
George Lyttelton (1709–73): Letters (1728–30)	23
Joseph Spence (1699–1768): Letters (1730–3)	81
James Boswell (1740–95): Letters (1764–6)	129
James Barry (1741–1806): Letters (1765–71)	169
Caroline Lennox (1723–74): Letters (1766–7)	213
Appendix A: The Hazards of Collecting Art on the Grand Tour	260
Appendix B: Advice to Travellers on the Grand Tour	270
Bibliography	278
Index	282

Preface

Fine travel writing in any century exists primarily in accounts by individual travellers recording their immediate personal responses to people, places, historic scenes, natural phenomena, seemingly strange diurnal activities and the like, which fascinate or repel, excite or instruct them. In the case of travellers on the Grand Tour, the immediacy of record was ensured by their addressing readers who were as eager to receive their intimacies as the writers to send them. Letters—the most intimate and direct form of written communication—were directed to individuals who were of great personal consequence to the senders: a parent, close relative, long-standing friend or patron who had a vivid existence in the writer's memory and imagination. Those imagined persons come alive to the modern reader: we cannot fail to create a multidimensional image of George Lyttelton's father or Joseph Spence's mother, Boswell's old friend Johnston, Barry's patron Edmund Burke, or Caroline Lennox's ennobled and much-loved sister Emilia. Their interests, anxieties, experiences and prejudices are readily deduced from letters written exclusively to them. Inevitably we become engaged in their concerns, as voyeurs perhaps—certainly as favourably-minded observers.

This volume, then, is not a guidebook for the Grand Tour. It provides an opportunity to explore the wide variety of motives, achievements and reactions of a diverse collection of specific individuals travelling. Their language is faithfully presented without modernisation or editorial interference, wherever possible direct from the actual autograph letters they sent.

Illustrations

George Lyttelton, 1st Baron Lyttelton; after Robert Dunkarton;   22
Benjamin West. Mezzotint, published 1774.
© National Portrait Gallery, London

Joseph Spence; after George Vertue; Isaac Whood. Line engraving, 1746.   80
© National Portrait Gallery, London

James Boswell; Sir Joshua Reynolds. Oil on canvas, 1785.   128
© National Portrait Gallery, London

James Barry; self-portrait. Oil on canvas, 1777.   168
© Victoria & Albert Museum, London

Lady Holland (Caroline Lennox); Allan Ramsay. Oil on canvas, 1766.   212
© Private collection, The Bridgeman Art Gallery, London

Acknowledgements

THE EDITORS wish to thank the following for help freely given: Ruthe Battestin, Jeremy Black, Harry Buglass, Brian Collins, Laura Dawkins, Suzanne Foster, James Harte, Martin Killeen, Heather Johnson, Avice-Claire McGovern, David Morrison, Colette O'Daly, Alvyn Pettersen, Joyce Purnell, Maria Singer, Zoë Stansell, Gordon Turnbull, Helen, Thomas, Joseph and especially Allan Wilcox.

'Old Style' and 'New Style' Dating

THE JULIAN CALENDAR—'Old Style' (OS)—was introduced by Julius Caesar in 45 BC; 'New Style' (NS) was based on the Gregorian calendar introduced by Pope Gregory III in 1582. The date of the adoption of NS in preference to OS varied from country to country. In England the change followed an Act of Parliament in March 1751; this decreed that the next 1 January should be the first day of 1752, and that 2 September 1752 should be followed by 14 September to eliminate the discrepancy between the two calendars. It became common in mid-century for correspondents to give both forms of date in their letters; where this occurs in letters printed here—as in the case of Joseph Spence—the writer's practice is strictly followed.

Principal places visited on the Grand Tour by travellers in this collection.
Map by Harry Buglass.

Introduction: The Grand Tour

The Grand Tour has in recent decades become the focus of much scholarly research and comment, which understandably treats it as a striking phenomenon, a significant cultural feature of eighteenth-century life. Scholars look, as it were, from the outside in. What this volume offers is a view from the inside. The travellers speak for themselves: each responded differently, was curious about different things, enjoyed different pleasures. The Tour emerges as a vast panorama of opportunities and experiences, far wider than any individual could take in. The point is all the more evident from the fact that none of these correspondents was writing with a view to publishing his or her letters; these have an immediacy unhampered or refined by thoughts of an eventual public readership. Spence did think of publishing, but nothing came of the idea. Others followed the fashion of disseminating their experiences to the general public. To publish one's letters meant shaping them as a corpus, endowing seemingly impromptu and personal letters with a kind of homogeneity, and providing a discursive unity. Such a volume could then be read and criticized as a crafted response to the Tour. For example William Beckford, who published his Tour letters as *Dreams, Waking Thoughts and Incidents* (1783), is said by one critic to illustrate 'the movement from North to South that the Tour entails'.[1] The letters in this collection are strictly 'familiar' and informal: that is part of their distinctive appeal.

One of the advantages of the informality of many of these letters is that they are full of detailed casual observations that catch the eye, or of unusual anecdotes. Lyttelton noticed the curious use of the ballot box during the election in Genoa and how easy it was to cheat (30 November 1729); he grows weary of losing money at cards, 'but tis no less certain that without them I shall soon be weary of Lorain. The Spirit of Codrill has possest the land; from Morning to Midnight there is nothing else in every house in town' (21 July 1728). Spence recounts how he nearly fell into a vat of wine:

---

1   Chloe Chard, *Pleasure and Guilt on the Grand Tour: Travel Writing and Imaginative Geography, 1600–1830* (Manchester: Manchester University Press, 1999), 14.

> I was rig[g]ed up a ladder that stood by the side of one to gape upon it; when—all at once—the ladder slips from under me, and in the hurry, I got hold of the brims and hung there. Had the Tub yeilded upon me, I shou'd at least have spoil'd my best Holyday Cloaths... (13 December 1732)

Boswell goes further than most, and is all the more interesting for it, in reflecting on the larger significance of what he notices. At Verona he visited the 'magnificent Amphitheatre':

> I have seen it put to a whimsical use this evening. In the *Arena* was erected a little Stage on which was acted an Opera Bouffé while the ancient rising seats were occupied by degenerate Italians. What a sad alteration time has made! Blackguards and effeminate Signori sit where the wise and brave and virt[u]ous of old bestowed their valuable applause. (23 July 1765)

The letters have glimpses of women's hairstyles, harvesting, the weather, and gossip. Italian women, writes Lennox from Naples, may be beautiful, but they are 'Noisy and Underbred, debauchd to a degree'. She goes on, 'Madame Gaetani tells me their Education is abominable, they are taught no one thing in their convents, not even to work, no musick which is the chief amusement here' (21 December 1766). This is the kind of detail that gives spice to accounts of the Tour.

As seen in Boswell, the letters are often interlaced with reflections on broader issues, particularly national characteristics. Lyttelton, young as he is, shows remarkably mature insights on what he regards as the degeneration of Europe: what he sees in Genoa prompts him to remark how 'the Modern Nobility is sunk in Ease and Sloth'; he bemoans 'the Decay of Learning' in Italy. His complaint of the 'Miseries abroad', meaning the plight of nations under oppressive rule, is a reminder that travellers repeatedly noted the absence of liberty so praised by poets and politicians at home. British visitors to the Continent took with them two underlying presumptions. The first was that, as a place to live, England was unquestionably preferable to anywhere on the Continent: as Spence puts it, 'indeed, tho' Italy be the Country for Sights, England is the Country to live in, for my money' (11 October 1732). The presumption brought with it the surprise at how little the general populace of the countries they passed through knew about England. Even the Italian Giuseppe Baretti, who had settled in England and was a friend of Boswell, was slightly shocked at how ignorant the run of Italians were:

> They have heard that the English do not believe the Pope to be infallible: of course they are not Christians. But what are they? No body knows for certain; but the English believe in transmigration, and that they shall be turned into some animal or other after death; mean while they are all Lords, and not men and women, but something else, no body knows what.

Such are the notions our low people have of the English; and what increases their absurdity is, that they see English travellers every day, who look as much like men as the Pope himself.[2]

The traveller's second presumption was that because Europe offered an engaging display of peoples, manners and culture that was certainly worth visiting, the experience would stimulate them to new ideas and bring them close to the sources of European culture. Much of what they saw would be educative in the sense that it would take them out of themselves and counteract any suggestion of a narrow or insular mind. As well as acquiring an understanding of how other nations conducted themselves, they would see for themselves the very places, architecture and art which had been the genesis of much of their own cultural heritage. Spence remarked, 'This is one of the pleasures of being at Rome, that you are continually seeing the very place and spot of ground, where some great thing or other was done, which one has so often admired before in reading their History.' (2 August 1732). Likewise Gibbon recalls, 'at the distance of twenty-five years, I can neither forget nor express the strong emotions which agitated my mind as I first approached and entered the *eternal city*. After a sleepless night, I trod, with a lofty step, the ruins of the Forum; each memorable spot where Romulus *stood*, or Tully spoke, or Caesar fell, was at once present to my eye'.[3] That was the tangible excitement of the Tour. The rider was the realization that Rome had fallen: Britain was now the home of those values once nurtured by Rome. Lyttelton encouraged Alexander Pope, 'Sing the land which yet alone can boast / The liberty corrupted Rome has lost'. Hence the eyes with which travellers saw this stimulating world were the eyes of Britons confident of their own moral viewpoint. Home was never far from their thoughts. Spence tells his mother that Dijon reminds him of Oxford: the public walks 'widen into a Circle, which serves here, in proper weather, as the Ring in Hide Park' (16 February 1731); 'the French women are not so beautiful as the English'; 'there's a great deal of difference between a Marquis in England, and a Marquis in France' (Spence, 2 July 1733). Britain was the moral yardstick.

---

2 Giuseppe Baretti, *A Journey from London to Genoa, through England, Portugal, Spain, and France*, 2 vols (London: Davies, 1770), i, 44.
3 Edward Gibbon, *Autobiography of Edward Gibbon* (New York: Turner and Hayden, 1846), 167.

The Tourists and Their Letters

Overview

An eighteenth-century guidebook for travellers on the Grand Tour starts with the remarks:

> Travelling, even in the remotest ages, was reckoned so useful a custom, as to be judged the only means of improving the understanding, and of acquiring a high degree of reputation... The first civilized nations had so exalted an idea of those who had been in foreign countries, that they honoured even such as made but short voyages, with the title of philosophers and conquerors.[4]

If the spirit of the Grand Tour could thus be traced back to the ancient Greeks, the concept and the term itself were relatively new. Its first use is often attributed to Richard Lassels (*c.*1603–68), a Catholic priest, who made the trip on several occasions as tutor to the sons of nobility; he died in Montpellier in France 'on what would heave been his sixth voyage to Italy'.[5] Among many other seventeenth-century travellers were Thomas Coryat (*c.*1577–1617), author of *Coryat's Crudities* (1611), the architect Inigo Jones (1573–1652), Thomas Hobbes (1588–1679), who went as tutor to the future Earl of Devonshire in 1614–15, and John Milton in 1638–9. William Bromley (1664–1732) added to a growing fashion by publishing an account of his journey, *Remarks in the Grand Tour of France and Italy. Perform'd by a Person of Quality, in the Year, 1691*, claiming with becoming modesty that 'when this Journal was writ, he had no Intentions of making it publick, and now is above the proposing to himself an Advantage thereby'.[6] The popularity of travel books by the early decades of

---

4 Thomas Nugent, Preface, *The Grand Tour, or, A Journey through the Netherlands, Germany, Italy and France*, 4 vols (London: A. Millar et al., 1756), i, i. This Preface replaced that in the 1749 edition.
5 Richard Lassels, (*c.*1603–68), Oxford Dictionary of National Biography (ODNB); his book, first published in Paris in 1670, was published in London the same year: *The Voyage of Italy, or A Compleat Journey through Italy* (London: John Starkey, 1670).
6 William Bromley, *Remarks in the Grand Tour of France and Italy: Perform'd by a Person of Quality, in the Year, 1691*, 2nd edn (London: John Nutt, 1705), 3.

the eighteenth century was such that Swift saw fit to satirise the vogue in his *Gulliver's Travels* (1726).

English, Scots and Irish, however, were by no means the only nationalities on the Grand Tour: Germans, French and Dutch (among others) made the cultural pilgrimage through Europe, ending up in Rome, all intent to learn about other cultures, to observe different social habits and political systems, and to marvel at the monuments of classical times and the renowned artworks of the Renaissance.[7] Guidebooks in various languages were available, with advice on what to see, what to avoid, and how to behave.[8] Travellers may have had different agendas — education, art, politics, natural philosophy, commerce — yet the bulk of those criss-crossing Europe on the Grand Tour were, by and large, from the nobility or professional classes. Invariably they saw themselves as more than just Tourists; a visit to Italy — to see St Peter's, to gaze on the sculptures of Michelangelo and the paintings of Raphael — was necessary for all 'who aspired to underwrite their authority as arbiters of taste'.[9] Thus 'improved', they were equipped to play their part in shaping their own country's cultural identity.

Although people all over Europe made the Tour, the phrase 'to make the Grand Tour' has an unambiguous resonance in English. The French phrase 'Le grand tour' can mean 'a long way round' in other contexts; 'Le tour d'Europe' has a general sense that does not necessarily take in Rome. The capital letters of 'Grand' and 'Tour' infuse the English term with an unmistakable sense of grandeur.

The Tour came into its own as a kind of cultural rite of passage for young British gentlemen in the eighteenth century. The typical young Tourist was in his early twenties, and after some years at Oxford or Cambridge spent a year or two travelling about Europe; the stops in Paris and Rome were *de rigueur*, and it was presumed there would be time to acquire a passing ability in French (and possibly Italian), mix with high society, and supplement his book-learning of classical authors with a first-hand view of scenery and places mentioned by Virgil, Horace and Cicero. The more serious or ambitious

---

7 For a recent study of the French on the Grand Tour to Italy, see Gilles Bertrand, *Le grand tour revisité: pour une archéologie du tourisme: le voyage des Français en Italie, milieu XVIIIe siècle-début XIXe siècle* (Rome : École française de Rome, 2008). In terms of numbers, the British outnumbered other nationalities on the Tour (Jeremy Black, *The British and the Grand Tour* (London: Routledge, 1985), 1).
8 See Antoni Mączak, translated by Ursula Phillips, 'Instructions and Good Advice', in *Travel in Early Modern Europe* (Cambridge: Cambridge University Press, 1995), chapter 7.
9 Richard Wrigley, 'Infectious Enthusiasms: Influence, Contagion, and the Experience of Rome', in *Transports: Travel, Pleasure, and Imaginative Geography, 1660–1830*, edited by Chloe Chard and Helen Langdon, Studies in British Art 3 (Yale University Press, 1996), 77.

traveller was attentive to the different political and economic systems of the countries he visited, and wanted to discuss politics and philosophy with people like Voltaire. Others saw the Tour as simply an opportunity to enjoy a different culture, particularly a more liberal, even sophisticated lifestyle, with fashion, manners and women the focus, rather than monuments. This too would count as a rite of passage. Where better to sow one's wild oats—and in style—than on the Continent?

By the 1740s the Grand Tour had acquired a quasi-institutional status with the establishment of the Dilettanti Society in London. What started out in 1734 as a dining club for gentlemen who had been on the Tour—with a reputation for bawdy revelry and drink—soon developed into a Society that promoted the serious study of antiquities, classical art and architecture in Italy and Greece. The point was not just to forward the study of classical civilization, but to encourage those who could afford it, when they returned, to reflect its splendours in the embellishments of their houses and their gardens: 'For the Dilettanti, ancient Greece was largely a giant pattern book for drawing rooms and garden temples'.[10] The Society sponsored archeological work, for example at Herculaneum, and published the results of research in such celebrated works as *The Antiquities of Athens Measured and Delineated*, published in three volumes between 1762 and 1794. The allure of the Grand Tour had become an almost indispensable part of a gentleman's education.

The number of people embarking on the Grand Tour during the eighteenth century varied from decade to decade, influenced not least by what wars were being fought on the Continent at the time.[11] Once Britain's war with France—the Seven Years' War—ended in 1763, the number of Tourists jumped dramatically. By August of that year over 7,000 passports for France had been issued.[12] Although, in the later eighteenth century, the focus of the Tour gradually turned to archeological sites—at Herculaneum and Sicily, for example—the attraction of the Tour continued until the French Revolution and the Napoleonic wars at the end of the century. At least two factors spelt the demise of the Grand Tour: domestic tourism in the British Isles had established itself as a new and inviting prospect, while, for many, France's

---

10 Rosemary Hill, 'Gentlemen Did Not Dig', *London Review of Books*, 24 June 2010, 26.
11 More than six thousand travellers are identified in John Ingamells, *A Dictionary of British and Irish Travellers in Italy, 1701–1800*, compiled from the Brinsley Ford Archive (New Haven: Yale University Press, 1997). Hereafter Ingamells, *Dictionary*.
12 *St James' Chronicle*, 23 August 1763, cited by Jeremy Black, *The Grand Tour in the Eighteenth Century* (Stroud: Sutton, 1992), 9. For more on the numbers who travelled, see John Ingamells, 'Discovering Italy: British Travellers in the Eighteenth Century', in *Grand Tour: The Lure of Italy in the Eighteenth Century*, edited by Andrew Wilton and Ilaria Bignamini (London: Tate Gallery, 1996), 21–30.

revolution made Paris seem dangerous rather than fascinating. The aims and attractions of the Grand Tour were overtaken by new ideas about Britain's relationship to Europe, about political philosophy, and about national culture.

Who Were the Travellers?

THE LETTERS in this volume indicate something of the variety of people who went on the Grand Tour, but as a corpus they are also a reminder of its unwritten prerequisites — money or patronage, and a good education. Lyttelton, Spence and Boswell were paid for by well-to-do family finances. The Irishman Barry, by contrast, had long wanted to go, but could not afford it. Only when the Burkes offered to pay for his journey and subsequent upkeep did he set out for Paris and Rome. Caroline Lennox, middle-aged and financially secure as the wife of the 1st Baron Holland, had a freedom that the others would have envied. Lyttelton, at 19, is a conscientious young graduate from Oxford, keen to develop his literary interests. Joseph Spence, who epitomizes the tutor-companion, travelled with Charles Sackville, the future Duke of Dorset. Spence, barely 19, and fresh from Christ Church, Oxford, was a man of extensive reading who meant not just to educate the nobleman in his charge, but to pursue his own interests. While he realized he was but 'my Lord's shadow', he delighted at his entrée into high society — 'I am now as well acquainted, as the strangeness of the Language will permit, with one Comtesse, two Comtes, a Marquis, and four Barons' (16 February 1731). Gardening and landscaping were other interests he could pursue during the Tour. Boswell's attitude to the Tour is a complex mix; he had serious intentions, if somewhat vaguely expressed as 'improving' himself, so that on his return he could be 'a usefull Member of Society'. He was also out to enjoy the experience. Few travellers write with such exuberance, frankness and delight. Barry is unusual in two respects: first, he had neither the money nor the educational background of the others included in this volume; second, he undertook the Tour with a clearly defined purpose — to develop his knowledge and skill in classical painting. His letters reflect his total immersion in what he saw and thought about while he visited galleries and developed his painting skills. The inclusion of Caroline Lennox shows that the Tour was not an exclusively male undertaking. Lady Mary Wortley Montagu (1689–1762) had been before her, and the Irish novelist Lady Sydney Morgan was to follow. Her account of her travels differs from the others in this collection in many ways: she travels with family members; there is not pressure to learn or 'improve'; there are pauses on her journey when she writes about people and places with an intelligent curiosity that gives us a rare insight into what travellers did when not visiting sites, or museums, or formal receptions. Her letters, along with the others, are a reminder of how diverse a clientele the Tour attracted.

What Were Their Intentions?

The general aim of 'improvement' on the Grand Tour is more often reflected than spelt out in these travellers' letters. Each of them writes to a recipient who is expectant of news. The letters are shaped and coloured by this understanding. Younger correspondents, like Lyttelton and Barry, are driven by a desire to satisfy the hopes of their elders that they are taking full advantage of the Tour: 'Gratitude and Duty' underlie their reasons for writing.[13] Boswell conveys no such duteous obligation to his friend John Johnston; rather he wants to share the stimulation and excitement of the Tour and to gather up 'rich ideas which will give much pleasure… many years hence'. Spence, writing as a tutor on the Tour, sends his mother a close account of places and incidents he thinks she would enjoy reading about. With Spence, the intensity in some of the other letter writers gives way to the relaxed observations of an anecdotist. While all would have agreed as to the broad aim of their journey, personal letters are not the place to harp on about it. The Tourist who published an account of his travels — and there were many of them — had a decidedly different purpose in writing from that of correspondents such as those illustrated here. These letter writers send home the news as it happens, as the Tour unfolded. To perceive their intentions and the expectations of their readers we would need to read between the lines.

Those intentions and expectations had been evolving for some 50 years before people like Lyttelton and Spence embarked on the Tour. The avowed purposes of the Grand Tour — education and improvement — had their genesis in the profound changes to the political and social structures in Britain that followed the 1688 Revolution. The Bill of Rights, the establishment of the Bank of England and the growth of a popular press were among the major innovations that contributed to the fashioning of a new kind of society in the early eighteenth century — a people guarded against authoritarianism, more open to secular ideas, marked by the increasing wealth from overseas commerce, and arguing in the press, and in the new medium of the novel, over the shift from the old securities of landed property to the new less certain and democratic power of money. Despite the ongoing struggle of ideas and power between the old aristocracy and the rising middle classes, Britons came to regard themselves as champions of liberty and enemies of arbitrary power. They

---

13 Lyttelton, Calais, 29 April 1728.

knew they were different from the French, who had an absolute monarch in Louis XIV, and more sensible than the Italians, who believed in the Pope. Yet, as an island nation, they accepted that for all their differences from Europe, their intellectual roots went deep into the classical writing and art of Greece and Rome. These had come to a second great flowering in the Renaissance of Dante, Michael Angelo and Titian. They saw no contradiction, as a Protestant people, in admiring the wonders of the Vatican galleries and the Catholic churches of Rome, Bologna, and Venice. If the English Reformation had put some distance between the British Isles and the Continent, this did not mean Britons had nothing to learn from Europe. As Spence puts it, 'There is certainly nothing equal to travelling for the improvement of the mind and the acquisition of knowledge' (4 February 1741). Samuel Johnson, thinking of going to Italy (something he never did), was more particular:

> A man who has not been in Italy, is always conscious of an inferiority, for his not having seen what it is expected a man should see. The grand object of travelling is to see the shores of the Mediterranean. On those shores were the four great Empires of the world; the Assyrian, the Persian, the Grecian, and the Roman.—All our religion, almost all our law, almost all our arts, almost all that sets us above savages, has come to us from the shores of the Mediterranean.[14]

Travellers went then, not with any sense of inferiority, but with a positive desire to engage with the cultural traditions that had shaped them and Europe. Whatever the wars between Britain and France and those in which Britain was embroiled on the Continent during the century, this desire to learn more of their cultural ties with European traditions was never dulled. A case could be made that writers and philosophers in England, as well as in Scotland and Ireland, became more European orientated during the eighteenth century. For example, the *Annual Register*, edited for some years by Edmund Burke from 1758, includes accounts of events in European capitals, essays by European writers, and Burke's own account of the history of Poland. Evidently there was a curiosity about Europe old and new. The best way to learn was to go on the Grand Tour.

Many travellers went for more specific reasons than simply to broaden their education: Robert Adam and his brother James saw the Tour as a necessary part of their professional training as architects. Their tours of 1755–7 gave them exposure to international ideas and contacts which were impossible to develop in Scotland. Barry's letters illustrate similarly serious intentions: thanks to the sponsorship from the Burkes he was able to spend nearly five years in Paris and Rome grounding himself in those skills and ideas that were a prerequisite

---

14 *James Boswell: Life of Johnson*, edited by R. W. Chapman, introduction by Pat Rogers (Oxford: Oxford University Press, 1980), 472, 11 April 1776.

to becoming a major neoclassical painter. An historian like Edward Gibbon found that Rome prompted a deeper questioning about, not just classical culture and politics, but the very meaning of human history: 'It was at Rome… as I sat musing amidst the ruins of the Capitol, while the bare-footed friars were singing vespers in the temple of Jupiter, that the idea of writing the decline and fall of the city first started to my mind'.[15] Writers as diverse as the essayist Joseph Addison (1672–1719) and the agricultural writer Arthur Young (1741–1820) took inspiration from the Tour, the latter producing one of his most celebrated books, *Travels During the Years 1787, 1788 and 1789, Undertaken More Particularly with a View of Ascertaining the Cultivation, Wealth, Resources and National Prosperity of the Kingdom of France* (1793). But then there were also Tourists who found the demands of sightseeing and learning just too much: the landscape painter Thomas Jones remarked on some travellers he noticed while sketching near Tivoli:

> three English Gentlemen arrived from Rome with Abbate Fraziotti as Antiquary who returned to Rome the next morning—NB This is the usual allowance of time that Our English Cavaliers take to see this extensive Scene of the Curiosities of Art & Nature—Many indeed come here & return in the same day—To such, & many Such there are—Seeing the Curiosities of Rome and its environs, is a Task that they think must be got through—but the sooner the better.[16]

Among the younger travellers was also the implicit acknowledgement that they would learn from the French how to improve their social graces, such as manners, 'politesse' and dress. French foppery was a regular butt of satirists like Hogarth, but there was no need to go to extremes. Letters by Lyttelton, as well as Boswell and Barry, indicate that having the right clothes for particular occasions was an ongoing concern. Lyttelton explains to his father that clothes are expensive:

> but in a court tis absolutely necessary to be Well drest. I have bought five suits since I am here. The first a Green hunting suit with a Border of Gold Lace: Every body wears them so trim'd, because they appear at court in them on hunting days. 2^d a handsome Summer Suit which cost about eighteen £ English for the Princesses Birthday and Tours de fete. 3^d, another for every day of a light Stuff, the Westcoat Blue Silk lac'd with Silver. (18 September 1728)

---

15 John, Lord Sheffield, *Autobiography of Edward Gibbon, Esq., Illustrated from his Letters, with Occasional Notes and Narratives* (New York: Buckland & Sumner, 1846), 169. Gibbon was on the Grand Tour in 1764.
16 Memoirs of Thomas Jones, 13 November 1777 <www.llgc.org.uk/pencerrig/thjones_s_005.htm>

Yet this apparent extravagance was not in any way an attempt to mimic the French or Italians; rather, it was part of the process of learning how to conduct themselves in ways of elegance, refinement and good taste—what Lyttelton calls the 'School of Breeding'.

An important task on the Tour, for people as different as Boswell and Barry, was to make contact with influential people on the ground. How to get known, and how to make a mark in Continental circles required planning, as well as letters of introduction: Lyttelton realised on his way across the Channel that he needed 'more Recommendations… the Reception I shall meet with at court depends upon them' (29 April 1728). Barry left London with letters of introduction from the Burkes to people of influence in Paris and Italy, including the antiquarian Sir Horace Mann, British envoy at the Court of Tuscany. The rewards, as Boswell found, were not just worth the effort but truly pleasurable: he writes to his friend Johnston: 'It is the court in Germany where a man is most at his ease. You would have loved it dearly. You would have been hand and Glove with his Highness. He would have called you Grange. You can scarcely beleive how simple and free he is, without Affectation, quite natural… We had a very excellent table both at dinner and Supper' (27 November 1764).

In between such pleasures the young traveller was expected to apply himself to study—be it books or music or art or fencing—and many did so. Barry is exceptional in that he did little else. Early in the eighteenth century William Blathwayt (?1649–1717) sent his two sons William, aged 16, and John, aged 14, along with a tutor, on the Tour in order to be educated in languages and music. He wrote to the tutor in Rome that he hoped John would compose 'in the style of Purcell a new *Te Deum*, which would be presented to the Queen on his return'.[17] Lyttelton attended an academy while in Luneville. Barry's contemporary George Dance (1741–1825) went to study architecture in Italy, as did the Scot James Byres (1734–1817), and he remained for 30 years. Several, including Barry, were made honorary members of academies in Italy at Rome, Bologna, and Florence.

One aspect of the Tour seldom mentioned in the letters selected here is the trade in sculptures and paintings. High on the agenda of some people on the Tour was the purchase of original artwork by well-known painters for export back to their country houses and private galleries. The Earl of Exeter made three visits to Italy in the late seventeenth century to make a substantial collection of Baroque paintings. However, many travellers had often to settle for copies or fakes. Contrary to the frequent charge that wealthy British collectors,

---

17 Brinsley Ford, 'The Blathwayt Brothers of Dyrham in Italy on the Grand Tour', in the *National Trust Yearbook* (London: National Trust, 1975/1976), 21.

like Charles Townley, took what paintings they wanted,[18] the papal authorities were extremely vigilant and their anti-exportation edicts surprisingly effective. There were rare cases when an agent acquired an outstanding original painting: James Byres, who irritated Barry by visiting his studio more often than he wanted, arranged the sale of Nicolas Poussin's *Assumption of the Virgin* for the Earl of Exeter. More often the Tourist was satisfied with souvenirs of one kind or another—cameos, prints, coins, and 'occasionally, a picture or a small statue'.[19] What agents like Byres realised was that there was a ready market among British travellers from the rising commercial class—be they from England, Scotland or Ireland—for artwork that would reflect well on the new owner, indicate taste and learning, and even suggest that the owner was a 'connoisseur'. Thomas Jenkins 'operated a cameo factory that produced objects that were sold as genuine antiquities to unsuspecting tourists'.[20] Barry looked on the trade and its agents with disgust. It flourished, as he says, because 'the Italians are all full of the idea of selling pictures to the English, who are full of money, and the richest, and consequently, the most respected people in the world'. However, neither Barry nor Boswell had any qualms about having their portrait painted, another accepted part of the Tour.

The Route

A *sine qua non* of the Tour was to have plenty of time. A certain leisureliness was presumed so that the traveller could soak up the sights, manners and *savoir vivre* of the various places and cultures he passed through. Barry took several months to return from Rome to London, largely because he wanted to spend time in Bologna and Venice. There were a number of books of advice on where to go and what to see on the Tour. One of the most widely used, because it was so comprehensive, was Thomas Nugent's *The Grand Tour, or, A Journey through the Netherlands, Germany, Italy and France* (1749). Here were descriptions of post-routes, distances from place to place, charges, lists of paintings (particularly galleries), climate, systems of government, cultural customs—in short, everything a person on the Tour might need to know. More specialized guidebooks included Addison's *Remarks on Several Parts of Italy, &c. in the*

---

18 This is not to deny the point made by J. H. Plumb that 'the wealthy had plundered the Continent to fill their houses with Italian fireplaces, French furniture and tapestries' (*England in the Eighteenth Century* (Harmondsworth: Penguin, 1959), 101).
19 Christopher M. S. Johns, 'The Entrepôt of Europe: Rome in the Eighteenth Century', in *Art in Rome in the Eighteenth Century*, edited by Edgar Peters Bowron and Joseph J. Rishel (London: Merrell, 2000), 39.
20 Johns, 'The Entrepôt of Europe: Rome in the Eighteenth Century', 39.

Years 1701, 1702, 1703 (1705) which went through ten editions by 1773[21] and, for the traveller interested in art, *Voyage d'Italie; ou, recueil de notes sur les ouvrages de peinture & sculpture, qu'on voit dans les principales villes d'Italie* (Paris, 1758) by Charles-Nicolas Cochin, used by Boswell. In addition, when the traveller reached Italy, a more serious person like Barry would have the help of classical texts like Pliny's *Natural History*, which described many of the classical places and objets d'art: Pliny was 'one of the most important sources of information for the historian of the ancient world, and, in particular, for historians of Classical art'.[22] It was Pliny who famously claimed that the monuments, sculptures and buildings of Rome summed up the wonders of the world.[23]

But the Tourist had first to decide which route to take. The customary itinerary, allowing for personal variations, is neatly summed up in the *Cambridge Companion to Travel Writing*:

> After crossing the Channel, the Tourist, having acquired a coach at Calais, would often proceed to the Loire Valley, where the purest French accent was supposed to have its home, and where the young Briton could spend some time preparing his tongue and his manner for the rigours of Paris society. A lengthy stay in the French capital might be followed by a visit to Geneva (and even, if one had the right connections, to Voltaire at his villa in the outskirts). One would then cross the Alps, as expeditiously as possible, proceeding via Turin or Milan down to Florence, to stay probably for some months. Venice might be next, then Rome, or vice versa. The Tourist might go as far as Naples. The return journey northward might include stays in Austria, the German university towns, Berlin and Amsterdam.[24]

The letter writers in this collection show a few differences to this, but all take in the two key destinations—Paris and Rome—without which the Tour would not be complete. Of particular interest on the journey into Italy, perhaps because it was so hazardous, was the passage across the Alps to Turin by Mont Cenis: special porters had to be engaged, the route being but a rough track through spectacular scenery. Lennox writes, 'one goes in open Chairs for six hours together, carry'd by Men up and down rocks that it seems quite impossible for any thing but Goats to walk upon, that one is often carryd within a hair's breadth of the most frightfull precipices, and yet they assure one there is no danger'. The experience was a locus classicus of the Tour. Thomas Gray wrote, 'Mont Cenis, I confess, carries the permission mountains have

---

21 Jeremy Black, *The British Abroad: The Grand Tour in the Eighteenth Century*, 3.
22 Sorcha Carey, *Pliny's Catalogue of Culture, Art and Empire in the 'Natural History'* (Oxford: Oxford University Press, 2003), 7.
23 Pliny, *Natural History*, 36, xxiv, 101.
24 *The Cambridge Companion to Travel Writing*, edited by Peter Hulme and Tim Youngs (Cambridge: Cambridge University Press, 2002), 39.

of being frightful rather too far; and its horrors were accompanied with too much danger to give one time to reflect upon their beauties'.[25] Once in Italy, the question was whether to go straight to Rome or to take in Bologna, Venice and Florence first. Naples, being south of Rome, was but an additional option, though the Lennox party chose to make that city their destination.

As to how the Tourists travelled, most took the diligence or public coach for the longer stretches of the journey. The coach went from 'post' to 'post', stopping at 'post-houses' where fresh horses were obtained for the onward journey. A carriage or chaise could be hired for shorter trips, which is what Barry sometimes did. He captures something of the tedium and irritations of travel in a letter written in February 1771 from Lyon on his way home:

> In order to divert my attention from disagreeable reflections upon the fatigues and extraordinary expenses of travelling in this time of the year, as I have also an idle day upon my hands in waiting for the diligence, and as there is nothing worth looking after here in Lyons, except trade and manufacture, in which I have neither knowledge nor taste, so I shall turn to my old resource of more pleasing memorial.

Where to Stay?

WHATEVER THE route decided upon, there was always some hazard in choosing where to stay; the inns varied greatly in cleanliness and comfort. Lennox remarks of the journey to Lyon, 'The Inns are dreadful'. Certain inns reminded her of her worst experiences on a previous Tour in 1763, when she wrote:

> Was it not for the abominable dirty inns I should delight in travelling about France, but they are bad beyond imagination. I do think the French are at least fifty years behind-hand in regard to the real conveniences and comforts of life, tho' they consult their ease much with regard to some things. Travel indeed they seldom do, and if by chance they do, 'tis the *bon ton* to go night and day without stopping to sleep, so the bad inns are not the same inconveniency to them as to us.[26]

On this Tour, however, she did find more fitting accommodation once she reached Italy. But her bad experiences are corroborated by many others on the

---

25 Gray to Richard West, 16 November 1739, *Letters of Thomas Gray*, selected by John Beresford (Oxford: Oxford University Press, 1951), 45–6.
26 Lady Holland to Marchioness of Kildare, 21 September [1763], *The Correspondence of Emily, Duchess of Leinster (1731–1814)*, edited by Barry Fitzgerald, 3 vols (Dublin: Irish Manuscripts Commission, 1949–57), i, 389.

Tour, both in France and Italy. Samuel Sharp, writing from Rome in 1765, gives some details of the discomforts met on the journey:

> Give what scope you please to your fancy, you will never imagine half the disagreeableness that *Italian* beds, *Italian* cooks, *Italian* post-horses, *Italian* postilions, and *Italian* nastiness, offer to an *Englishman*.[27]

He fared no better once he had found accommodation in Rome: the bedding was damp and coarse, the drapes dirty, no curtains, and bare walls. 'The total of *Italian* nastiness, your chamber, which you would wish to be the sweetest, is by far the most offensive room in the house, for reasons I shall not explain'.[28] However, as Jeremy Black notes, inns varied greatly from the 'justifiably famous' to what Arthur Young called 'execrable'.[29]

However, travellers in this collection had the means to ensure a relatively comfortable stay; this was something Boswell made a point of throughout his Tour. He writes from Neufchatel:

> I am now at the old Government of My Lord Marischal, where upon his Lordship's Recommendation I have been extremely well received. It is a fine healthy Place. The air is fresh. The beautiful lake yields most delicious large trout, and the hills arround in vines abound. I have realy lived luxuriously. (9 December 1764)

Spence too presumed comfortable quarters: he writes from Venice, 'We live in a very good house, in the great street, just in sight of the great Bridge, the Rialto' (22 November 1731). He also gives a good deal of attention to the wine and food on offer during the journey:

> The best Burgundy at the Taverns costs but 8 pence a bottle: and from the finest Cellars of the great Merchants but 16 pence. The common people buy worse sorts cheaper and cheaper: and tis matter of fact that the Lowest of all is but a half-penny a bottle. I had almost forgot to tell you, that about the beginning of last Month, I had the pleasure of tasting a Frigassee of Frogs, for the first time. It had a sort of Chickeny taste; but something of an odd Sowerness at the bottom that I did not quite like. (12 May 1731)

The cost of such a lifestyle was not inconsiderable and young gentlemen had problems living within their budget. There are periodic crisis moments when a correspondent has to confess that he has spent more than his father expected. Lyttelton apologises, but says he needs further funds, adding in a letter not printed here 'I know you are willing to supply me. You would sacrifice anything

---

27 Samuel Sharp, Letter XI, Rome, October 1765, *Letters from Italy, Describing the Customs and Manners of that Country in the Years 1765 and 1766* (London: R. Cave, 1766), 43.
28 Sharp, *Letters from Italy*, 44.
29 Black, *The Grand Tour in the Eighteenth Century*, 141.

to my education' (15 August 1728). His next letter goes into details on expenses for new clothes, and for a chair: 'my Money runs away very fast' (18 September 1728). The argument becomes ingenuous: 'This is the time of my life in which Money will be ill sav'd' (27 September 1729). Not surprisingly, his extravagance draws an angry response from his father (1 December 1729). Barry had less money to draw on, yet he too takes to explaining to the Burkes that costs, whether of clothes or chaises, are more than anticipated. On his return journey, while at Bologna, he finds he hasn't even the money to pay for his lodgings. His money, it seems, had all gone on his trip to Venice.

Posting and Receiving Letters

Posting and receiving letters in the eighteenth century was more complicated than it is today. Because so much was informal, it is difficult to be precise about how exactly it worked. The very word 'post' in eighteenth-century England referred not to letters, but to the staging points on the roads from one place to another—the 'posts' at which carriages and chaises had a change of horses and where travellers found refreshment. There was one post office in Britain—in London's Lombard Street—and no postage stamps. A 'post book' was a book informing the traveller where those stage 'posts' were. The business of posting and receiving letters as we know it had still to be formalised. Yet, as the letters in this volume show, correspondents knew there was a system and, despite all its hazards, it worked.

If the writer of a letter was at all troubled about costs, the first consideration concerned the length of the letter. Often it would consist of a single folio sheet which would be folded and sealed; an envelope was optional. The charge for letters between London and Paris, for example, was 10 pence for one sheet; the price increased according to the number of sheets used. Letters to or from Italy cost one shilling three pence for the first sheet.[30] This helps to explain why James Barry normally wrote in a small hand and filled the entire page, leaving no margins. Costs were usually met by the addressee, not the sender. Joseph Spence in Dijon remarks that four letters 'did not cost above 18 pence', which sounds cheaper than the standard rate. However, receiving mail could be expensive for the recipient if he received a great deal of it, which explains why Boswell decided to retain his letters rather than posting each one to his friend Johnston.

---

30 M. M. Raguin, *British Post Office Notices 1666–1899*, 6 vols (Medford: Michel M. Raguin, 1991), i, 98.

Once the letter was written, the next decision was how to send it. If the writer was in London it could be sent from the Lombard Street Post Office.[31] Since the late seventeenth century there were also a number of designated 'Receiving Houses' around London, appointed by the Postmaster General—business houses, taverns, and even individuals—where letters could be left or collected. Posted letters would then be lodged at the Lombard Street Post Office the same evening.[32] There they would be stamped with a bishop mark to indicate the date of sending.[33] Letters from London to Paris went twice a week, on Tuesdays and Fridays, and from Paris to London on Mondays and Thursdays.[34]

Letters could also be sent or received through the office of one of the Secretaries of State. Edmund Burke's friend, as well as Barry's, William Burke, was an official there, so they probably used that route. For many travellers, including most of those in this collection, a reliable route was through a bank. Smollett notes that he was staying on in Lyon 'until I should receive some letters I expected from my banker at Paris'.[35] Another option was to give the letter to a friend who was travelling, or to a private courier. Horace Walpole writes from London to the diplomat, Sir Horace Mann in Florence: 'This will be delivered to you by Mr Pars, a painter, who is going to Italy to improve himself'.[36] The Lyttelton family used intermediaries to re-direct mail for George when he was on the move. Caroline Lennox suggests her sister sends letters to her 'in Picadilly, and my porter has orders to send them to us' (21 September 1766). The reverse would also hold good for Lennox.

Sending letters from the Continent to England could be more hazardous. The handling of letters in France was the task of individuals who had purchased a licence from the King to run the carriage routes and to set the charges. They therefore controlled the transmission and costs of letters and packages throughout France. The downside of this lucrative business was that operators were more concerned for the payments received than for the delivery of letters.[37] Italy was particularly noted for what one critic calls 'a

---

31 This included a 'foreign office' that dealt, *inter alia*, with mail to Europe.
32 *London Gazette*, 2 November 1682.
33 A bishop mark was a small round postmark in black ink giving the day and month; it was first used in 1661 and continued in use till the end of the eighteenth century.
34 *London Gazette*, 2 April 1763.
35 Tobias Smollett, *Travels through France and Italy*, 2 vols (London: Baldwin, 1778), i, 123. Letters from Paris to Lyon took two days, and from Paris to Marseilles four days.
36 *Letters of Horace Walpole to Horace Mann*, 2 vols (Philadelphia: Lea and Blanchard, 1844), i, 389.
37 <www.laposte.fr/legroupe/LeGroupe2/Nous-connaitre/Histoire/Histoire-de-La-Poste/Histoire-de-La-Poste>

dawdling inefficiency'.[38] Lady Mary Wortley Montagu, writing from Turin in 1741, remarks: 'all letters are opened both here and in other places, which occasions them to be lost'.[39] However, the evidence of the letters in this volume suggests the system was fairly reliable and regular; Lennox confidently remarks, for example, in a letter of 30 October 1766 from Turin: 'the post goes tomorrow [Thursday] and Saturday.' Letters from Italy to London took three to four weeks. William Burke, in London, thanks Barry on 3 December 1766 for a letter sent from Rome on 4 November. Although sending and receiving letters was more varied and informal than in the nineteenth century, none of the correspondents in this collection expresses any doubt that the letters would reach their destination. Likewise Barry in Rome was sure that if anyone had written to him, he would find the letter waiting for him at the English coffee house in the Piazza di Spagna near the Spanish Steps.

Reading the Letters

A STRIKING FEATURE of the letters in this collection is that the voices are so different. Here is a medley of voices with different tones, different interests, different perspectives, even though they are all motivated by the same desire to benefit from what the Tour offers. But each sees those benefits differently. The point becomes clearer if we look at a couple of examples to catch what is distinctive about one or two of the writers.

These are private letters addressed to family or close friends: Lyttelton writes to his father, Spence to his mother, Boswell to his friend Johnston, Barry to close friends, Lennox to her sister. Moments of introspection are very uncommon: much of the content touches on places seen, incidents, and people. This is in keeping with the comment that the distinguishing mark of the best familiar letters of the eighteenth century is 'that the writer revealed his own character through candid accounts of matters other than simply himself'.[40] What is curious in this collection is the variety of ways in which each gives an individual account of the Tour.

Lyttelton writes with a certain formality, conscious of the conventional obeisance expected of a son to his father. Yet he is perceptive of the new people

---

38 W. E. Mead, *The Grand Tour in the Eighteenth Century* (Ayer, 1972), 168.
39 Mead, *Grand Tour*, 168; Walpole makes the same point to Mann: 'The great pleasure I receive from your letters is a little abated by my continually finding that they have been opened' (15 April 1742).
40 *The Familiar Letter in the Eighteenth Century*, edited by Howard Anderson, Philip B. Daghlian, and Irvin Ehrenpreis (Lawrence: University of Kansas Press, 1966), 272.

he meets, and even gives hints of enjoying himself: he writes of Soissons 'tis one of the agreablest towns in France: The people are infinitely obliging and well bred to strangers, we are of all their partys and perpetually share with them in their pleasures' (20 November 1728). What those 'pleasures' were he does not say. This is because the voice, as for instance in his letter of 16 September 1729, is deferential, not relaxed or familiar; even family affections are expressed with respect and restraint. His political news is businesslike and impersonal; the language has a ring of duty; he wants to give the impression that he is attentive to affairs of state: that is what his father expected to hear. When he comes to the point of his letter, to what he personally wants — namely to have permission to move on to Italy — he becomes more terse and direct; the comments are more specific and carefully argued. Lyttelton comes across as a serious young man for whom the Tour is an opportunity 'to improve myself considerably'.

Boswell has none of this earnestness or attempt to impress. Writing to his friend Grange Johnston, he strikes a much freer, even ebullient note. He did write to his father, but not to tell him about his Tour. His letters to Johnston have immediacy — a sense of pleasure at what he saw and did. What delights him on the Tour is the here and now — a card assembly, a dinner with the French ambassador, mass in the chapel of the Prince of Baden-Baden. Boswell is on the Tour, not just for the cultural, social and sexual pleasures, but to mingle with the great, to know and to get known: 'whatever may be the essential nature of man, sure I am that his happiness or misery his Abilitys or his Weakness depend almost entirely on his Position' (28 November 1764).

Neither Lyttelton nor Caroline Lennox needed to go on the Tour to enhance their 'Position'. They, as well as Boswell, would have found Barry's Tour too intense, narrow, and uneventful. As his letters show, Barry visited more galleries, saw more monuments, and learned more about classical history and art than any of them, yet he visited relatively few places. Spence, by contrast, comes across as an acute observer of the men, customs, and places he passed along the route; his account of the ascent to Mont Cenis is wonderfully dramatic and amusing. Spence is not driven by social ambition, or some cultural agenda. He has the sharp eye of a gifted and kindly raconteur, seeming to imagine his mother by his side as he tells her how the day has passed. He writes from Milan, 'I hope you are furnished with a good Map of Italy; and a pair of Jackboots to travel thorough it with me. I left you in my last at Turin.' (5 November 1731). The Tour for Spence was an opportunity to watch the French and the Italians in all kinds of mundane situations, to notice a waiter laying a table, to describe the old Marquis Scipio Massei dancing in Verona; the Tour gave him the opportunity to extend and deepen his knowledge of human nature as manifested in the manners and customs of everyday life.

The Benefits

The benefits of the Tour are impossible to measure. For some, like Spence and Caroline Lennox, little more can be claimed than a personal satisfaction. More tangible advantages are clear for young men like Boswell and Barry: for them it proved the stepping stone to celebrated careers in writing and painting. The presumption for most travellers was that when they returned from the Tour they would see Britain and its place in Europe in a fresh cultural, social and historical light; the Tour gave a breadth and depth to their way of thinking; it so challenged their values—social, political, cultural—as to prompt them to reflect on what they had and what they presumed was worth having. Notable men of the century, like Burke and Johnson, who missed out on the Tour, often regretted the fact. The career of Sir Joshua Reynolds (1723–92) illustrates more clearly than most the long term substantial significance of the Tour. His two years in Italy (1750–2) grounded him in ideas and skills that marked the rest of his working life as England's leading portrait painter and first President of the Royal Academy (1768). In his annual lectures to the Academy he encouraged his students again and again to work at the Greek sculptors and the Renaissance artists he had himself studied in his youth in Rome. He spoke in one such lecture of 'the greatest names of antiquity' because he hoped 'to excite in you a desire of knowing, the principles and conduct of the great masters, of our art, and respect and veneration for them when known'.[41] He argues that only by looking at the great work of the past can students produce something to equal or better it in the future. In many ways Reynolds changed the face of art in England. Burke remarked, 'He was the first Englishman who added the praise of the elegant Arts to the other Glories of his Country'.[42] The benefits of Reynolds' early years on the Tour reached into the very fabric of British culture.

---

41 Discourse VII, *Sir Joshua Reynolds: Discourses*, edited by Pat Rogers (London: Penguin, 1992), 203.
42 'Burke's Tribute to Reynolds', Appendix D, in *Sir Joshua Reynolds: Discourses*, 363.

George Lyttelton, 1st Baron Lyttelton; after Robert Dunkarton; Benjamin West. Mezzotint, published 1774

George Lyttelton (1709–73): Letters (1728–30)

With a single exception, all the letters printed here, written while George Lyttelton was on the Grand Tour, were addressed to his father, Sir Thomas Lyttelton (1685–1751), landowner and politician, of Hagley Hall in Worcestershire (the exception being a letter from father to son). His mother, Christian, née Temple (1688–1748), was the sister of Richard Temple (1675–1749), first Viscount Cobham, owner of the renowned estate at Stowe, which she often visited and which Lyttelton later attempted to rival by his development of the grounds at Hagley. George was the eldest of his parents' 12 children, four of whom died young; the letters contain occasional affectionate references to his siblings, especially his sisters Christian ('Chrissy') wife of Thomas Pitt (1705–61), and Molly.

The young man who embarked on the Grand Tour in February 1728 was highly educated—at Eton and Christ Church, Oxford—with strong scholarly inclinations, as well as political interests and ambitions: exactly the kind of person likely to benefit from the social and cultural experiences awaiting him in Europe. His literary bent was obvious, even before his departure. He had already published 'Blenheim'—a poem in Miltonic blank verse—in praise of the Churchill family: as is clear from the opening letter below, Sarah, widow of the illustrious Duke of Marlborough, rejoiced in the poetic compliments paid to her—'in her mind/ [Marlborough] Found greatness equal to his own'.

It was apparently natural for Lyttelton to express himself in verse; two occasions during his European tour confirm it. On the first, in Paris in 1728, he wrote lines 'To Mr Poyntz, Ambassador at the Congress of Soissons'. Stephen Poyntz (1685–1750), whom he met for the first time at Soissons, was a distinguished diplomat, a product of Eton and King's College, Cambridge, widely travelled in Europe, highly respected by leading politicians, and influential at Court. Undoubtedly he provided a rôle model for Lyttelton whose almost extravagant admiration for him is evident both in letters and in the opening lines of the poem:

O Thou whose friendship is my joy and pride,
Whose virtues warm me, and whose precepts guide;

> Thou, to whom greatness, rightly understood,
> Is but a larger power of being good.

The second notable piece of verse written on the Tour was the 'Epistle to Mr Pope, from Rome, 1730': its existence underlines the important relationship established between the distinguished 42 year-old poet, author most recently of the *Dunciad*, and the aspiring writer who had just attained his majority. The 'Epistle' acknowledges Pope as the only great contemporary poet, but has the audacity to advise him to shun the 'thorny', the 'unpleasing way' of satire, urging him:

> To sing the land which yet alone can boast
> The liberty corrupted Rome has lost.

The young man had confided to his father in August 1729: 'Nobody can have a higher opinion of [Pope's] poetry than I, but I am sorry he writ the Dunciad.' Pope, for his part, later acknowledged Lyttelton's benign influence on Frederick, Prince of Wales, and complimented him by name in the *Epilogue to the Satires* (1738), a poem he had seen in manuscript. He was described by Pope in a letter to Swift (October 1738) as 'one of the worthiest of the rising generation'; Swift unhesitatingly accepted the description.

His literary friendships were not limited to the two eminent satirists, Swift and Pope. James Thomson, author of *The Seasons*, was a frequent visitor to Hagley; after Thomson's death in 1748, the posthumous edition of his poems was prepared by Lyttelton himself. The soundness of his literary judgment was tacitly acknowledged by his friend Henry Fielding who sought Lyttelton's opinion on the manuscript of the novel, *Tom Jones* (published in 1749). Furthermore, James Boswell sought his opinion on *An Account of Corsica* published in 1768; the effusive letter that Lyttelton wrote in response to the invitation was added to the third edition of *Corsica* in 1769, thus giving Boswell the opportunity to lavish praise on 'this worthy and respectable Nobleman, to whom genius, learning and virtue owe so much'.

It comes as no surprise then to find evidence of scholarly and literary interests in his letters. He is scarcely out of his father's sight when the two men are engaged in a robust, well-informed debate about what their own century would call some sublime characteristics of Milton's *Paradise Lost*. Conversely, Lyttelton was obviously ill at ease among the pretentious but ill-bred courtiers in Lunéville, both French and English, who paraded their ignorance and provinciality: 'Men of Learning… is a character they despise. A Man of Quality caught me the other day reading a Latin Author, and askt me with an Air of contempt, whether I was designd for the Church'. His irony is also directed at the frenzy of enthusiasm for the newly discovered game of quadrille which had quite ousted interest in any serious pursuit. Later he admits that he had made 'schoolboy blunders' in his use of foreign languages while at Lunéville and is reluctant to return, but one suspects that he is principally offended by the philistinism he had encountered there.

The life of a courtier had one consequence which strained Lyttelton's relationship with his father, as Sir Thomas's solitary letter makes very plain: financial extravagance. The young traveller's defence against the charge of prodigality gives us insights into the cost and the standard of living at even a provincial Court, in this case at Lunéville, the residence of the Duke of Lorraine: 'tis absolutely necessary to be Well drest'. He felt it essential to buy five suits: 'a Green hunting suit with a Border of Gold Lace'; 'a handsome Summer Suit'; 'another for every day of a light Stuff, the Westcoat Blue Silk lac'd with Silver'; 'a fine Cloath Suit for the Duke's Birthday'; and 'a Black Suit of Mourning', the Duchess's sister having just died. Add to these his 'Footman's Livery', and the total cost comes to 'about 100 pounds sterling'. Then there is the sedan chair at 30 crowns monthly, payments to grooms and waiters, doctor's bills, 'Chair Hire in foul weather', and so on. Sir Thomas was obliged to recognise his son's predicament — and to underwrite his expenditure; we, for our part, benefit from the insights which flow from the situation.

Though the relationship between father and son was frequently under some strain, Lyttelton was responsive to Sir Thomas's wishes whenever possible — and convenient. He acknowledges the power of his father's purse in the remark: 'If you send me to Italy next Spring [1729] as you once designd to do...'; but then he proceeds to offer an alternative plan. Except for the sudden, unforeseen need to accompany Stephen Poyntz from Soissons to Paris, the places which occur in his own plan were largely those he actually visited. Lyttelton proposed first to explore France in order to acquire a 'perfect' knowledge of the language, and then to visit Italy so as to become equally skilled in Italian. In France it seemed to him important to see Orleans, Lyon and Bordeaux; in Italy, Tuscany en route for Rome and Naples, and finally Venice, Padua, Verona, Milan, Siena and Turin. The plan is instructive. It reveals the ways in which a young gentleman, cultivated and intelligent, hoped to benefit from the Grand Tour: with an enhanced capacity to speak foreign languages, increased classical, literary, and historical knowledge, a greater understanding of forms of government different from the British, and a familiarity with a wide variety of landscapes and cityscapes that Europe could provide. His response to the latter is best exemplified in his excited description of the spectacular scenery surrounding the monastery of La Grande Chartreuse, as well as his fascination with the monastic life itself: he writes about both aspects more vividly, and in greater detail, than about any other place on his journey.

Another way in which Lyttelton benefited from the Tour may broadly be labelled political. From this viewpoint it was a happy accident that enabled him to become a privileged person in the entourage of an Ambassador — Poyntz — at the Congress of Soissons. There can be little doubt that the experience extended his political awareness: he enjoyed not only the opportunity to participate in discussions about international affairs — even if he was only on the edge of the inner circle — but also the chance to meet and engage with men of considerable political importance. He grew in self-confidence when he could report on the negotiations between Prussia and Great Britain and her allies, offer his father gossip about the Spanish court, put up a spirited defence of the French monarch, Louis XV, or comment authoritatively on the political and economic weakness of the city-state Genoa. Perhaps Sir Thomas would greet, with a wry smile, his son's assurance that letters of recommendation to 'any of the Italian courts' were not required, he 'being acquainted with their Ministers here [in Paris] and not doubting to have as many as [he would] want'. The pride and self-satisfaction evident in the remarks were pardonable in a young man of 20 years old who had a far greater range of character-forming experience of politics than was available to most men of his age. One significant consequence is clearly stated at the conclusion of his lengthy account and assessment of the governmental system in France, and just when he is on the point of moving on to Italy: 'I am more strongly attached to my own Country by what I see of the Miseries abroad, and find the Spirit of Wiggism grow[s] upon me under the Influence of Arbitrary Pow'r. It will still encrease when I come into Italy where the Oppression is more sensible in its effects' (16 October 1729).

Undoubtedly Lyttelton's personality matured during the course of his European tour. The range of his social experiences was transformed through living in Soissons in the company of Stephen Poyntz. 'Tous les jours Bals, Festins, Partis du Plaisir' [Every day balls, banquets, fun parties]. He admits that he will have to forfeit the instruction in horsemanship that he had in Lunéville but, as for dancing, his tutor in Soissons is 'worth a hundred times more than the one in Lunéville.' 'The fashionable place is here where I shall best learn how to live. People of breeding will teach me the best manners… My character will improve at the same time'. Without question, it grew stronger. Although, for example, he was always ready to acknowledge his extravagance, the longer he was away from home the more he was confidently prepared to justify his spending: 'I am sensible I spent too much at Paris, that is more than a good Manager wou'd have done, but I repent less of it because it was in a place and at a Time and Circumstance of life when it was necessary to exceed the ordinary course of limited Expence'. He was now able to see the two places; Hagley on the one hand, and Paris on the other, in perspective.

National politics became Lyttelton's principal concern after his return from the Grand Tour in June 1730. He was elected MP for Okehampton in 1735; he allied himself with Frederick, Prince of Wales, and was thus identified with the opposition to the government. His friendship with the Prince was close and not merely political; he became Frederick's secretary in 1737, a position he held for seven years. The high point of his political career was reached in November 1755 when he became Chancellor of the Exchequer in the Newcastle administration; however, he resigned, along with the Duke of Newcastle, a year later; he was then created the first Baron Lyttelton of Frankley.

The energy with which he had participated in politics was, in his later years, devoted to literary activity. In 1756 he wrote *An Account of a Journey into Wales*, one of the earliest tourist accounts of North Wales; its publication in 1774 coincided with the two-week tour of the region by the painter, Paul Sandby (1730–1809), with his patron Sir Watkin Williams-Wynn (1749–89), that resulted in Sandby's influential *XII Views in North Wales* (1776). Lyttelton's published description of Mount Snowdon's sublimity is striking evidence of a sensibility in tune with the temper of the times, coming midway between Edmund Burke's *Sublime and Beautiful*, 1757, and the theorist of the picturesque, William Gilpin's *Three Essays on Picturesque Beauty*, 1792.

Finally, his *Dialogues of the Dead* was first published anonymously in 1760; its popularity encouraged Lyttelton to enlarge the volume with four new Dialogues in 1765. But the project which dominated the last 30 years of his life was the *History of the Life of Henry II*, the third and final volume of which appeared in 1771, just two years before his death.

The letters are published from MSS by kind permission of Christopher Lyttelton, 12th Viscount Cobham.

Letters of George Lyttelton

Feb ye 4th [1728]

Dear Papa.

I am mighty glad you have made choice of so agreable a place as Lorain to send me to: I shall be impatient to hear that you have got a Servant for me, that my stay here may be the Shorter: in the mean while you may be sure I shant neglect to make the best use of my time. I am proud that the D[uchess] approves my Verses, for her Judgement does great honour to those that please her. The subject is Blenheim Castle; I woud have sent you a Copy of them, but I thought if they were good you woud see them, if otherwise twas better you shou'd not.[43]

The news you tell me of Ld Henry[44] does not a little please me. What ever does him honour in your Opinion, is of advantage to me, as it will render the friendship that is between us more agreable to you: for my satisfaction in his acquaintance has been always checked, by observing that you had not that Esteem for him as I could wish and might have for all my Friends. But I hope he will deserve it better every day, and Confirm himself in my good Opinion by gaining yours.

I am glad that you are pleas'd with my *Persian Letters* and Criticism upon Voltaire.[45] But with Submission to your Judgement I don't see how what I have said of Milton can destroy all Poetical Licence. That Term has indeed been so much abus'd, and the Liberty it allows has been pleaded in defense of such extravagant fictions that one cou'd almost wish there were no such Words. But yet this is no reason why good Authors mayn't Raise and Animate their Works with Flights and Sallies of Imagination, provided they are cautious of Restraining them within the bounds of Justness and Propriety. For nothing can license a Poet to offend against Truth and Reason, which are as much the Rules of the Sublime, as less exalted Poetry. We meet with a thousand instances of the true Nobleness of Thought in Milton, where the Liberty you contend for is made use of yet Nature very strictly observ'd: it woud be useless to point out the Beauties of this kind in the *Paradise Lost* where the Boldness of his Genius appears without shocking us with the least Impropriety. We are Surpris'd, we are Warn'd, we are Transported; but we are not hurried out of our Senses or forc'd to believe Impossibilities. The sixth book is, I fear, in too many places an Exception to this: The Poetica Licentia is strech'd too far, and the Just is sacrificed to the Wonderful. (You will pardon me if I talk too much in the language of the Schools.) To set this point in a clearer light, let us compare the Fiction in the *Lusiads*[46] of the Giant that appears to the Portuguese and

---

43 'Blenheim. Written at the University of Oxford in the year 1727', in *George Lyttelton, Works*, edited by G. E. Ayscough (London: J. Dodsley, 1774), 593–8.
44 Unidentified.
45 At least part of Lyttelton's *Letters from a Persian in England to his Friend at Ispahan* (modelled on Montesquieu's *Lettres Persanes* of 1721) was obviously in existence in 1728, even though the complete work was not published until 1735. The series of fictional letters had a clear anti-Walpole bias. In his *Criticism of Voltaire*, GL concentrated on Voltaire's *Essay on Epic Poetry* published in the previous year; it included a wide-ranging assessment of Camoëns.
46 In Canto V of the epic poem, *Os Lusiades* (1572) by Portuguese poet, Luis e Camoëns (1524–80), the giant Adamastor symbolises the forces of nature encountered by Portuguese navigators, especially when they tried to round the Cape of Storms (Cape of Good Hope). In *Paradise Lost*, vi, 628–79, the Angels uproot heaven's mountains in

the Battle of Angels in Milton. The Storms, the Thunders, and the Lightnings that hang about him, are proper and Natural to that Mountain he represents. We are pleas'd with seeing him thus arm'd, because there is nothing in the description that is not founded upon Truth. But how do the Swords, and coats of Mail, and Cannons Agree with Angels. Such a fiction never can be beautiful, because it wants Probability to support it. We can easily imagine the Cape extending its arms over the Sea, and guarding it from the bold Invaders; the Tempests that Mariners always meet with upon that coast render such a Supposition very just. But with what grounds of reason can we suppose that the Angels to defend the Throne of God threw Mountains upon the heads of the Rebel Army?

>   Non tali auxilio, nec Defensoribus istis
>   Numen egit:——[47]

The Liberty in one Fable is restrain'd to Nature, and Good Sense; in the other it is wild and unbounded, so as frequently to lose sight of both.——

Pardon the freedom I have taken to contradict your Opinion and defend my own; I shall be very ready to give it up to you, if after this you continue to think me in the wrong. Tis prudence to Argue with those who have such Regard to our Judgement as to correct it.

You ended a letter of good news very ill in telling me that you had got the headach. I can have very little pleasure in anything, though it be never so agreable, when I know that you are ill.

Your dutiful Son,
G.L.

———

Calais. April ye 29th

Dear Papa.

After a passage of sixteen hours without any thing to eat or drink I came here very well and very hungry having had no sickness worth speaking of. I have bought a mighty good Italian Chaise for twelve guineas, and shall set out tomorrow for St Omers. The way from there to Luneville is as plain and good as can be, so I hope I shall have nothing to retard me. I went over in the packet boat with a Gentleman who had been some time in Lorain, and who tells me it

---

order to bury the engine that uses fire and sounds like thunder, invented by Satan to attack them.
47 Virgil, *Aeneid*, ii, 531–2 ['Non… istis tempus eget': 'Not such aid nor such defenders does the time require']

will be of great advantage to me to get more Recommendations to other people besides Prince Craon particularly from Ld Malpas and Ld Sunderland,[48] for that the Reception I shall meet with at court depends upon them.

I cant recollect the tenderness you shewd to me at parting without the warmest sentiments of Gratitude and Duty to you: To reply to our long discourse I only beg leave to say, That there is a certain Degree of Folly excusable in Youth, which I have never yet exceeded, and beyond which I desire no Pardon.

I hope Mama has dryd her tears: My Duty to her and Love to Chrissy; I'll write to both when I come to Luneville.

    I am, Dear Papa,
      Your very Dutiful and Obedient Son
        G. L.

        Luneville May ye 13th 1728[49]

Dear Papa.

The inclosd is in answer to Sr Robert Walpole from Monsieur le Prince de Craon, who has shewn me all the Favour and Civility that I might expect from so powerful a Recommendation. The Duke himself was pleasd to tell me that he would endeavour to render my stay here as agreable to me as possible.

You will let Sr Robert Walpole know how much I am oblig'd to his letter and do justice to the Prince de Craon, who has exprest his Regard to it in the strongest Manner, and by a kindness which I cant enough acknowledge.

I hope every thing goes on to your Satisfaction in the affair I left you engaged in: it will be the greatest Happiness to me to hear that you are pleasd and in good health.

    I am Dear Papa
   Your most Dutiful and Obedient Son
     G. Lyttelton

Monsieur

J'ai recu par Monsieur Littleton la letter don't vous m'honore, je tacherai de Repondre a ce que vous souhaitez de moi en lui procurant ici aupres de son

---

48 Marc, Prince de Craon (1679–1754), minister to Duke Léopold of Lorraine. The ducal court was in Lunéville. Sir George Cholmondeley (1703–70), styled as Viscount Malpas, 1725–33; succeeded to the title as 3rd Viscount Malpas in 1733; MP for Windsor, 1727–33. Robert Spencer, 4th Earl of Sunderland (b.1701); he died in Paris in November 1729.

49 GL had arrived in Eastern France at Lunéville, dubbed by Voltaire as 'Le Versailles Lorrain', a sobriquet exemplified in Laurent Charpentier's painting *Le Rocher* (1742).

altesse Royalle les agreements dus a sa naissance et a votre recommandation et je men rapporte au fidel compte qu'il vous en Rendra. Rien n'est plus flatteur pour Moy Monsieur que the Souvenir de Milord Walpol, je nai perdu aucune occasion de me renouveller dans les bonne graces depuis Son retour en angleterre et jai Charge tous mes amis qui ont passé de Me Menager une amitie qui mest si precieuse, accorder la votre Monsieur au desir que jai de la meriter, et a lattachement avec lequel jay l'honneur d'etre
>Monsieur votre tres humble obeissant serviteur
>Le Prince de Craon

A Luneville le 11 May 1728
[Sir,

I received from Mr Lyttelton the letter you kindly sent, I will endeavour to respond as you have asked of me in obtaining here from the court of his Royal Highness the respect due to him because of his birth and of your recommendation and I am confident his Royal Highness will agree to this. Nothing is more gratifying to me, Sir, than the memory of my Lord Walpole, I have not lost any opportunity to keep in his favour since his return to England and I have instructed all my friends who have gone there to cultivate a friendship which is so precious to me; may your friendship Sir accord with the desire I have to merit it, and with the regard with which I have the honour to be
>Sir, your very humble and obedient servant,
>Prince de Craon]

>Luneville June ye 8th. N. S.

I thank my dear Papa for so kindly complying with my Inclinations to board out of the Academy, and assure you that I am every day more convinced how inconvenient I should have found it to be there.

I shall eat as you direct me, though I don't know any settled Ordinary[50] in the town; but there are Taverns where Gentlemen eat together, and where I generally dine.

I heartily congratulate you upon my Sister's Marriage,[51] and wish you may Dispose of all your children as much to your Satisfaction and their own: Would to God Billy Pitt had a fortune equal to his Brother's that he might make a present of it to my pretty little Molly[52] but unhappily they have neither of them

---

50 A place where a meal was provided at a fixed price.
51 GL's sister Christian ('Chrissy') married the wealthy (but, as it proved, malevolent) Thomas Pitt on 2 May 1728.
52 Billy Pitt was GL's brother-in-law; Molly was GL's sister.

any Portion but an uncommon Share of Merit which the World wont think them much the Richer for. I condole with poor Mrs Hunt[53] upon the abrupt departure of her intended Husband: To be sure she takes it much to heart, for the Loss of an only Lover when a Lady is past three and twenty, is as afflicting as the Loss of an only Child after fifty five.

You tell me Mama desires a particular Journal of my Travels and the Remarks I have made upon them after the manner of the Sage Mr Bromley.[54] Alas I am utterly unfit for so great a Work. My Genius is light and Superficial, and lets slip a Thousand Observations which woud make a figure in his book. It requires much Industry and Application as well as a prodigious Memory, to know how many houses there are in Paris, how many Vestments in a Procession, how many Saints in the Romish Calendar, and how many Miracles to each Saint. And yet to such a pitch of Exactness the curious Traveller must arrive who woud Imitate Mr Bromley: Not to mention the pains he must be at in examining all the Tombs in a great Church, and faithfully Transcribing the Inscriptions, though they had no better Author than the Sexton or Curate of the Parish. For my part, I was so shamefully negligent as not to set down how many Crosses are in the Road from Calais to Lorain; nay, I did not so much as take an Inventory of the Relicks in the Churches I went to see. You may judge by this what a poor account I shall give you of my Travels and how ill the money is bestowd that you spend upon them. But however if Mama insists upon it, I shall have so much complaisance for the Curiosity natural to her sex as to write her a short Particular of what Rarities I have seen; but of all Ordinary Spectacles such as Miracles Rareeshows and the like, I beg her permission to be Silent.

As for my way of living here, tis agreable enough. I see the best company in the place, am regular at my Exercises, Read and Pray by Stealth, Give the Ladys hopes of
[End of MS]

July ye 21st N. S.

I thank you, my dear Papa, for so kindly forgiving the piece of Negligence I acquainted you of in my last. Young fellows are often guilty of voluntary forgetfulness in those affairs, but I assure you, mine was purely accidental.

---

53   Widow of John Hunt of Bewdley (about 10 miles from Hagley).
54   William Bromley (?1663–1732), author of *Remarks in the Grande Tour of France and Italy* (London: John Nutt, 1692; 2nd edition, 1705), and *Several Years Travels Through Portugal, Spain, Italy, Germany, Prussia, Sweden, Denmark and the United Provinces* (London: A. Roper, 1702).

I am glad to hear Tom is come from Clent.[55] No doubt he will make more improvement under the care of Mr Le Place than under the Rod of Dr Bland. He writes me a very particular letter in which he tells me that Charles is gone to school to learn to Petifogg,[56] but that for his part he is putting on the Sword to get Honour as well as Fortune. I am sorry these fine things cant be done without great expense to you, but I am sure you don't complain of what you bestow on us to so good an end. Dansel[57] tells you true that I am weary of losing money at cards, but tis no less certain that without them I shall soon be weary of Lorain. The Spirit of Codrill has possest the land;[58] from Morning to Midnight there is nothing else in every house in town. This Court is fond of Strangers; but with a proviso that Strangers love Codrill: Wou'd you win the hearts of the Maids of Honour you must lose your Money at Codrill? Wou'd you be thought a well-bred Man? You must play genteely at Codrill: Wou'd you get a reputation of good Sense? Shew Judgement at Codrill—However in summer one may contrive to pass a day without Codrill because there are agreable promenades and little parties out of doors; but in Winter you are reduc'd to play Codrill, or sleep like a fly till the return of Spring. Indeed in a Morning the Duke[59] hunts, but my malicious stars have so contriv'd it that I am no more a Sportsman than a Gamester. Men of Learning there are none in the whole countrey on the contrary tis a character they despise. A Man of Quality caught me the other day reading a Latin Author, and askt me with an Air of contempt, whether I was designd for the Church?

All this wou'd be tolerable if I was not doomed to converse with a set of English who are still more ignorant than the French: and from whom with my utmost endeavours I cant be absent six hours in the day. My Lord Hermitage[60] is the only one among them who has common Sense, and he is so scandalously debauch'd in his principles as well as practice that his conversation is equally shocking to my Morals and my Reason. My only Improvement here is in the company of the Duke and Prince Craon, and in the exercises of the Academy.

---

55 Sir Thomas Lyttelton's second son, Thomas (?1710–29) was made Page of Honour to the Princess Royal in 1728; consequently he left Eton, where Dr Bland was headmaster, in order to carry out his courtly duties. He was sent to a noted school at Marylebone run by M. La Place. His uncle and aunt lived in Clent, a village close to Hagley; he may have been staying with them.
56 Sir Thomas's third son, Charles (1714–68), later Dean of Exeter and (in 1762) Bishop of Carlisle, but in 1728 expected to follow the law—unless GL's use of the term 'petifogg' was jocular.
57 Dansell was the servant provided by GL's father as requested in the first letter.
58 Quadrille began to replace ombre as the fashionable card game c.1726 (OED).
59 Duke Léopold Joseph of Lorraine (1679–1729), married Elisabeth Charlotte d'Orléans (1676–1744).
60 Perhaps Henry Scott, Earl of Delorain (1676–1730), 1st Viscount of Hermitage.

I have been absent from the last near three weeks by reason of a Sprain I got in the Sinews of my Leg which is not yet quite cur'd.

Duty to Dear Mama; I hope you and she continue well.

I hope Chrissy and her Dear had my letters but I haven't heard from neither.

Luneville August ye 14th 1728

Dear Papa

There has been for about six weeks past a sort of contagious fever reigning in Luneville attended with excessive pains in the head, and sometimes with bloody flux. I have been attackd with it but I thank God without the last Symptom, and have sufferd a good deal. I am now taking the Bark[61] which I hope will prevent the Return of it though Relapses here are very common. We have two English Gentlemen who had it at the beginning of last Month and thought themselves well recover'd, who are down again and in great danger. The Physicians advise me by all means to change of Air as soon as I am able; for the town lying in a bottom and being all surrounded with Waters which putrifie in this season makes it very unwholesome to breath in especially for sick people: Besides that the Water and Wine here are both so bad that tis dangerous to drink them.

If you think it proper that I shou'd Remove for a Month or six weeks I shou'd be glad to go to Soissons, which lies not far from hence, and where I shall be very agreably. The Stories you have heard of it's being crouded are very false for the neighbourhood of Paris carrys off so many people that every body is lodg'd commodiously, and the town is not near full. Every thing is as cheap as Lorain and you are oblig'd to no greater expence. The People of the town are extremely civil and obliging to all Strangers which makes the place perfectly agreable. Our Embassadors there have Countrey Houses where they often pass a week or two and carry all the English along with them. Mr Windham[62] who is just gone back from hence gives me this account; he stayed but two days here being afraid of catching the distemper.

We felt a Shock of an Earthquake the 3d of August N. S. about five in the Afternoon which lasted something about half a Minute. It threw down all the Goods in the Shops, split a Staircase in two, and in some places was attended with a bellowing Noise. It extended over all Lorain but not with

---

61 The bark of various species of cinchona tree from which quinine is obtained, ground into powder and taken to counteract a fever; Boswell took it when he suffered from malaria.
62 Perhaps William Windham (?1706–89), MP 1766–8.

equal Violence. The Thing was very unusual in this country, and frightened them pretty much.

I suppose Chris is at Hagley, the enclos'd is to her. If you stay any time at Hagley, and the house be not too full, you wou'd much oblige me to send for Poor Ayscough[63] down to you. I have Letters from him expressing an Affection which cannot be feign'd. Duty to Dear Mama I raved of her in my fever and thought she was dead.

Compliments to everybody.
Adieu

Luneville Sep: ye 18th

I thank my dear Papa for giving me leave to go to Soissons; it is true, I have a great mind to the Journey, and as to my health, I have always found that whatever Pleases me does me Good. You will laugh at the Regimen, but I appeal to dear Mama whether the Sight of the Stowe Gardens had not a better effect upon her, than Burgesses Shop.[64] My Spirits were very low when I writ you my last letter, and I had not then Judgement enough to consider that the way to relieve your Melancholy was to appear Chearful myself. However I beg you to believe that what I said was the Language of my heart though it needed not have been said with so much Warmth: I most sincerely love you and cannot help being deeply affected at your least Complaint: But don't let this deprive me of your Confidence, for I have no greater Pleasure in life than seeing myself honored with it.

I am oblig'd to lay before you the Account of my chief expense at Luneville, I mean the Article of Cloaths. They amount to a great Expense, but in a court tis absolutely necessary to be Well drest. I have bought five suits since I am here. The first a Green hunting suit with a Border of Gold Lace: Every body wears them so trim'd, because they appear at court in them on hunting days. 2^d a handsome Summer Suit which cost about eighteen £ English for the Princesses Birthday and Tours de fete. 3^d, another for every day of a light Stuff, the Westcoat Blue Silk lac'd with Silver. I have since been oblig'd to make a fine Cloath Suit for the Duke's Birthday which cost about thirty four pounds English, and a Black Suit of Mourning for the Queen of Sardinia[65]

---

63 Probably Francis Ayscough (1700–63), who married GL's sister, Anne Lyttelton, in 1744. He was tutor to George III; then Dean of Bristol, 1761–3. His son, George Edward Ayscough (d.1779), edited GL's *Works* (1774).
64 Burgess is unidentified.
65 Anna Maria, Queen of Sardinia (1669–1728).

the Duchess Sister. I must make another Winter Suit for every day; all which with my Footman's Livery will come to about 100 pounds ster[ling]: I believe you will think the last Birthday Suit a little too extravagant, but I assure you all the English here were finer than me. Every thing is dearer here than at Paris, for Cloath Silk Lace and all are fetchd from thence to us — But then S^r you will consider that next Year I shall have so many good Suits by me, that I shall have no occasion to buy more; unless perhaps an every day Suit to save my best, which will come to no great Matter. This Article with my Lodging Eating and Exercises has oblig'd me to take up another hundred pound and break in upon the Third. You see S^r it will be necessary to allow me Credit for something more if you intend I shou'd pass the Winter here. Besides the Addition of Firing[66] I must keep a Chair at thirty Crowns a Month, the lowest price. As for my Pocket expences, I play as little as I can, and seldom drink but at my Meals; and yet with Fees to Grooms and Waiters, Doctors and Apothecarys Bills, little Rides about the country, and Chair Hire in foul weather, my Money runs away very fast. Lorain is a dearer place than it is thought to be. The Tradesmen are the greatest villains in the Universe, and make us pay double for all we have. The Court obliges us to Fine Cloaths, the Academy requires a good Sum, and yet people fancy one can live for nothing. Mr Fitz William's Governour[67] told me that he found himself so mistaken in the Notion he had of Expences here, that he was determind to persuade my Lord either to Remove his Son or allow him more. Indeed Sr I believe I should have been better at Angiers or Geneva, I am sure I shou'd be much Cheaper. However I shall make myself easy here as long as you think fit that I shou'd stay, which I hope will be only till next Spring. I am frighted at the Sickness in Worcestershire: Pray God preserve you and your whole Family. Duty to Dear Mama, and Love and Service to every body. I have receivd no letter from Brother Pitt. Pray S^r love Molly the better for being so good to write often to me; she is worth a thousand of her Sisters in this point. I am very angry at Madam Pitt.
[End of MS]

---

66 Fuel for a fire. In 1667 Pepys remarked on 'the dearness of firing' (OED).
67 A governor, or tutor, was responsible for a young man's education and well-being (e.g. when 2nd Earl Fitzwilliam, at the age of 16, went on the Grand Tour in 1765–6, he was accompanied by a clergyman, Thomas Crofts, as his tutor). The Fitzwilliam mentioned here may have been Richard (1711–76), who succeeded as 6th Viscount Fitzwilliam of Merrion on the death of his father, Richard (?1677–1743).

Soissons September ye 28th

Le voici, Mon cher Pere, fort a mes Souhaits, charmè du Bonté de Monsieur Poyntz, et profitant du commerce agreable des Anglois qui sont auprès du luy. Tous les jours Bals, Festins Partis du Plaisir, enfin tous les Agrémens qu'on peut desirer; Et tout ça avec moins du depense que je n'ay fait en Loraine pour entretenir une Vie triste et ennuïeuse. Vrayment Mon cher Pere vous ferez mieux de me laisser passer ici deux ou trios mois, que de me renvoyer sitôt dans une ville ou il y'a peu de profit a faire et bien des Chagrins a souffrir. Qu'est que je perdrai en restant ici? Je ne monterai pas a Cheval; voila tout—Car pour la Danse, j'ai pris un Maitre ici qui vaut cent fois celui de Luneville—Je suis assez bien placé a Cheval pour monter hardiment, et j'aurai assès du temp depuis pour bien apprendu le Manege: L'Affaire ne presse pas, et cet Intervale ne me fera rien perdu la dessus. Mais d'autre coté je m'instruirai plus dans trois mois de sejours a Soissons, que dans trois Ans a Luneville: C'est ici l'endroit du Monde ou j'apprendrai le mieux a Vivre. La bonne Compagnie me façonnera de toutes Manieres, et etant toujours dans le grand Monde, j'en attraperai l'Air plus facilement. Mon esprit se formera en meme temp; et la Conversation d'un aussi habile homme que Monsieur Poyntz me donnera des Leçons don't j'ay besoin, et qui me serviront utilement un jour.—En un Mot, je conservois[?] mon interet, et je le trouve plus ici qu'ailleurs; ce n'est pas le Plaisir qui me seduit, c'est le Profit qui m'attire. Je vous parle peutetre trop hardiment, mais je vous parle comme a mon Ami: Toutefois je me souviens du Respect que je dois a la Volonté de mon Pere, et je partirai d'ici sans Regret quand vous me l'ordonnerez. Mr Walpole est a Paris a present, mais on l'attend dans un mois ou cinq semaines. Je mange tous les jours chez M.Poyntz, et je vous assure qu'on y fait bonne chêre. Il me caresse de la Maniere du Monde la plus Obligeante, et autant que pourroit faire Mr Walpole.—J'espere que tout se porte bien a Hagley, mais ce Maudit Fievre m'inquiete. Dieu vielle sur votre Santé, Mon cher Pere. C'est ma priere la plus ardenté. Je fais bien mes Compliments a tout le Monde; je baisse ma chere Mere et je l'embrasse. Adieu, pardonnez les fautes que vous trouvez dans ma lettre, car j'ecris fort a la hâte, et sans y'prendre Garde. On ne peut pas vous Aimer plus que moy.—

[Here I am, my dear Papa, very much as I would have wished, delighted by the kindness of Mr Poyntz, and profiting from the pleasurable acquaintance of the English who are close to him. Every day balls, banquets, fun parties, in short all the pleasures one could desire; and all this for less expense than I would have paid in Lorrain to lead a dreary and boring existence. Without question, Papa, you will do better to let me stay here for two or three months than to send me back so soon to a town where there is little of advantage to do and a great deal of vexation to endure. What shall I lose by staying here? I will not get on a horse; that is all—as for dancing, I have a tutor here who is worth a hundred times more than the one in Lunéville—I sit well enough on a horse to get on to it without trepidation, and I will have plenty of time to learn horsemanship thoroughly: the matter is not urgent and I shall lose nothing by the hiatus. On the other hand, I shall improve far more in a three-month stay in Soissons than in three years in Lunéville. The fashionable place is here where I shall best learn how to live. People of good breeding will teach me the best manners, and being at all times in the higher social circles I shall become accustomed to the appropriate style most easily. My character will improve at the same time and the conversation of such a talented man as Mr Poyntz will provide the instruction which I need and which will be profitable to me one day. In a word, I look after my own interest and find that better here than anywhere else; it is not the pleasure that attracts me, it's the advantage that accrues to me. Perhaps I speak too frankly to you, but I speak to you as my friend. I always remember the respect that I owe to my Father's wishes, and I will leave here without regret when you direct me to do so. Mr Walpole is now in Paris, but we expect him in four to five weeks. I eat every day in Mr Poyntz's house and I assure you that we live very well. He makes much of me in the kindest possible way of the fashionable world and Mr Walpole does the same as far as he can. I hope all is well at Hagley but that wretched fever alarms me. God's blessing on your health, my dear Papa. That is my most fervent prayer. I send my best wishes to everyone. I send kisses and my best love to my dear Mother. Adieu, forgive the errors which you discover in my letter because I write in great haste and without taking care. No one can have greater affection for you than I have.]

Soissons, Oct. 28[68]

I thank you, my dear Papa, for complying so much with my inclinations, as to let me stay some time at Soissons; but, as you have not fixed how long, I wait for further orders. One of my chief reasons for disliking Luneville was the multitude of English there, who most of them were such worthless fellows, that they were a dishonour to the name and nation. With these I was obliged to dine and sup, and pass a great part of my time.

You may be sure I avoided it as much as possible; but, *malgré moi*, I suffered a great deal. To prevent any comfort from other people, they had made a law among themselves not to admit any foreigner into their company; so that there

---

68 The manuscript of this letter has unaccountably disappeared; the text is taken from the version printed in Ayscough's edition of GL's letters, 648–9.

was nothing but English talked from June to January. On the contrary, my countrymen at Soissons are men of virtue and good sense; they mix perpetually with the French, and converse for the most part in that language. I will trouble you no more upon this subject; but give me leave to say, that, however capricious I may have been in other things, my sentiments in this particular are the surest proofs I ever gave you of my strong and hereditary aversion to vice and folly. Mr. Stanhope is always at Fontainbleu. I went with Mr. Poyntz to Paris for four days, when the colonel was there, to meet him: he received me with great civility and kindness. We have done expecting Mr. Walpole, who is obliged to keep strict guard over the cardinal, for fear the German ministers should take him from us: they pull and haul the old gentleman so many ways, that he does not know where to turn, or into whose arms to throw himself.[69]

Ripperda's escape to England will very much embroil affairs, which did not seem to want another obstacle to hinder them from coming to an accommodation.[70] If the devil is not very much wanting to his own interests in this business, it is impossible that the good work of peace should go on much longer. After all, most young fellow are of his party, and wish he may bring matters to a war: for they make but ill ministers at a congress, but would make good soldiers in a campaign.

No news from [?Christian][71] and her beloved husband: their unreasonable fondness for each other can never last; they will soon grow as cold to one another as the town to the Beggar's Opera. Pray Heaven I may prove a false prophet! but married love, and English musick, are too domestick to continue long in favour.

---

69 These few sentences provide a glimpse into the complicated negotiations for peace at Soissons. William Stanhope (?1690–1756), a principal British negotiator, was frequently at the French royal residence at Fontainebleu; Poyntz, his fellow commissioner for the British government, was in Paris where significant discussions were taking place with Cardinal Fleury, head of the French government; and Horatio Walpole (1678–1757), a third commissioner, ensured that the cardinal was 'protected' from the influence of German negotiators. (The colonel has not been identified.) Stanhope was created first Earl of Harrington in 1730; Walpole became Baron Walpole of Wolterton in 1756.
70 John William, Baron Ripperda (?1680–1737) political adventurer, and one-time Spanish Minister. He misappropriated public funds and incurred the hostility of the Spanish government. In vain, he sought refuge with William Stanhope. He betrayed Spanish government secrets, was imprisoned in Spain, but escaped. He died in Morocco.
71 Ayscough omits the name, but in the light of GL's expression of astonishment about Thomas Pitt's behaviour on p. 59, the unnamed person was probably GL's sister Christian (see also n. 130). GL's reference to *The Beggar's Opera* by John Gay (1685–1732) proved wide of the mark: the ballad opera received its premiere on 29 January 1728; it was staged 62 times in the first season and, unlike Christian's marriage, went on to achieve unparalleled success.

My duty to my dear mother; I am glad she has no complaint. You say nothing relating to your own health, which makes me hope you are well. I fondly love my brothers and sisters as if I was their parent.

There is no need of my concluding with a handsome period; you are above forced efforts of the head. I shall therefore end this letter with a plain truth of the heart, that I am,

Your most affectionate and dutiful son,
G. L.

[Soissons, 20 November 1728]

Dear Papa.
I am highly sensible of the two last proofs of your goodness and affection to me, in allowing me to take up money as I want it, and to stay longer in a place I like so well. There will be no difficulty in doing of the first, Mr Arbuthnot[72] being willing to supply me upon demand provided you don't protest his bills. I shall not draw upon you till after Christmas according to your commands, though I want the money pretty much, this place being more expensive than I thought it was. In every other respect tis one of the agreablest towns in France: The people are infinitely obliging and well bred to strangers, we are of all their partys and perpetually share with them in their pleasures. I have learn't more French since I came here than I shou'd have picked up in twelve month at Lorraine. The desire of a further progress and improvement in that tongue has led me into some thoughts relating to the continuation of my Travels which I beg leave to lay before you.

If you send me to Italy next Spring as you once designd to do, one great inconvenience will arise, viz, that before I am perfect in speaking French I must leave it to apply myself to Italian; from which it may probably come to pass that I shall not know much of either. I shou'd therefore think it more for my advantage to make the Tour of France before I set out for Italy than after I come back. There is another reason which at least will weigh with Dear Mama; that is, that after the month of May when the Violent Heats begin, Rome (where it will be necessary to settle first upon account of the Purity of its language which is spoke corruptly in other places) is so unwholesome as to endanger the life of any Foreigner unaccustomed to the Air; and therefore most Travellers go thither about September and leave it towards April. I fancy these two objections to the foregoing Scheme will incline you rather to give

---

72 Robert Arbuthnot (d.1741), a Scot who became a banker in Paris.

into mine which is as follows. Suppose I stay here till after February, I may in March April May and June see Orleans Lions and Bourdeaux, and pass July August and September in the southern Provinces. The Air of those Countries is so pure that the great heats do nobody any harms. From Provence to Genova is the shortest road I can take for Italy and so through Tuscany to Rome where I shall arrive about December having seen what is curious in my way. I may pass two Months at Rome and go from thence to Naples the most delightful part of Italy and the finest Air: allowing me three months in that country I may take a little voyage to Messina, and from thence to Malta which lies fast by. From thence I may travel along the Coasts of the Adriatick Sea by Ancona and Loretto to Venice; where if I stay but till the end of July, I shall have August September and October to see Padoua Verona Milan and the other parts of Italy that lie North West of the Venetian Gulph. In the winter I may settle at Sienna where there is a mighty good Academy, and where they are not troubled with many English. From thence I may go to Turin where I may continue my Riding if you please, and stay there till April. After which to avoid returning through Provence a second time, I may go by Lauzanne and Berne to Franche Comté, and so by Dijon to Paris. When I am there it will be wholly in your breast how long you wou'd have me stay abroad, and whether I shou'd come home the shortest Way or have the pleasure of seeing Holland. This S^r is the Plan that I offer to you which I hope you will approve of in the main, and agree to for me: I don't pretend to have laid it so exact as never to depart from it, but am persuaded that generally speaking I shall find it agreable and commode. I have not brought Lorraine into it, because it lies quite out of my way, and because to say the truth I am unwilling to go thither. I know my dear Papa you expect I shou'd acquaint you with my reasons for the Dislike I have exprest against that place. This is not so easy an Eclaircissement as you may think it. Our Notions of Places and of Persons depend upon a combination of circumstances many of which are in themselves minute, but have weight from their assemblage with the rest. Our Minds are like our Bodies, they owe their pain or pleasure to the good or ill Assortment of a thousand causes each of which is a Trifle by itself. How small and imperceptible are the qualities in the Air or Soil or Climate where we live. And yet how sensible are the impressions they make upon us and the Delight or Uneasiness they create. So it is with our Minds from the little Accidents that concur to Sooth or to Disorder them: But in both the impressions are more strong as the Frames which they act upon are more Delicate and refin'd. I must therefore impute many of my complaints to the natural Delicacy of my temper, and I flatter myself you will not think that reason the worst I cou'd have given you.

But there are others more gross and evident which I have already in part informd you of, and which I shall here set forth more at large.

It is natural to us to hate the school in which we take the first lessons of any Art: the reason is that the awkwardness we have shewn in such beginnings, lessens us in the Eyes of people there, and the disadvantageous Prejudice it has given of us is never quite to be got over.

Luneville was my School of Breeding, and I was more unavoidably subject a quelque Bevues d'Ecolier,[73] as the Politesse practisd in that place is fuller of Ceremony than elsewhere and has a good deal peculiar to itself. The Memory of these Mistakes though lost perhaps to others hangs upon my mind when I am there, and depresses my Spirits to a degree that I am not like myself. One is never agreable in company where one fears too much to [be] disapprov'd, and the very Notion of being ill receiv'd has as bad an effect upon one's Gayety as the thing itself. This is the first and strongest reason why I despair of being happy in Lorraine. I have already complaind of the foppish Ignorance and contempt for all I have been taught to value that is so fashionable there. You have heard me describe the greater part of the English I knew there in colours that ought to make you fear the infection of such company for your Son. But supposing no danger in it; this brutal unimproving Society is no little Grievance: To what barbarous insults does it expose our Morals and Understanding: A Fool with a Majority on his side is the greatest Tyrant in the World. —Don't imagine dear S^r that I am setting up for a Reformer of Mankind, because I express some impatience at the Folly and Immorality of my acquaintance. I am far from expecting they shou'd all be Wits much less Philosophers. My own Weaknesses are too well known to me not to prejudice me in favour of other people's when they go but to a certain point. There are Extravagances that have always an excuse; sometimes a Grace attending them: Youth is agreable in its Sallies and wou'd lose its beauty if it looked too grave. But a Reasonable Head and an honest heart are never to be dispens'd with.—

Not that I am so severe upon Luneville and my English friends as to pretend that there [are] not Men of Merit and good Sense among them; There are some undoubtedly but all I know are uneasy at finding themselves in such ill company. I shall trouble you no farther on this head; if you enter into my way of thinking what I have said will be enough, if you don't all I can say will have no effect.

I shou'd not have engaged in this long detail but that I love to open my heart to you, and make you the Confident of all my thoughts: Till I have the Honour and Happiness of conversing with you in a nearer manner, indulge me dear Sr in this distant way of conveying my notions to you and let me talk to you as I wou'd to my dearest Freind, without Awe Correctness or Reserve.

---

73 'to schoolboy blunders'

Though I have taken up so much of your time before, I cant help giving myself the pleasure of acquainting you with the extraordinary Civilities I receive from Mr Poyntz. He has in a manner taken me into his family; I have the honour of his conversation at all hours, and he delights to turn it to my improvement. He was so good to desire me to ask your leave to pass the Winter with him, and to encourage me to do it promised me that I shoud not be without my share of Publick Business. The first packet that comes from Fountaineblau I expect to be employd which is no small pleasure to me, and will I hope be of service.

Don't you think S^r that it woud not be improper for you to write to Mr Poyntz, thank him for the honours he has done me, and desire him to excuse it if his Civilities make me troublesome to him longer than you designd. You know so well how to do those things that I am persuaded it woud have a good effect.

The only News I have to tell you is a Secret intelligence from Vienna that Count Zinzendorff[74] is going out of favour; this is of consequence to the Negociations, but you must not mention it: while I am not trusted with Affairs you shall know all I hear; but afterwards ne Patri quidem[75] —I was saying to Mr Poyntz that Ripperda was undoubtedly very happy to come out of Prison into the land of Liberty. He replyd, that whatever the Duke might think he was in danger of going to prison again. This was said some time ago and things may have alterd since. I writ to Lord Cob[ham]: in English but to my Lady in French just after.[76] Adieu. I hope you continue well; duty to dear Mama.—

Soissons December ye 20th NS

Dear Papa,

A sudden Order to Mr Poyntz has broke all my measures; He goes to morrow to Paris to stay there in the room of Mr Stanhope and Walpole who are on their return for England. His Excellency is so kind and good as to desire me to accompany him to Paris and live there with him en Famille at least till I hear from you. As the expence will not be great having the convenience of his Table, and as a winter Journey to Lorrain is impracticable I have ventured to take this Step without your Orders—Tis with me as it is with Embassadours who

---

74 Count Nicholas Ludwig von Zinzendorf (1700–60), initially destined for international diplomacy, gradually developed a sympathetic interest in the Moravian Church and eventually became its leader.
75 Seneca the Elder, *Controversiae*, I, ii, 10 ['Not even about my native country'].
76 Anne Halsey (d.1760) married, in 1715, Richard Temple (1675–1749); he was created Viscount and Baron Cobham in 1718; uncle to GL.

though never so desirous of keeping close to the letter of their instructions, are some times oblig'd to act without them, and follow their own Judgement without consulting their Superiors. The prospect of being let into Business and the Advantage of Mr Poyntz's conversation make me very unwilling to quit him now when I begin to know him more intimately, and to gain his Confidence and Trust. I have already copied some papers for him and don't doubt but he will continue to employ me. I will if you give me leave learn to dance at Paris, though the Price there is very high —

I have troubled you so often with Ripperda that I am almost ashamed to mention him again; but the conclusive Answer of Mr Stanhope to the Spanish Minister was that when Spain woud give up the Duke of Ormond[77] and the other English Rebels England woud send back Ripperda.

Prince Fredericks Journey was very secret,[78] Mr Poyntz did not hear of it till Friday last; at least he had no publick Notice of it.

There will be fine struggling for places; I hope Brother Tom will come in for one.

   Adieu S^r believe me always
     Your very dutiful and obedient Son
                  G. L.

Duty to Mama.

[Paris] Jan. ye 22d 1729

Dear Papa,

I have so much to thank you for that I have not words to do it; So kind a Complaisance for all my wishes surpasses my acknowledgement. Your two letters to Mr Poyntz had their effect and were answerd with a profusion of Civilities and Marks of Friendship and Esteem: But the inclos'd will instruct you better in the Obligations I have to you and him. How happy I am in your permission to quit Loraine you may Judge by my letter on that head; I think you have mistaken my Sense in some Arguments made use of there, but tis needless to set you right, your Kindness and Indulgence to my desires is an Argument more persuasive than all the rest, and in which only I confide.

---

77 James Butler (1665–1745), 2nd Duke of Ormonde, Irish statesman and soldier. He took part in the Jacobite rebellion in 1715, settled in Spain, and supported the Spanish plan to invade England in 1719 to put the Old Pretender on the throne.

78 Prince Frederick (1707–51) eldest son of Prince George of Hanover (later George II) and Princess Caroline of Ansbach; his parents were required to leave Germany in 1714 and did not see him again until he arrived in England in 1728. There was hostility between them and him from then onwards.

You tell me in your last that I have spent a great deal of Money considering my Business here is Improvement and not Show. I have indeed spent a great deal more than I cou'd wish, and the Necessity of doing it has given me no small uneasiness; but it is an undoubted Truth that without Show abroad there is no Improvement. You yourself confess it when you say that the French are only fond of Strangers who have Money to pay them for their compliments. You express a great Uneasiness for fear I shou'd grow fond of Games of Chance; I have sometimes risqued a little at them, but without any passion or delight. Gaming is too unreasonable and dishonest, for a Gentleman who has either Sense or Honour to addict himself to it; but to set you quite easy in that point. I give you my word and honour and desire no pardon if I recede from it, that I will never hazard a farthing more while afterwards at any Game of Chance. I have been a great Sufferer at Quadrille, and must even suffer on, for point de Societe sans cela; c'est un Article preliminaire a tout Commerce avec le Beau Monde.[79]

I am going to send Dansel to Luneville to pay off my lodgings there, which in the uncertainty of leaving it I was obligd to keep till I had Orders from you to return no more: besides this there is a Month at the Academy which I had just enterd upon, and must pay entire, and some other little debts which I left unpaid in expectation of going there again. The Court being still in second mourning I was oblig'd to make me a new Suit upon coming here, and to buy new Wigs and Stockings being but ill furnishd with both. As the Devil wou'd have it my Chaise which has often been broken and repaird is so shatterd with the Journey from Soissons that it is all to pieces and absolutely unfit for Service. I must be forc'd to buy another to continue my Travels south.

I may venture to assure [you] that all Thoughts of Peace are not laid aside as you apprehend.

[Enclosure]

Paris 22d Jany. 1729 N. S.

Sir,

I have received your two kind letters, in which you are pleasd very much to overvalue the small civilities it has lain in my power to shew to Mr Lyttelton. (I have more reason to thank you, Sir, for giving me so convincing a mark of your regard as to interrupt the course of his travels on my account, which will lay me under a double obligation to do all I can towards making his stay agreeable and useful for him; tho' I shall still remain the greatest gainer by the pleasure of his company, which no services of mine can sufficiently requite.) He

---

79 'There's no social life without that; it is a first requirement in all dealings with fashionable and influential people.'

is now in the same house with me, and by that means more constantly under my eye than ever at Soissons; but I should be very unjust to him if I left you under the imagination that his inclinations stand in the least need of any such ungenerous restraint. Depend upon it, Sir, from the observation of one who would abhorr to deceive a Father in so tender a point, that he retains the same virtuous and studious dispositions which nature and your care planted in him, only strengthen'd and improv'd by age and experience, so that I dare promise you, the bad example of Paris or any other place, will never have any other effect upon him, but to confirm him in the right choice he has made. Under these happy circumstances, he can have little occasion for any other advice, but that of sustaining the character he has so early got, and of supporting the hope he has rais'd (I wish it were in my power to [do] him any part of the service you suppose me capable of), I shall not be wanting to employ him as occasion offers, and to assist him with my advice where it may be necessary, tho' your cares (which he ever mentions with the greatest gratitude) have made this task very easy. He cant fail of making you and himself happy, and of being a great ornament to our Country, if with that refind tast and delicacy of genius he can but recall his mind at a proper age from the Pleasures of Learning and gay scenes of Imagination, to the dull road and fatigues of Business. This I have sometimes taken the liberty to hint to him, tho' his own good judgment made it very unnecessary.

Tho' I have only the happiness of knowing you, Sir, by your reputation, and by this common object of our friendship and affections, your Son; I beg you woud be persuaded that I am, with the most particular respect Sir

Your most humble and obedient Servant

S. Poyntz

A l'Hotel de Treville ye 15th de Fev:

Dear Papa

I made your compliments to Mr Poyntz as handsomely as I cou'd, and read him that part of your letter where you leave it to his determination how long I shall stay with him, provided it be no ways inconvenient. He assured me with the same obliging Air of Sincerity and goodness as you are charm'd with in his letter, that it was not in the least so, and that my company again at Soissons woud be the greatest Relief and pleasure to him; with many other kind expressions which you woud be glad to hear but which I can't repeat. I have a thousand thanks to pay you Sir, for so kindly preventing[80] my desires, and

---

80 anticipating

continuing me in the possession of a Happiness which I was afraid was almost at an end. The Time I spend with Mr Poyntz is certainly the most agreable as well as the most improving part of my Life; He is a second Father to me, and it is in his Society that I am least sensible of the want of Your's.

I sent Dansel to Loraine not only to pay my debts, but to take care of cloaths and other things of value, (which I had nobody else to charge with in whom I cou'd well confide. I had a Suit sent from Luneville some time agoe which was a good deal damaged by the careless way of packing up. And I was afraid my others might be serv'd so too if I left them to the same hands.).

Besides as I writ to Prince Craon and other people of Quality, I thought it a more respectfull way of sending my letters than by the post: They are wonderfully Ceremonious at that court, and take notice of such little points as these.

I must entreat you dear Papa to allow me extraordinarily for the time I stay at Paris which will be about six weeks longer, for there are really so many occasions of spending money here and this is so necessary to make some figure, that I don't know which way I can avoid it: When I return to Soissons I will make it up to you, and as I hope to stay there till the end of Summer, you may depend upon my not spending above a hundred pound in all that time.

I must buy a new Suit here will cost me upwards of fifteen pounds and a Nightgown, my old one being so dirty that it is not fitt to wear.

Of all expence abroad that in cloaths is the most necessary and the worst saved, especially to a Gentleman as I am in the Suite of an Ambassador. However I am almost furnish'd, and don't expect to trouble you again till this time twelvemonth. I equip myself here throughout, because an ordinary Suit made at Paris will do me more honour than a fine one by a Countrey Tailor. I have drawn for forty pounds since my last Remittances were paid, and expect by the beginning of April to make it up a hundred. That cursed Article of Coach Hire undoes me here. I fence and dance at a great price but tis better so than learning of bad Masters who are dearer tho' they ask you less.

You will be applied to upon my Recommendation and My lord Kintore[81] by a dependant of his who wants a Surgeon's place in some Ship of any of the Squadrons that we send out this Spring. You will much oblige me to do him service, My lord Kintore being my particular Freind, and one whom I shall have the honour of bringing you acquainted with at his Return to England. He is of a great Jacobite Family in Scotland, but being wiser than his Relations has a mind to Reconcile himself to the Government, and desires me to obtain him your protection to introduce him to Sr Rob.[82] I dare say you wont be

---

81 Most likely the Scottish John Keith, 3rd Earl of Kintore (*c.*1699–1758).
82 Sir Robert Walpole (1676–1745), regarded as the first Prime Minister; knighted in 1725, and created 1st Earl of Orford 1742.

sorry for the office, the rather that he may perhaps have a mind to one of your pretty Girls. He is sober and a Man of good understanding, but bashfull and somewhat awkward. I shall write to you more formally by him a month or two hence.

I find you are uneasy at the Situation the King's Speech has left us in,[83] but depend upon it notwithstanding the little Triumph that the Enemies of the Government may shew upon the present seeming Uncertainty of Affairs, they will be concluded to their confusion, and to the honour of the Councils they oppose. The greatest Mischief that has been done us and which you are not sensible of, was by the Number of disaffected papers full of false and malicious insinuations, which being translated and shewn to foreign Ministers unacquainted with the Lenity of our Constitution and the Liberty of Scandal it allows, made them think that the Nation wou'd disavow the Measures taken by the Court, and were the principal cause of the delays and difficulties that retard the publick peace. The Vigorous resolution of both Houses to support his Majesty in his councils will, no doubt undeceive them, and contribute very much to bring affairs to that Decision we desire. Adieu my dear Papa.

Paris Mars ye 11th NS

Dear Papa.

The Affair of the Gosport Man of War has rais'd a most extravagant Spirit of Resentment in the French: They talk of nothing less than hanging their own officer, and seem to expect that Our's shall come off as ill.[84] I have talked to his

---

83 Addressing Parliament on 21 January 1729, George II spoke of the proposal by the Allies (Britain, Austria, France and the Netherlands) for a Provisional Treaty of Soissons to secure European peace; he referred to his 'reasonable hopes of the concurrence of the Imperial Court and the Court of Madrid'; but 'no definitive answer being returned by either of them, nor the project of the Provisional Treaty either accepted or rejected, the fate of Europe is still held in suspence.' Resumption of hostilities with Spain remained possible.

84 The furore resulted from the zeal of a junior lieutenant, Thomas Smith (?1707–62) on the *Gosport*. In late November 1728 the ship lay at anchor at Plymouth; other officers had gone ashore, leaving Smith in command, when a French corvette took shelter in the sound. As she left she came close to the *Gosport* whereupon Lieutenant Smith required her captain 'to haul in his pennant in respect to the king of Great Britain's colours.' The captain having arranged to salute the citadel felt insulted; a letter of complaint was addressed to the British government by the French authorities; and, following an Admiralty enquiry, Smith was dismissed from the service on 27 March 1729. The severity of this sentence provoked such a public outcry that, on 12 May, Smith was pardoned and restored to his former rank. Promotion followed at intervals; he achieved the rank of admiral in 1757.

Excell: about it; he says he has had no account of it from England, but desires me to tell you that he is in hopes the French Officer has made a false report, and that if nothing very extraordinary has been done as the case must have happened frequently he shou'd thin[k] it very proper that as many precedents as can be found shoud be collected and sent him over. He apprehends as much as you a popular declamation from the Craftsman[85] on this unlucky Subject; The Imbarkation you speak of is uncertain (as far as I can know from him) and intended only to reinforce our Garrisons. Perhaps there may be more in it which he does not think fitt to trust me with, tho' I hardly imagine so, because I have such marks of his Confidence as convince me he does not doubt of my Discretion.

Love to my Brother Tom, I dare say he will be a gainer in the end by this warm action, though it happened to be ill tim'd: I am glad the Young fellow has so much of the Lyttelton Spirit in him.

What you tell me of Tom Pitt amazes me.[86] I shall obey your advice in being cautious how I think any man my friend too soon, since he whose affection I was surest of has so injuriously convinced me of my mistake. I confess I thought Malice or Illnature as great Strangers to him as to poor Chriss, but what are the Judgements of Young Men? Indeed my dear Papa, We are very silly fellows. I am glad you are so happy in your Daughter; You may assure her from me that I love her dearly, and resent any Infamy to her, much more than if it was done to me. I am much concernd to hear she has been ill, and expect impatiently to know she's better. I cannot help transcribing a few lines of Sister Molly's letter of the 10th, to shew you that your Goodness to your children meets at least with a Grateful Sense. "We shoud pass our time but ill if the good humour of Mama did not make us all chearful, and made amends for the loss of those diversions which London woud afford us. My Dear the oftener I converse with her the more I love her, and every one of her Actions shews me a Virtue I wish to imitate. This you must be sensible of as well as I, but there is such a pleasure in praising those we love that I must dwell upon the subject which I dare say will be as grateful to you as it is to me. How happy are we blest with such Parents! When I see my Papa quite spent with the Cares of his

---

    Smith's story is remarkable; it becomes the more so when viewed in the context of GL's letter. Thomas Smith—affectionately referred to by GL as 'my brother Tom' in the next paragraph—was Sir Thomas Lyttelton's illegitimate son. For the whole of his life he was treated as a member of the Lyttelton family; his portrait was painted by Benjamin Wilson (1721–88) and hangs in Hagley Hall; he lived at Rockingham Hall on the Hagley estate and died there on 28 August 1762. (See ODNB.)

85 The anti-Walpole periodical that began in 1726; the title was intended to label Walpole as a 'man of craft'.

86 See n. 130 below.

family; Mama confined here for the Good of her Children; I'm overpowered with Gratitude and Love. May You and They continue well, and I want nothing else to compleat my Happiness."

This Sr is a faithful extract, and speaks the language of all our hearts.

I am afraid there is an honest Gentleman at Christchurch Security for the plate you promis'd, without which I coud not have had the money; but I am not very certain.

Adieu My Dear Papa

[Paris August 1729]

Dear Papa.

I am glad you find the news I sent you so generally confirmd, but must beg pardon for an incorrect expression that escap'd me in my last, having said that the A[llies] of H[anover] guaranteed the Succession of D[on] C[arlos] which I believe is only true of England France and Holland.

Pour ce que regarde M. Keene[87] je puis seulement vous dire qu'il me semble que nos Ministres ont toujours fait beaucoup de cas de son Habilité, et qu'ils ont beaucoup deferé á ses conseils en tout ce qui regarde la Cour d'Espagne. Je sçais aussi que son Sentiment a toujours été de n'employer jamais les Menaces en traitant avec cette Cour; parce que connaissant la fierté Espagnole il croyoit qu'on ne pourroit rien gagner d'eux par ces moyens; c'est pourquoi il etoit d'avis ou de venir à une guerre ouverte sans nous arréter a faire des Menaces, ou de proceder par des voyes de Douceur comme nous avons fait jusqu'icy. Voila son système et on s'est bien trouvé de l'avoir suivi.

Il me paroit d'autant plus raisonable que je ne croy pas qu'on auroit jamais pû intimider la Reine d'Espagne, qui de l'Humeur dont elle est ne se feroit pas mise en peine de voir le Royaume de son Mari plongé dans tous les maux de la Guerre pourvû que ca n'eut pas empechéses Desseins en faveur de son Fils. Elle se regarde comme une Etrangere, et ne s'attend pas a rester deux jours en Espagne si le roy venoit à mourir, ou à abdiquer la Couronne. Mais enfin je ne pretens pas justifier tous les Pas de Mr Keene, dont quelquesuns peuvent avoir eté trop peu respectueux aux orders qu'il a reçus. Vous dites que l'Article de la Guarantée pourroit bien etre contestéen d'autres endroits qu'à Vienné; je le crois, car il y a un certain parti chez nous qui est fort dans les interêts de l'Empereur et qui sera sans doute fort faché de voir le peu de soins que nous

---

87 Benjamin Keene (1697–1747), British Ambassador at Madrid, 1727–39; he helped to negotiate the Treaty of Seville, 1729; knighted in 1754.

en prenons; mais laissons murmurer ces Messieurs là, et faisons toujours une bonne Paix sans nous soucier de leur mecontentments. Je ne puis pas vous repondre decisivement sur le Dedommagement des Pertes de nos Marchands; c'est une chose a souhaiter; mais je doute de son execution: Ce qu'il y a d'assurer c'est qu'on reparera les torts de notre Commerce, et qu'on le mettera en seureté pour l'Avenir.

Je suis charmé de la letter du petit Dicky et je vous prie de lui remercier de ma part.

La Maladie de Tom m'afflige mais j'espere qu'il n'est pas dangereux.

J'ay grande pitié de la pauvre Nanny Pitt; elle n'etoit pas belle auparavant, mais à present elle deviendra Effroiable.

Dieu scait si ce que je vous ecris est bon Francais, car je n'ay pas assez de tems pour l'etudier, ni pour en corriger le moindre mot.

[About Mr Keene I can only tell you that it seems to me our ministers have always thought highly of his competence, and invariably deferred to his advice on everything regarding the Spanish court. I also know his view has always been never to use threats when negotiating with that court; because, recognising the pride of the Spanish, he believed you can get nothing from them by those means; therefore his advice was either to declare open war without our waiting to issue threats, or to proceed by gentle methods such as we have used so far. That is his system and it has proved to our advantage having adopted it.

It seems to me all the more reasonable since I don't believe we should ever be able to intimidate the Spanish queen who, given her disposition, would not risk seeing her husband's kingdom plunged into all the evils of war, provided that did not obstruct her plans for her son. She regards herself as a foreigner and would not be expected to remain a couple of days in Spain if the king were to die or renounce his crown. But finally, I don't pretend to justify all the steps taken by Mr. Keene some of which may have been too distant from the instructions he was given. You say that the Article of Guarantee could easily have been disputed elsewhere than in Vienna; I believe it because there is a certain party at home which strongly supports the interests of the emperor and which undoubtedly will be very aggrieved to see the minimal interest that we show in the matter. But let those people grumble, and let us hold fast to a sound peace without troubling ourselves about their discontents. I cannot give you a positive answer about the losses of our merchants: it is highly desirable but I doubt if it will be realised. What is certain is that the damage to our trade will be repaired and that it will be made secure for the future.

I am delighted by the letter from little Dicky and beg you to thank him for me.

Tom's illness worries me but I hope it isn't serious.

I'm very sorry about poor Nanny Pitt; she wasn't beautiful before but now she will become frightful.[88]

God knows if what I have written for you is good French because I have neither enough time to check it nor to correct the smallest word.]

Paris August ye 30th. *N. S.*

Monsieur

Nous avons recus des Nouvelles fort extraordinaire d'Hanovre scavoir que le Roy se voit sur le point d'etre Attaqué dans ses Etats par son Voisin le Roy de Prusse. Ce Prince a une si forte Inclination pour les Grands Hommes qu'il les prend par tout ou il les trouve, et il vient nouvellement de faire enlever par ses officiers plusieurs sujets d'Hanovre qui avoient le malheur d'etre propres par leur taille a entrer dans ses troupes sans demander leur consentement ou celuy du Roy leur Maitre. S[a] M[ajesté] se croyant oblige à faire des Reprisailles arreta tous les Prussiens qui se trouvoient alors dans ses Etâts, mais il promit en meme temps au Roy de Prusse de les mettre tous en liberté aussitôt, que Luy de son coté auroit congedié les Hannoveriens. Le procedé etoit fort equitable mais Frederic declara que si le Roy ne luy envoyoit pas une autre Reponse plus satisfactoire avant un jour qu'il luy marqua, il viendra s'en faire raison à la tete de quatrevingt Mille Hommes. Comme le Roy ne se mit pas en peine de ses Menaces et laissa passer le tems prescript, S[a] M[ajesté] P[russe] donna ordres à cinquante mille Hommes de ses Troupes de marcher en diligence aux Frontieres, et pour faire voir qu'il etoit bien serieux il deboursa une grosse Somme pour les entretenir. De façon que nous sommes a la veille d'une Guerre au milieu de nos Negotiations pour la Paix, et pour un sujet qui n'a aucun raport aux Differents que nous travaillons à terminer. Nous ne doutons pas que l'Empereur ne fomente sous main la Querelle et qu'il ne tache d'allumer un feu de cette etincelle qui embraseroit toute l'Allemagne. On travaille pourtant a l'etouffer avant qu'il eclate, mais on a tout à craindre de la Folie du Roy de Prusse et des Artifices de la Cour Imperiale. Comme ce Roy a une Armée sur pied beaucoup plus forte que celle de S[a] M[ajesté] B[ritannique] et que le Pays d'Hanovre est tout ouvert il est à craindre que l'Ennemi n'y faisse de grands progress avanat que le Roy pourra se mettre en etat de l'empecher. Les suites d'une pareille enterprise seroient assurement funestes à l'Aggresseur, mais les Commencements pourront bien etre facheux pour Sa Majesté. Ce

---

88 GL was much concerned when inoculation against smallpox threated Nanny (Anne) Pitt with disfigurement; he developed a strong affection for her and their friendship was long lasting.

n'est pas la premiere Extravagance de cette nature que le Roy de Prusse a faite; il a autrefois enlevé un Marchand Suedois qui voyageoit dans le Voisinage de ses Etats, et plusieurs Saxons pour les forcer de servir dans ses Troupes; et on a en beaucoup de peine a luy persuader de les rendre aux Instances et aux Menaces des Puissances interessées. Je croy que de toutes les Tetes couronnées de l'Univers c'est la plus insensée que la sienne. Il se peut bien que vous avez deja entendu cette Nouvelle, mais comme je la tiens de Son Excellence, j'ay cru qu'il ne seroit pas mal à propos de vous la mander. Je me flatte que si la guerre se faisoit tout de bon vous m'envoyerez à Hanovre pour ne pas manquer à une si belle occasion de me signaler au service et à la vue du Roy. C'est une Grace que j'attends de votre Bonté et du Regard que vous m'avez toujours temoigné pour mon Honneur et ma Reputation. Mais en trois semaines d'icy nous en parlerons plus certainement, et alors je prendrai le parti que vous jugerez le plus convenable. Son Excellence a eté fort indisposé mais il commence a se retablir. J'espere que vous vous portez bien et que Madame est arrivée sans accident a Hagley.

Your most Dutiful Son
G. L.

[Papa

We have received very extraordinary news from Hanover to the effect that the King appears on the point of being attacked in his states by his neighbour the King of Prussia. This prince has a strong inclination towards Tall Men that he seizes them wherever he finds them, and recently he had his officers carry off several Hanoverian subjects who had the misfortune to be suitably tall to be part of his troops without their consent or that of their master, the King. His Majesty believing himself obliged to take reprisals arrested all the Prussians who were then in his territory, but he promised the Prussian King at the same time that they would all be set free as soon as he, for his part, freed the Hanoverians. The procedure was very fair but Frederick declared that if the King did not send him a more satisfactory reply within a day that he would determine, he would proceed to take the law into his own hands at the head of eighty thousand men. As the King did not make himself uneasy on account of these threats and allowed the prescribed time to pass, his Prussian Majesty ordered fifty thousand men from his army to march with speed to the frontiers, and in order to make it clear that he was very serious he made a large sum of money available to maintain them. Thus we are on the brink of war in the middle of our negotiations about peace, and about a subject which has no connection whatever with the disputes we are working to resolve. We have no doubt that the Emperor is not secretly fomenting the quarrel and that he will not blurt out so as to ignite a fire with this spark which would inflame the whole of Germany. Attempts continue, however, to damp the situation down before it explodes, but there is always the fear of the lunacy of the Prussian King and the stratagems of the Imperial Court. As this King has an army on the march very much stronger than than that of his Britannic Majesty and because the country of Hanover is wholly unprotected it is feared that the enemy will not hesitate to make great progress before the King puts himself in a position to halt it. The consequences of such an enterprise will certainly be disastrous for the aggressor but the early stages could well be vexatious for his Majesty. It is not the first extravagant act of this kind that the Prussian King has committed; in the past he kidnapped a Swedish merchant who was travelling in the vicinity of his lands, and several Saxons in order to compel them to serve in his forces; and there was considerable difficulty in persuading him to give them back by entreaties and by threats from the Powers concerned. I am convinced that of all the crowned heads of the world he is the most absurd. It might possibly be that you have already heard this news, but as I have it from his Excellency, I thought it not inappropriate to pass it on to you. I flatter myself that if the war comes about in earnest you will send me to Hanover so as not to miss such a glorious opportunity to reveal myself in the service of, and to catch the attention of, the King. It is a mercy that I can hope for your blessing and the regard you have always shown for my honour and my reputation. But in three weeks from now we shall talk about it more positively, and then I will take the course you judge the most advisable. His Excellency has been very unwell but he is now beginning to recover. I hope that you are keeping well, and that my Mother has reached Hagley safe and sound.]

[Paris 7 September 1729]

Dear Papa.

Sunday by four a clock we had the good news of a Dauphin,[89] and since that time I have thought myself in Bedlam. The natural Gayety of the Nation is so improv'd on this occasion that they are all stark mad with Joy, and do nothing but Dance and Sing about the streets by hundreds and by thousands. The Expressions of their Joy are admirable. One fellow gives notice to the Publick that he designs to draw Teeth for a Week together upon the Pont Neuf Gratis — The King is as proud of what he has done as if he had gaind a kingdom and tells every body that he sees, Qu'il scaura bien faire des Fils tant qu'il voudra.[90] We are to have a firework to Morrow, his Majesty to sup in town.

---

89 Louis, Dauphin of France, son of Louis XV, born 4 September 1729, died 1765. The event was commemorated by Giovanni Paolo Panini in his painting, *Preparations for the festivities to celebrate the birth of the Dauphin in Piazza Navona in 1729* (1731).
90 'He knew how to make as many sons as he wanted.'

The Duke of Orleans[91] was sincerely and without any suspicion of affectation transported at the Birth of a Dauphin. The Succession was a Burden too heavy for his Indolence to support and he piously sings Halleluja for his happy Delivery from it. The Good old Cardinal[92] cryd for Joy—It is very late and I have not slept these three nights for the Squibs and Crackers and other Noises that the People make in the Streets, so must beg leave to conclude—with assuring that I am with the greatest

Dear Papa.
Your very Dutiful
And Obedient Son—
G. Lyttelton

Paris September ye 16th N. S.

Dear Papa,

The Difference with Prussia is nigh compos'd, that King being intimidated with the firmness he found in his Majesty's Allies to stand by him in case of a rupture which he flattered himself they wou'd not have done especially the French. On the other side Seckendorf[93] the Imperial Minister who had intimated in private Discourse with the Danish Secretary that if the K[ing] of G[reat] B[ritain] calld in any of his Allies to his Assistance against Prussia his Master wou'd think himself oblig'd to assist that kingdom with his forces, being askd in Council whether the King of Prussia might depend upon Succours from his Imperial Majesty replyd that he had no Orders to promise any. I suppose you have a more ample account of this Affair from Mr West,[94] so shall say no more of it. Mr Poyntz has been very ill but is I thank God on the mending hand.

We are now in the middle of September, and tho' the thoughts of leaving so kind a Freind are very unpleasing to me, yet as I am now at the latest term I ever propos'd, and as a further Delay wou'd make my journey to Italy

---

91   Louis of Bourbon, Duke of Orléans (1703–52), directly descended from Louis XIV; a pious and cultured prince who took little part in politics.
92   Cardinal Andrè-Hercule de Fleury (1653–1743), appointed Chief Minister in 1726, effectively controlling the government of Louis XV until 1743.
93   Frederick Graf von Seckendorf (1673–1763), distinguished soldier. In 1726 he became Austrian representative at the Prussian court where he exercised considerable influence on Frederick William I (father of Frederick the Great). In the same year he was appointed General of Cavalry in the Imperial Army.
94   Gilbert West (1706–56), friend of GL's since their days at Eton, had obtained a place in the Secretary of State's office in April 1728; he shared GL's literary and political interests, wrote poetry, and translated Pindar.

impracticable, I am oblig'd to mention it to you, and to desire immediate leave to set out that way.

His Excellency himself advises me not to Defer it any longer the Winter being the proper Season for seeing Rome, and this we are now in for passing the Alps.

It is probable He will not be long in France, and therefore it is not worth my while for a month or two longer to lose the opportunity of travelling as I always design'd.

I hope I have given you no reasons to alter your first intention of sending me to Italy a Countrey I long to see and where I may expect to improve myself considerably.

You will undoubtedly thank Mr Poyntz upon my taking leave of him, for the many infinite Obligations I have to him which do me so much honour, and of which I have so deep a Sense. I protest to you my Dear Papa that as you are the only Person in the world to whom I am more indebted than to Him, so after you there is Nobody whom I Love and Honour, and to serve whom I wou'd sacrifice Life and Fortune so willingly as to Mr Poyntz. Were he a private Man and divested of that lustre which great Abilities and Employments give him, his Virtues only woud gain him the Veneration and Love of all the World. My Nearness to him has given me opportunity to study his character, and I have found it more beautiful and Perfect the closer I lookd into and examind it. I propose to myself a great deal of pleasure in telling you some particulars of his conduct which his Modesty conceald from Eyes that were less intent upon him than mine. You need not give yourself the trouble of looking out for Recommendations for me to any of the Italian Courts, I being acquainted with their Ministers here and not doubting to have as many as I shall want. We have had news of Mr Halsey's Death at Stowe[95] but it being contradicted afterwards I waited for the Confirmation of it from you. The Tumult of the people for the Dauphin's birth is now a little over and the Nation are returning to their senses. I hope soon to hear of Chrissy's safe Delivery and of a little Prince of Swallowfield[96] being the fruits of it.

    I am Dear Papa
      Your very Dutiful
        And Obedient Son
           G. L.

---

95 Edmund Halsey died in 1729 at Stowe, the home of his daughter, Anne, wife of the owner, Richard Temple (later Viscount Cobham). Halsey owned the Anchor Brewery from 1696 till his death when ownership passed to Ralph Thrale, friend of Dr Johnson.

96 The seventeenth-century manor house, Swallowfield, and its lands in Berkshire were bought by Thomas Pitt's grandfather in 1719.

Paris Sep: ye 27 N. S.

Dear Papa.

Stanhope is on his way to Spain: the Caprice and Stubbornness of the King of Spain not always to be govern'd even by his Wife[97] made it necessary to send a Minister to that Court of too much weight and Authority to be trifled with. It is a melancholy Reflexion that the Wisest Councils and best Measures for the Publick Good are sometimes to be frustrated by the Folly and Incapacity of One Man. How low is the Servitude of Humankind when they are reduc'd to respect the Extravagance and court the Pride of a senseless creature who has no other character of Royalty than pow'r to do Mischief! However I hope all will come out well, and that his Catholick Majesty will behave himself a little like a King since the Queen will have him be one in spite of his teeth. About three months ago she caught him going down stairs at Midnight to Abdicate in his nightgown. He was so incensed at the Surprise and Disappointment that he beat her cruelly, and wou'd have strangled her if she had not call'd for help. This Attempt of his alarm'd her terribly, and put her upon carrying him about Spain to amuse him with seeing sights, and keep St Ildefonso out of his head.[98] The Journey has cost immense sums, so that the Indult and Treasure they expect from Lima is already mortgaged, and the King more in debt than ever.

 I have a word of two to add to my French Letter upon the Succession of Don Carlos. There is a secret Article in the Quadr^le Alliance,[99] not much attended to which says that in case the Dutch should be unwilling to pay their share of ye Neutral Garrisons, the King of Spain should if he pleas'd take upon himself to furnish their Quota for them. (i.e. two thousand Men)

Article Separé

Que si les Seigneurs Etats Generaux des Provinces Unies des Pais Bas trouvoient, qu'il leur fut trop à charge de fournir leur quotepart des Subsides qui seront payez aux Cantons Suisses, pour les Garrisons de Livourne, Porto Feraio, de Parme, et de Plaisance, selon la teneur du Traité d'Alliance conclu ce jourd'huy, il a eté declare expressement par cet Article Separé et convenu entre les quatre Parties Contractantes que dans ce cas le Roy Cath[olique]: pourra se charger de la portion qu'auroient à payer les Seigneurs Etats Generaux.

---

97 Philip V (1683–1746), dominated by his second wife, Elizabeth Farnese of Parma.
98 After his summer palace was destroyed by fire in 1719, Philip became obsessed with building a grandiose replacement at San Ildefonso, 34 miles north-west of Madrid; it was modelled on Versailles, built by his grandfather Louis XIV of France.
99 The Quadruple Alliance had been formed in 1718 between Britain, Austria, France and the Netherlands to resist the attempt by Philip V of Spain to annex Sardinia and Sicily, thereby nullifying the Peace of Utrecht, 1713, at the end of the War of Spanish Succession.

[That if the members of the Dutch Parliament found that it was too burdensome for them to afford their share of the subsidies which were to be paid to the Swiss Cantons for the garrisons at Livorno, Porto Feraio, Parma, and Plaisance, according to the terms of the Treaty of the Alliance concluded this day, it has been expressly stated in this separate article and and agreed by the four contracting parties that in this case his Catholic Majesty will accept responsibility for the share that should be paid by the Dutch Parliament.]

By which it is plain that the fifth Article was not designd to be strictly understood, but that notwithstanding the Prohibition there exprest a Proportion of Troops in Spanish Pay might be admitted into Italy. But what is of much greater importance, there is a private Article in the Vienna Treaty by which the Emperour is allow'd expressly to send a Body of eight thousand Imperialists into Tuscany and Parma upon the Death of the present Possessours. This is so certain, that upon the late Illness of the Grand Duke which was apprehended to be Mortal, the Imperial Minister actually writ to hasten the March of the Troops that way. This Point the Emperour obtain'd without our Knowledge or Consent in contradiction to the terms of a Treaty which we made in favour of his Interests and in prejudice to our own: And yet He and his Friends complain of us for securing ourselves against his Breach of Treaty by giving up an Article we are no ways concernd in and which he had made so light of himself. One woud be astonish'd how Spain cou'd be prevaild on to to yield him such a point, but the whole Vienna Treaty is perfect Infatuation on that side where every real Advantage is given up to the Chimerical Marriage with the A[rch] Duchess.

Mr Poyntz is better; but the deep concern he takes in every incident that affects the Negotiation, much retards his Recovery. Never man lov'd his countrey better or was more active in its service.

I have been much out of order with a Distemper that has been universal at Paris and is probably owing to the Seine Water, but I am very well again.

I am troubl'd and uneasy at my expences here though you are too kind and generous to mention them in any of your letters. I am guilty of no extravagance but dont know how to Save as some people do. Since I come here I have bought a new suit of Mourning, my old being quite worn out, and a handsome Summer Suit my best not being good enough for Paris although it was for Hautefontaine. Besides this I have furnishd myself with new Linnen, bought a new Livery for my Man, and a hundred necessary Bagatelles which one finds at Paris better than any where else. I must make a good cloath Suit to travel in, my last Winters Cloaths being too fine for that purpose. I shant enumerate the other expences, you know them having been here yourself.

This is the time of my life in which Money will be ill sav'd, and your Goodness is lavish of it to me, I think without offending your Prudence. My

Dear Papa I know no happiness but in your kindness and if ever I lose that I am the worst of Wretches.

Your very Dutiful

And Obedient Son.

G. L.

Paris October ye 6th. NS 1729

Dear Papa.

I have the greatest thanks to return you for the many proofs of Confidence and Affection you gave me in your last, and shall labour to deserve that Goodness which is so kind and complaisant to my Desires. I shall in obedience to your Orders set out for Italy to morrow where I hope to make such improvements as will answer the expences of the Journey.

But whatever advantage or pleasure I may propose I cannot without a sensible affliction take leave of my Dear Freind Mr Poyntz of whose favours to me I have so deep a Sense that I cannot too often express my acknowledgements. The time I have enjoyed his Company has been spent so happily and so much to my honour and advantage that I don't know how to reconcile my thoughts to a Period of it. It is not so much the liveliness of his Wit and uncommon Strength of Judgement that charm me in his conversation as those Great and Noble Sentiments which wou'd have been admir'd by Ancient Rome, and have done honour to the most Virtuous Ages. He is going to his Country seat where I hope the Air and a little Repose from the fatigue of Business will entirely restore his health.

I shall observe your caution against Grapes, new Wine and pretty Women tho they are all very tempting things as you will own. I have credit from Mr Arbuthnot for several places in Italy, and have drawn upon you for a hundred pounds in present at two usances[100] to clear me here and carry me on: I will let you know as often as I take up considerable sums. I shall go alone as far as Florence but there I expect to meet with Mr Williams[101] who is a young Gentleman of a very good character. I don't know who the Baronet is against whom you caution me at Rome but there is one Sr Rob. Myrton there whom I had the Misfortune of living with at Luneville who is the most contemptible odious Rake I ever knew.[102] I hope you will find dear Mama entirely recovered,

---

100 At twice the normal period allowed for the repayment of a loan.
101 (Sir) Charles Hanbury Williams (1708–59), satirist, poet and diplomat; he was in Florence by November 1729, en route to Rome and Bologna.
102 Sir Robert Myrton, 2nd Baronet of Gogar (d.1774).

and all your family in good health. My kind Love to all of them, and to the absent when you write.

You shall hear from me from Lions, I have time for no more now but to assure you of my Duty and Affection. I have wrote to Ld Cobham upon my going to Italy.

Direct all your letters for me chez Mr Arbuthnot Banquier dans la Rue Argenteuil proche de la bute St Roch à Paris. I have directed him to send them after me.

(Post.) I have the pleasure of being able to assure you that the final Project of a Treaty sent to Spain is entirely Satisfactory and Honourable and that it contains a full Redress and Reparation of all Abuses Greivances and Wrongs.

His Excellency thanks you for your letter and will write to you as soon as he gets to Hautefontaine.

Lions, October ye 16th. NS. 1729

Dear Papa

I came well to Lions Friday last after a very pleasant journey if the Roads had been a little better. I am mightily pleas'd with this fine City, and cou'd be willing to stay longer int; but it begins to rain and I must make haste to pass the Alps. I cannot take leave of France without sending you a few Observations upon the present state of it but I do it upon condition that you shall shew them to Nobody though they shou'd have the good fortune to please you.

The present King[103] is so little known either to his Subjects or Foreigners, that the first have not much to say in his praise and the latter are at full liberty to Suppose what they please to his disadvantage: For this reason and perhaps from a little pleasure we take in Mortifying the French, we have generally a worse notion of him in England than he really Deserves. We represent him as Ill-natur'd, Brutal, and Incapable of Affairs: but this character does not justly belong to him in any one particular. I have enquir'd into the Truth of the Stories we are told of his Barbarity, and find them entirely false. He [has] shewn great Marks of Good nature; particularly to the Queen, in being the only Man in France that did not hate her for not bringing him a Son: His Behaviour to those about him is perfectly affable and easy, I think more so than is consistent with Majesty. There is no one Act of Violence or Injustice that can be laid to his charge, nothing Vicious or Irregular in his conduct. As to his Incapacity for Business they are much mistaken who suppose that he

---

103   Louis XV (1710–74) succeeded to the throne aged only five; married Maria, daughter of the deposed King of Poland, in 1725.

does nothing but hunt and Sleep. I know for certain that there is no affair of moment either Foreign or Domestick that the Cardinal does not communicate to him. I believe indeed he always acquiesces in his Minister's Opinion but he is constantly consulted, and let into all the Secret of Affairs before any body else is trusted with it, even the Garde des Sceaux[104] himself. Nor is this Confidence ever Prejudicial, for he is Master of an impenetrable Secrecy, which is a good deal owing to the natural Phlegm and Reservedness of his temper. It is hard to say whether he has courage, but the Cardinal thinks he has and dreads to engage him in a War for fear he should grow too fond of it. He is cold, unactive, and insensible to all kind of Pleasures; his very Hunting does not delight him; and this is what the French are angry at: They love that their Monarch shou'd be Galant, Magnificent and Ambitious, and don't care what price they pay for it provided there be great news from Flanders and fine Entertainments at Versailles. Louis the fourteenth understood their Genius, and humoured it in his Wars and his Amours: But the Frugality of the present Court and the Dulness of a continued Peace are Things they cannot relish.

In truth his Majesty's worst fault is a kind of bashful Timidity which makes him shun all occasions of shewing himself and has very much the Air of Heaviness. He is Devout, which may degenerate into Bigottry, as it did in his Grandfather.

It is to be feard from the Eagerness he expresses of Winning Money at Play, that he may grow avaricious. But that is not always a certain Sign. His Virtues and Vices will probably remain as much conceald as they are now during the Life of the Cardinal; but at his Death Flattery and Love may give him a new turn, or his Disposition being no longer under any check may exert itself more conspicuously: Upon the whole there appears Nothing shining, nothing Elevated, or Commanding in his Character, but such a Mediocrity as may make his People easy, and very capable of Governing a kingdom where there are no Factions to contend with, and no Disaffection to overcome.

His first Minister is the most Absolute that ever exercis'd that Authority in France not excepting even Richelieu. There is not one Man in the whole Nation dares speak of any Business to the King besides Himself, and those immediately under his Direction. The Parliament is hardly the Shadow of what it was; the Princes of the Blood and the Nobility are all Pensionarys and Dependants of the Court from the Dukes and Marshalls of France to the lowest officer in the service. Their Interest once so formidable to the Power of the Ministry is reduc'd to such a degree of Weakness that not one of them if he had courage to Rebell, is able to raise fifty Soldiers against the King. And what is of no less moment the Women are quite out of play, and oblig'd to

---

104 The Keeper of the Seals.

content themselves with Love Intrigues instead of Cabals against the Ministry to which they have a more violent Inclination. So that the Authority of the Cardinal is without bounds, the Disposal of all Dignities and Employments is solely in his hands, and all Business both at home and abroad is managed by his Ministry and Orders. The use he has made of this Authority has been so just and Beneficial to the State that except the Jansenists whom he treats with too much Rigour, the Nation is generally satisfied with his Administration…[105]

I am more strongly attachd to my own Country by what I see of the Miseries abroad, and find the Spirit of Wiggism grow[s] upon me under the Influence of Arbitrary Pow'r. It will still encrease when I come into Italy where the Oppression is more sensible in its effects, and where the finest country in the world is quite dispeopled by it. I set out to morrow for Genova in company with Sr. Will. Wyndham's son[106], and shall go from thence to Turin.

I have sufficiently tir'd you with so long a letter so shall end with assuring you of the Respect and Affection with which I am

Dear Papa Your very Dutiful and Obedient Son

G. L.

———

Geneva October ye 26th NS 1729

Mon cher Pere,

Il y a trois jours que je suis à Geneve et je vous assure que j'en suis tout à fait charmé. Le Lac, les Montagnes, et les Promenades qui sont autour de cette belle ville, presentent la vue la plus riante et la plus agreable qu'on puisse voir, et la Societé en dedans est aussi polie et aussi scavante que dans aucun endroit de l'Europe. Il me paroit qu'on aurait beaucoup de peine à trouver ailleurs une si jolie Retraite pour l'Exercice et pour l'Etude.

En venant de Lions icy je me suis un peu detourné de ma Route pour voir le Grand Couvent de Chartreux,[107] qui est situé dans un Desert affreux parmi des Rochers et des Precipices presqu' inaccessibles ou de tout coté on voit tomber des Torrents du plus haut sommet des Montagnes pour former une petite Rivière qui remplit la profondeur du Vallon et coule avec beaucoup de Rapidité entre des Bois et des Forets sauvages dont tout le Païs est couvert.

---

105 Of the eight folio pages GL devoted to an account of the political situation in France, five have been omitted.

106 Sir William Wyndham (1687–1740), prominent parliamentarian; his son Charles (1710–63), later Earl of Egremont (1750) was GL's contemporary at Christ Church, Oxford.

107 The Carthusian monastery of La Grande Chartreuse was founded *c*.1084 by St Bruno (d.1101) at an altitude of 3,300 feet.

Jamais Situation n'a eté plus conforme au Genie des Chartreux que celle cy que choisit leur Fondateur pour y batir leur Couvent, ni plus propre a leur faire oublier le monde par l'Eloignement de toute Societé humaine, et de tout ce qui peut reveiller leurs Desirs. La Maison est batie simplement et ne consiste que dans un long arrangement de Cloitres et de Cellules separées les unes des autres, avec une Eglise et une Salle à manger. Vous scavez qu'ils ne parlent que les Dimanches et les jours de Fête et qu'ils mangent maigre toute l'année. Une Solitude et une Discipline si rigoureuse les rend sans doute trés miserables, ils vivent pourtant long tems, et jouissent d'une tranquillité apparante. Leur Temperance conserve leur santé, et ils s'amusent dans leurs cellules a des occupations mechaniques et laborieuses qui servent a vaincre l'ennui de leur Prison. Il y en a cependant quelquesuns qui n'etant pas propres au travail languissent dans une oisivité penible, et se tuent à force de rever. Ils nous ont recu Mr Windham et moy avec beaucoup de civilité, et nous ont fait les honneurs de leur Maison en nous donnant un bon souper en Maigre, et des Lits assez commodes dans leurs cellules. Leur Ordre est riche quoiqu'il ne paroit pas dans leur maniere de vivre; le Couvent où j'ay eté possede tous les Bois et toutes les Montagnes qui l'environnent par l'espace de trois ou quatre Lieux. Je souhaitrois que le Recit que je viens de faire pourroit vous donner quelque Idee du Plaisir que j'ay eprouvé en voyant une Solitude plus sauvage et plus rude qu'aucune des celles qu'on nous depeint dans les Romans, et où Don Quichote n'auroit pas manqué de trouver des Geans et des Enchanteurs. La Hauteur prodigieuse des Rochers, le bruit des Eaux qui en tombent, l'Ombre des Bois dont ils sont ornée et la Riviere qui en arrose les pieds, forment une Scene si nouvelle et si etonnante que le plus habile pinceau ne viendra jamais a bout d'en peindre la bizarrerie et la beauté.—

Je partirai en deux jours pour Turin, ou je ferai un sejour de deux ou trois semaines. Je m'attends a trouver beaucoup d'Incommodité en passant les Alpes, parceque les Nieges commencent dèja à tomber. J'espere de recevoir bientot de vos nouvelles et de pouvoir me rejouir de la certitude qu'elles me donneront de votre Santé, et de celle de ma chere Mere et de mes Freres et Sœurs.

Duty to Dear Mama,
Adieu.

[My dear Papa,
I have been in Geneva for three days and I assure you I found it completely charming. The lake, the mountains, and the paved walks which surround this beautiful town offer the most attractive and the most satisfying prospect that one could ever see, and the townspeople are also civilised as well as learned as any place in Europe. It seems to me that one would have a great deal of trouble to find anywhere else such a lovely spot for exercise and for study.

On my way here from Lyons I took a little detour from my route in order to see the great Monastery of Chartreux which is situated in a fearful wasteland among rocks and virtually inaccessible precipices where you see on every side waterfalls from the highest mountain peaks which form a small river that fills the very depth of the valley to overflowing and rushes at great speed between woods and untamed forests with which all the countryside is covered. There never was a location more in keeping with the unique character of the brethren of Chartreux than that which was chosen by their founder as the place for building their monastery, nor more appropriate to their purpose to forget the world by distancing themselves from all human society and from everything that could stir their desires. The house has a simple design consisting only of a lengthy arrangement of cloisters and cells separated one from another, with a church and a refectory. You know that they talk only on Sundays and feast days, and that they eat frugally all the year round. Solitude and such a rigorous discipline undoubtedly make them very miserable; however they live a long time, and enjoy an obvious peacefulness. Temperance preserves their health, and they busy themselves in their cells with routine and laborious activities that help to ameliorate the boredom of their prison. Some of them, however, being unable to work, languish in the trials of idleness, wearing themselves out by dint of dreaming. They received Mr Windham and me with great politeness, and did us the honours of their establishment by giving us a good vegetarian supper, and beds which were comfortable enough in their cells. Their Order is rich though that is not obvious from their way of life; the monastery where I have been owns all the surrounding woods and mountains for a distance of three or four leagues. I hope that the account I have just given will give you some idea of the pleasure that I have experienced in seeing solitude wilder and more terrible than anything presented to us in fiction, and where Don Quixote would not have failed to discover giants and magicians. The enormous height of the rocks, the noise of the waterfalls, the gloom of the woods with which they are adorned and the river which waters their roots, make up a scene that is so unique and so astonishing that the most skilful paintbrush will never succeed in depicting its fantastic and beautiful nature!

In a couple of days I shall leave for Turin where I shall stay for two or three weeks. I expect to encounter considerable trouble in crossing the Alps because snow has already started to fall. I hope soon to receive news from you and to be able to rejoice in the certainty it will give me of your good health, and that of my dear mother and my brothers and sisters.]

My duty to dear Mama.

Adieu.

Turin November 16th NS.

Mon Cher Pere

Il y a dix ou douze jours que je suis icy j'ay trouvé un reception fort honnete dont je suis redevable aux Recommendations de Monsieur le Marq. de Santacru[108] Ambassadeur d'Espagne au Congré qui a demeuré longtemps a cette Cour et est fort considere: Si la Paix se fait il ira en Angleterre ou je vous prie Monsieur de vouloir bien le remercier pour moy des civilités gentil qu'il m'a faites. J'ay en une assez rude passage sur le Mont Cenis la neige tombant avec beaucoup de violence, et le Vent bise qui nous donna dans le visage nous causant un Froid epouventable. Danzel en a eu le plus grand mal, car une grosse fievre l'a pris, et il reste toujours fort malade. Nous montâmes sur des Mulets, mais pour descendre il nous fallut des chaises à Porteurs à cause des Precipices que la neige rendoit plus glisants, et qui veritablement faisoient peur. Les Brouillards etoient si epais qu'ils nous empechoient de voir les autres Alpes qui nous environnoient et qui sont beaucoup plus hautes que le Mont Cenis quoique celuyci a trois lieuies de Hauteur.

Ce qui nous faisoit le plus de plaisir etoit un Torrent qui peut s'appeller une Rivière, qui tomboit *de la cime* de la cime de la Montagne et formoit des magnifiques Cascades entre les Rochers qui s'opposoient a sa chute. La Plaine de Piedmont est belle et fort bien cultivée, ce qui nous a charmé d'autant plus que nous sortîmes du Pays le plus deforme et le plus Desert du monde. Je ne vous fourni pas la description de Turin, c'est une ville assez connue. Le Roy[109] nous a recu fort gracieusement Monsieur Windham et moy. Il est toujours a sa Maison de Campagne dont nous sommes très fachés parce que nous souhaiterions de luy faire notre Cour. He has his eyes very intent upon what we are doing on the side of Tuscany and would be glad to give us some Disturbance. The Milanese is the object of his Ambition and as a Peace would be an Obstacle to any new acquisitions he is very much out of humour with the thoughts of it. They would not let him send a Minister to the Congress because they knew the part he wou'd have acted there would not be very favourable to the Repose of Europe. He is a great General and has a fine Army and never lost by a War. Je conte de rester icy sept ou huit jours encore ensuite j'iray a Genes et de la à Milan. J'ay partout de bonnes Recommendations qui sont des choses fort nécessaires pour les voyageurs. Je suis dans la dernière impatience de recevoir de vos nouvelles et d'apprendre que Ma chere Mere se porte bien et que ma Sœur est heureusement accouchée. Monsieur Windham voyage toujours avec moy ce qi me fait beaucoup de plaisir comme ce jeune Seigneur

---

108   Alvaro Benavides Bazan, 7th Marquis de Santa Cruz (d.1737).
109   Perhaps Victor Amadeus II (1666–1732), Duke of Savoy; he became King of Sardinia in 1720.

a infiniment d'Esprit et du Savoir vivre, et qu'il est bien recu de tout le monde. Vous aurez de mes nouvelles aussitôt que j'arriverai à Milan si je ne vous ecris pas de Genes.

In my English Letter from Geneva I mentioned Marshall Tallard, but I recollect now that he has been dead some Months and beg pardon for the Mistake. You may put Marshall Villars in his stead. We have one great Enemy in the Army, the Marshall d'Uxelles,[110] but that is of no consequence to our Affairs. I long to hear Mr Stanhopes Success at the Court of Spain.

Duty to Mama.
      Your most Dutiful Son
      G. L.

[I arrived here ten or twelve days ago and met with a splendid reception for which I am indebted to the recommendation of the Marquis of Santa Cruz the Spanish Ambassador to the Congress who has lived at the Court for a long time and is very highly regarded. If peace is made he will go to England where I beg you, Sir, to have the kindness to thank him on my behalf for the generous courtesy that he has shown towards me. I had a rather rough crossing over Mont Cenis, snow falling with great force and the bitter north wind blowing directly into our faces made us frightfully cold. Dansell was extremely ill as a result, he developed a high fever and he is still very unwell. We made the ascent on mules, but for the descent we had to use sedan chairs because of the steep places which the snow made very slippery and were particularly frightening. The mists were so dense that they prevented us from seeing the other alps surrounding us and which are very much higher than Mont Cenis though that is about 7,000 feet high.

What gave us the greatest pleasure was a cataract that could be called a river, which fell from the very summit of the mountain and formed wonderful waterfalls between the rocks that got in the way of its downward path. The plain of Piedmont is beautiful and highly cultivated which pleased us all the more because we had left countryside that was unattractive and and the most desolate on earth. I am not providing you with a description of Turin, it is a town sufficiently known. The King received Mr Windham and me most graciously. He is still at his country seat which grieves us because we wanted to pay our respects to him.] He has his eyes…never lost by a war. [I intend staying here seven or eight days more, then I shall go to Genoa and from there to

---

110 Camille d'Hostun de la Baume, Duc de Tallard, captured at the Battle of Blenheim, August 1704, where he commanded the French and Bavarian armies; Claude Louis Hector de Villars (1653–1734) Duc de Villars, one of the most able of French commanders; Nicholas Chalon du Blè d'Uxelles (1652–1730), made Marshall of France in 1703.

Milan. I have good references from all quarters which are absolutely essential things for travellers. I am extremely impatient to receive your news and to know that my dear mother is well and that my sister is safely delivered of her child. Mr Windham is still travelling with me which gives me a great deal of pleasure because this young gentleman is extremely witty and well mannered, and he is well received on all sides. You will hear from me as soon as I get to Milan if I don't write you from Genoa.]

In my English Letter…

Genova November ye 30th

Dear Papa

I have been at Genova four days and shall sett out to morrow for Milan. I am extreamly pleased with the magnificence and beauty of this town whch is one of the finest in Italy. Nothing can be more noble than its situation which rises in an amphitheatre from the sea, and has a spacious Port before it that is defended with a tolerable fortification and is generally well filled with Merchant Ships. Its Palaces are fitt to lodge Kings; but I shall reserve the description of them to entertain you at Hagley fireside. The form of its Government is so well known and so nearly resembles that of Venice, that I need say nothing to you about it. The low state of its commerce and the Weakness of its once powerful fleet which is now reduced to five Galleys, have been observ'd by every Traveller these thirty years: but what the Republick suffers most is in the Decline of Genius and Spirit in its Governours; the great families of Doria, Spinola, and Grimaldi[111] which are famous over all Europe for having produc'd so many illustrious Generals cannot now boast of one Soldier in all their branches; the Modern Nobility is sunk in Ease and Sloth without Courage or Ability to Act either for their own Honour or their Country's: so that the State must necessarily languish and wou'd probably fall into the hands of some powerful Neighbour if the Jealousy of other Princes did not hinder, which is at present its best Security.

They are in great apprehensions of the King of Sardinia[112] who is continually undertaking something to their prejudice, and demanding concessions from them which they ought not to grant, but are not able to Refuse. The greater part of the Nobility are Slaves to the interests of the Emperour from the Estates

---

111 The Doria and Spinola families dominated the political, commercial and military life of Genoa from the twelfth century onwards; a Grimaldi reigned over the state in 1297, and the family continued to be prominent thereafter. The Doge in 1729 was Luca Grimaldi (he was succeeded by Domenico Spinola).

112 King Carlo Emanuele III (1701–73).

they possess in the Milanese and Kingdom of Naples which render them obnoxious to that Prince's pow'r, and destroy the Liberty of the State: He often extorts Sums of Money from them greater or less as he finds occasion besides Taxing them higher than his other Subjects in those countries. The present Doge is a Grimaldi but his dignity is almost expir'd. I must just take notice of some little Arts that they practice here in their Elections and Resolutions of State, to lett you see that the Method of voting by Ballot may be abused as well as any other. The Box is divided into two partitions one White, the other Red; to each Member of the Council they give a Ball which thrown into the White consents, into the Red, denies; After all have putt in, they count the Balls on either side, and so decide the Question by the Majority: but it often happens that some person has Address enough to convey in two Balls instead of One, so that when they come to reckon they find a Vote too much, which renders the Election void, and obliges them to begin again, or put off the Affair till another day as is generally the case: This gains time to the losing party for new business and frequently changes the Event. There are more tricks that they play of the same Nature, as stopping up the Hole by paper thrust about half way in but the first is the most successfull. I have drawn upon you for a hundred pounds in two Bills at Lions and Turin, the journey over the Alps being very expensive and my chaise having cost a great deal to make it fitt for Travelling. Money in Italy is very low and much is lost by the Exchange.

My Duty to Dear Mama, Love to all your fireside.
                    Your ever Obedient Son
                          G. L.

By a Ship arriv'd here from Cales[113] in fourteen days we have the welcome news that the Court of Spain has sign'd the Treaty of Peace with Mr Stanhope; I heartily wish you joy.

                                              Hagley Dec: ye 1st 1729

Dear George[114]

I have receiv'd only two letters from you since you left Paris one dated from Lyons the other from Geneva. I acknowledged the first on the 20th of Oct. and the last on the 3rd of Novr in wch I inclos'd a Copy of the former. I hope both are receiv'd being not very proper for others eyes.

---

113   Calvi, in north-west Corsica.
114   This is the only surviving letter to GL from his father written while the young man was on his Grand Tour.

I have since receiv'd to my very great surprise and no less concern Sr Joseph Eyles's[115] Account in wch he charges me with £400 you had drawn for since the £1500 wch I paid in June viz one 500 paid the 5th of July another the 15th of Sep a third the 5th of Nov and the last wch was the only sum you made any mention of due the 25th d[itt]o and wch I concluded was all you had taken up you having told me that the abovementioned £1500 wou'd serve you till the end of rhe summer and indeed I cannot conceive without some extravagance wch you say you were not guilty of how you cou'd contrive to exceed so vastly, considering the advantages you had of Mr Poyntz's Table and House wch were very considerable Articles, The several particulars you enumerated in the Apology you made for your expences God knows do not swell the Account in any degree of comparison therefore if I must not lay profusion to your charge you will allow me to impute it to extreme carelessness in letting every body impose upon and cheat you.

My Dearest George you have many rare and excellent qualities for wch I love you from my Soul and have no pleasure equal to that of making you happy, there is nothing you can wish for in my power to gratifie you that an honest man may do wch you may not command but I have not wherewithal to support you at this rate nor do I know wch way to procure it for as I told you in my last I am already at the End of my Tether and cannot go a step further without hazard to my honour and good name wch you will give me leave to value above all things in the World. I have a numerous family wch I am sure you wou'd be as sorry as myself to see unprovided. I must if possible give them a good Education because I have very little else to bestow upon them and what makes it indispensibly incumbent upon me to avoid running deeper into the Mire is that the nature of my fathers Settlement is such as puts it out of your power to relieve me till all your brothers are of age to concur with you in any act for that purpose wch is a prospect so very remote that it cannot be regarded to conclude this disagreable subject wch I am griev'd to have said so much upon. I expect since I have shewn you the necessity you are under of doing it that you put your self into a less expensive way of living and don't imagine you are to spend your mony for the honour of your Country abroad wch you will find the want of when you come home.

I long to hear you are safe in Italy your account of the present state of France gave me so much pleasure I cou'd not forbear shewing it to some friends wch you may forgive me when I assure you it has done you great honour: Chriss is brought to bed of a brave boy and is pure well, your Mother cannot get the better yet of her Disorder nor is poor Molly much mended having lately had

---

115 Sir Joseph Eyles (c.1690–1740), wealthy city merchant, director of the East India Company; Lord Mayor of London, 1726.

a severe return of the Ague, tis no wonder the Country shou'd be sickly for we have not had twenty4 hours dry weather together I'm sure in six weeks: thank God we have at last got our peace with Spain and Mr Stanhope has receiv'd the reward of his labours being created Lord Harrington. I wish your good [MS ends]

Venise Decem: ye 30th NS.
Dear Papa.
After seeing abundance of fine things and suffering a great many fatigues I am got through the worst roads in Europe as far as Venise: My pleasure at coming to this town wou'd have been much greater if I had found any letters here from You and my other freinds as I had reason to expect; but whether it is my Banker's negligence or some Disorder in the Posts, I have not reciev'd a line from any body, which makes me very uneasy and gives me a thousand fears. The publick Papers bring good News, the Peace is signd with Spain of which I wish you joy and hope it will soon lead us to a General One.

They tell us here in Italy that the Emperour is extremely dissatisfied, and determind to oppose our new engagements: I believe they are not thoroughly inform'd, but if it be true I am sure he complains without any justice: If he was sincere in the Quadruple Alliance he cannot be averse to the Establishment of Don Carlos in Italy; why then shou'd he be so angry at what is done for the better securing that Establishment? If he was not sincere, how can we be blamed for taking our Precautions against him? But it seems he is jealous of a Spanish Pow'r getting foot in Italy; woud not the Quadruple Alliance have brought in one after the Death of the present Duke? And what else does this Treaty do but a little advance the same Design? The introducing Spanish Garrisons into Tuscany during the Great Duke's life is thought a Hardship; but wou'd it not have been an equal Grievance to have imposed Neutral ones upon him? Are Swiss Troops more immediately under his dependance than Spanish Ones will be, or are not all foreign forces equally offensive to a Prince in his own Dominions. It is indeed a Hardship but a necessary one for the Peace of Europe and not at all greater than it wou'd have been by the former Treaty.—

I hear Mr Stanhope is made a Lord and they say that Mr Walpole will be Secretary of State but nothing is talk'd of for Mr Poyntz: I hope his Modesty wont be a reason for leaving his other Virtues unrewarded. I am sure he had as great a share in the Merit of the present Treaty as either of his Collegues. You will pardon me if I give you no account of my journey from Genova hither; the Number of Things that pleased me is too great, and must be reserv'd for conversation. Venise is the place in the World that a Traveller sees with most

Surprise: We have a very fine Opera, Calzona and Farinelli sing, the last is a Prodigy, beyond Senesino and every body.[116] Duty to Dear Mama and Love to all your Fireside.

    Your ever Dutifull Son
        G. L.

            Venice January ye 13th 1730

Dear Papa

Last post brought me two of yours dated October ye 20th and November ye 3rd which were extreamly welcome. I writ to you from Turin and from Genova, and last post from Venice to let you know that I was got well hither. Mr Windham came with me all the way and I assure you is a very good Whig as well as a very pretty Gentleman. How far his Father's authority may force him to change his sentiments when he comes to England I cannot tell,[117] but they are now entirely agreable to the excellent Understanding he is Master of. I receive your Lesson of Oeconomy as a great and important Truth, which I cannot too often sett before me, and which I have too much neglected. I know that Extravagance and Illmanagement have made as many rogues as Avarice, and that Liberty is inconsistent with the Dependance which a broken fortune subjects every man to.

 These Reflexions will always save me from the natural Carelessness of my Temper, and you shall find when I come to have a fortune that may suffer from a want of Exactness that nobody shall look into their Affairs with more Attention than I. I am sensible I spent too much at Paris, that is more than a good Manager wou'd have done, but I repent less of it because it was in a place and at a Time and Circumstance of life when it was necessary to exceed the ordinary course of limited Expence. It is true I was myself surprisd at paying off a great number of little Bills to find how high they rose when putt together, and it was in that chiefly that I experienced the great fault I had been guilty of in not looking more regularly to my accounts.

 Since I have begun my Italian Journey I am able to give an account of every Livre that I have laid out, neither have I spent a farthing more than the

---

116 Calzona has not been identified. Farinelli (1705–82), real name Carlo Broschi, was one of the most famous soprano castrato singers of the eighteenth century; Handel visited Venice in an unsuccessful attempt to secure him for his London company. Senesino (1686–1758), real name Francesco Bernardi, a celebrated alto castrato singer who sang in Venice in 1729; he is particularly remembered for his long collaboration with Handel.
117 Charles Wyndham's father, Sir William, was a leading Tory; Charles served as a Whig MP from 1734–50.

Necessarys upon the road obliged me to, or than other Gentlem[e]n of my Quality spend in places where they make any stay. Every thing is excessive dear in this part of Italy especially in Carnival Time. When I have the Happiness of seeing you in England you shall find me resolv'd to take any course that you shall point out to me to make us both easy in our fortunes, and to repay you the expences of my travels as far as it is possible for me to do; and I must need say that it wou'd be much less uneasy to me to live there upon a small allowance, than in a Countrey where the figure that I make must introduce me to the best part of my improvement and at a time of Life which will in a manner decide of the Good or Ill of all the rest. I shall draw for a Hundred pounds here and shall go from hence to Rome in about fifteen days. The Caution you give me in relation to the Gentlemen of the Pretender's[118] party whom I may chance to meet with there is what I constantly observ'd towards some of the same kidney whom I knew at Paris: It is indeed a common Principle of good Manners to shock nobody's sentiments upon a point in which you know they are determin'd. I shall wait upon Mr Plowden[119] with a great deal of pleasure. I hope you will have an easy Session of Parliament, for sure the Peace with Spain is a very popular one; and I am every day more convinced that the Emperours Opposition will come to nothing. Mama's and Molly's indisposition give me the greatest uneasiness, but as you say there is no danger of either I am not much alarm'd. I hope by this time Sister Pitt[120] has given you a Grandson, pray my kindest Love to her and her Husband. I send a Duplicate of this by next post as you advise me. The subject of this letter wont lett me conclude it without assuring you what a grateful Sense I have of your Goodness to me which are infinitely beyond my Deserts and demand such Returns as I can never make though my Life be spent in obeying you, as I fully resolve it shall be. Adieu my Dear Papa, let me often know that you are well and that you continue to Love me; I honour esteem and Love you more than any other person upon Earth.

Venice Jan ye 21st NS. 1730

Dear Papa,

I have your's of the first of December, and am so struck with the Indulgence and Goodness you are pleas'd to shew me upon an occasion where I had reason

---

118   Prince James Francis Edward Stuart (1688–1766), known as the Old Pretender; he laid claim to the thrones of England (as James III) and Scotland (as James VII). In 1729 he was living in Rome at the invitation of the Pope.
119   Probably William Plowden (1666–1741), Catholic and Jacobite.
120   GL's eldest sister, Christian, wife of Thomas Pitt.

to fear your Severity, that I can neither express my confusion at having too much deserved another treatment, nor my Gratitude for that which I have receiv'd. My last of which the inclosed is a copy will deliver you a great part of my Sentiments on the point you write upon, in so ample and sincere a Manner, that I need not repeat them in this; give me leave Dear Sir only to assure you, that if it pleases God to allow me life and Health I will so behave myself to you, and make such a use of the Improvements that you purchase for me, as will justify an extraordinary Liberality for these few years both to yourself and your family. I beg pardon if I just observe that the assurance I gave you last Spring that the Money I then drew for wou'd be sufficient to serve me till the end of Summer was wholly grounded on the Confidence I had of passing that Season in the Countrey as his Excellency talked of doing; but I cou'd certainly never think of living upon that sum in such a town as Paris; and I thought it so evident to you that it was impossible I shou'd, that I did not judge it necessary to tell you so, any otherwise than by letting you know that I was come to town and expected to continue there.

I hope that by living prudently and circumspectly while I am in Italy I shall spend considerably less than I did last year but it is in vain to promise you I will retrench any part of my reasonable expence for my Spirit wont lett me do it, and I am sure you wou'd not demand it of me. I heartily wish you joy of your Grandson. Neddy Walpole is here and goes with me to Rome; he is a Youth of uncommon parts and great expectations; I am very glad to cultivate a friendship with him.[121] I beg my Duty to Dear Mama if she is with you or when you write.

I am Dear Papa
Your ever Dutiful Son
G. L.

Venice Feb ye 11th 1730

Dear Papa,

I have yours of Decem: ye 24th with the Duplicate; I answrd that the post before last and enclosed a Copy of a former which I hope you receiv'd. I am glad to hear the Land tax is diminish'd; tis no wonder that the City is discontent for if I don't mistake it is at present govern'd by Tory Magistrates and they are not of a humour to be pleas'd with any good success to Court Measures. You have by this time no doubt been publickly acquainted with all the Terms of the

---

121 GL's hopes to have Sir Robert Walpole's son, Edward (1706–84) as his travelling companion were to be disappointed.

Spanish Treaty, and I am persuaded that you have found them honourable and advantageous: I cannot be of your opinion that the Congress will last much longer or terminate in a War: The Emperour has little to gain in Italy and much to lose; neither has he other reason of complaint except that he did not give the Law to Europe as he wou'd have done.

I know that he is marching troops, I think they say forty thousand men into his Dominions here; but I shant believe the rest of Italy in any dangers till I see him send a hundred thousand, which he is not in a condition to do; and even if he did make his utmost efforts I shou'd doubt of his power to oppose so formidable a Confederacy. But it is the Opinion of this Republick which is a very good judge of Politicks that all these Menaces will end in Smoke, and that he is only doing as he has done at almost every Treaty that has been sign'd these thirty years, Delaying his Acquiescence on Accession, in order to be courted a little and save his honour. I have more particular reasons for thinking so but they are such as I cant trust to the common post –

I have writt to the good Parson.[122] Your having been so ill with the headach afflicts me mightily and so does poor Mama's weakness; I will write to her very soon. I am sorry for poor Chrissy's loss.[123] I stay'd here a fortnight longer than I design'd in hopes of going to Rome with Mr Walpole, but an unforseen Accident having fixd him here I shall sett out to morrow quite alone which will be very melancholy. I beg my Dear Papa to believe that no Son ever lov'd a father with more tenderness or felt his obligations to him with more gratitude than I do. My Duty to Lord and Lady Cobham, Love to Chriss and her Husband.

      I am your ever Obedient Son
          G. L.

When you see my Lord Harrington I beg you wou'd make him my compliments upon his Negotiation and the Reward of it.

                Rome April ye 12th 1730
Dear Papa.
I have three of yours the last of which is dated Feb: ye 22d in answer to those I writ from Venise. I am infinitely obliged to you for your kind offices in favour of poor Ayscough and I dont doubt but you and his other friends will obtain ample Justice for him. I am very glad that all your family have got so

---

122 Francis Ayscough.
123 Christian's infant son, born late November, died mid-December.

well through so many distempers, but Chrissy's frequent miscarriages are ugly things, and may bring an ill habit upon her. It is impossible to tell you my Dear Papa how sincerely I am afflicted at your complaints about your Head. I wou'd willingly suffer any share of them if it was possible to ease you by it: It is so natural to give advice upon these occasions to those for whom we are much concernd, that I cant help saying you wou'd do mighty well to try a journey to Spa if it was only for exercise and change of Air: I have known great cures perform'd that way upon people in your case, and it is a Remedy you have not yet experience'd.—

I writ to you about ten days agoe only to tell you that I was pleasd with Rome and that I had seen Mr Plowden who is in good Health, tho a little upon the Decline. I am going to Naples to morrow, to stay about eight days and to come back hither where I propose to settle till the beginning of June; After that time there is no stirring out of Rome till the end of September on account of the infectious Air in the Campagna, so that unwilling as I am to leave a place so agreable to me, I am oblig'd to it for fear of being a Prisoner. I propose to pass the great Heats at Milan tho' I cannot say I have any fixd Design, because my stay in any place will depend upon my Liking the company. Mr Arbuthnot has no correspondence in Italy except here, at Venice and Leghorn, so it will be necessary for me to draw upon Mr Alexander at Paris or what I shall like as well upon Mr Joseph Eyeles directly, for which purpose you will be so good to desire Mr Joseph Eyeles to send me a Letter of general Credit, or else to settle it with Mr Alexander as you think proper. My Direction here is to Mr Jean Angelo Belloni Banker. I believe you will have a mind to see me next summer in England, so I shall endeavour to get out of Italy by the end of Autumn. I have receivd a most kind letter from Mr Poyntz in which he gives me very strong assurances of a general Peace and that I may pursue my Travels through Italy without impediment. Speaking of the manner the Treaty of Seville is receiv'd in England he says:: The Satisfaction that it gives will much encrease when it comes to be known and felt that far from having made a *Paix Platree*[124] we are really upon better terms with Spain than ever and have the predilection over all the pow'rs of Europe in her Freindship, which I may venture to assure you in confidence is really the case.—

I hope you have the Verses to his Excell.^{cy} which I sent you from Venice.[125]

I beg my compliments to Lord Hervey;[126] I saw him just before he set out for Italy, and had his orders not to write to him till I heard first from him,

---

124 'A papered-over peace'.
125 Presumably a copy of the verses 'To Mr Poyntz, Ambassador at the Congress of Soissons', which GL had written in Paris the previous year.
126 John Hervey (1696–1743), known by the title Lord Hervey on the death of his older brother in 1723. Courtier, political writer and memorist, Hervey gained notoriety

which I waited a good while for, and then writ to Rome without any certainty of his being there, which letter I suppose miscarryd: It woud be a great Affliction to me if I thought that in losing his correspondence I had forfeited his Esteem. My Duty and Services where due.

Your most Dutiful
And Obedient Son
G. L.

I have a letter from Lady Cobham for which I will thank her in a post or two. I writ to her Ladyship just before I left Venice to acquaint her that I had sent her some Musick in a box of books directed to you. I shall be glad to hear they arrive safe. We have yet no certainty who will be Pope. One Cardinal Zonzandari is most talk'd of.[127]

Rome May ye 7th 1730

Dear Papa.

Your Commands shall always be receiv'd with an implicit Obedience from me, however contrary they may be to my inclinations; or to speak more justly, I have no inclination so strong as that of doing all I can to convince you of my Love and Duty to the best of Fathers. I have been at Naples since my last which I am very glad of because it lies quite out of my present Road and I must have left it unseen. I shall go from Rome with a very imperfect knowledge of the great Variety of fine things that are in it, more time than I have past here being requisite to see them as one shou'd do. I shall pass through Florence and Bologna which are the most considerable Places where I have not been, and embark at Genova for Marseilles. I shall expect to find a letter from you at Paris where I hope to arrive in about six weeks if no accident prevents.

I shou'd be insensible of Praise to a Fault if I were not proud of the Honour her Majesty does me so much beyond anything I cou'd flatter myself with the hopes of; but I cant help being very apprehensive that I shall not answer the advantageous Opinion she has been pleas'd to entertain of me from the partial Report of my Friends.[128]

---

through political hostility, his alleged homosexuality, and the severe attacks on him in Pope's satirical poems.

127 Pope Benedict XIII died on 21 February 1730; he was succeeded in July 1730 by Cardinal Lorenzo Corsini as Clement XII (1652–1740). Zonzandari is unidentified; GL probably confused him with Cardinal Antonio Felice Zondadari (d.1737) who did attend the conclave.

128 Apparently the Queen had intimated to Sir Thomas some kind of preferment for GL when he returned home; the nature of it is unknown.

Your ill state of Health makes me so uneasy that it wont let me take much pleasure in anything. I am sorry for poor Lane's Death;[129] I beg the Note you found among his papers may be placed in the number of my past Faults which your Goodness has already forgiven, and which my future conduct shall make amends for. Chrissy's banishment so far from all her friends is a great Affliction to me, as I am afraid it will be to her in spite of Conjugal Love.[130] If you like the inclos'd Verses I desire you wou'd give them to Mr Pope to whom I have taken the liberty to address them: they contain a good piece of Advice, and I hope it is given in a manner that will make it acceptable.[131] In speaking of Italy I have confind myself to the Decay of Learning there, because Mr Addison has wrote so finely on every other point in his verses to Lord Hallifax[132] that I durst not think of attempting them after him. I have drawn here for about two hundred and twenty pounds and have credit for more at Genova. Lodging, Eating, and Equipage are dearer vastly here than at Paris, and I was obliged to lose twenty pounds at Cards to introduce myself to the Roman Assemblies: My Antiquary and the Expence of seeing things, run away with a good deal more, not to mention my journey to Naples. I set out to morrow morning, and my letter must stay here till Thursday. I received your's but a Week agoe.
   With great Impatience to see you, I am
     Your most Dutiful Son,
       G. L.

            Paris June ye 16th 1730
Dear Sir.
I arrived at Paris ye 14th having seen Florence Modena Parma and a great part of the South of France in my way. I had but an indifferent passage to Marseilles

---

129 Lane is unidentified.
130 Christian's marriage to Thomas Pitt inflicted endless misery on her; life on the isolated estate of Boconnoc (bought by Pitt's grandfather) in Cornwall eventually became intolerable and, many years later, she took refuge at Hagley; Pitt agreed to a separation on condition that she never saw her three children again.
131 GL's 'Epistle to Mr Pope, from Rome, 1730' contains the clear advice:
  No more let meaner satire dim the rays
  That flow majestic from thy nobler lays…
  Of thee more worthy were the talk, to raise
  A lasting column to thy country's praise
  To sing the land, which yet alone can boast
  That liberty corrupted Rome has lost.
132 Addison's poem that GL had in mind was entitled: 'A Letter from Italy to the Rt Hon Charles Lord Halifax, in the year 1701'.

having been six days a making it and in some danger of being cast away: I came in three days and a half from Lions hither the most part a horse back which makes about a weeks rest necessary for me and delays a little the Impatience I have to pay my Duty to you in England. I am very sorry for one article in your letter: I hope there was nothing else of moment in those you sent to Rome for I have lost them. I hear with a great deal of pleasure that Ayscough is restored. God be thanked that you are so well recover'd of your last Illness; if I find you and all my freinds in good Health my wishes will be compleat. I am mightily pleasd to hear that I shall enjoy my Dear Sister Pitt at Hagley this summer. Mr Poyntz is still here. Dear Papa I beg you woud assure all my Freinds particularly Mama of the extream Joy I have in the hopes of seeing them which will be the happiest moment of my life: if a constant uninterrupted course of Duty and Affection to You and Her, can acquit me of any part of the Obligations I have to both, you may depend upon such a Return from

        Dear Sir
        Your ever Obedient Son
               G. L.

His Excell^{cy} desires his compliments.

Joseph Spence; after George Vertue; Isaac Whood. Line engraving, 1746

Joseph Spence (1699–1768): Letters (1730–3)

As the eldest son of the rector of Winnal, a small parish partly in Winchester, Joseph Spence appeared to have no special prospects at birth; they were not enhanced by his mother's connection with minor aristocracy (through her grandfather, Sir Thomas Lunsford, of dubious reputation, who died in Virginia in 1653). His education began in the Berkshire village of Mortimer. Not until a generous and wealthy relative offered to pay for his transfer to Winchester College did his fortunes improve; but then they most certainly did—by the move to Winchester he became a Wykehamist, and thereby a member of an élite group who would expect and achieve accelerated advancement. Spence went up to New College, Oxford, in 1720, and was elected a full Fellow of the College in 1722, one year after his Wykehamist friend Christopher Pitt (1699–1748) and two years ahead of Wykehamist Glocester Ridley (1702–74)—both men who achieved some reputation, Pitt as a poet and translator of Virgil, and Ridley as an Oxford don, prebendary of Salisbury Cathedral, and miscellaneous writer. Already established in Oxford with an All Souls Fellowship was Wykehamist and poet, Edward Young (1683–1765); then, younger than Spence, came yet another Wykehamist, Robert Lowth (1710–87) who was to become Bishop of London and also author of the significant *Lectures on the Sacred Poetry of the Hebrews* (translated in 1787). Collegiate loyalty was important, as were social cachet and scholarly distinction; Spence's friends, equipped in both respects, were prepared to exert their influence on his behalf. One result was that, combined with his own literary efforts and the blessing of Alexander Pope—Spence published his *Essay on Pope's 'Odyssey'* in 1726—he was elected Oxford Professor of Poetry in 1728 at the age of 29. He held the appointment for the maximum permitted 10 years; shortly after the end of his tenure Robert Lowth succeeded him.

With increasing scholarly prominence and social contacts—Pope's friendship being of considerable importance—Spence began to move freely in wealthy influential circles. One sure sign of this was the frequency with which he was invited to act as mentor to young men sent by their upper-class families on the Grand Tour. On his first Tour, 1730–3, Spence accompanied Charles

Sackville (1711–69), Lord Middlesex (later 2nd Duke of Dorset), who had been to Westminster School and Christ Church, Oxford. In the same decade Spence acted as 'governor' on two further Tours: 1737–8, in the Low Countries and France, with John Morley Trevor (1716–43), a distant relative of the Duke of Newcastle, and 1739–41, in Italy, with Henry Fiennes Clinton (1720–94), Earl of Lincoln. It is with the first that we are concerned here.

His subsequent career was largely determined by his function as a priest of the established church, as well as by his literary and associated interests. The first can quite rapidly be disposed of. A couple of years after his ordination at Oxford in 1726, Spence accepted the living of Birchanger in Essex, his own college being the patron; he moved from there in 1742 to the richer New College living of Great Horwood, Buckinghamshire; and, finally, he became a prebendary of Durham in 1754. He owed this preferment to Bishop Richard Trevor (1707–71) who had inherited the family estate of Glynde in Sussex on the death in 1743 of his cousin, John Morley Trevor, for whom Spence had been governor on his second Grand Tour.

His literary interests were extensive — as was his learning. This last was most evident in his *Polymetis* (1747) whose 'principal design was', to quote Nicholas Tindal, author of an abridgment (1764):

> To compare the descriptions and expressions… in the Latin poets, relating to the Roman deities, with the allegorical representation of the same by painters and sculptors… in order to illustrate them mutually from one another.

Spence's work draws on massive reading: Tindal claims that his abridgment itself contains over 3,000 translated passages from classical authors. To view it as no more than an exercise in scholarly research, worthy but dull, would be, however, to limit its wider importance. As a source of mythological imagery its influence is beyond exact estimate — except for the example of Keats. Keats was directly indebted to it. His presentation of Cupid and Psyche in the *Ode to Psyche*, for instance, almost certainly derived from Plate VI in *Polymetis* which shows the kiss between the two main figures as engraved on a statue in Florence. (Plate VI also illustrates the intimate connection existing between Spence's travels and his scholarship.)

His literary activities were not confined to the study of classical authors. In many respects he was a 'miscellaneous writer' like so many of his contemporaries: he was poet, satirist, essayist, translator, biographer and anecdotist. The last two deserve most attention. Spence's principal contribution to the art of biography rests on his studies of the literary achievements of men of 'natural genius' and of humble origin: Stephen Duck (1705–56), the Wiltshire thresher; Thomas Blacklock (1721–91), the blind poet of Edinburgh; and Robert Hill (1699–1777), the learned tailor of Buckingham. Spence compared Hill to the extraordinarily learned bibliophile and scholar, Antonio Magliabechi (1633–1714), the famous Florentine librarian to the Grand Duke of Tuscany—which underlines the difficulty in keeping the subject in perspective. Similarly, those contemporaries who 'discovered' 'natural poets' such as Mary Collier, washerwoman, Henry Jones, bricklayer, or Ann Yearsley, Bristol milkwoman, sometimes preferred the importance of unlettered backgrounds and origin in the lower working class to evidence of superior poetical talent. For his part, Spence contributed through meticulous analysis of, say, Blacklock's verse, to the proper appraisal of hitherto unacknowledged creativity.

Nevertheless, it is as an anecdotist without rival that he is now best known. The authoritative edition of *Spence's Anecdotes*, edited by James M. Osborn (1966), shows his having recorded numerous conversations with Pope, others that contained valuable observations on British writers from Dryden and Wycherley to Bolingbroke and Swift, and still others arising from conversations Spence had with distinguished people encountered on the Grand Tour. There is no reason to doubt the reliability of any. Literary people, especially Pope, enjoyed Spence's dinner-table company; they discussed freely, and he recorded the essence of what was said. It seems appropriate to apply to Spence the remark made by Pope about Gay: '[he] was quite a natural man, wholly without art or design, and spoke just what he thought and as he thought it' (Anecdote No. 239). Or, to quote James Sambrook, the *Anecdotes*, itself, 'reflects its scribe: self-effacing, conscientious, discriminating, knowledgeable, and kindly' (ODNB).

Some of these same characteristics appear in the letters he wrote to his mother during his first Grand Tour when he accompanied the nineteen year-old Lord Middlesex to Italy via Calais, Dijon, Lyon and Geneva. He was invariably alert to his mother's interests, careful always to involve her as in an imaginary conversation: 'you and I should sit down and talk a little more'; 'all the Chat we have had together across the Water'; he promises to provide her with a vivid and memorable picture of all the considerable cities visited in order 'to bring 'em home to you and to talk over the places together.' He describes for her minute details of French women's hair and dress, amuses her with an account of the flirtatiousness of his landlady in Dijon, and boasts that he could cuckold his landlord if he had a mind to it, but assures her that 'such a villainy is not in my nature.' Spence's account of the journey between Rome and Naples is meticulously detailed for her, as is the vivid and lengthy description of his ascent of Vesuvius. He is determined to share with her his own delight in 'seeing the very place and spot of ground where some great thing was done': '*This* is the place where Julius Caesar was stabbed by Brutus... *Here* stood Manilius', and so forth. He makes certain assumptions about his mother. He presumes that she is following his route by reference to a map: 'I hope the

Map lyes just at your right hand.' The suddenness with which one season is replaced by the one succeeding it prompts him to refer to Horace—'summer enters in a hurry, turns the spring out of doors, and treads on her heels as she is going out'—but he does it with full confidence that she shares his pleasure in the allusion: 'I'me sure you know Horace very well.' And he is confident that Mrs Spence would respect his wish that she should not utter 'one word of any kind, relating either to Religion or Politics' when writing to him in Italy. It is therefore noteworthy that Spence himself would not write to her about Rome while he was in the capital—'the Pope's Town'—but only when he and his companion 'are got safe to Florence': 'I may talk my bellyful of it.'

Among his keenest interests was landscape gardening, a popular subject in his day. It was given free rein when he (with his mother) moved to Byfleet in Surrey in 1748 to live on the estate given for his lifetime by Lord Lincoln. His near neighbour, Philip Southcote, was credited by Spence with having 'brought in the garden farm, or *ferme ornée*' in 1734 (Anecdotes Nos. 1,125 and 1,126). Several years later Spence followed his example. His aim was 'to imitate Nature in what she is pleasing' (Anecdote No. 1,069n): that such 'beautiful Nature' fascinated him wherever he found it in landscape or in painting is clear in his letters. He is painterly in his description of the 'prospect' between Chalon and Mâcon en route from Dijon to Lyon. First there was 'a continual rising and chain of Hills of a moderate height'; beyond that 'the Country spread every way for a vast length, first in delicious Meadows, then in Cornfields, and then in Woodlands. At the end of all… the mountains of Switzerland, all coverd with snow.' Here at work, in embryo, are Spence's principles for judging 'the finest landscapes of the best painters' as elaborated in Anecdote 1,084 nearly 20 years later. The same features are present in his account of crossing the Apennines, his evocation of the vale of Arno 'the most beautiful Vale in the whole world,' or his description of the Florentine pleasure gardens and landscape: trees, groves, arbours, the river Arno, and 'wild crocus's as thick as the Stars in Heaven.' His descriptive language often becomes imaginative as when he sees spray from an impressive waterfall 'like a plume of feathers gilded with the Sun' or when he compares the Apennines with the Alps, the former 'seem only to be like the Son of a vast Giant, about 7 or 8 Years old.' Occasionally imagery drawn from the natural world is applied to human features: fashionable women who tastelessly paint their faces 'look like a bed of old overblown Piony's.'

Spence's dominant manner, however, is usually more genial and gently humorous than acerbic. He mocks 'by what degrees [he] creeps into the Habit of a Gentleman… every day my Barber persecutes [my hair] with an ounce of Pomatum; and then plaisters it down with half a Pound of Powder.' Italian preachers are a source of comedy:

those I have seen, make a terrible noise and hubbub in their Pulpits: but tis more excusable in them for they talk there prodigiously often of the Devil... they have very much the Advantage of us on frosty Mornings; for let the weather be as cold as it will, they are sure to bawl till they are all over in a Sweat.

But it is the scene of his own folly and misfortune that attracts the most genial humour.
When visiting the Duke of Florence's vineyard he was curious about the wine fermenting in large tubs:

> I was rig[ge]d up a ladder that stood by the side of one, to gape upon it; when—all at once—the ladder slips from under me, and in the hurry, I got hold of the brims and hung there. Had the Tub yielded upon me, I shou'd at least have spoil'd my best Holyday Cloaths, or perhaps have gon out of the world almost in the way of the Earl of Clarence; if 'twas he that was drown'd in Malmsy.

The incident was subsequently referred to as his 'Tale of a Tub'.

Such a man would have proved an agreeable, entertaining and instructive 'governor' for his young companions; he would have convinced them of the view expressed in a letter written on his third Tour: 'There is certainly nothing equal to travelling for the improvement of the mind and the acquisition of knowledge.' The young men would also have been persuaded, having explored one city or landscape after another under Spence's direction—as he told his fellow Oxonian, Henry Rolle—that 'tho'' Italy be the Country for Sights, England is the Country to live in... the most beautiful, the most delicious, the most improv'd of any under the Moon.'

By kind permission of the British Library the letters are printed from Egerton MSS 2234; some annotation is indebted to the edition by Slava Klima of *Joseph Spence: Letters from the Grand Tour* (Montreal: McGill-Queen's University Press, 1975).

Letters of Joseph Spence

[Calais]
Thursday Decr: 24, 1730 [OS]

Dear Mother,[133]

—I believe that Wednesday night you receiv'd a letter to let you know, that we shoud not leave England, in 6 or 7 days. This comes to tell you, that I was then at Dover, where we had waited a day or two for a good wind: and am now at Calais; where we came this morning, with a very pleasant passage, in three hours. We have been since (beside eating a hearty dinner) all over the fortifications of this place; at a Roman Catholic Church Service; in two religious Houses, and one Nunnery. To morrow we get into the Chaise, for Dunkirk. I was huge Sea Sick for about half an hour; which did me a great deal of good, and made me eat an unreasonable good dinner. The Captain of the Vessel now stays for this: My next shall be longer. I am ever

Your dutiful and Affectionate

Jo: Spence

[Dijon]
Jan: 26 1731 here, with you ye 15th [134]

Dear Mother,

We are at last got safe to Dijon. The place where my Lord is to pass all the rest of the winter.[135] Twas a long and tedious journey hither: I mean as to the time of Year; and generally, the badness of the roads; but a Chaise made both less troublesome. Generally speaking, we sat so easy in it, that we coud sleep, or read: we had a perfect Study of books round us, in Books contriv'd on each side in the inside of the Chaise; and every day we read a Play or two of Shakespeare, or two or three Poems of Mr Pope's. Sometimes, the Prospects took us off from our Book, which even in this Season are sometimes agreable. The first part from Calais, we came 140 miles, without seeing any such thing as a Hill; even any where at a distance often by the Sea Side, and more by the Side of a large Canal. Since Namur, the 3 or 4 last days hither have been thro Vinyards or between a Variety of little Hills on each side, coverd with woods,

---

133 Mirabella Spence (?1670–?1755); other than her having a very limited income from some small inherited properties, few biographical details are available.
134 France had already adopted New Style dating; England remained with Old Style.
135 Charles Sackville (1711–69), Earl of Middlesex from 1720 when his father was created Duke of Dorset.

here and there Rocks, and now [and] then an old Castle on the Top of them: we went on a raisd causeway, which runs all through the vale between these Hills, with a River all the way on the left hand, which winds along the Vales, and falls often in the oddest little Cascades that ever I saw. I thank Heaven, I have been all the way, and am now in perfect good health: and we are now settled for 4 or 5 months: a house is taking for my Lord here, where I shall have a Servant and a Separate apartment: and may live just as if I were at Oxford. Only we can have more diversions here in the Afternoons, and evenings; and I am all the while with a Gentleman of so much good sense and good nature as Ld Middlesex, who excells most people in both. I hope you and my Sister[136] and all friends are very well: I sent a letter from Namur to Mr Rolle,[137] which I hope came safe to you; as yet I have receiv'd none: but hope to do it, when we are settled at a place. I find that the bringing about a Year, will not be near so expensive to me here as it was in England. The [MS damaged] below. I am ever
          Your dutiful and affectionate
              Jo: Spence

              Dijon:
            Febr: 16, 1731

Dear Mother,

I have written to you From Calais and this place, and to Mr Rolle (which I reckon much the same thing) from Namur. We have not yet receivd a single letter from any body.

We are now above three weeks old at Dijon: the situation of it is very agreable, and has in some parts of the Prospect, just resemblance enough to put one in mind of Oxford. Almost ever since we have been here, there has been the deepest snow that has been seen in these parts these fifteen years: the common depth of it has been two foot. Towards our first coming here was a thaw of two or three days. I took the advantage of it to see the Public Walks, which are just without the East Gate of the City. They are extremely handsome; a full mile in length: the middle walk 20 Yards over: and those on each side, 10 Yards. In the midst they all widen into a Circle; which serves here, in proper weather, as the Ring in Hide Park.[138] At the Farther end of the Walks, is a

---

136 She was known as Belle; no other details are known.
137 Edward Rolle (1703–91), Fellow of New College, Oxford; he acted as Spence's deputy in his absence.
138 A circular course in London's Hyde Park used by members of the upper classes for riding on horseback or in open horse-drawn carriages.

Public Park, where the walks are all Star-fashion: and at the End of that, is half a Circle, planted entirely with Firs, Pines, and ever-greens: all along this runs an open walk, and that is bounded by a very wide and very particular Canal. The first time of finding out all this, one piece after another, was extremely agreable: and I have not yet had any room for a Second View: the Snow being still knee-deep as we call it, in the Country. However I don't lose my Morning Walks: for in the Town, they clear away the snow in a good degree, every time after it falls: and my favourite walk, now, is on top of the Walls on the Sunny Side of the Town.

Tho' I used to have 8 or 10 Colds every winter at Oxford, both in our journey hither and ever since we have been here, I have not had any such thing and am, I thank Heaven, is all respects entirely well; at this present writing. I shoud be very happy in hearing that You and my Sister, &c, are so too.

This place does not at all want for company: at our Concerts of Music, and our Masquirades, which all the Carnival time were every Sunday Night, I have seen above 150 people of fashion. Tho tis Lent, the Concerts continue still at the same time; for Sunday here is the high day of diversion. Their Music at least to us, is not near so agreable as the English. They have above thirty hands and voices: In the Front of 'em are six Women, who all sing; but to me in the most howling manner that ever I heard: indeed all except one (who is the Governour's[139] Mistress) are extremely ugly, and without any exception painted to a gross degree, both the red and the white. In the midst of these is a desk rais'd, on which stands the Master of the Music: he has a roll of paper in his hand, with which, his Head, and his whole body, he is continually keeping time; in so violent a manner, that I can hardly think of him without laughing.

I believe all the great Cities here, abound in a little sort of Noblemen, of all sorts of titles. With the benefit of being my Lord's Shadow (and following him every where) I am now as well acquainted, as the strangeness of the Language will permit, with one Comtesse, two Comtes, a Marquis, and four Barons. If I have forgot any of my new Quality Friends in this calculation, I hope they will have the goodness to forgive me. Three of my Barons, are strangers, Germans who are now in this place: and the Fourth is (God bless him) an Englishman.[140] Both he and his Lady talk English very well; so that tis the most comfortable thing in the world to go and see them.

We begin all to long very much to hear from England: pray how does Mr Wavil do and all his good family?[141] And Mrs Kelly and her fireside?[142] The

---

139 Louis-Henri (1692–1740), Duke of Bourbon, 4th Governor of Burgundy.
140 Perhaps Sir George Colgrave.
141 Daniel Wavell (b.1676), Vicar of South Hayling near Portsmouth.
142 Probably the wife of Dr George Kelly, a neighbour in Winchester.

Nun-Letters lay still as quiet as lambs,[143] and as we seem inclind, I don't know whether Paris will not be the very last place we shall be at. Next October we are for Italy. When you write any letter for me, please not to send it to my brother as I first desird:[144] the best way will be to direct it as below: and to put it as you wd any other letter, into your post. Never but half a sheet, but in that, pray let me have as much as you can. My Service to Mr and Mrs Morecroft[145] and all friends. I am ever

Your dutiful and affectionate
J. Spence

À Monsieur
> Monsieur Spence, chez Mr Cotheret,
> Proche la Place Royale
> à Dijon *Par Paris*

Dijon
March 1, NS
feb. 17 old stile

Dear Mother

To day morning, just as the Servant had lighted the fire in my chamber and before I cared for stirring out of my bed, in came the Postmaster, with an armful of letters. Among the rest I had the pleasure of receiving one of Yours (dated Jan: 30), one from my brother Dick, and another from my brother Rolle. I'm so particular, because they are the first Packet I have receivd from England; and to see your hand, after longing for it so long, was an extreme pleasure to me. I'm overjoyed to find you are all well; and beg you'd return my services to every body, and particularly to Mr Wavil. Your being acquainted so well with my dear deputy at Oxford (Cap: Rolle) and owning him for your Son, in my absence, is just what I wisht. I beg you'd write to him on all occasions, for you know what, just as you wd to me if I were at Oxford. I thank God I am in a better situation than I cou'd be there. My dear Lord has every thing in him that is agreable: the finest sense, and the best nature.

I have talkt to you as yet only of the Roads and Walks: 'tis proper one s[houl]d let you know a word or two about the people. In deference to the Fair Sex, I shall begin with them. One may say it safely, for 'tis own'd over here, that the French Women are not so beautiful as the English: but then they make it

---

143 Addressed to Miss Belson, who proposed to enter a French nunnery, but see p. 91.
144 Richard Spence (b.1701), an employee of the African Company.
145 Friends of Mrs Spence in Winchester; she was staying with them.

up in a Sprightliness and Freedom of behaviour, that is universal among them. Their Head Dress here for the people of Fashion is cald Tête des Muttons; tis a very small Head just on the Top; without flaps or anything coming down on the sides. Their hair is short, and formd all into little Curls, row after row, quite down to the Neck every way. They wear a sort of Sultanas:[146] or at least a Vest of silk that comes up almost quite to the Neck, and falls loose every way down to the feet. The breast is invisible; and there's no pretence to a Waist in this dress: but yet I must say it has something very graceful in it. One thing that I was surprizd at, was a Compliment[147] that is very common both here and at Namur. You have heard of the Dutch women sitting at Market with a Pan of Coals under them. There's a great many of these pans here: and at an Assembly, you'll frequently see a Gentleman scuttle along with a Pan of Coals, and put it himself under a Ladie's Pettycoats; who bows kindly in her seat; and plays on her Cards at Quadrille all the while, with great serenity and satisfaction.

We have had an extreme hard winter here; Snow two feet deep for these five weeks: tis now almost gone, and this afternoon I had a very dry and pleasant walk half round the Town upon the Ramparts. But to return: My Lord lives in part of a Merchants house, whose wife and I are grown extremely acquainted. I believe I might make a Cuckold of my Landlord, whenever I had a mind to it: but such a villainy is not in my nature. She is sometimes half the day together in my Chamber: and as she is eternally talking French, and I always endeavouring to answer her, she has really done me more good that way than my Fr[ench] Master. She is about five and thirty, or by our Lady, Forty Years old: but for ever brisk, and more talkative than seventeen Parrots. When I don't understand what she says, or she does not understand what I say, we always fall a laughing: so that tis a very merry method of learning a language. I laugh till I hold my sides; and then we talk again. I told Capt: Rolle in my last [about] my top Dress here; but I must repeat it to you, for fear his s[houl]d miscarry. Tis a black Velvet Coat lined with red Silk, a black silk Waistcoat lin'd with white, black Velvet Britches, and Black-silk stockings: a Sword always tuckt to my side, and a Cane never out of my hands: and to Crown all, a French Wig in a Bag, with two large black pieces of Silk that come on each side under my Chin, and are lost in the buttoning of the Breast. Beside this, I have just begun to learn to dance; and I believe verily shall come home very much a Gentleman. – My hearty Service to my Sister: I hope she, and you, and all friends are well; and am ever

Your most affectionate

Jo: Spence

---

146   A richly decorated gown, fashionable at the time.
147   An act of courtesy.

I find by our letters, that tis but 10 days fro' hence to London; and 12 to Winton[148]: rather less than more!

I wrote to you fro' Calais, but know not w[hethe]r it came to hand.

Dijon
Mar: 27, NS.
16. old stile

Dear Mother,

I have had the pleasure of receiving a whole Covey of your letters together: There were 4 of them: the first dated Decr 20; and the last, Feb: 21. I am very glad you did not think time enough of writing to Dick to curtail them; for I wd not have had them otherwise than they are for twice the Postage. Indeed the Post hither is very tolerable, as well as very expeditious: all four together with Dick's, did not cost me above 18 pence; and they got hither from Dick in 8 days.

I'me glad my Cheat succeeded so well, to let you know that I was at Calais; before you thought I had left England. I wish Mr Wavil all the Health that is necessary to hold him out twenty years longer, tho' I hope to see him in two: I wrote to him the 13 of this Month, NS. I am very glad Miss Belson is to be in England again; for a Nunnery here wou'd be a terrible thing for a Lady of her constitution: I'le bring the letters very gladly back with me. I just came home from a Walk when I receiv'd your letters, and am now just return'd from another, when I sat down to write this. Our Weather here has been, almost this fortnight, as warm as May in England; nothing can be more delicious than the air; and abroad all round us they are busy in their Vinyards, setting up the Sticks and tying the Vines to them. They don't seem to make half the Figure that I expected: the Sticks (or Hop-poles in Miniature) are not above breast-high: and a whole Vinyard , when the Poles are set looks only like a large regular plantation of Raspberry's.

About a Fortnight ago we walk'd out to see a College of the Chartreux, ab[ou]t half a mile without the Walls. These are, generally speaking, some of the strictest Religious people among the Roman Catholicks. Our English Friend conducted us thither, as he does almost every where. He led us directly to the Warden (the Pryor) of the College; who was a plump, goodnaturd, cunning, bald pated, old Gentleman. After staying the time of a Civil visit

---

148   Part of the borough of Christchurch in Hampshire.

with him, we had leave to speak with one of the Society; or rather, we carried him leave to answer us, when we spoke to him: for they are all under an Oath of Silence. The Society consists of 24, beside Mr Abbot. There is a little hole in the Wall, abt a foot square, belonging to each chamber: the Cook keeps the key of it, and puts in their dinner without speaking a word. Each day, each 24 hours, they have eight hours for Public prayer, eight for sleep, and eight for their business, reading, or working in their little gardens. They go to bed at six, Winter and Summer; rise at ten at night; pray till two; then in bed again till six; and then pray again till 10. From that to six in the Evening is their hours, at their own disposal. The Brother we saw had very neat little Lodgings, and a pretty Garden: and the rest have all the same. They never speak, but for two hours two days in the week; nor stir out of their foredore even into their own Cloysters, but for an hour or two on stated days. Then they walk each singly: and if one happens to cross another, all he is allowd to say is, Remember your Death Bed; in Latin. They keep a Fast for life; and never taste any thing but Fish or Herbs. I was mightily pleasd with one thing. A bird here, something like our Morehens, that lives chiefly on the water they will have to be a Fish; I mean they always eat it as a Water Creature: They do the same to Otters; which the Abbot assur'd us were excellent good, when well drest. For their 8 hours of Diversion, each has some employment or handy craft; as Painting, making of Statues, Music &c. The Brother we visited was a Turner and made little Tunbridge-Ware things.[149] After I came home, I cou'd not help being really concern'd, to think that Religion, which was designd to make men goodnatur'd and sociable, s[houl]d ever be perverted so very far from its original intent as to make people plant themselves, one by one, like Orange Trees in their particular boxes; and even forswear the use of their tongues, which I have a strong notion were given them to talk with.

 I begin myself to come little and little to the use of my tongue again, and (Heaven be prais'd) have taken no oath as yet of Silence. I have a Priest that comes to me every day to teach me the Language; and, after Easter he is to come twice a day. I can now hold a little sort of a broken conversation with any body I meet: and every day it will grow easier and easier. We dine generally at a large Inne, where there is an Ordinary kept every day for all strangers, to help on Learning the Languages: and yesterday we had the pleasure of having no less a man, than a Knight of Malta for one of the company.

 I desire my hearty service to Mrs Page: and tell her 'twas a fine day the 24th of December on the Sea between England and France, as well as in Culver's

---

149 The local industry at Tunbridge Wells in Kent was making wooden work boxes and toys from beech, holly &c and inlaid; they were known as 'Tunbridge ware'

Close. My very hearty service to my Sister, Mr Wavil, and all friends round the Reking.[150] I am, thank Heaven, very well: and ever
 Your most Affectionate and Dutiful
Jo: Spence

Dijon
May 1,
12, 1731.

Dear Mother

I'me very glad you mention'd Mr Wavil in your last, for I expected a letter from him and forgot to write to him in answer to what he mention'd of his Son. I have now made amends for it, and sent to him by this Post. Mr Rolle is got to Oxford again as I take it; for Dick has wrote to him, and receivd an answer. I'le answer for him he will be always glad of receiving your letters, and in writing to you again.

Among all the Chat we have had together across the Water, I dont know that I have once mention'd our eating here. They delight mightily in Fowl, in particular: and I dont know that I have once either on the Road or here, set down to dinner or supper without a pullet, or Capon, on the Table. At present we never miss of that, and pidgeons: with 2 plates of Sparagrass,[151] one drest with oyl and vinegar for the good people of the country: and another with honest butter, for us poor Englishmen. The Dinner always begins with a Soupe: and both that and the Supper end with a disert. As soon as this is set on the Table, the Serv[an]ts place a glass by each person, and a bottle of Burgundy at each end of the table; make their bows, and retire. The Disert and Cloth stay as long as you do: which keeps the table dry, and gives you sweet-meats whenever you have a mind for 'em. In the Winter, we never mis[se]d of Grapes preservd in the bunches as they grow, and a plate of Almonds in their neighbourhood. At present we have generally a Preserve which is very much my Favourite: 'tis made of Barberries, in which there is a Mixture of Sharpness and Sweetness, that is extremely agreable. They have now too, always Curds and Cream in the desert; but tis always sower. The best Burgundy at the Taverns costs but 8 pence a bottle: and from the finest Cellars of the great Merchants but 16 pence. The common people buy worse sorts cheaper and cheaper: and tis matter of fact that the Lowest of all is but a half-penny a bottle. I had almost forgot to tell you, that about the beginning of last Month, I had the pleasure of tasting

---

150 Possibly the Wrekin, a prominent hill (1,342 feet) eight miles south-east of Shrewsbury.
151 asparagus

a Frigassee of Frogs, for the first time. It had a sort of a Chickeny taste; but something of an odd Sowerness at the bottom that I did not quite like.

This week two gentlemen of Oxford came hither: one of 'em is son of Mr Shuttleworth,[152] Knight of the Shire (I think for Lancashire) and the other a very sinsible pretty Gentleman, one Mr Denny.[153] They stay here for some time, but we are going next week for Lyons, more towards Italy. I expect to be there for 3 or 4 Months. The other Gentlemen are for Italy too; and I believe will probably follow us to Lyons in 4 or 5 weeks. The next direction to me is in all it's form, according to the French Fashion, as follows:

  à Monsieur,
 Monsieur Spence,
Avec Milord Middlesex,
 Au Palais Royal
   à
Par Paris Lyon

Tis a very pleasant place, by the Pictures of it: I hope to give you account of it in my next: and am

   Your most Aff:
   And Dutiful Son,
   Mr. Spence.

       Lyons
       May 17 1731

Dear Mother

We set out from Dijon on Monday Morning, and came here to Lyons time enough to dine on Tuesday; that is a hundred and twenty miles. We had not been here above five minutes, when the Post-woman came in with the letters, one for My Lord; and, as good luck wou'd have it, another for me. My brother had been with the Duke's Secretary; and so had learnd how to direct to me here, sooner than I expected.

We came out of Dijon a little after the rising of the Sun. You know the Post-Chaise[154] is as easy as a great chair; so that we cou'd set and enjoy all the

---

152 Richard, son of Sir Richard Shuttleworth (1683–1749). A Knight of the Shire represented a county in Parliament.
153 William Denny (1709–?1770), an army officer; member of the Society of Dilettanti; later governor of Pennsylvania.
154 A closed four-wheeled horse-drawn coach used for the rapid transport of mail and passengers.

Prospects at leisure. The first four and twenty miles was all through Vinyards; the leaves as yet only beginning to come out: but the variety and neatness of em still made it agreable enough. After that the Country mended much to the Eye; there are two Towns in the way call'd Chalons and Maçon about 30 miles apart: all the way between I never yet saw as fine a Prospect in my life. On the left hand was a continual rising and chain of Hills of a moderate height; or rather one Hill rising and sinking at least every quarter of a mile unequally: this was generally about a mile or two off from us: on the right hand about the same distance commonly, was a river not much inferior to the Thames. Beyond that, the Country spread every way for a vast length; first in delicious Meadows, then in Cornfields, and then in Woodlands. At the end of all, almost all the way, we cou'd see the mountains of Switzerland, all coverd with Snow, whilst we were sometimes sweating with heat in the Chaise. Our Prospect on that side was almost always above 60 mile, for the mountains were generally about that distance from us. In spite of the Prospect I wishd to be nearer to them for as we were, we c[oul]d not discern the Snow so plain as I cou'd have desir'd. Twas so indistinct that twas difficult to distinguish their Tops from Clouds gilded a little with the Sun. All the Country on, quite to Lyons, was I think verily more beautiful than Dorsetshire: but by no means equal to the Thirty Miles I have been speaking of.—

There was one thing that added a good deal to the pleasure of the Journey. The two days that we were upon the road happened to be Whitson Monday and Tuesday with us here. In a hundred places the roads were full of Country People, drest all in their best, and in their different fashions. I think all the women had hats, some like mens, some odd high Crowns, some neat straw hats, very wide brim'd and with little steeples upon 'em like the black high crowned hats in England. For one part of the Course, all the Women wore odd black things on their heads, of wool, and fashion'd like Turkish Turbans. We had the Pleasure too, as twas a great Holy Day, of seeing two Country Processions of the Priests and poor people with the Cross carried before 'em and the picture of their favourite Saint swinging on a banner in the air. The other had all this with Kittledrums and Musick, and the Militia on Horseback; and so was much finer and much more pleasing to God Almighty no doubt.—I did not think of lengthening out my letter at this rate: but as I have no room left to tell you anything of Lyons, at present, I must keep that for next time. I am
  Your dutiful and affect:
  Jo: Spence

Lyons,
July 30)
Aug' 10) 1731

Dear Mother

I recd your letter yesterday, and this I hope will set out for you to morrow. Beside being a very good boy, I write this with the more dispatch; and beg you wd answer it as soon after receiving it as you can; because we shall set out for Italy about the middle of next month. I hope to let you know, in my next, what particular route we are to take; which is not yet fixt.

The poor Nun, whose execution we were at, lookd very much like a dying creature. She was extremely pale, and had a Face that was neither handsome, nor agreable. My acquaintance, as yet, in the Nunneries does not reach far enough to say whether they are generally pretty. I believe, for the most part they are not. If there are two daughters in a family, and one of 'em to be a Nun, they generally chuse out the less handsome; because the other will be more fit to scuffle in the world for a Husband.[155] What may make people generally think that Nuns are pretty, may be this. In all their Houses, they have Needle Work and little Trinkets to sell: and when Strangers come to the grate, they always send the prettiest Noviciate they have to offer their ware: there she stands like a Milliner; and the prettiest Milliners have always the best Custom.

I ought to let you know the progress of my Dress and by what degrees I creep into the Habit of a Gentleman. Ever since we have been at Lyons, my Hair (which had six weeks growth on my Forehead and Temples at Dijon) has been comb'd back on a light brown natural Wigg. It did not comply so well with the Mode at first; but every day my Barber persecutes it with an ounce of Pomatum; and then plaisters it down with half a Pound of Powder. After the operation, I walk out with what passes for a Head of Hair very well Frosted. My Coat is a light Camlet[156] with Silver Buttons; a Green Silk Wastcoate sufficiently daubd with silver lace; and I seem upon the brink of having a pair of Stockings to it with Silver-Clocks. With all this, I shall look upon myself to be as much a Gentleman, as that half of the Gentlemen in England, who are only so from the Cloaths they wear.

I have often told you of the fine River that runs under my window. Between my writing and reading in the morning it furnishes one with perpetual diversion. Beside the River itself, which has always boats upon it going and coming; just on my right hand is a bridge over it, that wants but very few yards of being as long as our famous bridge at Rochester: and there is always a flux of

---

155 Successfully to fight for a husband.
156 Material made of wool and silk.

People and Carriages upon it. On the River we have often Great Boats which go and come weekly from the Cities that lie up or down the Soane. They call 'em Water-Coaches, and indeed they use 'em just as we do our Stage Coaches in England. They bring sometimes 30 or 40 Passengers at a time, and they are such an odd mixture of people that tis very agreable to be at their arrival. For the little Boats and Scullers, they are almost always rowd by women, and yet we don't abound so much with water-language here as on the Thames; which, considering the difference of the Sexes as to the Faculty of Talking, surprizes me very much. T'other day we saw a Boy fishing for Swallows on my Bridge. Perhaps you may think I have got the knack of a Traveller: but 'tis literally true. They bait for 'em not with meat, but Feathers: tis at the time the creatures make their nests. The Feather waves about in the air; three or four of the Swallows will skim at it after one another, and if either of 'em has the luck of snapping the Feather, tis ten to one but she snaps the Hook too and so is flung up on top of the Bridge. The Boats are not so neat and good as ours: and sometimes they use only a single board to pass the water. I have see three men go down the stream on one. They stood on it very steady, two of 'em helpd to row and guide it; and the middle man was playing upon a Flute, very much at his ease. Their boys use these boards too, particularly when they first learn to swim. You will sometimes see five or six of them swimming round one; and, as either of 'em is tir'd he gets and rests upon the board. 'Tis a little floating island for 'em that attends 'em wherever they please. It was about a month ago that I was passing in a boat going thro' the Town; beyond us is a bridge where the water is not above breast-high under the Arches; I had heard nothing of the custom and you may imagine how much I was surprizd to see the Arch I was going under, one half full of boats; and the other, almost full of Ladies, up to the Chin in water. When the weather is hot, they do it to cool themselves; they have alway[s some]thing on, like our Women at the Bath: but they don't at all shriek to have men among them. Some of 'em sit on great stones that are in the water: up to the Chin all. You see 'em in little parties; two or three with their faces chatting together; and one gentleman, perhaps, in the Circle with 'em: others in couples, or threes, and there perhaps two or three holding their little children in their arms, with only their little heads and a silk Cap and Feather above water. They all look mighty serene and well pleasd: and tis no manner of affront to pass close by 'em or to stop the boat to look upon 'em. Tis really a very odd and very agreable sight.

Your most dutiful
[signature missing]

Lyons
August 24)
Sept' 4) 1731.

Dear Mother

I don't know whether we may not stay here long enough to receive another letter; at least the best way will be to direct your next hither as usual; and if we go, orders will be left here how to send it after us. The violence of the Heats in Sicily need not have put you in any fright. We have had very good luck here, and indeed have had (I dare say) a much more temperate Summer than yours at Winchester. We came hither abt the middle of May: the last week of that month, and the first of June, were so extreme hot, that if it had gone on increasing in proportion, we must have kept in entirely all day, or been roasted to death: but the Convenience is that we have North Winds which we call the *Bise*, that travel thro the snow on the tip of the Alps, and cool the Air here and keep it from taking fire. They have their inconvenience too; for sometimes after a day that has been much hotter than any I ever felt in England, the next day comes a wind that puts us all at once in the middle of December. We actually had a great Christmas Fire one day in the Dining-Room, at the end of June; and I had one here in my chamber, the 24th of August. At present neither the Cold, nor the Heats are so extreme. In all this tryal of one's constitution, I thank Heaven I have not been out of order any one day since I came to this place.

The Ladies here wou'd really frighten you, to see how very unconcern'd they are in their watry Situation. The same impudence runs thorough 'em all. If they were prettier, this wd take away a great deal from their agreableness; but the misfortune is that Lyons is not a city of Fine Faces. Tho' 'tis recon'd the Second City for size in France, and is certainly one of the best peopled; I dare say that Winchester cou'd beat 'em for Beauties. I own I have a great regard for my own dear Country; but I believe I may say this, without any manner of partiality for the fair Ladies of the Capital of Ham[p]shire.

The Cool days that we have had intermixt with our hot have given me, beside our other expeditions, very often the opportunity of taking my walks. One day, in particular, I was resolv'd for a long one: to see the Aqueducts, that in the time of the Romans brought fine water from twenty miles distant hence, quite to the City. 'Twas a Channel for water raisd up into the Air on vast Arches of Stone-work. The Remains of 'em are still considerable. I set out at 6 a clock in the Morning with a Priest. As soon as we got out of Town we met with a great piece of it, of 10 or 12 Arches; then it ceasd and at intervals we found traces of it again. About 4 miles from the Town, we came to a place that seemd formerly to have been the channel of a vast River; but there was not any water left in it. This the Arches crost, and remain all along it very thick and very high. On farther, abt half a mile off, on the Hill, we cou'd see another range of

it that seemd to be 70 or 80 of these Arches all together: however, we thought it time to turn towards Lyons, and as we were for making new discoveries, we took a round on the Left hand towards another Roman Castle that appeard on a Hill. We walkd all along thro' the bed of the River, for a great way; and then thorough Meads, that led us to some odd dark walks, the most Romantic I ever saw in my life. The place was so agreable, that we wanderd about and lost our great Path. At last we found out a Meadow, at the back of a Gentleman's House. Every body is obliging in France: so we knock'd without any scruple at the Gates, to pass thorough, and to be put into the right way. When the Gate open'd, it discoverd an odd Figure of a man, very much like our Country Squires, with five dogs about him, and a hunting-Pole in his hand. He was the Master of the Castle. We told him our case: and he was so obliging, that he wd make us enter the Palace and take a Refreshment with him. His Servants were all abroad, some at work and some at Mass; and so he was forcd to take care of us himself. Never was a man more bustling or more obliging. 'Twas between 9 and 10 in the Morning, a very good time for people to break fast that had been so long a walk. Our good Gentleman brought us every thing, as fast as he coud, by degrees. He spread the Table himself, and laid the Napkins. After that he disappeard for a considerable time for indeed the poor man had enough to do. At last he return'd with a very large plate of Ham that he had cut very nicely into slices; and another of Bologna sausages: they were set off with pickles and Anchovies. His next journey produc'd a bottle of very good Burgundy: he set us each a Glass; and then we had nothing to do but to fall to eating, and drinking, very much in earnest. After the first heat, we began to come a little into regular conversation and 'twas then that we found out that he was an old officer. He had serv'd all the war, almost, both against K[ing] William and the D[uke] of Marlborough. Beside a good tolerable number of wounds, he had twice been taken Prisoner and had once been set out to be sent as such to London, but met the day before he was to go with a lucky Exchange of one of our Officers for him. He got enough by the war, to purchase a very pretty estate, and now lives in that delicious old place: where, as he told us, he passes all his time in Walking, or Reading. He is a very sensible man, speaks very honourably of the English: and when our bottle of Burgundy was out, gave us another: so that we came off very chippant,[157] and very much in love with him and his dwelling place. He was very pressing that we should stay and dine with him; but his breakfast (tho 'tis a very common one in France) was so new to me, that I thought it might pass for Breakfast and Dinner too: so we took our leave with many thanks, and arrived safe here by 12 a clock.
[MS ends]

---

157 lively, cheerful

>Geneva;
Oct: 3)
Sept 22) 1731.
Sent away Oct: 5.

Dear Mother

We made three days of it in coming from Lyons hither: in most parts of France the Posts[158] are so managed, that we have a change of horses every six mile; in some places at 9, and in others at 12: but for this journey we were forc'd to take one set of Horses for the whole, and were forc'd to pass a good deal of hilly Country, into the bargain. At our first setting out, we past by the Course of the Rhone. Before us, at a distance, lay a whole range of hills, that we thought all along we were to pass, but when we came to them were agreably enough surpriz'd, to find that there was a double range of 'em, and that we passd all between both. 'Twas a very odd and uncommon sight all the way: the plain between them was generally not above 3 or 4 hundred yards wide, then the ground rose with little Vinyards and fields: the rising was often full of woods, which went sometimes up to the top of the ground. The highest part of the hills on each side was all solid rock which came down strait to the woods and fields, like the great Quarry at Giles' Hill.[159] This sort of road continu'd for about 15 miles and tho' twas, in general, like what I have mention'd: there were several varieties in it, that were still new and surprizing. In one place the Stone at top had form'd the Ruins of a Castle; and tho' there were several real ones in the way which we had just seen, we were a good while before we cou'd distinguish whether this was real or natural stonework. Sometimes the Meadows and rising fields took a greater stretch , and in one place made a View exactly like the picture of Tempe which I left with you, and which was reckon'd the most agreable spot in the world.[160] In one place, we had a Fall of water in a strait Line from the Top of the Rock to the bottom; and in another the stones on each side form'd a street of ruin'd houses, which the more you look'd upon it, look'd the more like a Town with broken pillars, and arch'd windows, in a thousand parts of it. The Cathedral of this Town, that was built by nature (possibly at the time of the deluge) was very distinguishable; and we passed

---

158   Originally posts were places where men with horses were stationed at intervals along the post-road to ride with the king's mail to the next stage; thus they were places where travellers could find a change of horses for their onward journey.
159   St Giles Hill is the summit of a chalk spur giving a panoramic view of the city of Winchester.
160   A cleft through thick marble by which the river Peneios penetrates the mountains in north-east Thessaly; it was celebrated in antiquity as the place where Apollo purified himself after slaying the python.

close by the Front of it: which was an old Gothic building (as your Cathedral is at Winton)[161] and look't grand tho' irregular. There was a real House or two sometimes stuck up against the side of the Hills; a few more about the middle of the plain; and two villages: one of which was the oddest dark street I ever saw. There was a slanting shed came from over all the first windows which shelved down for half the height of the houses, then began another that came down quite to the ground. 'Twas so on both sides; the way and between 'em was nothing but a little stream of water that a frog might jump over without straining himself. The people walk on both sides under the ugliest Pent-house in the world: and I can't imagine why they are so cover'd, except it be to save 'em from the snows; especially those heaps, that might fall from the Tops of the Hills over 'em in the beginning of the Summer, and knock the Citizens on the head.—Geneva is a very neat place; and there is an air of Liberty and Happiness all over it. I have not yet seen a beggar in the Streets: tho' I have walk'd 'em considerably for the time we have been here. Yesterday morning I took one of My Lords footmen with me to show me to the Great Church. Just before we came to it, I saw the Head of the Professors here, old Turretin,[162] reading a lecture in the German Church; and as I was willing to hear so famous a man, I bid the servant stay at the door and went and sat me down in the circle of Students. After I had satisfied my curiosity, and was coming out, I found the servant was gone and s[houl]d have been at a loss if it had not been for a worthy old Gentleman whom I took by his dress to be a Lawyer. He offerd his service to me, to show me all about the Town, and all over their fortifications: and whatever I cou'd say to the Contrary, forc'd me at least to take his servant with me to the places I was to see, and left me with half a dozen compliments on each side: as soon as I was got some distance from him, I ask'd the servant who was that very obliging gentleman his Master; and who shd it be, but the head Magistrate, at present, of all the state of Geneva?[163] I mention this only just as one instance of the politeness and obligingness of the people of this City of which one cd not say too much. Tis confidently reported here, that the King of Sardinia, our neighbour at present, has put his Father the Duke of Savoy in Prison for attempting to resume the Crown.[164] I am

Your dutiful Son
J. Spence

---

161 The Cathedral Church of the Holy Trinity at Winchester (archaically called Winton) is the longest Gothic Cathedral in Europe.
162 Jean Alphonse Turretin (1671–1731), Swiss theologian.
163 Barthelémy Gallatin (1662–1748).
164 Victor Amadeus II (1666–1732) had renounced the crown in 1730 in favour of his son, Charles (see n. 112).

Turin,
Oct. 13)
24) 1731.

Dear Mother

I wrote to you a long letter from Geneva, Octr 5 (Septr 24 with you) with an account of the Road thither, and the most remarkable of our adventures in our present state of Knight-Errantry. I then talkd to you of Hills; and I really thought they had been pretty handsome ones then, because they were as big again as any I had ever seen in my life: but now I can fairly look upon 'em as Pigmies. In short we have passed the Alps. All the way from Geneva, for five days, we kept rising higher and higher. The first day we were in a confusion of Hills: and the rest, between two ranges of 'em again; with a line of fields and Meadows between; which grew each day narrower and narrower, and more and more barren. The Fifth day brought us to a stop. It was the vast Mount Cenis, the general Passage into Italy. We had for a good while before passed thorough a road where each side of us was generally a wild face of Nature, quite untaught and unmanaged by man. Rock above Rock, with vast wild Quarries of loose stone, the Tops of the Hills coverd often with snow, and often hid part in the Clouds; and sometimes, part appearing above them: little streams of water breaking down the Hills, sometimes falls of water all at once, that at a distance look'd like white smoak tumbling downward, a River at the bottom, that was almost all the way labring over a bed of broken pieces of the rocks; and look'd often more like a stream of boiling, than running water. Nothing that lookt human or agreable; except sometimes great woods of Firs and Pine trees that grew all up some of the Hills, and Rocks; where one wd think it impossible for them to grow: and a little village now and then in the bottom with people in it with sweld Necks, and such shapes and faces as made 'em look very little like men and women; in spite of their having something of cloaths on: whatever they are, they live to be very old; and in one of these little villages we past in the last 12 miles toward Mount Cenis, they say scarce any one dies before they are 100 Years old. They live upon nothing but milk indeed, and the water there which tho' it gives 'em vast swellings in their Necks, is (they say) otherwise very wholesome. We lay at a Village just at the foot of Mount Cenis, where the people seem to be much of the same kind: they can say, Yes or No; laugh when you speak to 'em; and I suppose eat and drink when they can get anything. I ask'd the moderate-aged woman, who lighted our Fire, how old she was: she said she did not know, but that she was young: perhaps you are past Thirty? Yes, Yes, I'me past thirty. Forty, perhaps? Ay, that I am.—Perhaps, fifty? I believe I may.—This is a true History of our Dialogue, and I did not carry it any farther for fear three more questions s[houl]d make her fourscore. This wild Road I have been talking of, was all in our last day and a half to Mount Cenis: we lay at the foot of that monster: the next day was designed wholly for passing it. We had often seen the Clouds, on each side of us, lower than the tops of the Mountains; but that day was the first that we were to take a Journey into 'em. Over night one of the Prime ministers of the King of Sardinia for that Village came to take measure of us: I mean, one of the Head Porters came to view each person, and see how many men wd be necessary to carry him up the Hill. Ld Middlesex had four assigned him; the D[uke] of Kingston, six; and his Governour who is a Portly plump gentleman,[165] no less than eight. For my part, when I view my own size by his, I was under horrible apprehensions, that they wd allow me only two: but was overjoyed when the Manager said that my little Lord (for we English are all Lorded abroad) must have four too. The Morning came; and the Moment we came out of doors, we were each plac'd imediately in our chairs, with our feet in a bag of Bears-skin; and our honest carriers began to move upward in a good sound trot. 'Tis surprising with what dispatch they shufle with you up the Hill. They call the Ascent itself three miles; and yet in comparison to the length we seemd to be up immediately. Half way up we passd thro' a grove of Pine Trees on each side, for a good way, like the Avenue to a gentlemans House, only the road serpentizes thorough 'em, running up generally in the shape of an S. We were so many in company (porters, Servants, and all, above fourscore men; and I believe at least fifty horse and mules with baggage &c) that sometimes you wd see one of these great S^s, all full of company, moving up together against the steep. When we conquerd the ascent we found ourselves in a great plain, on a level with the Clouds, the Hill rising in peices all round us, and the Clouds rolling against their sides. This plain we passd for above 3 miles; we went by a Lake there (of a mile long as they say) well stockt with fish; and a Religious House built in the Clouds to the beginning of the Descent. The Descent is about 6 Miles; and I'me glad that I am got to the end of my letter, for 'tis in some places so rough and so wild, that it wd be very difficult to describe it. We are all very well: and I am

Your dutiful and Affectionate
J. Spence

---

165 Dr Hickman.

Milan,
Nov. 5, 1731

Dear Mother

I hope you are furnisht with a good Map of Italy; and a pair of Jackboots to travel thorough it with me. I left you in my last at Turin. After the pleasures of that delicious City, we went to Milan. I never saw so large a Town, so very ill inhabited. They call it 10 miles about; and when we enterd it, it lookd almost like a Desert. It is but poorly inhabited, and as the women never walk the Streets (but to go to Church) it seems much less inhabited, perhaps, than it is. Here we begin to see the care of the Italian Husbands, very sensibly. The women do not only keep generally within; but appear too very rarely in the Shops or any public part of their own houses. They keep mostly in their own chamber, and their chief diversion is looking out of [the] Window. Even when they do that you must not expect to see their faces: there's a sort of wooden lattice (they call 'em Jealousies) that generally hangs down all over the outside of the Window: 'tis made moveable to about half a foot before 'em; there they poke out their heads and see about them without being fairly seen. By what one cd discover of em, I believe there were several faces among them that deserve better usage. The Dress of the Head, especially, is very becoming. The Common people wear nothing upon their heads: their hair is twisted in two long Breeds[166] behind: these Breeds are then drawn round and round a Silver Bodkin on the Top of their heads and looks like a Crown of Hair: the rest they set very prettily to the face: and if they have any ornament at all on the Head, tis two or three Rose buds, or a Sprig of Jessamin. The Ladies come very often near this; or if they go farther tis often nothing but a little Cap all of short red Ribbons; and for the graver gentry, black. In Assemblies they dress pretty much in the French Fashion; in the Churches and Streets you lose most of their head dress by a Veil that covers that and most of their faces. One of the things that I saw with the greatest pleasure at Milan, was the Great Hospital. There is one large Court, and 4 less on each side of it. Each Court has a Canal of clear water running round it; they are serv'd with all conveniences and every thing looks neat about them. In one Square are religious women, in another the Sick, in another the Decrepid, and in a fourth Children that come by chance into the world; &c. The latter, if Boys, they prentice out when about 14 Years old: and the Girls are kept there till they can get husbands; or some method of living out of it, if they choose it. The Income for the maintenance of the Hospital is very great; and they are all kept very well. The number of the Bastards upon the Spot there, or now prenticed with the Hospital money, amounts to between 11 or 12 Thousand: in a modest computation, they have about 10 fresh ones every

---

166 braids

week. We were in the Chamber of Infants; and I never saw any anything that pleasd me more. There between 50 and 60 little creatures perhaps; all from a day or two to 7 or 8 weeks old; and about 10 neat nurses in the Room, that seemd as busy and as pleasd about them, as cou'd be. Above half the Chitts[167] were asleep, in little long beds with bolsters at both ends; and sometimes you'd see two little heads together, at each end. Some were feeding, and scarce any one whimpering; for they manage them extremely carefully and well. I believe most of the Nurses had been of the same Breed themselves; and as they grew up were taught to take care of their new little Cosins as they came in. We have something of this kind in all the great Cities where I have been; there is a noble one at Venice; and before it was establisht, they usd to find numbers of little children drown'd continually in their Canals: Tho the Hospital at Milan, where we saw the little Nursery I have been talking of, is so rich; there are still people continually leaving money to it. They have a great Hall, with the Pictures of their Benefactors in it: among which there is one in a shabby dress who was a small Coal man but managd his gains so well that he died worth a hundred Thousand Crowns and left it all to the Hospital. With hearty services to all friends, I wish you and Belle a happy New Year; and am ever

Your affect: and Dutiful
Jo: Spence

Venice:
Novr 22, 1731.

Dear Mother,

I am now by a good fire side with the Sea all round me (for the middle of our streets, here at Venice, are pav'd with nothing but water) and two of your letters before me. I'me very sorry to find that your Eyes trouble you again; and beg you wou'd spare 'em as much as possible. If my sister will be so good as to write for you, it will be a great satisfaction to me, for then I shall be sure you take care of 'em. When I hear from you, which can't be too often I shou'd be glad always of your Winchester News; who is married and who dead; for I wou'd willingly know all the terrible accidents there. As for the length of my letters, you need never fear 'em: the only danger is, that they shou'd be too long.

My last letter to you (Octr 24) brought us safe over the Alps to Turin. From thence we came with the Duke of Kingston to Milan, where we staid about a week. There we changed companys: the Duke with his attendance went for Genoa; and Ld Middlesex, with a brother of the D[uke] of Manchester, and

---

167 very young children

Ld Ferrers's brother[168] (two of the best naturd gentlemen in the world) for Venice: we stopt in the road 4 or 5 days at Verona and 2 at Padua, from whence we came hither in a day, by water: I think 'twas the most agreable day I ever had in my life. The River Brenta, by which we came into the Sea, is a great passage; we meet with boats perpetually; the weather was of a right heat, neither too warm, nor too cold; the side of the River is full of Gentlemen's and Noblemen's seats; we eat and drank with a particular good appetite; and were all as merry as Fiddlers. When first you fall in upon the Sea, you first see Venice before you: a fine City, spreading very much each way and, as it were, floating upon the waters. You see nothing but buildings and ocean.

If ever there was an agreable place in the world to live in for two or three months, it must be Venice: especially at this time of year. It looks like nothing else in the world. The Streets are all full of Sea; and instead of a Coach, you have always a boat (they call 'em Gondolas here) waiting for you. They are the best contriv'd for swiftness, and the snuggest things to be in as I ever saw in my life. We have three always at the door: and if you want to go a mile or two in the Town, tis but stepping into one of 'em and away they go with you, either conceal'd or with the windows open if you please; and there you are carried on, in the most agreable, or at least the most indolent, manner in the world. We live in a very good house, in the great street, just in sight of the great Bridge, the Rialto, the picture of which, if I don't mistake it, is at Mrs Kellys, to whom and all her good family, I beg my humble service. After dinner we never go out without our Masking habits; for tho' 'tis not yet Carnival, in the publick places there is not one in ten but what is maskt. The best Opera House is just by us; and we can go to it afoot, which is particular enough in this place: you'd be charm'd with their singing: Faustina and Bernacchi,[169] who were both in England last winter, I heard there last night, and the former of them sings certainly most exquisitely well. You know, I am a Judge[170]: but I speak rather from those that are so, than from myself. There's no place where perhaps a greater number of fine-looking Pictures than in Venice. The Collections of them are without number and the going to see one or other of them is the business of the morning. When you are once got into your boat, you are surprizd to find yourself so soon at the place you are designd for: they shoot along like Arrows tho' there are such multitudes going and coming in every

---

168 Robert Montagu (?1710–62), later 3rd Duke of Manchester, and the Honourable Sewallis Shirley (1709–65), son of 1st Earl Ferrers, subsequently Comptroller of the Household to Queen Charlotte.
169 Fustina Bordoni Hasse (1693–1781), famous soprano; Antonio Bernacchi (1685–1756), famous castrato.
170 Perhaps Spence intended to write 'I am no Judge'; the sense seems to require a negative.

street, they are so dextrous in the management of 'em that you scarce ever see any two of 'em hindering one another. We shall stay here two or three months; and then for Rome. I believe I have told you, that if you have any commands to the Pope, I shall be very ready to execute them.

I'me very much oblig'd to Mr Wavil for giving my direction to Mr Cheyney: and am glad to hear his Son Dicky is Commoner at the College. That will be a tryal to him; and, in my mind, I shou'd not fear to put him in upon the foundation afterwards, if he goes on well there, especially as he is pretty high in the School, and will grow more so daily, and consequently more considerable in that Commonwealth. I hear the praises of the School even here as I am wandering about the world: and this day am told that the D[uke] of Queensborough waits for a place in the Schoolmasters Lodgings for his Son.[171] Tis a particular happiness to me ever to hear of the Success of things there and more so in regard to the Schoolmaster, who has been so particularly a friend to me.

I s[houl]d be glad to know whether you are entirely with Mr Morecroft again, or whether you are in Sestos's Tower only by the by. I cou'd go and see the Original Sestos's Tower,[172] if you please; for as we are upon the Mediterranean at present, we are upon the high road to it. I beg my humble Services to my Sister, and all friends; and am ever

      Your Dutiful and Affectionate

          Jo: Spence

         Venice
       Feb: 29, [17]32

Dear Mother

We are now preparing to leave Venice; and in all probability shall have the pleasure of being in Rome before this comes to your hands. They tell me that we are going to meet the Spring; and I am the more apt to believe it because (tho' we have no Spring yet in Venice itself) I see, every day, the Flowers that are brought from the Continent, and which are ranged in several of the Markets here for the Ladies who buy 'em, to put 'em in their Head-dresses. The Carnival died last Tuesday; and every body now is got into mourning for it. Instead of the Multitudes of fine dresses we usd to see every where, one can

---

171 Henry Douglas (1722–56), elder son of Charles, 3rd Duke of Queensberry; he was about to begin at Winchester where he was a pupil 1731–9.
172 Sestos, a town at the narrowest point of the Dardanelles; at the terminus of the bridge of boats built by Xerxes in 481 BC to provide a crossing for his invading army.

now only meet with old Women, and now and then a young one, buried alive in a black Veil. But I must not forestall things: I hope to give you an account of what we have seen here, from Rome: and 'tis proper to tell you some thing of the Life of the Carnival, before I talk to you of the Death of it.

The last considerable place before we came to Venice was Padua: 'tis a large City, and the Number and Situation of the Spires (which lay in a line before the Eye) put us very much in mind of Oxford. We begun to expect very fine things of it, but upon our entrance were very much disappointed. 'Tis much less inhabited than Milan; and, in reality, the grass gets the better of them in several of the Streets, for want of feet enough to tread it down: in short it looks like the Ghost of a great City: and is rather famous for what it has been, than what it is. We saw there the Stone that Mr Addison speaks of, which Debtors for a moderate sum are to set upon in a pretty scandalous manner, instead of paying what they owe.[173] 'Tis come in play again lately: and last year there were three or four that caught Colds upon it. In going thorough the University there, we saw a famous Doctor that was instructing the young gentlemen. His subject and stile were both as plain as the calmest chapter of the Bible; and yet he spoke every word with more Action and Noise than any of our people on the Stage, in the most violent of Tragedies. I thought he wou'd have talk'd his Wigg off; tho' that wd have been no great misfortune, for twas so bad that no body wou'd have stoop'd to take it up again, tho' they might have had it for their pains. Tis the same with the Italian Preachers; those I have seen, make a terrible noise and hubbub in their Pulpits: but tis more excusable in them; for they talk there prodigiously often of the Devil. One observation I have made in my Travels which is, that 'tis much more wholesome to be a Parson in Italy than in England: for Preaching here is really a very strong Exercise; and must conduce very much to their continuing in a good State of Health: beside that they have very much the Advantage of us on frosty Mornings; for let the weather be as cold as it will, they are sure to bawl till they are all over in a Sweat. You see that I am not prejudic'd in my Religion; but wd give the Papists the Preference, where they really deserve it.

As the Small Pox is very much in Winchester I shall pray heartily for the Preservation of the many pretty Faces in it: and am very glad to hear 'tis so favourable a sort. Pray who is it that is going to marry some body at Southampton? For I can't recollect who you should mean. The Papers from England tell us that Mr Nicholls is made a Knight of the Bath:[174] I was extremely glad to hear it, and have some reasons to hope tis true.—I am glad to hear the happinesses of Mr Wavill's family; and long often to be in the Dean's

---

173 Addison, *Remarks*, 77.
174 Sir Charles Gunter Nicholl, KB (d.1733).

Garden with him talking about Predestination.[175] Hearty services to my Sister, and all friends from

>>>Your Dutiful and Affectionate

>>>Jo: Spence

>>[Rome]
>>March 4
>>15, 1732.

Dear Mother,

Yesterday we arriv'd safe to the City of Rome; and this morning only I have already seen enough to make one most sincerely amaz'd at the magnificence of it. All the time we staid at Venice, I did not care to mention anything relating to it: now we are four hundred miles out of their Dominions, I think I may do it with some safety. The Situation of their City is not more particular than their manners. They seem wholly to be divided between Debauchery and Devotion: and of course 'tis the most Melancholy, and the most gay place, in the world. In the Carnival, they give a loose to all their passions; and 'twou'd be a modest thing to say they are only half mad. The great diversion is appearing in the great Square, which is call'd the Place of S: Mark, in all the odd habits they can invent: their faces are hidd, and, in short, 'tis a Mascarade of six weeks continuance. The pleasure of Foreigners there is to see them act over their parts: for it requires a good deal of practise to behave so properly as they do and the Venetians are grown very eminent for the noble Art of Mimicking. You see always after dinner numbers of all sorts of people flocking to The Place of S: Mark. An odd blundering Harlequin pushes you on one side, as you are walking the Streets; and while you are recovering your self, you stumble perhaps against a Milk-maid who ten to one is a Lady of the first Quality. There are great numbers of Gentlemen drest up like Country fellows, with wooden shoes: and I have seen one of 'em, all cover'd with Sheepskin and playing upon a Bagpipe, before 30 couple at least of People of fashion drest up like Country people. There are others like Turks, Indians, and Sclavonians &c. The Character[s] that gave me the most pleasure were the Lawyers. You'd always have five or six of 'em together, with very scurvy black gowns and weather beaten wiggs. They were always in a hurry, and the noisyest people

---

175 The family's pleasure probably resulted from the election in 1732 of their son, Richard Wavell (1717–79) as a scholar at Winchester College (he was a commoner 1731–2). His father, Reverend Daniel Wavell (1675–1738), was Rector of St Maurice in Winchester; the title 'Dean' may have been associated with that Church.

upon the Place. They catch people, as they bustle along in the crowd, and swear they have a Lawsuite against some of their neighbours. Upon these occasions every moment the dispute grows louder and louder, and the poor occasional client has a very bad time of it. I once saw six of these Lawyers mounted on some rails near the Church of S: Mark, and disputing with much impetuosity, when, as Heaven would have it, in the perfection of their bawling, in comes a company of Harlequins upon 'em, a dozen at least in number, who scamperd up att 'em all at once; drew their wooden daggers; set upon the disputants; beat em all off their higher station; and then mounted in their places, and chatterd at one another like so many monkeys. One day there was two excellent wild Indians, a male and a female, walkd up and down very sagely thro' the crowd. The female one was a little polisht for an Indian; for she had a Muff made of a hollow piece of a mossy oak that became her extremely. Another time there was a great fat fellow drest up like a Nurse; and one of the tallest gentlemen in Venice like an Infant in swaddling cloaths: the poor child bawld every minute as loud as it cou'd roar for more pap; and as fast as the Nurse fed him sputterd it out again; very much to the diversion of the Spectators. I was by him at the instant that an unfortunate English sailor, who had ventur'd from the Port (which is just by) to the Place; stood to gape upon him; and the Great Child was so mischievous, and aimd so well, as to give him a mouthful he did not care for. My countryman took it very ill, and clinchd his fist very furiously at him; and I believe verily, if we had not interceded with him, wd have beat the Baby's Teeth down his throat. Between the Port and the Place is an Opening from the great Square, where I have gaped away many a good hour. Tis the Region of Mountebanks, Ballad singers, Rope dancers, and Conjurors. There were never less than three Mountebanks stages, the Gentlemen on 'em all haranguing together; and at least seven seats of Conjurors. One Conjuror was a gentleman drest in scarlet trimd with Gold, and his Wife by him, a Lady of the same profession. They sit in chairs on a table; they have their books by 'em, and a long trumpet in their laps. When the Curious come to be inform'd of their future fortunes, they apply the little end of the Trumpet to their ear, and speak down the great end of it. The patients listen at bottom with all the anxiety in the world. Tis surprizing how many customers they have. I have observ'd my friend in scarlet for an hour together; on purpose; and in all that time, he has not been a minute together without some new Fool at the end of his trumpet. I have no more room; and am

       Your dut[iful]: and Aff[ectionate]:
            J:Spence

Rome,
April 16, 1732

Dear Mother,

My last of the 15th of March I wrote to you from Rome; we then staid there for the present only two days, to take a little breath: and then went on, 150 miles farther, to Naples. Naples is the very farthest point we are to go from England; and the Morning we set out to return from thence hither, 'twas a common observation among us all, that we were then first returning homeward again. As much as I long to see you, I shou'd not care to forward our Journey on homeward, till we have enjoy'd some months in this City. 'Tis the place I always had such an eager longing to see; and I assure you in many things it more than answers all the expectations I had of it. I long to talk more of it at present, but I must follow my old way, and let you travel on with me regularly, as we usd to do.

From Venice we set out in a large cover'd boat for Ferrara. We were two days and a night upon the Adriatic Sea, or rather coasting along in the Marshes belonging to it. The first Night was the first time I had ever seen the Sun set on the Sea: 'twas really a very beautiful sight. Our Vessel follow'd a great channel; the Earth between us and the main land is very high, for five or six miles length: at low water it appears; and at high is all floated, and looks like the ocean. 'Twas a very odd sight to us that Evening to see hundreds of Fisherboys walking upon the Water. They were fishing for Cockles: and had left their boats at a good distance from them; the water did not come up above their Ankles, and at the distance we were they seem'd to tread the surface of the water. They trod the shallows for the Fish; and as fast as they caught any put 'em into little wicker-baskets they had about their middle. Tho' we were a jolly company, Seven (beside the Servants and Sailors), the Night did not pass on so agreably. In the Morning we found ourselves gaining toward the Mouth of the Po, the largest River in Italy; and came up it the rest of the day to the City where we were to stay. This was Ferrara: it lies quite in a flat, and when you view the whole town from the top of a Cardinal's house there is not a Hill to be seen in the whole circle round about you. The Streets are prodigiously strait and regular; but as for the people, they are departed; and 'tis more the Ghost town than Padua itself. Bologna makes up for it: the most populous Town in the Popes Dominions in which almost all the Streets are built with piazzas on each side so that the people have every where dry walking in Winter, and cool in Summer. In going on toward Loretto we ran sometimes twelve miles together on the sea-shore, one wheel often in the water: like one of the days we had in Flanders. We often pasd stragling Pilgrims, and the nearer we came the thicker they grew: for the last 5 or 6 miles the road was extremely well stocked with 'em. The Holy House, or rather room is cased all with a marble cover to secure it from the Devotion of the Pilgrims who wd else have carry'd it away piece by piece, by way of reliques. There's a good handsome Church built over it, and it stands in its Marble doublet just under the Dome.[176] Loretto is a little Town, poorly walld, and of no strength tho' on a hill. We came to it of a Sunday Night, while the people were at Vespers: 'tis incredible the numbers that streamd from the Church after the Service was over; we thought the Run of 'em wd never have done. Next day we went all to pay a Visit to the Holy House: the first thing they show you is the Image of the Virgin; some of her cloaths, that always keep their colours, as fresh as when she first bought 'em out of the Shop: and a little dish that she usd to break fast &c. This Image is all over Gold, Diamonds, and precious Stones; on one side of her is an Angel of Gold, giv'n by James the 2^{nds} Queen towards a birth; and opposite to it, one in silver giv'n by her mother to help on that great affair.[177] The riches of the House and of the Treasury just by, are beyond all ones expectation. Out of many gold lamps that hang up before the Image, there's one only which is valued at twenty thousand pound; and that whole room is perfectly wainscoted with Gold and Silver: and yet all the Gold and Silver together wd be inconsiderable in comparison of the Value of the jewels if they are all or only one half of them real ones. How many millions of poor people might be made happy, with what is now made useless, out of Piety and Religion. I s[houl]d be very glad to receive a letter from Mr Wavil. Services to my Sister and all friends. I am ever

Your Dut[iful]: and Aff[ectionate]:
J. Spence

⇒►◉◄⇐

Rome,
May 1)
Apr: 20) 1732.

Dear Mother,

My last, I think, left us at Loreto: all our Journey from thence to Rome was hilly or mountainous. We pas'd the Apennines, sometimes had snow lying close by the Chaise wheels; and sometimes the road all strewed with Violets. 'Tis in this part of his travels, that Mr Addison says he saw the four Seasons of the Year all in six days:[178] we came farther up toward the Spring than he did and traveld the same ground, from Loreto to Rome (almost all across Italy) in three

---

176 The Holy House was thought to be the place where the Annunciation took place; to save it from destruction by the Turks it was supposed to have been carried by angels and deposited in Loreto in 1295. The basilica was built over the House in 1469.
177 The birth of the Pretender, 1688.
178 Addison, *Remarks*, 165.

days which wd have made such a sight the more surprising; however, we had not the good luck to see all those Seasons: we had then really the Spring abt as forward as in England now, and as Italy abounds in Evergreens of many sorts it sometimes lookd much forwarder. On the Tops of the highest hills all was snow above us at a distance, and we were as cold as in December, for an hour now and then, and in the Sunny Vales sometimes as hot as Summer. Thus far we had a shifting of the Seasons; and no farther: for I wou'd not tell fibs to my mother for all the world. Between Spoleto and Terni (you may trace the places in your Map) we went out of our way to see one of the finest sights in Italy, of a Natural Curiosity. 'Tis a River (as broad as the Wares at Winchester) which falls all at once down a Precipice of 100 Yards high. It falls into a vast hollow between two Rocks which are separated from each other in the middle; and rises again, with a rebound, all in a vast Arch of Mist about 50 Yards high: the rest of the river rolls out, at the bottom, between the two rocks, roars and froths unequally over the Stones and broken pieces of rock, spreads itself in a course it made for itself; and then gathering itself into a regular stream again, falls into the river Nar; and so runs on with it to the City of Narni. The fall itself is a prodigious and a beautiful sight. The Brow of the Precipice is worn into hollows with the Mist and Vapours that rise from it; the descent and slopes on each side are cover'd, chiefly with olive trees and other evergreens, the leaves of which for a good way on each side are tarnisht from the same cause. This, and the sudden fall, make it terrible; but the rising again of the water, in that scatterd pretty manner, like a plume of feathers gilded with the Sun, is very pretty. I don't doubt but in a proper situation you might see rainbows in this mist, but we were just opposite to it, and the Sun on our right hand. This is call'd the Cascade of Terni; of old the river was call'd Velino. There were some parts of the Apennines that put us in mind of the Alps; but 'twas only a faint resemblance and a picture of 'em in miniature. They can't compare to them for rudeness,[179] natural ruins or height: and when you think of them together these seem only to be like the Son of a vast Giant, about 7 or 8 Years old; however, sturdy and gross enough for its age!

I have had the pleasure of meeting Mr Holdsworth,[180] the Poet, here at Rome, talking with him about Ham[p]shire and Nurse Page.[181] He has now left us. About 3 weeks ago he was robd of his cloaths, watch, a Diamond Ring and some money, by a fellow that got into his chamber at Midnight. He slept all the while. The villain came into his room with a lighted candle which he left

---

179   Being rugged or wild.
180   Edward Holdsworth (1684–1746), poet and learned Virgilian scholar; he specialised in relating passages in Virgil or Horace with the actual site where they had been written; Spence found his conversations valuable.
181   Unidentified; perhaps the same person as 'Mrs Page' on p. 92.

behind him; so that 'tis concluded, that if he had stird the fellow was prepar'd to murther him. The Rogue is since taken; and is to be put to the Torture to confess. He pawn'd the Cloaths; and the Pawnbroker appears against him. 'Tis probable he will be sent to the Gallies: as for his Life, Mr Holdsworth was unwilling that he shoud lose that because he had spard his, when 'twas evident he might easily have taken it away. Such a Robbery as this makes the more noise here, because tis a very uncommon thing. The Italians love to pick pockets, and pilfer every thing they can steal slily; but seldom rise to such a Robbery as this.

The Queen of Sardinia's Father is a poor Prince of Germany (as there are thousands of poor Princes there) call'd the Prince of Hesse-Rheinfields.[182] I wish I may see the old Gentleman to give your service to him: however we are pretty likely to see one of his daughters, the Dutchess of Bourbon,[183] the first beauty of France, and not car[e]d one farthing for by her husband, who is so civil generally as to let her have a bed all to herself. Last week I sent Capt Rolle a full and true account of the delightfull Spot we live in here; and shan't trouble you with anything of it at present, because ten to one he will be so dutiful a child as to send his mother word of it. Nothing pleases me so much as that you have been able to write all your letters yourself the whole winter; I was terribly frightend at what you said about your eyes [at] the beginning of it; but now hope they are pretty well. Ten thousand services to all friends from

Your Dutiful and Affectionate

J. Spence

Rome,
May 22)
11) 1732.

Dear Mother.

When we got first from Loreto to Rome we only staid three days to take breath (in which I wrote you my first from Rome) and went on for Naples. In going to Naples we often pasd old Roman roads, in many places all laid with large smooth stone, and as entire still as the Pavement of a great Hall, tho' near 2 thousand years old. Tis for me the most surprizing thing, of Art, which we have seen abroad. This noble Pavement, sometimes for miles together is border'd with Myrtles and a hundred other evergreens; and on each side of it you see perpetually the ruins of old Tombs and Monuments; for the Romans

---

182   Prince Ernest-Leopold (1684–1749).
183   Caroline Hesse-Rheinfels (1714–41), married Louis-Henri in 1728 (see n. 139).

always buried by great Roads: (perhaps to put people in mind that this life is but a Journey; and that in this world we are not properly at home.) There are sometimes Orange-Trees in the road; and at Mola, a little Sea-port in the way to Naples, all the Orchards were full of 'em, just like apple trees with us. Within abt 30 miles of Naples, we came into a vast plain, the richest soil and the best cultivated in Italy: whence the Italians call it *Campania Felice*, or 'the Happy Country'. It was soon after that we discern'd the top of the famous Mount Vesuvius; and the Smoke which it perpetually flings out, look'd at that distance, like a cloud gilded with the Sun. Naples is perhaps the most delicious Sea-Port in the World: it lies down a sloping ground, all in a large Half Moon, to the Sea. The Shore on for a great way humours the same shape of a half-moon; in one side of it, about 6 miles on the left-hand from Naples, is Vesuvius; and on the right, the Grotto of Pausilippo and the Tomb of Virgil. The Grotto of Pausilippo is a road made in a strait line, quite thro' the bottom of a Hill; broad enough every where for two coaches to pass, and the lowest part 15 foot high. At the Entrance 'tis 80, but the archt top goes sloping down to fling the light in. 'Tis near half a mile long; and when you are in the middle 'tis absolutely dark. I pasd it twice, and 'tis certainly the oddest travelling in the world. You are for some minutes w[ithou]t seeing anything, except a gloomy light, at a distance, at each end: you can there discern people entring and going out (for 'tis a great road;) who amidst the dust they raise and the odd light, look like a stream of Ghosts flitting backward and forward, and hear Coaches running by you, and confusd voices, without seeing anything about you. At the Entrance of this gloomy passage, on the side of a high rock is the Tomb of Virgil, the greatest Poet old Rome ever produc'd: it stands like a little round Temple; and on the Top of it grow three or four Laurel trees (of which I have sent a leaf to Kitt Pitt,[184] inclosd in a letter) and the ground where he lyes, I have kisd three times, so that I reckon his Ghost very much oblig'd to me. The dark hollow road below, leads to a Country full of Curiosities. A little way beyond it is a grotto, the air in which is so poysonous that most creatures, when held down in it, are kill'd in a few minutes; just by is a Lake, the water of which boyls up in several places like the water in your Tea-kettle. Indeed 'tis not only Vesuvius, but all the ground (perhaps for many and many miles about Naples) has a bed of Sulphur all under it, which makes a number of Hot Baths thereabouts; and sometimes breaks out in irruptions of Fire: as now often in Mount Vesuvius, and formerly in a vast Bason twelve miles on the other side. This Horror and Beauty of the Country so oddly mixt together, made the old Poets perhaps

---

184   Christopher Pitt (1699–1748), fellow student with Spence at Winchester and New College; he was translating the *Aeneid*, having published his *Essay on Virgil's Aeneid* in 1728.

place their Hell and Elysian Fields both in the neighbourhood of Naples. Don't be frightend if I tell you that I have seen both. We were in Hell on a very fine morning. Crossing a league or two of the Mediterranean Sea brought us to the Lake of Avernus, one of the Rivers of the old Heathen Hell: by it is a deep passage under ground to the Grotto of a Sibill, into whose chamber, at the end, we rode on the backs of our Guides who were up to the knees in Water. This letter will look most like a traveller's to you; but I have several noble witnesses to the truth of every word of it. I have not time now to tell you the particulars of our journey up Mount Vesuvius; that for my next: with services &c I am

Your Dut[iful]: and Affect[ionate]

J Spence

I am particularly obligd to Mrs Pitt for her Visit to you, and her Kindness to me.

Rome,
May 24)
June 5) 1732.

Dear Mother,

It was with a great deal of impatience that I waited for the morning when we were to go up Mount Vesuvius; which was heighten'd by my seeing it every morning. The Tops of the Houses are all flat at Naples, and as smooth as a floor; they often set 'em out with Flower-pots or Orange-Trees: and 'tis a great place for diversion with them. From the top of our House, we had a most distinct view of Vesuvius; and I usd to run up there every morning the first thing I did; to see whether he encreasd in his smoking or not. At last the morning came: four mile we went along the beautiful shore of Naples in chaises; which we were then to quit, from the rising and badness of the way, for horses; these carried us 2 mile more; and then the way is so steep and bad, that you are forcd to quit even them, and be drag'd up the two last mile by men; who make a trade of it, and so are the more ready in help to you. A mile before you come to their help you pass a dry stream of black earth for a great way together; this is the way that the Mountain formerly has boild over into the Sea: 'tis melted brass, lead, brimstone, and earth all mixt together, which after the fury of the irruption, as it grew cold, settled and hardend all along to the earth. After passing this a horseback and creeping up along the Hill, you come to the place where the men are to help you. This at the Foot of the part they call the Sugar loaf; 'tis much like it in its make, having been flung up in an Irruption, and encreasd by several since (for the great Vent for the Fire is in the midst of it) by the Earths pouring down on each side of it, like the lower Sand in an Hourglass. However, if 'tis a Sugar loaf, 'tis a pretty sizeable one: for 'tis 2 mile up to the very top of it. At the Bottom of it, when we came all together (for we were a very jolly company) there were I believe a hundred and fifty fellows stript to their wastecoats, ready to help us up. Two of these honest men get just before you, with strong girdles on; you take hold of the Girdles, and then they draw and you trudge up as fast as you can. Both they and we are forcd to rest very often; and then tug and trudge up again. The first 2 stages were pretty tolerable; then we get up thro' a vast solid river, of what had been all running Fire formerly; it lyes now all in ragged pieces; in colour and make, like the cinders of a Smith's forge, only larger and spread for a vast way. In some of the resting places here, we felt the Earth hot under us as we sat down; in others the Smoak and Vapours burst out here and there, so hot that you can't suffer your hand two instants in it. The last stage is infinitely the worst; 'tis all a loose crumbled earth in which your two draggers and you sink every step up to the knees: beside which it often yields under you; and tis often impossible not to slip back half a yard, or a yard with it together: but the Eagerness to get to the Top w[he]n so near makes it nothing to one. When there, you have a ragged rocky edge all round a vast Caldron, of perhaps, half a mile deep, and a mile round; all full of Smoak. The wind every three of four minutes clears away the smoak, and then you have a view of it. It sinks irregularly and raggedly all down on the inside. There are several places in it that look of a fire colour, blewish, greenish, and principally yellow. Paper held to it lights; tho' it looks rather of a flame-colour than as actual flames. A Stone is a vast time rattling down the Hole; and sometimes sounds as if twas dashing thro' melted metal. The Smoak often fills up the whole Hollow: and by fits the wind clears it, that you see the Sides distinctly, and the bottom. In a minute or two you are all clouded again: there seemd to be something like a regular Pulse in its venting smoak. One of my Guides was an extraordinary honest fellow; I was got very intimately acquainted with him in our journey up. He told me, That to be sure the Devil liv'd in that Hill, and wish'd very heartily that all the Frenchmen were in there with him. Upon my telling him that we were all Frenchmen, he said He was sorry for it, but it cou'd not be helpt. Our Descent (from this Devilish place which I was very sorry to leave) was rather flying, than walking: we were down I think in 15 minutes; which is pretty swift for two Mile. I forgot to mention one part of the sight: when the Wind blew away the Smoak from between the Crags of the opposite Side of the Caldron we had a View of a beautiful piece of Country, Green fields, Meadow-grounds, &c thick set with houses; on the right hand, appeard a part of the delicious Bay of Naples: twas but turning the head and we had a full view of all the City and Bay: this mixture of the most beautiful things, with the most horrid in the world, had a very particular effect and struck one in a manner that I never felt upon any other occasion. I cou'd wish myself there again was not I now a hundred and fifty Miles nearer Winchester. We have almost finish'd our affairs at Rome; and shall not stay here much longer. In 9 or 10 Months (which is about the time I us'd to stay at Oxford together) I hope to see how you do in Ham[p]shire, and to walk up Giles' Hill instead of Vesuvius. In the mean time with all services to all friends I am

Yours Dutiful and Affect[ionate]: Son
J: Spence

Florence,
Augt 2,)
July 22.) 1732

Dear Mother,

We are at last got to this City, from whence I shou'd rather chuse to write to you about Rome, than to have done it from that capital itself. I did not care to talk much to you about Rome till now, that I can assure you I have left the Pope's Town without turning Papist. We are now got safe to Florence; and so I may talk my bellyful of it. Rome is above 13 miles round the Walls; but not a third of the inside of it is fairly inhabited. There are several Vinyards within the Walls, as there are Hop-gardens in Winchester, and several of the nobler Palaces have Gardens to them as large as if they were in the Country. 'Tis common for the first Noblemen to have a Palace in the Heart of the Town; and a House and Gardens (which they call their Country-seat) within the Walls; but in the less inhabited part of it. I have taken a walk of a mile in a strait line to one of the Gates, with hedges and not one house on either side of me. This mixture of City, Country, and Gardens, with the inequalities of the ground (for Rome is built on above 7 hills, and in many other places is made strangely unequal by successive Ruins;) gives several views of an uncommon sort and more beautiful than I ever saw in any City. In many parts you have little Groves of Pine-trees, rising above the houses; here you see a long Garden, with Statues and fountains sloping down half the Side of a Hill; and the other half full of buildings and regular streets; and there a dark wood running along the side of a market-place. St Peters, and the vast Palace of the Vatican, lay at a distance in a line before our house: and between that and our part of the Town is a pretty run of Meadow-ground and the River Tiber. It was from this very Meadow that the Romans formerly took an honest man from the Plow, to be General of their Armies and Sole Governour of the State. He beat their Enemies, settled every thing extremely well in the Government, and then retired again to his 4 or 5 acres of Land which he plowd and managed all himself to the best advantage to get Bread for his Wife and Children. His name, you must know, was Quintius Cincinnatus;[185] and the meadow I'me talking of is call'd the Meadow of Quintius to this day. This is one of the pleasures of being at Rome, that you are continually seeing the very place and spot of ground, where some great thing or other was done, which one has so often admired before in reading their History. *This* is the place where Julius Caesar was stabd by Brutus; at the foot of *that* Statue he fell, and gave his last groan; *Here* stood Manlius to defend the Capitol against the Gauls; and *there* afterwards, was he flung down *that* Rock for endeavouring to make himself the Tirant of his Country: thorough *that*, and *that*, and *that* Arch always mov'd the Triumphs to this Hill; *there* did one famous soldier alone defend the Bridge against a whole army of enemies, and *here* did another plunge himself down the precipice, because the Oracles had declar'd that, if any one of the Soldiers wou'd voluntarily sacrifice his life there, he shoud save his Country from Ruin. All these places I have seen over and over: but there's one thing that mortifys one, that they turn these old Roman things into modern Popish ones. Thus by the Hole that the last Gentleman flung himself into to save his Country; they have now built a Church to the Virgin Mary, and call her over the door, the *Saviour* of Mankind. In a round old Temple just by, was a Statue of Romulus, and Remus, and their Wolf; which the Heathens usd to carry their children to when despaird of by the Physicians, to beg Romulus to save 'em or take them to himself: Tis now dedicated to some Saint; and the good women now, when their children are despaird of, play just the same trick. There was another fine church dedicated formerly to *Juno the Royal*, and now to *Mary the Great*, where the Roman Ladies once a Year usd to prostrate themselves on the steps to beg Children and good luck; the Christian Ladies, one day every year, now do the same thing there. Just by is a Church formerly dedicated to Diana, the Patroness of all beasts; and now to S: Antony, the Patron Saint of all cattle: on his day, they bring Horses, Mules, and Asses, from all parts to be blesd for about a shilling a head or what the good farmer can afford to give. To a Lover of Antiquities this is a great fault, to see these old things and customs turnd into modern ones. The great Amphitheater is daubd over with Pictures of Saints, in 50 places; and the Rotonda (the finest Temple left of the Antients) which was dedicated to Jupiter and all the Gods, is now dedicated to the Virgin and all the Saints. All our warm Antiquarians in England wou'd go to loggerheads with them for this mixture of Antient and Modern things together: for my part, I am glad to see Religion still go on in

---

185   In 458 BC Cincinnatus was called from the plough to become dictator; in 16 days he saved the Roman army, defeated the enemy, and returned to his farm.

a better way; and to see that Devotion has got the better of every thing else among them. With services to my Sister and all friends, I am

>Your most Affect[ionate]: and Dutiful
>J: Spence.

>Florence;
>Aug: 12)
>23) 1732.

Dear Mother

I'me heartily glad to hear that [Nanny Rhimes ?][186] is paid off, and that that affair is now entirely over. I'me afraid that you streighten'd yourself too much; if you did, whenever Dick has anything for me, you may make it up to you again: and then I shall be quite easy.

By the 2nd of August N. S. I sent you a little account of Rome; as to the Particular Palaces, Churches, Fountains, Pictures, and Statues, they are in such numbers, that they are only to be talkd over when we meet round our Coal fire.—At Rome, there is what they call, the Mala Aria, what we s[houl]d call a Bad Air, at a particular part of the Summer. They have great superstitions about it; and are so exact as to name the very day that it comes in. The Country about Rome is almost a Desert; very little ground that is made anything of, and sometimes not a house to be seen for 5, or 6, miles together. This is one great occasion of the Mala Aria, which lyes over Rome in July and August, and in some parts for 40 mile round it. We left Rome the 30th of June and came all over a hillyish Country to *Viterbo*. (I hope the Map lyes just at your right hand.) Just before Viterbo is a very steep hill, from which you see one of the prettiest views of a Lake in the world: on its right, and on its left, are two Hills all cover'd with Woods; in the middle lyes the Lake, as clear and as smooth as a Looking-glass; all along beyond it is a ridge of little Hills rising one above another, till they look blew, and are lost in the clouds. The next day we past another Lake (much larger, and with a great Rocky Island toward the middle of it) and then got over a Ridge of Hills, which are the Boundaries of the Great Duke of Tuscany's Dominions. The next great City is *Sienna*, where we came on their great Feast day;[187] and saw a Race, after their fashion without Saddles and Stirrups. The Women of Sienna are extremely pretty; and their dress is still prettier. Their Hair, brought up generally in three Breeds and twisted round at top like a Coronet, a little white hat abt as broad as my hand set on one side,

---

186 The name of the unidentified person was obliterated in manuscript.
187 The 'Corsa del Palio' is held on the Feast of the Visitation of the Blessed Virgin, 2 July, and also on 15 August, the Feast of the Assumption of the Blessed Virgin.

and a bunch of Flowers on the other, is their general Head-dress. From Sienna we went 60 mile of one of the best and most beautiful Roads in the world, to *Leghorne*. As Leghorne is a great Port for Trade, there are abt 300 English settled in the place; and there were then 10 English Ships in the Harbour. There are seldom so few; and they have had above 50 at a time there. The English Consul[188] carried us to see a Play there. 'Twas an Italian Don John; but as they mix buffoonery with every thing, when Don John sits down to supper he is attended by an Harlequin, who blunders abt every thing he is sent for, and eats every thing that comes to the Table, without any compassion for his Master. It was a Scene longer than our Don John;[189] for he appears the last Scene in Hell, with a flame colourd Doublet on, and 3 or 4 Devils on each side of him; and made a very good Speech there if twas not interrupted so much by the Devils pulling him by the sleave, and spitting fire in his face so very plentifully. In Leghorne you see immediately the benefits of trade and business: the town looks all alive; the people have an air of Gayety: 'tis a mighty place for Pipes and Fiddles, and the people are dancing somewhere or another all night long in the streets. They say their great Church was built by Inigo Jones;[190] and there are Piazzas on each side of it, not unlike those in Covent-garden. The Mole too, out at Sea, is said to have been built by the direction of an Englishman, a Son of the Great Earl of Leicester, in Queen Elizabeths time:[191] so that from the people, the place, the Seaport and every thing, one seem'd at Leghorne to be half at least in England. I beg my Service to my Sister and all friends; and am ever

Your Dutiful and Affectionate
J. Spence

Flor[ence]:
Dec. 13, [17]32

Dear Mother

I have receiv'd all your letters safe; and indeed I believe there has not a single one of yours miscarried since I have been abroad. We arriv'd here with so temperate an air till the last week in November, that I us'd to set and write

---

188 Brinley Skinner (d.1764).
189 *The Libertine* (London, 1675) by Thomas Shadwell (?1642–92) was often performed under the title *Don John; or, The Libertine Destroy'd*.
190 Inigo Jones (1573–1652), the English architect, designed the façade of the Duomo, 1613–14.
191 Sir Robert Dudley (1574–1649), Earl of Warwick, was one of the architects of the new mole in 1611.

with my chamber windows open; to enjoy the fresh air, and the Sun: but I find now that we are to have our share of winter too, for 'tis now sufficiently cold for one to shut all the windows and doors, and keep a good fire into the bargain. The Seasons here are not distinguisht by a gentle going off from one into the other, as they are in England. After the winter, you fall almost all at once into the Heats: and after the summer Heats are quite conquerd, Winter steps in all in a day. One of the old Roman Poets (but I need not talk at such a distance, for I'me sure you know Horace very well) says that their Summer comes in in a hurry, turns the Spring out of Doors, and treads on her heels as she is going out:[192] and I have seen a picture of the four Seasons, at Rome, done by one of their great Painters, in which the Spring and Summer are kissing one another to shew that they come as it were at the same time, and the Winter and Autumn are hand in hand.[193] The latter are really not so much huddled together as the former; for they may happen to have six weeks of Autumn in Italy, but I believe they seldom have three weeks of Spring. Indeed the Autumn is the pleasantest part of the year here: every thing begins to bud afresh in it; and 'tis rather a false Spring, that is kill'd before it comes to maturity, by the succeeding Colds.

A little way out of the Gate that we live next to (and Florence, I can assure you, is worth no less than ten Gates) is a place made for the pleasure of the Great Duke, and his good subjects.[194] You go to it thro' a range of vast Scotch fir-Trees; on your left hand is a long run of Groves, and pretty artificial Islands full of Arbors; and on your right lyes the Vinyards and Cornfields interspersd, which is the manner all about Florence (as in Lombardy:) This leads into a large beautiful Meadow. The walk of Firs is continud on, all the length of it; the Groves and Wood, with a variety of a thousand different walks on the left: and beyond them, all along, runs the River Arno. These woods are at last brought rounding to join the Fir-Walk, and so terminate the Meadow. This Meadow all our Autumn was almost as fresh a Green as we have in England (a very uncommon thing here) and was all sprinkled with wild Crocus's as thick as the Stars in Heaven. Many of the Trees in the Woody part wanted to shew another crop of Leaves; and the wild Vines that are very frequent in it, hung over your head from tree to tree with their glistning black bunches of Grapes that were left there for the happiness of the Birds that inhabit those woods very plentifully. In short, all the Autumn this place was the most like a Paradise

---

192 Horace, *Carmina*, IV, vii, 9–10.
193 Francesco Albani (1578–1660), Italian baroque artist who painted ceiling frescoes of *Apollo and the Seasons* in the Palazzo Verospi.
194 The Cascine.

of any thing I ever met with: but I have not seen it these three weeks, and I believe it now begins to look as rough as the rest of the World.

However we have still a great deal of Benefit from the Cassini (so they call this delicious place). In the Entrance to it is a Country house which is the Great Dukes Dairy: they make his butter there, and we have from it fresh and fresh every morning: a Blessing, which I assure you is very valuable and very uncommon out of England. Just by, they make some of his Wine. Mr Sm[yth] and I went in one day to see 'em at it. The grapes were left in so many Tubs on very high Stands: whether they had squeez'd 'em, or whether they had squeez'd themselves by their own weight, the juice was all fermenting so strong that it playd up like a little fountain thro' the Tunnels. I was rig[ge]d up[195] a ladder that stood by the side of one to gape upon it; when—all at once—the ladder slips from under me, and in the hurry, I got hold of the brims and hung there. Had the Tub yeilded upon me, I shou'd at least have spoil'd my best Holyday Cloaths; or perhaps have gon out of the world almost in the way of the Earl of Clarence; if 'twas he that was drown'd in Malmsy:[196] but being somewhat light and the tub very large and heavy, it stood firm; and so did no manner of dammage to

Your Humble Serv[an]t
J. Spence

Florence;
Feb: 3)
14) 1733.

Dear Mother

I'me very sorry my Tale of a Tub shoud have given you any concern; for as my good friend Mr Smith was by, I verily believe that at the worst it wou'd only have spoilt me a Suite of Cloaths. However, I thank God, I came off very well; and continue at this writing, in very good health.

We are now in the liveliest part of our Carnival; for it is always in most vigour towards its end; and we have now but five or six days of it to come. There's one particular here, which we cd not have at Venice: the different manner of setting themselves out in their Coaches. The Vehicle usd on this occasion wd be like our Coaches with their Tops off, and the back, before and behind, coming up no higher than your shoulders. In one of these you will sometimes see, a Turk and a Christian Lady forward, and an Empress

---

195 Climbed up (as in a ship's rigging).
196 The Duke of Clarence is drowned in a butt of malmsey in *Richard III*, I. iv. 270.

and Chimney Sweeper backward: every body has some disguise or other: the Coachman is generally dressd as a Harlequin; and the Footmen as Piero's. The General Rendezvous is a Place as big as St James' Square: the Coaches go round in a ring, all in Masquerade; and the Fools on foot have all the Middle raild in, to walk at their ease; and see as great Fools as themselves, go round in the Coaches. The Inside is always well crowded. I have had a Pharisee there tread upon my toes; and upon recovering myself, with some confusion, have run my head full into the face of a Roman Emperour. The very Coach Horses are in a sort of Masquerade: for I have seen for instance, a Coach and six Horses, with their hair drest out in a particular manner, all with ribbons and bells, and a Marquis drest in an Harlequin's habit riding Postillion. They go a regular Trott; and, as their bells sound all at the same time, make a very pretty sort of music. Today we had a Stage built up, and some of the first Noblemen (very probably) acting the parts of a Mountebank and his attendants, all in Fools-coats. One of the great diversions upon the place, is Fishing. I have seen this at Venice, when two gentlemen have walkd together with fishing-rods, bated with Sugard-Almonds; and two or three score of little boys nibbling at 'em. Sometimes they got the bait, very dexterously; and sometimes the hook got a piece of their lips: but a boy that's well exercisd will play the Fish very successfully. Here they have had the same sport, more in form. One day a fellow was got with all his baits and implements, on a little stage raisd on purpose: and a Heap of Sausages of a Yard or two high lay by him, which his servant fryd off in a pan of oyl with great expedition. As fast as one bait was snapt off, he supplyd his master with new ones, hot out of the pan. The Gentleman had so many Bites, that all that monstrous heap of Sausages was vanisht in less than an Hour. It wou'd have done you good to see the Number of Hungry faces, and open mouths, in the Circle round him, in the Heighth of his Sport. The nearest wou'd often bite whilst the bait was so hot, that they were forc'd to quit it again when 'twas half way down their throats, to the great baulking of their Appetites, and Distortion of their features. The Italians are generally reckon'd men of Spirit, and of a Character rather serious than light: but when the Season requires Foolery, there are no people in the world that give into it so much. I have often enquired what may be the reason of this, but cou'd never get one that was satisfactory. At the same time 'tis very odd to see numbers of people every day, of five or six and twenty years old only, going about the Streets with a vast pair of Spectacles upon their noses, to be thought older and wiser than they are: and these very people, at other times, playing the Fool together in the silliest and most childish manner that can be imagin'd. I'me growing too grave for Carnival-time; and therefore shall leave off with being

Your most Dutiful and Affectionate

J: Spence

This very morning I am packing up a box of Books to send, by Sea, to London; so that, you see, I begin to think in earnest of returning to you; tho' I have been astray now upward of two Years.

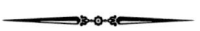

Hotel de Luynes. Paris.
June 4)
15) 1733.

Dear Mother,

This is just to let you know that we are so near you, that we cou'd almost shake hands across the water: we came hither last night, and in that day and the day before had run 246 mile in our chaises: by which you may guess we were pretty desirous to get to Paris and so near to you. There is nothing yet that surprizes me so much here as the Silence about us, in comparison of London. We are in the Faubourg St Germain, one of the best parts of the Town, and they say one of the most active; and yet I am retired now to a Window that looks into a good handsome garden, without either noise, heat or dust: and yet the Summer is the chief time for company at Paris. Indeed the Heat there may be, and I not feel it; for coming out of Italy and Provence, the warmths here were so cold to us, that we were forcd to wear our greatcoats in the Chaises; and for all that, were often shivering as if 'twas winter. This was a great blessing to us; for the only insufferable thing on the road is Heat: and we expected enough of it, because the Summer (which has been very backward this year both in France and Italy) they said, was just come in when we got to Montpellier. We are all perfectly well, and with services to Belle, and all friends, I am ever

Your dutiful and affectionate
J Spence

My brother knows how to direct to me here.

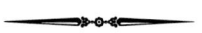

Paris
June 21)
July 2) 1733.

Dear Mother

Your straggling, wandering, Prodigal Son, is at last coming home in earnest: we ought to be in London the 20th of this Month NS. that is the 9th of July with you. I think my best Gown and Cassock is with you: I beg you wou'd send it up to Dick, in all haste with a tolerable proportion of Bands:[197] and (if I have any such thing with you) a black suite of cloaths; but I much question whether I'me worth any; and if you have none, I can take care to get some when I come; let the worst come to the worst. I desire my service to Belle and to all friends, and hope I shall find you all in very good health.

Paris is a very agreable place: and more full of nobility, [su]ch as they are, than London: but there's a great deal of difference between a Marquis in England, and a Marquis in France. Here to be in possession of such a Mansion-House, or such a particular Farm, very often makes all the family Lords, when with us the head of that family wou'd be only a tolerable Lord of a mannor. I have often seen the pretty Dutchess of Bourbon, who is one of the three Sisters I have talk'd to you of in a former: tho' she's as pretty as an Angel, she's forc'd to paint here, for there's no being in fashion without it. The Actresses on the Stage and the Ladies of the first quality, in particular, lay on the Red so unmercifully; that in the side-boxes they look like a bed of old overblown Piony's; and as we are now in the month of July, it really makes one sweat to walk thorough them in the Public Gardens in some one or other of which all the company is every evening. I have not mist a night since we have been at Paris of being either at the Opera or the Play: these diversions begin early, and after they are done, we go regularly to the public Walks. Their Plays are good; and not ill acted, very often: but their Opera's are things that I wou'd not advise any body to go to who has not lost his Hearing, or has no mind to lose it. Beside the Actors, there are generally six or seven women rang'd, on each side of the Stage, to make the Chorus, and stun all good Christians that come to hear them. They really place the Perfection of musick in Bawling; and the Ladies (who, in all the countries that I have yet travel'd thro', are particularly fond of hearing themselves either speak or sing) are so very vigorous here in lifting up their voices to an agreable Squall, that t'other night when it thunder'd we were at the Opera, it was really a sort of refreshment between whiles when they were low enough to let us hear it. However to morrow we must go thorough the persecution of hearing them again because the Queen and King Stanislaus are to be there, whom we have not yet seen.[198] The Court is out of town; this is only an afternoon's visit they make to Paris: for the King of France never lays a night in his Capital City. The letter I had to deliver here, I will bring safe with me to Winchester. Mr Rolle I have not seen, nor heard

---

197 As a cleric properly attired, JS would require his cassock, and the bands, which were a pair of short strips of white material that hung down, in front, from his collar.
198 Maria Leszczynska (1703–68) married Louis XV in 1725. Her father, Stanislas Leszczyski (1677–1766), was King of Poland, 1704–9.

of in these parts, and know not whether he is in England or France. I believe I shall not stay above a fortnight or three weeks at London: for I shall come to you as soon as I can; and in the mean time am

Your Dutiful and Affect[ionate]:
J: Spence

James Boswell; Sir Joshua Reynolds. Oil on canvas, 1785

James Boswell (1740–95): Letters (1764–6)

It was not unusual for a young man with an eye to a legal career to spend a year studying law in Holland; Boswell's father, a senior Scottish judge, Lord Auchinleck, had done so in Leyden; his son chose Utrecht, where he went in August 1763. Once there he was determined to make Utrecht the launching pad for the Grand Tour. His father was strenuously opposed to the idea, insisting that he should complete his studies and establish himself in the practice of the law. The prospect of his son loose on the Continent, and spending parental money without restraint, no doubt alarmed Auchinleck. It is more than likely that he entertained 'gloomy suspicions' about his son's prodigality. He wrote in August 1765 expressing the hope that Boswell would 'return with a proper taste and relish for [his] own country'; otherwise,

> I should most heartily repent that ever I agreed to your going abroad, and shall consider the money spent in the tour you have made as much worse than thrown away.[199]

Both the message and the tone recall Sir Thomas Lyttelton's warning to his son George.

However, as Boswell told his friend John Johnston, Laird of Grange (in Annandale, Dumfriesshire), his 'worthy Father' eventually and reluctantly agreed that he should accept an invitation from the 10th Earl Marischal, George Keith, to accompany him to Berlin. The young traveller would also be able to draw on 'a genteel credit' provided by his father.[200] Not that Boswell and his father had reached a common view about the purpose of a Continental tour. 'There is no end nor use of strolling through the world to see sights before unseen': that was the Auchinleck view;[201] another was that of Boswell's new

---

199 *Boswell on the Grand Tour: Italy, Corsica, and France 1765–1766*, edited by F. Brady and F. A. Pottle (London: Heinemann, 1955), 223, hereafter *Journal*.
200 The *Correspondence of James Boswell and John Johnston of Grange*, edited by Ralph S. Walker (London: Heinemann, 1966), 126, hereafter *Corr.*
201 F. A. Pottle, *Boswell: the Earlier Years, 1740–69* (London: McGraw-Hill, 1966), 234.

friend, Samuel Johnson: 'A man who has not been in Italy, is always conscious of an inferiority, from his not having seen what it is expected a man should see. The grand object of travelling is to see the shores of the Mediterranean'.[202] Boswell's own view is implicit in his Journal entry, 21 December 1765, where he records meeting a Colonel Ross in Marseilles: 'He served me as a proof how much I must be improved since I came abroad… at least in assurance.' Perhaps he was recalling Dr Johnson's advice that he should go abroad 'with a manly resolution to improve', which he translated for Johnston: 'I shall, while abroad, lay up a store of pleasing ideas. I shall return composed and put on the [lawyer's] gown and be a usefull Member of Society as well as an agreable private friend'.[203] To what extent this aspiration accorded with Boswell's ecstatic outburst on his homeward journey from Italy remained to be seen:

> O Italy! Land of felicity! True seat of all elegant delight! My mind shall ever soothe itself with the image of thy charms. Thy divine music has harmonised my soul. That nature, that sweet simplicity, that easy grace which has pleased me so often in thy theatres, shall never fade from my memory.[204]

The Grand Tour, then, for Boswell was intended to be a journey of self-discovery and moral growth. Its stages were recorded in his letters—54 of them to Johnston—and also in his Journal. He proposed to write a letter 'at every city or Court where [he resided] three days'; and though his plan was not fulfilled, in every detail he made a sustained attempt to be faithful to it. Partly to avoid putting Johnston to great expense (in postal charges), Boswell explained that he would keep the letters until the end of the tour; 'then Johnston shall you and I open these letters and read them in their order. The pleasure will be mutual. I shall be pleased to see my freind pleased. Besides I shall have forgotten the contents of the letters and they will appear as new to myself as to you'.[205] They would also form an adjunct to Boswell's Journal, which 'will be a treasure to us.'

The first letter was written from Berlin on 10 September 1764. His goal was Rome, but initially it appeared that he might not reach it: his father strenuously opposed the plan—he was 'averse to my going to that intoxicating Region'—and virtually instructed Boswell to spend the winter in Geneva. In late September, therefore, he set off in the direction of Geneva via Dresden, Mannheim ('a very bad court'), Baden-Baden (admirable Court with 'some very handsom women' and fine wines), Soleure, Motiers (the home of 'that

---

202 Boswell, *Life of Johnson*, edited by G. B. Hill and L. F. Powell, 3 vols (Oxford: Oxford University Press, 1934), iii, 457–8.
203 *Corr*, 127.
204 *Journal*, 254.
205 *Corr*, 135.

Sublime Sage' Rousseau), and Neuchâtel. It was from there that he told Johnston in great excitement: 'I have obtained my Father's permission to make the tour of Italy. It is impossible for me to express my happiness... I shall have the richest enjoyment of all the fine arts'.[206] He visited Geneva but wrote no letter there.

Boswell crossed from Switzerland by Mont Cenis to Italy on 6 January 1765. The Alpine crossing did not produce the kind of vividness to be found in the correspondence of other Tourists: 'I have passed the Alps' was all that Johnston was told; using fashionable Burkian language, the Journal in its fuller account recorded that 'the prospect was horribly grand'.[207] Similarly muted was his reference to a visit to Voltaire at Ferney in late December. Only when he arrived in Italy at Turin, then Milan, did Boswell's literary vitality return. He was especially delighted to be 'for the first time, in a City [Milan] described by a Latin Classic' (Ausonius) and, as he had done at Soleure, to acknowledge Addison as, to some extent, his guide and mentor.

From Milan Boswell followed a south-easterly route, via Parma and Bologna, to the east coast at Rimini and Ancona, and then, on a south-westerly tack he moved inland to Spoleto and Terni, before arriving in Rome in mid-February. Remarkably, there was no letter to record his first impressions of the capital. After ten days he departed thence 'by that rough Appian Way' for Naples, where he caught up with the renowned radical John Wilkes whose exploits and conversation engrossed his attention. The classical antiquities in and near Naples delighted him, as did 'the finest Bay diversified with Islands and bordered by feilds where Virgil's Muses charmed the Creation.' This 'Romanising' continued when he returned to the capital on 24 March 1765, and at once began a six-day 'Course in Antiquities and Arts', clearly aimed at the Tourist trade. Perhaps being surrounded by historical evidence of human successes and failures, Boswell felt impelled to take stock of his past life and future prospects; he despaired of satisfying his father's aspirations for him, but took heart from the importance of his present occupation 'storing [his] memory with rich ideas which will give much pleasure... many years hence.' Like Tourists before and after him, Boswell assured himself that 'to be in illustrious Rome itself and to walk the scenes of classical enthusiasm is indeed noble'. That 'enthusiasm' continued with equal fervour when, having left Rome, he visited Horace's villa—'Divine Horace whose Poetry has charmed my youthfull Soul'—and delighted in the scenes which were reflected in 'the scattered beauties of Horace's finest odes'. The same enthusiasm—even if not strictly 'classical'—persisted in Venice, where Boswell recalled characters and

---

206   *Corr*, 149.
207   *Journal*, 23.

scenes in Thomas Otway's *Venice Preserv'd*, and in Verona where Shakespeare was centre stage. His pleasures, however, were not exclusively cerebral. He found time in Rome to have his portrait painted, to commission a miniature derived from it, and to run 'about among the Prostitutes', thereby contracting venereal disease.

Boswell's route from Milan to Florence took him 'journeying from one classical town [Cremona] to another [Mantua]'; inevitably this encouraged him to draw on his considerable knowledge of Virgil to such an extent that he feared his letters might 'resemble the pages of a German Commentator, where quotations come so thick upon one another that half the Book is brown with Italics'.[208] Johnston learned little about Boswell's fortnight in Florence, principally about 'the delirium of love' he experienced in Siena, and virtually nothing about Pisa and Leghorn. Then came his 'very singular Expedition to visit the Island of Corsica' from 11 October to 30 November 1765, after which he boldly visited Genoa, the centre of strenuous and sustained opposition to General Paoli. He records his fear that, because of his well-known intimacy with the Corsican General, the Genoese 'despicable Republic' might have designs upon his life. Nothing untoward happened.

At Antibes Boswell formally entered France. From here he proceeded to Toulon and thence to Marseilles, 'one of the prettiest towns in france'. His letter from Aix-en-Provence was brief, on account of his being 'hurried by a rascal of a Postilion who insists on my mounting a vile hack this instant'. He delighted in the Christmas Midnight Mass in Avignon's cathedral, and the same city allowed him to enjoy the company of some 'true old Scots Nobility' who supported the Stuart cause. Boswell's final letter was written in the diligence that would take him from Auxerres to Paris; in it he expanded on the relationship between the traveller and the coachman:

> The Coachman is a Personage of very great Consequence, for besides his being Chief Conductor of our Coach, It is He who orders every thing at the Inns where we have most excellent entertainment I promise you and very good beds. If any of us is not content with what the Inn has furnished him, The Coachman is called in and talked to with such manly vigour as the Cook of a College at Oxford or Cambridge is chid by the eaters of Commons.[209]

Getting this relationship right—a combination of dependence, authority and mutual respect—was essential to the satisfaction of the traveller on the Grand Tour.

The reader of Boswell's letters should not expect to find in them an account of what he saw on his journey—that was the function of his Journal. 'These my

---

208 *Corr*, 183–4.
209 *Corr*, 206–7.

letters are intended rather to tell you what I feel, to give you the ideas which employ my mind at the time I write'. Broadly speaking this was an accurate description, even though, inevitably, the letters do contain some record of his experiences. Nevertheless it is his feelings that are dominant, and Boswell makes no effort to disguise or restrain them; indeed he delights in their extravagance as if he wanted to justify his remarkable claims: 'I am one of the most engaging Men that ever lived'; 'Few People of any nation can boast an Imagination more lively than mine'.[210] Fortunately such boasts were balanced by equally frank self-assessment: 'long study of myself has convinced me that my Constitution was never intended for great labour of Mind… I find myself an amiable pretty [i.e. skilful] Man of moderate abilitys'.[211]

That he was blest with a lively imagination is true; it is the source of some of the most memorable features of the letters. The tone of his writing confirms that he was constantly alive to the need, at the end of his Tour, to engage Johnston's interest in what he had written: the letters were imaginatively designed for oral delivery by Boswell himself. When, for example, he muses on Ausonius's reaction to modern Milan, he shoots a question to Johnston who was assumed to be the eager listener: 'What think you would be his notion of the pompous Mass and of the variety of Religious orders?' Or, having visited the court at Baden-Baden and enthused about the charms of Mlle de Geismar, Boswell rebukes his friend in a manner reminiscent of Laurence Sterne: 'Come come Johnston, compose yourself: Be upon your good behaviour. Consider where you are. You must not think to get up and take the charming Creature in your arms…'. Again, confessing that he feels 'very dull… realy stupid', Boswell, with mock solemnity, pleads: 'What clumsy attempts am I making to entertain You! I beg you may not laugh at me. At least laugh as gently as you can. Make not the whole Neighbourhood ring with thy unrestrained bursts of merriment'.[212] The element of self-mockery here is more extensively found when, writing from Brescia, where he bought a small gun, Boswell 'slung it carelessly over my left arm like a handsom fowler or a Captain of a marching Regiment and… even shoulder'd my firelock like any bold Brother Soldier… and giving my broad gold-lac'd hat a gracefull turn to one side of my head I thought myself a very great Man'. The same tone reappears when he pokes fun at the myths surrounding Virgil's career, including 'the Neapolitan tradition that he kept a school, or the tradition which I myself invented that he stood a furious siege of Swans'.[213]

---

210 *Corr*, 137, 153.
211 *Corr*, 164–5.
212 *Corr*, 154, 144, 139.
213 *Corr*, 179, 185.

The good humour that one finds in every letter contributes significantly to Boswell's attractive epistolary manner. It takes several forms. The imaginative energy generated by his visit to Rousseau, 'that Sublime Sage', enables him to dare to open a letter: 'Art thou alive o! my freind? or has thy spirit quitted it's earthly habitation. To hear of thy death would not now distress me. I would glory to think of thy exaltation.' Only good-natured humour ensures that this kind of relationship will flourish. Or there is his skilful development of an allusion to Swift's country bumpkins, Dermot and Sheelah, which he owes to John Wilkes, into an ironic comment on his own garrulity via a further allusion to Swift, this time to his 'Thoughts on Various Subjects'. And finally, we have the reverie on the subject of Gray's *Elegy* in which Boswell contemplates, with gentle humour, the possibility that an orator superior to Pitt, a statesman more popular than Bute, an uncorrupted Wilkes, a Johnston 'Philosopher enough to be content with a small fortune, hoping to have it made better' may be buried in the country churchyard. 'And who knows but what we might find here a Boswell solemn and gay by turns who is sometimes the favourite of the Ladies, but more often a pensive and gloomy Metaphysician'.[214]

By kind permission of Gordon Turnbull, General Editor, and the Editorial Committee of the Yale Editions of the Private Papers of James Boswell, the text of the letters printed here derives from Ralph Walker's edition of the *Correspondence of James Boswell and John Johnston of Grange* (London: Heinemann, 1966).

Letters of James Boswell

Berlin
10 Septr. 1764

My Dear Sir:

Why have you not written to me, since I left Utrecht? Davie would have given you my address.[215] But, I excuse you; for, although I wrote you the last letter, you are waiting for a letter from Berlin.

How do our minds alter with the times! How easily do we submit ourselves with contentment to Circumstances! While I was in London, you would have

---

214   *Corr*, 147, 160, 186–7.
215   JB's brother, David (1748–1826), apprenticed to a banking house in Edinburgh; he held Johnston in particularly high regard.

been very uneasy if you had been a week without hearing from me; and when you now and then neglected a Post, you was sure to receive from me a very warm letter, in which anger, anxiety and affection were mingled, so as to show the heart of a most sincere friend, who suffered so much from the apprehensions of a tender and gloomy mind, as realy to upbraid Him whose innocent neglect caused his Uneasiness. Now our situation is very different. We are at such a distance from each other, that frequent Correspondence cannot be carried on, but at a great expence. We have therefore set our minds at ease, and as we have no fixed time of expectation, we are never dissappointed. Yet, my freind, beleive me, three months is a long time. I think we might correspond once in two months. What say you?

To give you my history since I emerged from Holland, would be to transcribe or abridge my Journal, neither of which would I wish to do. For, I hope to have the satisfaction of reading it with you at length. I shall therefore give you a sort of Index to the later part of my Journal, by giving you the principal lines of my Story since I left Utrecht. I had a most agreable Journey with My worthy Lord Marischal.[216] You can scarcely imagine what satisfaction I felt in the company of the venerable old Earl, a true Scottish Chieftain, I do assure you. He has an infinite fund of good storys, and tells them to great Advantage. The Turkish Lady was indolent, but now and then very amusing.[217] My Lord presented me at the court of Brunswic, where we stayed two days. We next came to Potzdam where I saw the King's Palace, as also Sans Souci, which is hard by. I then came to Berlin, where I saw a large and beautifull City. I enjoyed for some time the instructive and agreable conversation of Mr Mitchell the British Envoy who is now gone.[218] He is a worthy and a very pretty man. I was presented to the Queen, and to many Princes and Princesses. But I found the Court very dull. I returned to Brunswic and past a forthnight during the Fair. I dined every day at Court and supped every evening but two. We had public diversions every day in the week, Sunday not excepted, on which we had a concert, or a grand court and cards. I was well received. I lived well. I was quite happy; and I assure you my Brunswic forthnight will ever supply me with pleasing recollection, which you and I have both agreed is often finer than the present enjoyment. At Berlin I am lodged in the house of the *President de Police* whose family is extremely agreable. I have got a pretty Acquaintance among the rich Bourgeois, who live like Princes. When I quitted Utrecht, I beleived it impossible to remove the

---

216   George Keith (?1693–1778), 10th Earl Marischal; greatly valued by Frederick the Great (whose Ambassador he had been in Paris and Spain), he was returning to live at Potsdam at the king's entreaty.
217   The Earl Marischal's adopted daughter.
218   Andrew Mitchell (1708–81), British Envoy to the court of Frederick; described by JB as 'very pretty', i.e. very astute.

clouds which hung over my Mind. I was allmost sunk with despair. And yet, Johnston, variety, good company, the exercises of the Academy[219] and regular living restored me to health and Joy. I have had such a strong instance that Melancholy may be overcome that you would think it impossible for me to despair, if I retain my memory and my Judgment. And yet, this very morning was I bad, and began to think I never should be well. I remembered my former woe, and I remembered that it was cured. I judged too from all probability of reasoning that my present woe must also be cured. And yet my imagination was so strong, that reason bowed before it. What shall we say of the human mind, dear freind? Every man must judge in a great measure from what he has experienced. You know what sort of experience mine has been.

As to the course which I am next to steer, I cannot as yet exactly inform you. I would wish to pass four months in Italy; But, my Father is averse to my going to that intoxicating Region. He wishes to have me pass the winter at Geneva, and go to Paris in the spring. I however still beg to be allowed to see Rome. My Lord Marischal and Mr. Mitchell have both written in my favour, so that I am not without hopes that my request may be granted. In the mean time, I am to leave this in ten days, make a tour by Dessau, Dresden, Gotha, Maanheim and some more courts to Geneva, where I shall receive my Father's final determination, and from whence I have a plain passage into France, or a mountainous one into Italy. If my Father is absolutely against my going to Italy, I shall see how I like Geneva. If it is agreable, I shall stay there till the spring. If otherwise, I shall go to some University town in france. I shall however have an opportunity of seeing Voltaire and Rousseau. I hope to be very well amused in the German Courts which I intend to visit. You shall hear from me when I get to Geneva. In the mean time do you write me a long letter proving that you are alive, that you have not forgot me your absent freind, and that you have no Antipathy at the Abbey of Holyroodhouse, or at the noble mountain of Arthur-scat.[220] Let your letter be sent to the care of Messrs. Splitzerber et Daum,[221] á Berlin.

I pray you Johnston give me consolation against the hour of Antiquity. Both you and I must lay our account to suffer such hours. Let us assist each other. I study Hypochondria as a Science.[222] I am allways picking up more knowledge

---

219 A riding school.
220 Two famous landmarks in the city of Edinburgh: the ruins of the Augustinian Holyrood Abbey sited in the grounds of the royal palace of Holyroodhouse, and Arthur's Seat, the main peak (820 feet) in a group of hills forming a remarkable highland landscape in the city itself.
221 Splitgerber & Daum, an influential business house.
222 JB published 70 essays in *The London Magazine*, 1777–83, using 'the Hypochondriack' as his pseudonym.

with regard to it. My Dear freind I feel sincerely the want of you to talk with. God grant that we may yet be much together. Encourage me in my plan of following the law in Scotland. May I not do pretty well between the Session-House and Auchinleck[223] with now and then a jaunt into England? You know my sad changeable humour. Help me to get the better of it.

You are now at Grange. Walk out on a sunny day and indulge pleasing Meditation. One thing is most sure that after the blackest gloom we may be quite happy. Strange is our existence. Let us hope for a better world and do as well as we can in this. Pray be kind to Davie. Make my kind compliments to the family of Schaw, to worthy Mr. Irvine, to Currie and to all our other freinds.

Give me any material news that is passing in the country. Your Lords of Session have died fast of late. Poor Lord Edgefield's death shocked me very much.[224] Pray do not forget to give my best compliments to Mr. Fergusson. Is he married? What is he doing? Remember me in the best manner to Provost Graham Mr. Orr and Mr. Hay and ever beleive me My Dear Johnston your affectionate freind

James Boswell

Anhalt Dessau
1 October 1764

My Dear Johnston:

Behold a new Project for the entertainment of our hours of freindly Sociality. I am now upon my travels. I cannot hear from you often, as you know not how to direct for me. Nor would I chuse to put you to the expence of hearing often from me. Yet as freindship is kept alive by continued by repeated exercise of the kind affections, I have formed a very excellent Scheme. At every city or Court where I reside three days I shall write you a letter and if I find time I shall even write where my stay is very short. These Letters I shall regularly seal and direct so that they shall be to me as if I had sent them to you. I shall put them up in a Bundle which I shall keep till I return to Scotland. Then Johnston shall you and I open these letters and read them in their order. The pleasure will be mutual. I shall be pleased to see my freind pleased. Besides I shall have forgotten the contents of the letters and they will appear as new to myself as to you.

---

223 Between his professional and legal obligations, and the pleasures of home.
224 Robert Pringle, Lord Edgefield (born c.1700) was admitted a Lord of Session (i.e. a member of the supreme civil court in Scotland) in 1754; he died on 8 April 1764. According to the official list of Lords of Session, George Sinclair, Lord Woodhall d.5 May 1764, and William Grant, Lord Preston Grange d.23 May 1764.

This first letter is written from Anhalt Dessau where I have past a week with much pleasure as will appear from my Journal. I have delayed writing till my Trunks are gone to the Post Waggon. I must set out immediatly. In time coming I shall write with more composure. In the mean time my scheme gives me great satisfaction. I ever remain your affectionate freind.

James Boswell

Leipsic
6 Octr. 1764

My Dear Johnston,

 I find myself perfectly well in this City which is much larger than I imagined. It is fair time: so there is here an immense concourse of all nations. The hurry the variety the novelty agitate my spirits and leave no entrance for the gloomy fiend. If he shows his black visage on the frontiers of my Mind a detachment of brisk animal spirits like a Corps of light troops give him a reception so smart that he is glad to retreat with grumbling precipitation.

 Do you know I past a week at Dessau in perfect happiness. So much was I employed, so well was I amused that during seven days I am sure I had not seven hours of Melancholy. I shall ever remember this agreable court with gay regard. Where We have been admitted to the embraces of fair felicity we feel an instantaneous joy spring up in our Souls. You know the famous story of the horse of Darius whose neighing made his Master a King.[225] Did My Sovereign wish to hear me express my gladness he must cause me be led to the noble forrests of Anhalt Dessau.

 I have come here without any letters of recommendation; so have had a fair tryal of my real Merit. And what have I found think you? I have found Johnston that your vaunting freind has not half the Pride that he ought to have. Sir I am one of the most engaging men that ever lived. Amidst the innumerable multitude of Existences that have past thro' this World I beleive upon my honour that very few have been blest with more agreable talents. I have made acquaintance with Professors here who have shown me an attention and a cordiality that would charm thy benevolent soul. Leipsic has ever been a distinguished Seat of learning. It still preserves it's reputation. I have seen two very noble Librarys, and some very elegant Gardens. Tomorrow I set out for Dresden. Congratulate with me Thou old and faithfull freind of Boswell thou

---

225 Darius was one of seven Persian chiefs who destroyed the usurper Smerdis; they agreed that the one of them whose horse neighed first should become king; Darius's horse neighed first. Herodotus, *History*, iii, 84–6.

firm Borderer who has allways stood by him in fair weather and foul. Live long and long be happy. I ever remain My Dear Sir your most sincere freind

James Boswell

Dresden
12 Octr. 1764

My Dear Johnston,

 The Capital of Saxony now contains your freind. I wish with all my heart that I had you here. Dresden is the most beautifull City that ever I saw. The houses are generally built of free Stone so that the Streets have a most elegant look. The Catholic Church and some other public edifices are very fine; very splendid I should say. There is a fine river here, over which is built a magnificent bridge. The Country on each side of the river is prettily varied with hill and dale and often ornamented with Vineyards. It fills me with agreable ideas and refreshes in my mind the fading pictures of my gay sensations in the days of Youth. But why talk so? Am I not young still? Am I not healthy? Am I not joyous? Yes I am. Without doubt I am so this afternoon. Well, and shall I not be so tomorrow? Ah! Johnston my worthy freind! Thou who knowest my gloomy as well as my gay disposition, thou knowest that eer the Sun has gone another round I shall probably be old, be sickly and be sad. What a strange temperament have I got! And pray My freind have not all mankind the same in a certain degree? Yes; all Mankind are more or less Hypochondriack. What think you of this method of entertaining you? Notwithstanding of all the Objects arround me, I cannot help reflecting on myself. O Johnston forgive me for harping upon this string which one would think must e'er now have been thrummed to pieces. What will you have Man? Will you have poetry? Well the whim seises me and I will give thee at all events two or four lines. This is a true Whim as much as if a Man who had an empty house should say, "Come Johnston You shall sup with me, and I'll give you two to four dishes." Never was honest man's house emptier than is my head just now, and never did any man know worse where to find Victuals than I just now know where to find rhimes.
 However Come on.

> Thou freind of Boswell! and thou Laird of Grange
> Preserve thy Lands, let not thy freindship change,
> Write not too much, lye not too long abed,
> Nor let strong liquors knock thee on the head.
> Hire a stout Nag and on the sands of Leith
> Ride like an English Rogue on Hounslow heath.
> Thus mayest thou purchase all the joys of health

And laugh at Hopetoun with his heaps of wealth.[226]
Thus to my freind my vigorous Sons be born
And future Granges Annandale adorn.

      Adieu My dear freind and beleive me ever yours
               James Boswell

                Manheim,
               7 Novr. 1764

My Dear Johnston:

 To find Boswell in bad humour is no new thing for you. You have seen him sulky as a Welchman who has been rejected in the Herald's court,[227] as an Englishman who has had his dinner spoiled, as an Irishman who has been detected in uttering five Bulls,[228] and in forming a project to carry off a rich widow, and as a Scotsman who has lost an Election, or who has got a younger officer put over his head. I could give you many comparisons as excellent as these, should I come upon the continent. But, at present I would not chuse to go out of his Majesty's dominions. If you ask me in a respectfull manner why I am in bad humour, I shall tell you. I say in a respectfull manner, because when a man is sulky he is also proud, and requires particular attention to be payed him, even by his best freinds. Well do you know this Johnston. Well may you remember how I begged of you one evening at Thom's not to lean upon the table, because it gave me pain.

 I am in bad humour at Manheim because I have found here a very bad court. The Elector wants forsooth to be a prodigious great man.[229] He gives an Opera and a French Comedy and a Concert or an academy of Music as he calls it, all of which entertainments are realy magnificent. But then he treats Strangers with a distance which makes some of them laugh at him, and others curse him, according to their temperaments. For my own part I have had an inclination to do both. As to his table I can say nothing. Strangers are very seldom invited to dine there. I have not been asked once. What an inhospitable dog! I have been obliged to dine at an Ordinary[230] amongst fellows of all sorts and sizes.

---

226 Hounslow Heath was renowned as the haunt of highwaymen. John Hope (1704–81), 2nd Earl of Hopetoun, was a very wealthy landowner.
227 One whose application for armorial bearings has been rejected by the College of Arms.
228 Ludicrous self-contradictory propositions for which the Irish were allegedly notorious.
229 The prince ruler who attracted JB's anger and contempt at Mannheim was Karl Theodor (1724–99); like the Margrave of Baden-Durlach (in the next letter), as an Elector he had the right to take part in the election of a new Emperor.
230 An inn where meals were served at a fixed price.

It was one of the best tables in town. But the company disgusted me sadly. O British take warning from me and shun the dominions of the Elector Palatine. I remain My Dear Johnston ever yours

James Boswell

Carlsrus,
9 Novr. 1764

My Dear Johnston:

I shall not here repeat the old song that The World is full of changes. But I shall not delay to inform you of a most agreable one for your freind. Instead of fretting at the Court of Manheim, I am now carousing at the court of Baden-Dourlach. The Marcgrave is a sensible, polite man. He has travelled a great deal, which one may soon find out from his Conversation and Address. He has been in England twice, and has liked it much, for he talks the language realy well, knows the history of Britain, and is even acquainted with the particular genius of the different parts of the Kingdom. His highness remembers the names of Streets and Squares and a thousand little particulars with regard to London, which prove that he has entered into the spirit of the Place. I have allready had the honour of talking a long time with him, and since dinner he has done me the honour to send me a parcel of English Newspapers. Ay Johnston this is treating a Stranger with politeness. And do you imagine that a Prince loses any thing by such a conduct? Have I not as much respect for his Highness as if he had held up his head and looked at me as a Bashaw[231] looks at a Slave? Indeed I respect him much more than the silent Negroe at Manheim. You must know that the Elector Palatine is exceedingly swarthy. I wish he was well drubbed.

And now Johnston I am contented and chearfull. My Servant[232] a good Suiss is not a little pleased to find me so; for, when I am vexed and consequently gloomy it is not a very agreable post to put my hair in papers.

All good things attend you My Dear Johnston. I ever remain Your Most Affectionate Freind

James Boswell

---

231 Obsolete form of 'pasha', a Turkish title of a provincial governor or military officer of high rank.
232 Jacob Hänni accompanied JB throughout the Grand Tour.

Strasbourg,
22 Novr. 1764

My Dear Johnston:

You must have often seen in an Edinburgh Advertisement the City of Strasbourg. "Strasbourg and St. Domingo Snuff." Who has not read this? In the City of Strasbourg am I now writing. Lest I should forget an anecdote of importance I will tell it you immediatly. The Tobacco trade here employs Six thousand hands. I must ask your pardon, My Dear Johnston, for having neglected to write to you from Ratstat where I past three days at the court of Baden Baden. The Prince[233] is Catholic, so we had high Mass in his Chappel, which pleased my solemn humour very much. It is the court in Germany where a man is most at his ease. You would have loved it dearly. You would have been hand and Glove with his Highness. He would have called you Grange. You can scarcely beleive how simple and free he is, without Affectation, quite natural. If he does not make you respect him I defy you not to like him. We had a very excellent table both at dinner and Supper. The Court is numerous, and there are some very handsom women there. Again, for you Johnston. Methinks I see your honest eyes glittering with delight to behold the sweet Mademoiselle de Geismar. So tall! so genteel! so loving! Come come Johnston, compose yourself: Be upon your good behaviour. Consider where you are. You must not think to get up and take the charming Creature in your arms and give her a kiss as you do to a bonny Lass on your *ain braes*.[234] I know a little the manners of courts: So be counselled by your freind. If you had her with you in the Garden, or in your Bedchamber, I should not oppose your tasting her delicious lips. But at present, taste something else. The Margrave's Rhenish and Burgundy are both excellent. Call for a couple of glasses of any of the two, and we'll drink your Mistress's health. You see Johnston how Imagination carrys me from Strasbourg to Ratstat. That may be true. But tomorrow morning early a coach comes to carry me forward to Basle; and that will be truer. So, my good Johnston good night. I am ever your true freind

James Boswell

---

233 August Georg (1706–71), Margrave of Baden-Baden.
234 'your own estates' (literally hillsides)

Soleure,
28 Novr. 1764

My Dear Johnston:

Man is a curious Animal: and I am not at all amazed that many Philosophers have tried to define him and Pope written a Poem[235] upon him as the Philosophers as well as the Poet were men themselves. But whatever may be the essential nature of man, sure I am that his happiness or misery his Abilitys or his Weakness depend allmost entirely on his Position. This evening Johnston, you are shivering with cold at Edinburgh: While I bid defiance to Winter at Soleure. You are probably thoughtfull and gloomy. I am thoughtfull and gay. And whence comes this mighty difference between two men who in many hours of their existence have differed less than most men. Why from no other cause but Position. You are in a Scots Town. I am in a Suiss Town. You are in a dirty Town. I am in a clean Town. You have past the day in Uniformity. I have past the day in Variety.

I have walked the ramparts. I have viewed from a Tour the Environs. I have been in the Jesuits and Franciscan Churches. I have been at a Card Assembly. I have kist (but no more) a comely healthy Maid at my Inn. I have dined and supt at the French Ambassador's. There is my day.

I must mention one circumstance as to Soleure which will please you much. It is the first town I have been in that Mr. Addison mentions in his travels.[236] Does not the Spectator's having been here give a value to it. It is mighty agreable to read Mr. Addison's observations and then look at what he has described. I have found many Alterations or more properly new works since his time. With these my Journal shall be enriched. With these my worthy freind shall be feasted.

My Dear Johnston! "Live well" as the good German says, and beleive me ever Your Most sincere Affectionate Freind

James Boswell

Vall de Travers,
5 Decr.1764

My Dear Johnston:

Art thou alive o! my freind? or has thy spirit quitted it's earthly habitation. To hear of thy death would not now distress me. I would glory to think of thy exaltation.

---

235 Pope's *Essay on Man* (1732–4).
236 Addison, *Remarks*, 481–2.

Johnston I am in the village which contains Rousseau.[237] These three days I have visited that Sublime Sage. He has enlightened my mind. He has kindled my Soul. Yes, we are Immortal. Yes. Jesus has given us a Revelation. I feel an enthusiasm beyond expression. Good Heaven am I so elevated? Where is Gloom? Where is Discontent? Where are all the little vexations of the World? O Johnston! Wert thou but here? I am in a beautifull wild Valley surrounded by immense mountains. I am just setting out for Neufchatel. But I return to Rousseau. I am to be alone on Horseback in a dark Winter night, while the earth is covered with Snow. My present Sentiments give me a force and a vigour like the Lion in the desert. Farewell My Dear Freind

James Boswell

Neufchatel,
9 Decr. 1764

My Dear Johnston:

I am now at the old Government of My Lord Marischal, where upon his Lordship's Recommendation I have been extremely well received. It is a fine healthy Place. The air is fresh. The beautifull lake yeilds most delicious large trout, and the Hills arround in vines abound. I have realy lived luxuriously. There is a great deal of good Company here very social very gay.

There is an English Captain of the Navy here an amiable young fellow. He has the true grave composure of a John Bull of good temperature. He looks at a jolly Suiss Girl, and says: "That now is what we call in England *a good piece*," and he never alters his countenance, not he.

A Parcel of his Countrymen threatened this winter to take a house here. The whole train consisted of Five Gentlemen, Five Tutors, twelve Servants twelve Horses and thirty Dogs. Was there ever such a Set? Luckily no house could be had, tho' they wrote in the true english stile, "Never mind moncy. We grudge no expence."

I have obtained my Father's permission to make the tour of Italy. It is impossible for me to express my happiness. My Dear Freind! I shall have the richest enjoyment of all the fine arts. Live and prosper o Johnston! and continue to regard your most affectionate freind

James Boswell

---

237 Jean-Jacques Rousseau (1712–78) lived in the Swiss village of Môtiers, seven miles from Neuchâtel.

Turin,
15 January 1765

My Dear Johnston:

It is now many a week since I last wrote to you. Since that time I have seen a great deal, but Dissipation has so overpowered me, that I have been a mere passive Existence driven along by a whirlwind of agitation. I have been at Geneva, I have been with Voltaire, I have passed the Alps.[238] You see I have had enough to say, could my mind have possessed half an hour of calm. But, I must own to you my freind, that my mind requires a little more of the sober influence of Old Father Time to give it that settled serenity which constitutes the true felicity of a rational Man. You will wonder that I did not become composed during my residence at Geneva, where John Calvin preached his gloomy orthodoxy, and where my Scots Presbyterian ideas might be supposed to return. But my good freind must know that Geneva is much more changed than Edinburgh. The Ghost of John Calvin would not be half so much dreaded at their Market place, as would the Ghost of John Knox at our Cross.[239] The Mutability of Mankind is every where to be observed. At Geneva I have seen a most remarkable proof of it.

And now Johnston I am in the City of Turin. I have found it different from what I expected. There is neither the elegance of taste nor the politeness of manners that I supposed. It contains a great many idle men, and a great many abandoned women. Gross gallantry is their occupation. They couple without sentiment, like the Beasts of the field, with this difference that the Beasts have some natural affection for their offspring and the People here have none. Yet among this good-for-nothing race have I been as dissipated as if I been among the most gay agreable Society on earth. O Johnston! I have lost my time here. I have been presented at court. The King of Sardinia is quiet and has no grand

---

238 In his Journal, JB recorded some details of the crossing at Mont Cenis on 6 January 1765: 'At six [a.m.] I mounted the Alps machine, which consisted of two trees between which were twisted some cords on which I sat. There was also a kind of back and arms, and a board hung before on which I put my feet. In this machine did four fellows (six I should say), changing two and two, carry me over the *saevas Alpes* [the savage Alps]. I drank some of the snow, that I might say, "I have climbed the rudest heights—and drunk the Alpine snow" [cf. Dryden's translation of Virgil, *Eclogues*, x, 71: 'And climb the frozen *Alps*, and tread th'eternal Snow']. The prospect was horridly grand. The snow was sometimes six foot deep, but the road had been well hardened by passengers.' *Boswell on the Grand Tour*, 23.

239 John Calvin (1509–64) exerted vast influence on European Protestantism from his base in Geneva where he lived, preached, and excited controversy in 1536–38, and 1541–64. His important *Institutes of the Christian Religion* was published in Basel, 1536. John Knox (1505–72), leader of the Reformation in Scotland and founder of Presbyterianism. The two men met in Geneva when Knox moved there in 1554, and again in 1556–8.

air. I was glad to view him as a Relation of our Royal House.[240] His Son the Duke of Savoy looks well. I can say no more to you here. After this I shall write to you more regularly.

I ever remain very sincerely yours.

James Boswell

Milan,
25 January 1765

My Dear Johnston:

My rule now is to write to you, the day on which I arrive at a town and thus dissipation shall never make me forget my regular tribute. How whimsical is my present suite of Epistles to You. Is it possible that they are to be composedly bundled up till we meet. I write every one of them as if my Servant waited to carry it to the Post directly. I imagine your happiness when you receive it, and if I omit to write at any place where I ought to do it, I fancy you are very angry with me. Few People of any nation can boast an Imagination more lively than mine. Vivacity I am certain of; but for strength for justness for continuance I must send you somewhere else. Perhaps however you are content with me and indeed take me as I am this evening, and you are much in the right.

You see from the date on this that I am now at Milan. Pleasing and curious are my ideas when I find myself for the first time in a City described by a Latin Classic. Milan is described by Ausonius as Mr. Addison has remarked.[241] I have great satisfaction in comparing ancient and modern sentiments manners and Buildings. Let Ausonius be placed in Milan as it now is and it would appear more strange to him an old Italian than it does to me a distant Caledonian. What think you would be his notion of the pompous Mass and of the variety of Religious orders. I suppose he would take the City of Milan for a Place of immense commerce, and the Monks for Merchants of different nations who are come hither to trade. As he would be extremely curious in asking questions he would be amazed to find the language so changed. When the Milanese would answer him in Italian he would take them also to be foreigners and finding very few People who could talk to him in the Roman tongue he would be much embarrassed. Perhaps he and I might meet, and bad as my Latin is, I would contrive to entertain him so well, that he would embrace me as a Countryman. In short honest Ausonius and I would be hale fellow well met. My Dear Johnston I am ever yours

James Boswell

---

240 Charles-Emmanuel III, of Sardinia, was a great-grandson of Charles I.
241 Ausonius, Roman poet born *c.*310; see Addison, *Remarks*, 50–51.

Bolonia,
5 February 1765

My Dear Johnston:

If Strasbourg is remarkable for it's snuff Bolonia is no less for it's Sausages. During all my travels I meet with places whose celebrity is made known to many only by the back or the Belly. Strasbourg and this Bolonia are allready mentioned. But I can give you a list to prove the truth of my assertion.

Westphalia is renowned for it's hams, Brunswic for it's Mum,[242] Leipsic for it's Larks, Neufchatel for it's wine, Florence for it's oil, Venice for it's Poplins, Genoa for it's velvets Rome for it's Purl[243] if we may beleive the London signs, Parma for it's cheese and so on till your Larder and wardrobe are compleatly filled.

My Dear Freind I am fatigued tonight. I have seen a great deal in this ancient city and it's environs, but for my account thereof you must be referred to that capacious Treatise my Journal and so we heartily bid you farewell.

James Boswell

Spoleto,
12 Febry. 1765

My Dear Johnston:

Had the Scots Militia taken place,[244] and you been a Colonel in the Annandale Battallion, this Letter would have highly suited you. I now write from a City whose gallant Inhabitants drove off the victorious Annibal when he was marching with flying colours to Rome after having defeated the Romans at Thrasymene.[245] Little did he expect that Spoleto would oppose him; but he found himself much mistaken, and received such a shock, that he fled like Sir John Cope from the field of Falkirk.[246] This People are surely of the same constitution as the Scots Highlanders. They are in the heart of the Appenines, and their City is built upon a Mountain. I have been patroling it this evening, and figuring to myself the spirited courage with which the Old Spoletti rushed down against the foe. I have also viewed the remains of

---

242 A kind of beer originally brewed in Brunswick.
243 A liquor made by mixing bitter herbs with beer; later, in the eighteenth century, a mixture of hot beer with gin was advertised as a stimulant to the appetite in the early morning.
244 Had a militia been formed in Scotland as in England.
245 Hannibal's victory in 217 BC at Lake Trasimeno near Perugia.
246 Charles Edward (1720–88), the Young Pretender, defeated Cope (d.1760) at Prestonpans in 1745.

a noble Aqueduct which has been a work of immense labour.[247] Johnston I am now Romanising every day. My Patriotism is inflamed, and every spark of generous sentiment which I contain is kindling. Adieu My Old freind worthy to be so were I as great as any Roman that ever dignified Humanity. I am ever Affectionately Your's

James Boswell

Naples,
19 March 1765

My Dear Johnston:

If a Man's Mind never failed to catch the spirit of the Climate in which he breathes I ought now to write you a most delicious letter: For Naples is indeed a delicious Spot *præter omnes ridet*.[248] I have been near three weeks here and have been constantly employed in seeing the Classical Places all arround. Is it possible to conceive a richer scene than the finest Bay diversified with Islands and bordered by fields where Virgil's Muses charmed the Creation, where the renowned of ancient Rome enjoyed the luxury of glorious retreat, and the true flow of Soul which they valued as much as triumphs. But My Dear Freind modern Naples has nothing of the ancient Parthenope[249] except it's heat and it's idleness. The People are the most shocking race eaters of garlic and catches of vermin an exercise which they scruple not to perform on the public Streets. Swift's Dermot and Sheelah would make a true Naples Eclogue. I owe this conceit to the famous John Wilkes who is now here and is to settle for some time in the Environs. I am so full of ideas that I cannot write. Swift's allusion to a Churchdoor is most applicable to my mouth this evening.[250]

The warmth of the air here has extracted the vicious humours from my blood, and covered my chin and neck with a prodigious scurvy which plagues me much. But as it probably has saved me a fever I do not complain tho' allmost

---

247 For another account of discovering an aqueduct, see Spence pp. 98–9.
248 'more charming than anywhere else,' Horace, *Odes*, II, vi, 13–14.
249 According to legend, when the Sirens drowned themselves, the body of one of them, Parthenope, was washed ashore in the bay which originally bore her name—as did the city (now Naples).
250 Swift's two Irish country bumpkins appear in his 'Pastoral Dialogue'. JB attributes the reference to his having met the outlawed radical MP, John Wilkes (1727–97) recently arrived in Naples. 'Swift's allusion to a Churchdoor' occurs in 'Thoughts on Various Subjects': 'common Speakers have only one Set of Ideas, and one Set of Words to cloath them in; and these are always ready at the Mouth. So People come faster out of a Church when it is almost empty, than when a Crowd is at the Door.'

certain that no Woman under fifty would give me a kiss without being payd for it as you have been payed for being the *Doer* of some old Lady.[251] Go on and prosper. Ever your's

James Boswell

Rome,
11 May 1765

My Dear Sir:

Your letter of the 1st of February has given me so much pleasure, that I have allmost forgot your eight months silence: That, Johnston, is a long time between old freinds: But you excuse yourself so well, and so much in your own natural stile, that I see your honest countenance full in my view, and as you ask me to do, I "forgive you frankly." When I look back to the day on which I wrote you last, what a variety fills up the space between that day and this! I left Berlin in September, and made a very agreable and improving tour through a good many of the German Courts, where I lived with Princes, and had the most advantageous opportunity of forming my manners, while, at the same time, I saw a great extent of country and many places worthy of attention. I then went into Switzerland, where I past some weeks with satisfaction. I went and visited the celebrated Rousseau in his wild retreat, and had some conversations with him which will have an influence on the whole of my future existence, for we talked much both of this world and of the next. I also past four days at the Country Seat of M. De Voltaire whose name carries lustre with it over Europe. I had much conversation with him too, and as you know how very faithfully I can record what I hear from Men of eminence, you may well beleive that my Papers contain a rich foreign treasure. I was a very short time at Geneva, from whence I certainly intended to have written to you, as I thought myself sure of having a letter from you lying there under my brother David's cover. But finding no such letter, I delayed writing till it should come, and so put it off from month to month till I did not well know what to think. The very day that your last arrived I had written to David begging that he would give me some account of you. I had sealed my letter to him and on receipt of yours, I burnt the one I had written and wrote him another. On the first of January I set out from Geneva and at the most rigorous season of the year, I had an excellent passage over the Alps. I stayed a forthnight at Turin, and then went by Milan, Placentia, Parma, Bologna, and the Holy House of Loretto[252] to Rome. I stayed a few

---

251 An advocate on behalf of an old lady unable to act for herself.
252 Reputed to have been the home of the Virgin Mary after the miraculous transporting of her house from Nazareth. Cf. Spence n. 176.

days and saw some of the principal things, and then went to Naples, where I past three weeks in viewing that City and it's classical environs. I past many an hour there with the famous Mr. Wilkes, who has chosen that Paradise as the Place of his Exile. He has hired an old Castle overlooking the delicious Bay, and has with him a beautifull Italian Girl.[253] He is as gay in his Exile, as when he used to make Aylesbury ring with his jovial mirth. He is publishing Churchill's Works with notes, and is writing a History of England from the Revolution to the fourth year of his present Majesty.[254] Wilkes is a most extraordinary Man. He has constant flow of health and spirits, and is allmost the only instance of a man of genius who enjoys continual happiness in this strange World. Upon my return from Naples to Rome, I employed an Antiquary, and in a regular course viewed the Remains of ancient grandeur, the Statues, and the Pictures.[255] I give you my word that without affecting to be a *Virtuoso*, I have had great satisfaction from this course, and have formed a taste for the arts which will contribute to calm my mind while I live. I regret only that my time of elegant Study at Rome is so short. However, I shall continue to study, with the assistance of Books and Prints, in the Library at Auchinleck. While I tell you what I have been doing, during my travels, I must not neglect to give you some account how I have been thinking. My natural sensibility and Anxiety of Mind has ever kept me exposed to the attacks of Hypochondria. By the great exercise and entertainment which I have had, the foul fiend has been often chaced away; but I have never been able to promise myself any long continuance of felicity. I have experienced, during the last half year, such changes of sentiment as would hardly be conceived to arise in a Mind where Judgment was not totally overthrown. I shall not enter into particulars, but leave you to imagine all the wild ideas which your gloomy fancy can suggest, on the wettest Sunday, while the Bell is ringing for the Tolbooth Kirk, and all the gay ideas which cheer your mind when the air is pure, and the Sun is bright, and you are lying luxuriously upon Arthur Seat,[256] or calmly musing in your wood at Grange. My great comfort is that I am ever firm in my attachment to the old Family of Auchinleck, to my worthy Parents, and to my Bosom Freinds. Were it not for Melancholy, I am one of the most fortunate young Men alive,

---

253 Gertrude Corrandini (b.1746).
254 Wilkes, at the manor of Aylesbury, with Sir Francis Dashwood at nearby Medmenham Abbey, hosted the orgies of the infamous Hellfire Club. The edition of Charles Churchill's poems never appeared; the history, of narrower compass than originally intended, was published in 1768 as *The History of England, from the Revolution to the Accession of the Brunswick Line*.
255 JB attended a six-day 'Course in Antiquities and Arts' that was designed for Tourists. His guide was the Scottish antiquary, Colin Morison (1732–1810).
256 Tolbooth Kirk, associated with rigid Calvinism. On Arthur's Seat (see n. 220).

for I know none who has more real advantages than I have. I must however own that I am uneasy when I think of returning to Scotland. My Father is very well satisfyd with me at present: But I much fear he will not be so when he finds me at home with him. By his way of writing I can discover that he expects me to be a sollid steady Man who shall apply to Business with persevering assiduity. But my Dear Freind You know that there is hardly any probability that I shall ever be such a Man. Years indeed may render me steady, but I despair of having application. God bestows his gifts as he thinks fit, and long study of myself has convinced me that my Constitution was never intended for great labour of Mind I can pore over books as long as any Man. I did so at Utrecht. But the effect was not improvement but sickness and perturbation. I swear to you that I seriously think it my truest Philosophy to be content with the Powers which my Maker has assigned me, and not to torment myself with inefectual struggles to change my Nature. I find myself an amiable pretty Man of moderate abilitys, but a Soul truly noble, a Soul which in reality sets me higher in the scale of being than if I had attained to the first honours which superiour talents procure, and been without such a Soul. I would however do what I can to promote the happiness of my fellow-creatures. I shall put on the gown as an Advocate and endeavour to acquit myself faithfully towards those who entrust me with their causes. But I shall not lay myself out for very much employment. If I can get a seat in the house for a Parliament, I shall like it much, but shall not absolutely set my heart upon it. I shall at all events hope to have a good Exchequer gown, and so enjoy *Otium cum dignitate*,[257] and have plenty of time to give to the cultivating our old Estate and following out the Studies which please me the most. The great point will be to begin properly when I return, and get My Father to see me as I realy am. Come, my good freind, encourage me. Who knows but I may yet rejoice my Father's heart. I call God to witness that I wish most earnestly to do so. His civilitys to you in my absence touch me sensibly. I hope to shew him that I am gratefull. I am just now quite well and happy, and storing my memory with rich ideas which will give much pleasure to us both many years hence. To be in illustrious Rome itself and to walk the scenes of classical enthusiasm is indeed noble. When I give you my warm account of all this, you will enjoy it very near as much as if you had been here. I know how to make your Soul feel joy. My Journal will be a treasure to us. Were you but with me this evening what store of entertainment would I pour forth! In a letter I can only give you a few ideas half-coloured. You must know I have travelled through Italy under the Protection of the Dominican Friers. The King of Sardinia's Antiquary recommended me to a

---

257 JB hopes to become a judge of the civil court responsible for trying Crown revenue cases… '*leisure with dignity*,' Cicero, *Pro Sestio*, xlv, 98.

Father of that order at Milan. I found him a learned pretty man, and after having had some conversation with him I discovered a very curious circumstance. This was the Father who converted to the Romish Faith Sir Alexander Jardine.[258] You may be sure I had a full account of that singular affair. The Reverend Monk recommended me to the Convent at Bolonia, and from thence I have had letters from Convent to Convent, and been treated with great distinction. The dress of this order is White with a black gown. This, Johnston is being quite in my own romantic stile. I have now been more than two months in Rome. I shall stay just a week longer. I have been presented to two Cardinals, and on Monday I am to kiss the Pope's toe. I go from hence to Florence, then to Venice, and afterwards come round by Parma to Genoa, where I am to embark for France. How long I shall yet be abroad I cannot say. My Father will no doubt expect to see me before winter. But I am very desirous to pass some time in France the country of gayety, and afterwards intend to travel through Flanders, where are a great many places well worth seeing, and so return to Holland and see my good Dutch Relations and Freinds.

I am by no means displeased to hear that Miss Stewart and Miss Colquhoun are both married.[259] My Matrimonial schemes were transient flights of restless fancy. You must know that I am very fond of the daughter of one of the Nobles of Utrecht.[260] She is well looked and has £8000. But she is an universal Genius and rather too learned. She is very amiable, but is too much of my own constitution being subject to inequality of spirits. I know not how two such lively souls could unite. Any yet if I take a plain sensible woman it will look aukward to me. At any rate I shall be in no hurry to *yoke* as my Father calls it. Mademoiselle De Zuylen likes me, and corresponds with me, as does her Father a sensible worthy Gentleman. Johnston what say you to my foreign Lady? You must go back to the dancing School and brush up your bows. My brother John's conduct has given me much uneasiness.[261] But from the knowledge which I have of human nature I can only pity him. David is a fine fellow. I glory in him. Between ourselves, He will make the best figure of any

---

258 Sir Alexander Jardine of Applegirth (1712–90), 4th Baronet; he was converted to Roman Catholicism sometime before 1765 and was elected as a Knight of the Order of Malta.
259 Margaret Stewart (?1742–1816), daughter of Sir Michael Stewart of Blackhall, 3rd Baronet; married Sir William Maxwell of Springkell, 3rd Baronet (1739–1804) on 24 March 1764. Katharine Colquhon (d.1804), daughter of Sir James Colquhon, married Sir Roderick Mackenzie of Scatwell, 4th Baronet (?1740–1811) on 7 April 1764.
260 Known as 'Belle de Zuylen' or, by JB, as Zélide, Isabella Agneta Elisabeth de Zuylen (1740–1805); initially encouraged JB's thoughts of marriage but, in 1768, rejected him.
261 John Boswell (1743–?98) suffered from periodic bouts of insanity; regarded by his father as 'full of pride and ill nature… an idle load upon the earth' (*Journal*, 227).

of us. I am pleased to hear of your Interview with Erskine. I hope he shall be provided for. He ought to have been born a Laird. Your Parliament house news entertained me. You may depend on having a miniature picture of me, which I shall either send to you or bring over when I return. I realy long to see you again and to enjoy with you such cordial evenings as make us thank God for our existence. In the mean time let us write pretty often. My Address is now Aux soins de Messieurs Vautier et Delarue á Gênes. My Dear Freind Farewell.

James Boswell

Padua,
26 June 1765

My Dear Johnston:

Were you to make the tour of Italy, I am certain you would stay some time at Padua. For surely you must have read of it, and if you have, must like it. What think you of a venerable City founded by Antenor the Brother of King Priam,[262] and besides it's antiquity renowned for learning and sanctity. It's university has been famous and has procured it the title of Padova la dotta:[263] And the celebrated Saint Anthony must ever keep up it's holy reputation.[264] It has truly an ancient look, and were I here alone, or in grave company, I should feel myself much of the Student and much of the Monk. But here I am with Lord Mount-Stuart whose ideas have no similarity with those which Padua ought to give.[265] A young handsom Nobleman of the highest fashion has thoughts more light and more gay. Besides it is now fairtime, and the town is full of Venetian Nobility. We have an elegant Opera, and genteel Coffeehouses; and so the hours run on as in all other places of dissipation.

My good Edinburgh old freind, you have no notion of the Coffeehouses of this country, in which you see crowds of Ladies and Gentlemen in full dress, some walking about, some set down to Card tables, and some making love in

---

262 Antenor was among the wisest of the Trojan elders; unsuccessfully he advised that Helen should be returned to Menelaus; when Troy fell, the Greeks spared him and his family on account of his impartiality.
263 'Padua the learned.'
264 St Anthony of Padua (1195–1231), famous preacher and follower of St Francis of Assisi; canonized in 1232; JB narrowly missed being in the city for his feast day, 13 June.
265 John Stuart (1744–1814), eldest son of 3rd Earl of Bute (George III's closest political ally) and grandson of Lady Mary Wortley Montagu; styled as Viscount Mountstuart; succeeded his father as 4th Earl, 1792. In 1765 he was making the Grand Tour with his governor, Colonel James Edmondstone (1722–93), and tutor, Paul-Henri Mallet (1730–1807), author and historian.

convenient corners. Johnston it will be long before you see such doings in the Forrest's Coffeehouse to which your letters are addressed. My Dear Freind, be assured that I am ever yours,

James Boswell

Monigo,
19 July 1765

My Dear Johnston:

It is not my fault if you have not received a very long letter written from Rome in answer to the excellent one which I had the pleasure to receive from you in that City. I could hardly expect a return before this time, and therefore have nothing to say against you. If you have been indolent it has been but for a few days, and that you know is not to be minded in you. It is sometimes of advantage to have a great fault: a man's freinds become accustomed to it, and overlook little offences of the same kind. Were you a very regular Man, I should be in a passion with you for neglecting me a Post. But as you are you may e'en indulge your goodhumoured ease, Post after Post, and not have a word said to you.

I intended to have left Rome before the middle of May; but I formed a great intimacy with Lord Mountstuart, who kept me on from week to week, and at last insisted with me to accompany him in the rest of his tour of Italy. He removed the objections which I made on my Father's account, by assuring me that he would take care to have my conduct represented to him in such a manner, that instead of being offended he should be highly satisfyd with me. You may be sure this made me very happy and on the fourteenth of June I set out with pride and pleasure as the distinguished Freind of an amiable young Nobleman son to the favourite of our Sovereign. I promised myself a sure interest for life, and I felt my heart warm with affection to a branch of the loyal house of Stuart. My Lord Mountstuart has with him Colonel Edmondstoune a worthy Scotsman who has attended him from the time that he left England, and M. Mallet of Geneva who was Preceptor to the Prince Royal of Denmark and has a handsom pension from My Lord Bute for instructing his Son in History. My Dear Freind can you conceive any thing more agreable? We had a good journey to Venice, where we past a forthnight. We lived at the house of General Graeme Brother to Bucklivie.[266] He is Commander in Chief of the troops of this Republic; and being an old freind of Lord Bute's, and a

---

266   William Graeme, commander of the Venetian army; his brother James had sold the estate of Bucklyvie, but kept the courtesy title, Graeme of Bucklyvie.

very sensible polite man, we have been entertained by him with the greatest cordiality and ease. We are now at his seat in the Country where fine air regular living and moderate amusement keep us in a state like what you have proved in your simple summer days at Schaw. This is a new strong proof to me that a man ought never to despair; for, after all my tossings in the variety of life, after all my dismal days of horrid gloom I am now clear as when my mind was rural, young, and undisturbed except one day in seven. And yet Johnston, I have reason to be unhappy for my conduct of late has not been that of a Sage. At Rome I ran about among the Prostitutes till I was interrupted by that distemper which scourges vice in this world. When I got to Venice I had still some small remains of disease, but strange gay ideas which I had formed of the Venetian Courtesans turned my head, and away I went to an Opera-Dancer, and took Lord Mountstuart with me. We both had her; and we both found ourselves taken in for the punishment which I had met with at Rome. Pretty doings! Our evil has been recompensed but moderately; but we are as much to blame as if we had suffered most sadly. I have blamed myself so much, and repented so sincerely, that I am now no more distrest. Besides I do assure you the climate of Italy affects me much. It inflamed my hot desires, and now it keeps my blood so warm, that I have all day long such spirits as a man has after having taken a chearfull glass.

Before I left Rome I took care to execute your Commission of having my Picture done in miniature. I had it painted by a Mr. Alves an Inverness Lad who is studying in Italy. It is thought like and well-painted. I wish it may please you. It has been sent off some weeks ago to Mr. Strange the Engraver,[267] who is to convey it to Mr. Thomas Boswell, from whom you will receive it upon asking for it. I left it at Rome to the care of a very worthy Exile, who is Secretary to a Scots Gentleman of a very ancient Family who is obliged to live abroad for particular reasons.[268] You see there is something romantic in the history of this same miniature.

I leave this in a day or two, and after going with My Lord as far as Verona, I shall separate from him, and go to Parma, where I have an amiable French Acquaintance[269] a Man of knowledge and taste and sensibility to whom I was

---

267 James Alves (?1738–1808), a fine miniaturist then in Rome, later in London. (Sir) Robert Strange (1721–92), distinguished engraver; knighted 1787. He was to convey the miniature to Thomas Boswell (no relative of Bos) who worked in the Edinburgh post office.
268 Andrew Lumisden (1720–1801) was secretary to the Chevalier de St Georges in Rome, and later to the Young Pretender. Brother-in-law to Robert Strange; an antiquarian, author of *The Antiquities of Rome*.
269 French *philosophe* Alexandre Deleyre (1726–97), librarian to the Duke of Parma and ardent disciple of Rousseau.

recommended by M. Rousseau. I may perhaps spend a little time at the court of Parma and then go straight to Florence, and after seeing the curiositys there, jaunt thro' the rest of Tuscany, embark at Leghorn and sail to Genoa where I shall embark for France. You must know I have been longer in Italy than my Father intended and have spent £440 since the month of January. I hope my worthy Father will not be uneasy; for I am determined to do what he inclines as far as may lye in my power. I think Johnston you have here a pretty full account of me. Let me add that my regard and Affection for you is just as when we walked upon Arthur Seat and that I will convince you of when we meet. Pray see Davie from time to time. My heart is bound up in him. He is the *flower of the flock*. I am uneasy to think that I am not yet Master of Myself; but I allways hope to be better. Remember me kindly to all freinds, and pray write soon. Adieu My Dear Freind I am ever your's

James Boswell

Verona,
23 July 1765

My Dear Johnston:

Would you beleive that I have been just now gravely studying how to write you this letter. I would needs have it a good one because forsooth Verona was the City of Romeo and Juliet, and because Shakespeare has a Comedy called *The Two Gentlemen of Verona*. I say nothing of the younger Pliny[270] and other great men of Antiquity who were born here but I think I ought at least to remember one pretty quotation from either of these Plays of Shakespeare which I have mentioned.

I have seen here some good pictures, and a Portico of the Museum Philarmonicum in which are collected a number of ancient inscriptions, some of which can no longer be read, as the language in which they are written is lost. Nothing appears more striking to me than the loss of a language. A stately edifice may be repaired when ruined, or rebuilt from Plans or from exact Memory; A City may be swallowed up and after remaining for ages in the heart of the earth may be discovered; but a Language if once forgotten is never to be recalled. Words are arbitrary marks and have seldom any original connection with the ideas which they represent. If therefore the meaning annexed to particular characters slips into desuetude, a language is for ever destroyed. Were the learned to put significations upon the old Tuscan characters, perhaps

---

270 It was Pliny the Elder (AD 23–79), whose birthplace was Verona; his nephew was born at Comum in AD 61.

in ten thousand words they would not hit upon three significations the same with those which the characters formerly stood for.

I have viewed the magnificent Amphitheatre of Verona the inside of which is surprisingly entire. I have seen it put to a whimsical use this evening. In the *Arena* was erected a little Stage on which was acted an Opera Bouffé[271] while the ancient rising seats were occupied by degenerate Italians. What a sad alteration has time made! Blackguards and effeminate Signori sit where the wise and brave and virtous of old bestowed their valuable applause, and on the spot where was formerly a fight with wild beasts, or a combat of Gladiators, a low *Scurra* a ludicrous wretch of a Harlequin cuts aukward capers and rattles out Infamous attempts at wit. My Dear Johnston, I am in a Passion; but not with you. So honest freind shake hands. Were there more such Men as your honour this age would be less despicable. I ever remain with strong Affection Your sincere Freind

James Boswell

Brescia,
24 July 1765

My Dear Johnston:

All that Addison says of this Town is only "Brescia is famous for it's iron works,"[272] and as Addison is my Classic while I travel in Italy, and the least expression of so favourite an Authour valued by me like the least bits of the precious diamond, iron has run in my head since ever I arrived and I could not rest till I had seen the firearms which are the works mostly esteemed. They are indeed excellent for they make vast quantitys of them; This is the country where assassination is most frequent and Men and Women go often armed. I have bought a gun for three zechins as a little specimen of Brescia ingenuity, and have been allready not a little amused with it. So young is still this fancifull head of mine that I had no sooner bought my Gun than the ideas returned which used to stir my blood at Auchinleck when I was eager to be a Soldier; I brandished my Gun (if the sword will permit me for once that expression) I slung it carelessly over my left arm like a handsom fowler[273] or a Captain of a marching Regiment and I must own that I even shoulder'd my firelock like any bold Brother Soldier in his Majesty King George's service; all these motions I performed to an English march which I whistled and upon the honour of a

---

271   a comic opera.
272   Addison, *Remarks*, 53.
273   One who hunts wild birds.

Man who is not ashamed to discover the simplicity of his sentiments at times I do declare I was as happy as I could wish and giving my broad gold-lac'd hat a gracefull turn to one side of my head I thought myself a very great Man. My Dear Johnston I give you leave to smile. But let me tell you that in whatever way we can enjoy an innocent happiness in this sad world let us not disdain to enjoy it. The illustrious Johnson once cured me of haughty pride which despised small amusements. He told me "Sir, nothing is too little for so little a creature as man."[274] We are all little at periods of our lives and if we were all as candid Philosophers as I am would just march as I have done. My Dear Freind adieu

James Boswell

Pavia,
27 July 1765

My Dear Johnston:

This has been a day of disappointments to me. I left Milan early in the morning very pleased with the thoughts of having a curious conversation with one of the Fathers of the famous Carthusian Convent about five miles from this City. He was a very gay young man but of a religious turn of mind and at the age of sixteen he felt himself strongly inclined to the severe monastic life. He went to the Convent where he now is and past eight days in all the strictness of the Order. He then returned to Milan and lived a year in the world during which time his inclination still continued so at the end of the year, He began his Noviciate through the whole of which he preserved a calm and firm resolution to follow the hard precepts of Saint Bruno[275] and thus being perswaded that he had a true Vocation from God he took the vows and has now been a Religious above fifteen years full of peace and hope of celestial happiness. His name is Padre Serafina Grassi, and as I had a letter to him from his Brother a very ingenious engraver, I promised myself an uncommon satisfaction from the study of a mind so much warmed with Piety. But on my arrival at the Convent I found that this was a day of silent retirement and that the Prior would not permit the Father to receive me. I however saw the excellent Convent and magnificent Gothic Church. My next disappointment has been my not seeing the field of Battle where Francis the first was taken Prisoner by the army of Charles the Fifth.[276] I hoped to have viewed with

---

274 See Boswell, *Life of Johnson*, 14 July 1763.
275 St Bruno (?1030–1101), writer and founder of the Carthusian order.
276 The battle, on 24 February 1525, was fought between Francis I of France and Charles

accuracy and enthusiasm this celebrated Scene and as Doctor Robertson in his *History of Charles the Fifth* will in all probability give some description of the Battel of Pavia I rejoyced forsooth in the prospect of some mistakes which I supposed him to make and which I should correct with an air of importance and if he should insist on his being right I thought of giving him a grave reply, "You'll excuse me, Doctor. I have been upon the spot." But I find that nobody can give any distinct account of the situation of this field which must have been chang'd in many different ways since the Battel was fought; so that I pass on my way just as wise to the point which I intended to pique myself upon, just as wise as any honest Tradesman who never travelled above four miles round his shop. However I have seen two curious Cells one ornamented with bones of the Pavians and one with bones of the french. Sculls and shin-bones and shoulder blades and other parts are arranged with singular art as you have seen pebbles in the grotto of a Virtuoso. I have never seen a Conceit that struck me more. It is the first time that I have look'd on dead mens bones without horror. I find my freind that in this world all depends upon the imagination which may be affected very different ways by very small circumstances. I speak for myself. Yours with much Affection

James Boswell

Mantua,
30 July 1765

My Dear Johnston:

If I go on journeying at this rate from one classical town to another, my letters will resemble the pages of a German Commentator, where quotations come so thick upon one another that half the Book is brown with Italics. Can I be here without introducing *Mantua me genuit*?[277] I have come forty miles out of my road in order to see this City, which I find much larger and handsomer than I had any notion of. The Princess of Spain who is to be married to the new Grand Duke of Tuscany past two days here on her way to Inspruck.[278] They entertained her with a pretty little Pastoral opera, and now she is gone, it has been repeated twice to do a courtesy to the People who are all gay upon

---

V. William Robertson's *History of the Reign of the Emperor Charles V* was in the course of preparation; it would be published in 1769.

277 'Mantua bore me,' words attributed to Virgil and taken from the inscription on his tomb.

278 Maria Luisa, daughter of Charles III of Spain, was to be married to Leopold (1747–92), Grand Duke of Tuscany, on 5 August 1765.

this occasion. I saw it tonight, and I assure you the Theatre is a very handsom one. It was agreable to see an Italian Pastoral played in the Town where Virgil wrote his Eclogues. But Virgil's Birth-place is two miles out of town. I shall go out to it tomorrow morning early sailing on the Mincius, and I am told I shall there see a true idea of the little humble village

> *quo sæpe solemus*
> *Pastores ovium teneros deponere fœtus.*[279]

I am also told that I shall see the very Palace where Virgil lived; but this I look upon as the Neapolitan tradition that he kept a school, or the tradition which I myself invented that he stood a furious siege of Swans.

My Dear Freind, Mantua will remain in my mind as one of those pleasing scenes the recollection of which cheers me in my dullest hours. I ever remain your sincere freind

James Boswell

Guastalla,
31 July 1765

My Dear Johnston:

When one finds in a little Country Church a young Lady of a tollerable good air with a cap somewhat fashionable and a few pretty ribbands, is not one mightily pleased, and does not Miss appear extremely agreable? And what think you is the reason of this? In short we are glad to find what we did not expect, and therefore the object has a superiour value to us. Just so my freind does the Town of Guastalla strike me with uncommon satisfaction. I had not the least idea of it, and supposed that I should find one of the poor Italian Villages which I have seen so many of with pitifull shattered houses, and narrow dirty streets. Instead of that I find Guastalla very well built. I find a very decent fortification, very good houses, handsom streets and even *Places* or Squares, and what is extraordinary, I have met with no bad building nothing little, nothing mean. I have walked about with a Jewish Merchant. He carried me into the Synagogue where I saw a Levite teaching some Boys to read the sacred Books. It was curious to find mere Children bawling out Hebrew.

I began this letter with a Country Church, and if you have no objection I will end it with a Country Church-Yard. I would imitate a little Mr. Gray's celebrated Elegy in that passage where he supposes that perhaps the Country

---

279 Virgil, *Eclogues*, i, 20–1 ['… teneros depellere…']: 'where we shepherds are accustomed to drive our newly-weaned lambs.'

Church-Yard may contain the bones of People equal to the greatest names whom we have preserved

>Some Village Hampden that with dauntless breast
>The little Tyrant of his fields withstood etc[280]

I cannot at present write a word of verse, so you must be contented with a prose imitation. Perhaps in this humble Village may be concealed an Abraham worthy to live in the primitive Patriarchal dignity to rule a numerous seed, and to possess vast herds and flocks.[281] Perhaps there is here a Pitt of superiour fire to Him whose Eloquence bears the British Senate along as a Tide sweeps away every thing near it. Perhaps there is here a Bute unexposed to the rude blasts of popular caprice. Perhaps a Wilkes uncorrupted by party

>Some Wilkes yet guiltless of the fall of Bute.[282]

Perhaps too there is here a Johnston who is Philosopher enough to be content with a small fortune, hoping to have made it better but in the mean time enjoying life with a consciousness of independence. And who knows but what we might find here a Boswell solemn and gay by turns who is sometimes the favourite of the Ladies, but more often a pensive and gloomy Metaphysician. Adieu Dear Johnston

James Boswell

Florence,
24 August 1765

My Dear Johnston:

You have often heard it observed that Men are carefull in small matters, and negligent in matters of consequence. I have this day been very near having a strong proof of that observation. You must consider that Consequence is merely proportional and then you will understand me. Since I began to write you the suite of letters, while upon my travels, there is hardly a little town where I have not been mindfull of my engagement and now when I am in Florence the Capital of Tuscany I have omitted it till within a few hours of my setting out and I can see that it has been by mere chance that I have at last recollected it. I must however own that it is easier and pleasanter to write

---

280 Thomas Gray (1716–71), *Elegy Written in a Country Churchyard* (1751), ll, 57–8.
281 See Genesis 27:7 and 24:35.
282 Cf. Gray, *Elegy*, l, 60: 'Some Cromwell guiltless of his country's blood.' JB was the friend both of Bute's son, Mountstuart (see n. 265), and of John Wilkes (see n. 326); in *The North Briton*, Wilkes had conducted a campaign against Bute, but it could not be claimed that he had brought about Bute's fall (which had recently occurred, in May 1765).

from little towns than from large towns for in a small place you have no crowd of ideas to confuse you whereas in such a Place as this there is so much to be seen that it cannot be described in a hasty letter. Therefore my good Friend I reserve an account of what has amused me at Florence till I have the happiness of meeting you in Edinburgh. I ever remain Yours with great truth

James Boswell

Island of Corsica,
14 Novr. 1765

My Dear Johnston:

I have written you many a letter when in good health; I now write you one when confined by a tertian fever. How does it affect you, old freind? Do you perceive a strong smell of Peruvian Bark?[283] Or does it act upon you like a cold Electrifyer, and make you shiver from head to foot?

After travelling over Mountains and Precipices which your comfortable Indolence would never have attempted, after passing ten days with Signor De Paoli General of the Corsican Nation and making myself acquainted with one of the greatest Men in Europe,[284] after having traversed the greatest part of this Island, and observed the free spirit of it's brave Inhabitants, I am very well satisfy'd with the singular tour which I have made, and shall reflect upon it with a manly pleasure, when five and twenty more years have fixed me in a good easy chair, and a good easy Philosophy; When you and I Johnston shall lay a log upon the fire with hearty complacency,[285] and tell old Storys over a bottle of old wine.

This tertian fever has distrest me much. I carried it about for eleven days, having no Assistance I could confine in. I arrived at last at Bastia, where is the Commander in Chief of the french troops in the Island, M. de Marbeuf, the best man I ever met with. He has insisted on my living in his house, where I am

---

283   Powdered bark from the Peruvian cinchona tree was used as a treatment for malaria ('tertian fever').

284   Pascal Paoli (1725–1807) led the Corsican rebellion against Genoese rule; in 1755 he was invited by the island's supreme council to become their generalissimo; after achieving considerable success, both politically and militarily, he was eventually defeated by the Genoese (with French support) and forced into exile in England in 1769. JB had a series of conversations with him, 22–28 October 1765; see JB's *Account of Corsica, The Journal of a Tour to That Island, and Memoirs of Pascal Paoli*, edited by James T. Boulton and T. O. McLoughlin (New York: OUP, 2006).

285   self-satisfaction

attended by a very able french Physician, and have every thing I can desire.[286] In short one would think that the ancient alliance between the french and the Scots is renewed. I am allmost quite well and sail for Genoa in a day or two. Dear Frcind Adieu.

James Boswell

Nice,
15 Decr. 1765

My Dear Johnston:

In a City where a famous General Council was held I ought surely to be in an orthodox humour, and whatever difficultys I may make to receive the hard doctrines of St. Athanasius I should for this evening at least be a firm Supporter of the Nicene Creed.[287] Just as I entered the City the ringing of bells and firing of guns proclaimed a grand Procession. It was that of the Madonna Annunciata which being a pleasing subject made a fine mixture of solemnity and elegant sweetness. Our Lady was borne by a number of white masks on a scaffold richly gilded. She was a handsom figure and stood upright with her hands modestly folded on her breast. "Be it unto thy Handmaid" etc.[288] She was drest in a scarlet gown and had over it a loose flowing robe of blue with gold flowers. Round her head was a garland of stars, and above hung a magnificent crown. She was preceeded by the Franciscan friars with torches and followed by a vast crowd many of whom also had torches. I own I think that Processions representing the principal facts of our Holy Religion may have a very good effect on people's minds. I am sure I felt it on this occasion. Warmed with devotion I entered a venerable church and payed fervent Adoration to the Father of Spirits. I was much of a Catholic. I find a Man now and then comes just round to what he has been and changes again he knows not how. But I enjoy a perfect tranquillity on that head. God grant it may last. Johnston I visited this day the little state of Monaco, from whence I ought to have written

---

286 Louis-Charles René (1712–86), comte de Marboeuf, commanded French troops sent to Corsica, at the request of Genoa, to occupy major coastal towns. The physician was Claude-François Passerat de la Chapelle (see *Account of Corsica*, 212).

287 The Nicene Creed adopted by the Catholic Church was composed at the first Oecumenical Council held, in 325, at Nicaea in Bithynia, not—as JB believed—at Nice. St Athanasius (?296–373) was present at the Council, but he did not formulate the creed.

288 The Feast of the Annunciation of the Blessed Virgin Mary, normally held on 25 March to commemorate the revelation by the angel Gabriel to Mary that she had been chosen to be the mother of Jesus; she responded, 'Behold the handmaid of the Lord; be it unto me according to thy word' (Luke 1:38).

you a letter, but was so hurried I realy forgot. To make up matters I here promise that I shall never stop at any town long enough to dine sup or sleep without writing to your honour. Adieu My Dear Johnston.

James Boswell

Avignon,
27 December 1765

My Dear Johnston:

You know I am half a Catholic. I love the solemn and magnificent worship of the Church of Rome and allthough I cannot beleive some of her tenets I have a great respect for the many learned and holy men that have lived and died in a firm perswasion of that faith, and therefore I treat with reverence what to my understanding appears strange. I came to this City on Christmas eve and heard high Mass at Midnight in the Cathedral. I contrived it so as to pass the agreable festival of the nativity of our Saviour in this ancient seat of the Dominion of the Pope. I have seen one or two of the Churches with satisfaction and have been in the best frame I could wish. The Jesuits have taken sanctuary here.[289] It rejoyces me to meet in my walks the genteel fathers of that Order so much distinguished for Science and for Nobility. I have been much with My Lord Dumbar and My Lady Inverness[290] who are most excellent People true old Scots Nobility with the ease of foreign manners. They are of that sort of people which is wearing out in this interested[291] debauched and republican age of Britain. Their attachment to the Royal Family of Stuart does them honour with liberal Minds. Their long acquaintance with the unfortunate Court has given them a turn of thinking which it is pleasing to sympathise with, and the variety of Anecdotes which they know makes them very entertaining. I have enjoyed a singular scene here. It is true I have my melancholy hours, but I own, that I am perswaded no man has tasted a greater diversity of ideas than I have. Adieu Dear Johnston

James Boswell

---

289 Avignon was the residence of the Popes from 1309–76 and remained under papal jurisdiction until 1791, when it was united to France. It was therefore legitimate for the Jesuits, when they were expelled from France in 1765, to take refuge in Avignon.

290 James Murray (?1690–1770) was created Earl of Dunbar by the Old Pretender, whose cause he served; he lived in Avignon, home to a significant number of Jacobites. Among them was his sister, Lady Marjorie Murray, whose husband had been given the earldom of Inverness, also by the Pretender.

291 self-interested, self-seeking

Montpelier,
30 December 1765

My Dear Johnston:

Allthough in a hurry to get to Paris, I have come a day out of my road in order to see this Seat of Salubrity where so many of our sickly Countrymen have been restored to the ordinary state of imperfect humanity, which by comparison appears to them a state of health.

What is the matter with me this morning I realy cannot say; but I find myself a formal and tedious talker, a man who gives you a long warped period for what might be very easily said in three words. I am a dull frenchman. I have past a day here, and seen what was curious, which does not require much time. I must not rob my Journal to tell you what I have seen. These my letters are intended rather to tell you what I feel, to give you the ideas which employ my mind at the time I write. If they have some connection with the place where I happen to be so much the better, if not they are always the thoughts or reveries of your freind who never fails to remember you in all Citys and in all Countrys. I have been kindly entertained here by Mr. Alexander Ray an honest east Lothian man and a most admirable Banker and what I like as well when my Purse is not empty He is a good Classical Scholar and an Antiquarian.[292] Adieu My Dear Freind Yours ever

James Boswell

Lyons,
5 Janry. 1766

My Dear Johnston:

Let me wish you many happy new years, as is the cordial custom in good Scotland, where you are now eating *Buns* and Short-bread of most excellent taste, savoury to your palate and comfortable to that honest Stomach which must always partake of the best. I can say hardly any thing of this ancient and stately City renowned for it's roman remains, for it's printing and for it's beautifull stuffs. I am lame Johnston.[293] I have got sore toes and in this severe

---

292 JB wrote in his Journal on 29 December 1765: 'I had sent a card to Mr. Ray, merchant here, to whom Mr. Lumisden had recommended me. He… was so much of the antiquarian that they gave him the name of Dr. Ray… a free, sensible, good-humoured man with a variety of agreeable knowledge… [We] talked Italian.'

293 JB's toenails were the source of his trouble. His Journal for 31 December 1765 records: 'One of my feet was now swelled prodigiously, by reason of an inflammation in the toe.' On 2 January 1766 he wrote: 'My feet were so bad that I could not walk across my room.'

frost it is necessary for me to stay quietly at home in my warm room; therefore Johnston I can only bid you good night. I might dash you down a few flashes of imagination; but I set out tomorrow morning at five in the Diligence for Paris and it is now Midnight so I must go and have a few hours repose. Adieu My Dear Freind

James Boswell

Auxerres,
9 Janry. 1766

My Dear Johnston:

My last from Lyons was written in a very great hurry and this from Auxerres will be written as the Scots Blackguards[294] say in *a couple of hurries,* for I am now upon my route to Paris in the *Diligence* of which you have certainly read. Let me assure you it is the best Stage Coach in the world. You pay a hundred livres for which you travel a hundred leagues and are *nourri* and *couché* the whole way.[295] The Coachman is a Personage of very great Consequence, for besides his being Chief Conductor of our Coach, It is He who orders every thing at the Inns where we have most excellent entertainment I promise you and very good beds. If any of us is not content with what the Inn has furnished him, The Coachman is called in and talked to with such manly vigour as the Cook of a College at Oxford or Cambridge is chid by the eaters of Commons.[296] But you Johnston know nothing of those Anecdotes of English Universitys. You must apply to my freind Temple[297] of Trinity Hall Cambridge who will soon instruct you as to this as much as he has done me. Diligence Passengers like University Students are glad to improve the little opportunity they have of domineering. The Coachman I have said is respectable, but not from his figure which is not like the bluff square jolly grumbling British Coachman. No no. The Materials of which Man is made in france cannot make a true Coachman. We are eight Passengers in The Diligence. When we meet, you shall laugh at our History. At present let me tell you that I have the health of a Hercules dining and supping heartily every day and sleeping soundly every Night. I have great vigour and a pure absence of thought. I have an existence without pain which some would

---

294 Servants who work in the kitchen among pots and pans.
295 A diligence was a relatively comfortable public stagecoach whose coachman was responsible for passengers' requirements for food and comfortable beds.
296 Food provided for members of a college and eaten at a common table.
297 William Johnson Temple (1739–96), JB's contemporary in the University of Edinburgh and a very close friend; they were law students together in London. Temple had been admitted at Trinity Hall in 1758.

prefer to the anxious sensibility of taste and passion; but for my part I prefer being an unhappy man with the prospect of perfection to being a contented Brute with no prospect. We have just time to sup before we go to bed as we are called up between two and three. I write you one Diligence letter. Adieu.

James Boswell

James Barry; self-portrait. Oil on canvas, 1777

James Barry (1741–1806): Letters (1765–71)

James Barry, the eldest child of John and Juliana Barry of Cork in Ireland, had shown promise as an artist from his earliest days. At just 20 he was awarded a premium at the Dublin Society's annual exhibition for his painting *The Baptism of the King of Cashel by St Patrick*. At about the same time he met Edmund Burke in Dublin through their mutual friend Dr Fenn Sleigh, a physician in Cork who had schooled Barry in the classics. Burke soon arranged for Barry to move to London where, in 1764, he found him a position as an assistant to the antiquarian and painter 'Athenian' Stuart. Both Sleigh and Burke recognised his talent and encouraged him to pursue his art studies on the Continent. But Barry could not afford that. By mid-1765, however, the finances of Burke and his kinsman William Burke had so improved that they agreed to pay for Barry to study on the Continent, and he left for Paris in October. Overwhelmed by the kindness of his patrons, and determined to live up to their expectations, he set off on a tour that would take him to the great art galleries of France and Italy. There he would study and practise art on the grand scale: his ambition was to be a great history painter. If the Grand Tour was designed to educate young gentlemen by exposure to the finest art of Classical and Renaissance culture, Barry was one of its exemplary pupils. Seldom had a traveller set out with such determination and dedication. He was ever busy, sketching as he travelled, taking notes in galleries, copying the masters when he could, writing to the Burkes about what he had seen, and giving them his impressions and opinions.

His letters are mostly to Edmund Burke, though addressed to the whole family, in the belief that these good friends would all be interested in his progress. Clearly he had become a close family friend while in London, caught up in the energetic bonhomie and intellectual animation of the household. Although he missed those stimuli on his travels, his letters show he wanted to maintain that kind of serious engagement by telling them of the paintings, the sculptures, the great galleries and palaces he saw in Paris and Rome. Art is virtually all he writes about, except when in financial difficulty. There is not much small talk or idle observation, little easy reflection or conversational relaxation. The underlying strain throughout is of gratitude—of a debt that could be repaid not in kind, but in fidelity, to the trust they had put in him.

Barry's approach to the Grand Tour was unusual in that its attraction was the prospect of serious stimulation of work: 'I am mightily pleased with several things in Paris,' he writes shortly after his arrival, 'but shall inform myself better of their merits, before I venture to say anything of them'. As he journeyed, he sketched, observed, made notes, trying all the time to think his way into a critical position about the great artists whose work he came across for the first time. Within a few weeks he had decided to copy one of the best pictures he had ever seen, Le Sueur's *La Maladie d'Alexandre*: that, he says, was the most 'profitable' thing he could do; later he made a present of the finished painting to Edmund Burke.

Barry, unlike so many other young gentlemen on the Tour, had no desire to throw himself into the social milieu of Paris. Instead, he gave his days to the galleries and his nights to his own work. For a time he enrolled at the Academy of St Luke, but was soon disappointed by his experience there:

> there are such mobs of blackguards go every night to acquire a trade there, as is enough to shock any one who has the least regard for the art. People send their children to make them painters and statuaries (without learning, genius, or indeed any thing else) only because it is less expensive than making them perukiers or shoemakers.

The academy was a scandal; a betrayal of serious artistic endeavour. This youthful response has its ironic echoes later when, in 1798, he openly criticised the Royal Academy, where he was Professor of Painting, for failing its mission to art and society.[298]

By the time Barry settled in Rome for a few years his letters reflected a young man caught between excitement at seeing and studying masters like Poussin, Titian, and Michael Angelo, and disappointment—even anger—with the contemporary state of the arts – the paintings, the critics, the institutions, the commerce – in both France and Italy. The serious note in so much he writes is underpinned by a desire that he himself would become a Master, a great historical painter. That ambition colours so much of what he writes. But his Tour was not a lone mission. The letters have an air of an imagined dialogue with Burke, whose opinions and intellect he had admired since the time he first read and copied out his *Philosophical Enquiry into… the Sublime and Beautiful*. In the background of his thoughts are painter friends back in London who he asks to be remembered to, like his Irish contemporaries George Barret and Hugh Hamilton. His respect for Sir Joshua Reynolds increased, in spite

---

298 James Barry, *A Letter to the Dilettanti Society*, (London: Walker, 1798).

of the distance: William Burke tells Barry that 'Reynolds really expects every thing of you, and so do we all'.[299] Barry drew energy from these expectations. Yet in a way they also fuelled his intellectual isolation, notably in Rome. The letters from Rome show no signs of his getting out and about—certainly no Boswellian desire to meet prominent or influential people. Painting took up most of his days.

Yet Barry was not unsocial: he enjoyed mingling with friends and artists at the English coffee house in the Place d'Espagne. But there were difficulties of personality:

> We are in number about thirty students, English, Scotch, and Irish; and as there is in our art every thing to set the passions of men afloat, all desiring consequence and superiority; it is no wonder if distrust, concealed hatred, and ungenerous attempts, are perhaps oftener experienced, than friendship, dignity of mind, or open square conduct.[300]

In Barry's case the problem went deeper than such 'passions of men'. The Burkes keep exhorting him to curb his abrasive temper, to be more tolerant: their knowledge of him suggests he had shown the same traits while still in London. If some of the habitués of the coffee house annoyed him, his problem was how to respond, and that problem remained with him well into his later years.[301] He felt they were either jealous or prejudiced against him. What he expected from others and, from all accounts, gave back, was 'open square conduct'.

Some letters, such as that to his Cork friend William O'Brien, reflect the more relaxed Barry, the man capable of 'warm and sincere' friendship. The letter to his parents on the sudden death of his younger brother Jack gives a rare view of the very private area of his feelings for his family. Suddenly, deeply entrenched preoccupations with Rome and the Tour evaporate on the news of a personal tragedy. The bulk of the letters, however, are dense with detailed descriptions and discussion about paintings and sculptures. Barry gives the impression of thinking his way through his own responses and ideas in long, sometimes tortuous, sentences that presume the reader will keep up with the flow of his thoughts. Writing about Titian, whom he so admired for his colouring, he remarks to Burke:

> There is nothing in his pictures whiter, bluer, or yellower—but they may be made now as much and even more so, if the merit consisted in that.

---

299 William Burke to Barry, 7 October 1766.
300 26 February 1768.
301 For example, Anthony Pasquin [John Williams] satirised Barry for 'ill manners and uncharitableness' as Jemmy O'Blarney in his farce *The Royal Academicians* (London: Denew and Grant, 1786).

> But the judicious application and mixing together of things is what puzzles in Titian, for he hardly ever laid on a colour simple, pure, and in its full force. Bassano, Rubens, Vandyke, and Paul Veronese, are all good colourists, though all different; with a little displacing of the favourite tints, less blue, less red, purple, or yellow, put on here, the other there, and you may change each of them into the other with respect to colouring, and you may transform any or all of them into Titian in the same manner.

This last sentence demonstrates a typical run of clauses, each enlarging or qualifying what has just been said: 'with a little… less…, less…, or…, the other…, and you may…, and you may…' When Barry explains something, he gives few occasions to draw breath or take stock. He was so absorbed in, and stimulated by what Titian—let alone Rome—offered, that he often used the letters to organise his responses.

But art was not Barry's only preoccupation. He was often worried about money. The Burkes had arranged to finance Barry on his travels. The arrangement was that they deposited money in their London bank and Barry could draw on that from wherever he was, be it Paris or Rome, as he needed. The agreed amount was about £40 per year, and the arrangement lasted for the duration of his tour, from 1765 to early 1771. The letters' periodic insight on Barry's anxiety about his finances also reflects his total dependence on the Burkes. Unable to pay his rent in Bologna on his way home, he wrote letter after letter trying to contact the Burkes. Weeks went by without a reply. Such was his plight he thought of 'running naked out of my lodging and turning friar, when I imagined that by the means of my art I should meet with a sort of reception—but this was a remedy that I thought much worse than the disease' (20 November 1770). Once the money had arrived he quickly slipped into the role he had cast for himself all along as a studious correspondent of everything worth noting in the galleries of Bologna and Parma.

He returned via Lyon and Paris, his head full of what he had seen. He starts a letter in Lyon,

> In order to divert my attention from disagreeable reflections upon the fatigues and extraordinary expenses of travelling in this time of the year, as I have also an idle day upon my hands in waiting for the diligence, and as there is nothing worth looking after here in Lyons, except trade and manufacture, in which I have neither knowledge nor taste, so I shall turn to my old resource of more pleasing memorial.

'My old resource', his memories of countless paintings, frescoes, and statues, is a fair summation of what so pleased him during his five years on the Tour. However, this satisfaction was tinged with apprehension that London would be no easy place to settle back into: news of the state of the arts in England—particularly reviews of recent exhibitions—depressed him. He well knew that in England there was little interest in, much less cultivation of, the grand classical style he had given his days and nights to: instead he had to expect portraits, landscapes, flowers. Barry expected to be out of key with the prevailing taste. So it turned out for much of his career. Although he was soon a member of the recently formed Royal Academy, where his friend Reynolds was its first President, and despite being appointed Professor of Painting there, he was never an establishment figure. Quite the reverse. He was expelled from the Royal Academy in 1799 for his public criticisms of the institution.

His major work was a series of six huge paintings that still decorate the walls of the Royal Society of Arts, *The Progress of Human Culture* (1777–83). These are scenes from Classical Greek mythology through to contemporary Britain, concluding with 'Elysium', in which he portrayed a vast array of writers, philosophers, scientists, artists and statesmen who had marked western civilisation. The genesis of this immense and celebrated project lies in the encouragement of people like the Burkes and Dr Fenn Sleigh; they were responsible for Barry's fascination with, and devotion to, the great art he discovered during the years of his Tour.

With one exception, the text for the Barry letters included in this volume is taken from the only known source, *The Works of James Barry, Esq: Historical Painter*, edited by E. Fryer, 2 vols (London: Cadell and Davies, 1809). The exception, Barry's letter to Sir William Hamilton (29 November 1768), is taken from the MS as transcribed in 'The Correspondence of James Barry', edited by T. O. McLoughlin at <http://www.texte.ie/barry/> No silent corrections have been made to spelling or punctuation as found in Fryer's edition.

Letters of James Barry

Paris, November 6, 1765.

My Dear Sirs,[302]

As I proposed keeping myself alive in your memory, I would have wrote to you from Calais on my arrival the 27th, but as there were only two things which offered themselves to me, either the deep and indelible sense I had of your good nature and affection, or the little things which I took notice of in my journey,

---

302 Except where stated otherwise, all letters were addressed to Edmund Burke ('Dear Sir'), or to the Burke family ('Dear Sirs'). The phrase 'you both' at the close of this letter suggests Barry was thinking mainly of Edmund and his kinsman William Burke.

I shall, until I see you again, mention nothing but the latter, knowing but too well how trifling and unseasonable my thanks, &c. must be to persons whose generosity and friendship to me could be the effect of nothing but their own goodness.

I shall begin then by telling you that I made as many sketches of the country between London and Dover as the velocity and uneasiness of the motion of the coach would permit:[303] I have done the same in the way to Paris; the vehicle I came in, which they call a diligens,[304] has been indeed very diligent, though not altogether expeditious, as we were in motion from four in the morning till eight or nine at night, and yet were from Monday the 29th till the Sunday night following, upon our journey.[305] I sat in one of the side places for the advantage of seeing the country and taking down such things as I could here; I got such a terrible cold as almost deprived me of the use of my speech, but thank God I am now pretty well got over it. The country is in many places very fine, particularly between Beauvais and Paris; there are some views near St. Denis pretty like those about Richmond, but much finer; it has not so much the appearance of improvement as our English grounds, but is more beautiful, and though it never rises to any thing more than beauty, yet it rarely comes short of it. The nave of the church at Beauvais is really very striking, it is Gothick, and has, I think, incomparably a better effect than any thing I ever saw before.[306] I had but half an hour to run about in it, and what makes it still worse, it was before day, between four and five o'clock. My hurry, and the multiplicity of views, put it out of my power to attend much to particulars, and generals, though not entirely satisfactory, yet are not totally without use.

I am mightily pleased with several things in Paris, but shall inform myself better of their merits, before I venture to say any thing of them. Col. Drumgold has received me very politely;[307] I shall see him soon again, but nothing could

---

303   The coach from London to Dover took a day and cost 20 shillings: *The Gentleman's Guide Through France Wrote by an Officer*, 4th edition (London: Kearsly, 1770), 14.
304   Normally, 'diligence': 'A public stage-coach' (OED); it went faster than the usual stage-coach.
305   Barry's route took him via Beauvais and St Denis; the Calais to Paris journey cost 30 livres, about twenty-five shillings (*Gentleman's Guide*, 260).
306   The Gothic Cathedral of St Pierre, noted for its arches, nearly 50 metres high, as well as for its stained-glass windows.
307   Colonel John Drumgold, (1720–81). Of Catholic Irish and Jacobite stock, he was educated in Navarre where he became Professor of Rhetoric; he joined the French army, rose to the rank of Colonel, and won the Royal and Military Order of St Louis for bravery, which carried a pension. George Lyttelton praised him in a verse epistle for 'Learning and wit, with sweet politeness graced' ('To Colonel Drumgold', *The Poetical Works of George Lord Lyttelton* (Glasgow: Foulis, 1787), 115).

equal the warmth and affection I met with in Mr. Macleane.[308] Yourselves could not be interested more about me than he is. He has introduced me to an English gentleman, whose name I forget; he is a great connoisseur,[309] and is very able, and I believe very willing, to procure me access to every thing that may be of use. My interest is so blended with your concerns, that I am at the greatest loss to know how to conclude. I suppress a thousand things that are breaking from me, and shall only take the liberty to say, that though you must be dear to all your friends, there is no one who loves and respects you both more sincerely than your humble servant,

James Barry.

P. S. My best respects to dear Mrs. Burke, to Dr. Nugent, Mr. Richard Burke, Master Richard,[310] to Messrs. English and Creagh.[311] You will oblige me, Sir, in presenting my respects to my friend Mr. Barrett, to Mr. Stuart, to Mr. Reynolds,[312] and to Mr. and Mrs. Cholmondely,[313] and to such of your friends as I had the honour of knowing.

---

308   Lauchlin Macleane (c.1728–78), friend of Edmund and William Burke, was admitted to Trinity College, Dublin, on 29 May 1746; he had a reputation as a stock market gambler and was involved in land speculation in the West Indies. He often travelled between London and Paris.
309   Not identified. A connoisseur is 'A critical judge of art or of matters of taste' (OED); cf. (Sir) Joshua Reynolds: 'The remembrance of a few names of painters, with their general characters, with a few rules of the Academy, which they may pick up among the painters, will go a great way towards making a very notable connoisseur' (*The Idler*, no. 76, 20 September 1759).
310   Members of the Burke family in Queen Anne Street, London: Mrs Jane Burke (1734–1812); Dr Christopher Nugent (1698–1775), father-in-law of Edmund Burke, an Irish physician and Catholic who had formerly practised in Bath; Burke's brother Mr Richard Burke Snr. (1733–94); Burke's son Richard Burke Jnr. (1758–94).
311   Thomas English (c.1725–98), Burke's principal assistant on the *Annual Register* at the time (see T. O. McLoughlin, *Edmund Burke and the First Ten Years of the 'Annual Register'* (Salisbury: University of Rhodesia, 1975). Creagh has not been identified.
312   George Barret (c.1728–84), Irish painter who had left Dublin for London in 1763. James Stuart (1713–88), under whom Barry worked when he first went to London; surveyor of Greenwich Hospital and painter to the Society of Dilettanti, often referred to as 'Athenian' Stuart. (Sir) Joshua Reynolds (1723–92), England's leading portrait painter of the day and friend of the Burke family; Burke had introduced Barry to him in London.
313   Robert Cholmondeley (1727–1804), Anglican priest, son of 3rd Earl of Cholmondeley; his wife Mary (c.1729–1811) was a noted hostess and friend of Dr Johnson.

Paris [*c*.20 December 1765]

My Dear Sirs,

I have since had but little time to myself to answer either of the kind letters I received from you by Mr. Morison,[314] and now that I have sat down to it I could wish myself some excuse to defer it still longer. I am confounded to think what I shall say to so much and so unmerited kindness.[315] Love and gratitude urge me on to expressions which I must lay aside to avoid the awkward situation of being detected in the language that is so common in the world, and which may be found in a person who has very little of what I think is in my bosom, when I remember what I owe you and the family whose friendship is alone what has counterpoised and sweetened the other circumstances of my life, which God knows have been disagreeable enough. Mr. Richard Burke's arrival has, you may conceive, given me no small pleasure and advantage. Every day lays me under new obligations to him and to you; all that union which is so visible in the family is as manifest in your carriage towards me as it is in every thing else, insomuch, that when I mention kindness and generosity, I am at a loss to know on which of you I shall first lay my finger. What you say of me in your letter to Mr. Richard is very flattering; yours and Mr. Reynolds's good opinions must be no small argument to me of my own importance, which you will have no difficulty of believing, as you know but too well how ready my vanity is to catch at any thing that may do me credit, and you must allow that it can no where meet with what is more grateful to it than in the present instance: to be at all thought of by such people is a stimulus that must oblige one to stretch every nerve to endeavour to merit it.

As soon as I can obtain permission I shall set about copying the Alexander I mentioned to you.[316] It will be more profitable to me to be about it than any thing else, and though you may not be inclined to keep it, you may give it to somebody or other. The academies are open at night only, so that copying that or any other picture will not interfere with my attendance there.[317]

---

314 Secretary to Burke's friend, Charles Lennox, 3rd Duke of Richmond (1735–1806), who had recently been appointed Ambassador in Paris.
315 An allusion not least to the fact that the Burkes were financing Barry's studies in France (and, later, Italy).
316 In his letter to Burke on 5 December 1765, Barry had expressed great admiration for the painting by Eustache Le Sueur (*c*.1616–55), *La maladie d'Alexandre*, which he wanted to copy for Edmund Burke.
317 Barry attended L'Académie de Saint-Luc, founded in 1649, in the rue du Haut-Moulin; classes were given in drawing, sculpture, architecture, geometry and perspective. The drawing classes were free and lasted two hours every day; the models changed on Mondays and Thursdays (Jules Guiffrey, *Histoire de l'Académie de Saint-Luc* (1915: Paris: Nobele, 1970), 26–7, 42). Courses were much the same as at the Académie Royale founded by Louis XIV in 1648.

The varnished paper which Mr. Richard Burke wrote to you of is to be had here,[318] we did not know it then, and you will excuse the mentioning it to you. My most sincere love and respects to the Doctor, to Mrs. Burke and the family, and to Mr. Macleane. Mr. Drumgold would be obliged to the Doctor to let him know the title of Malcom's book on the Scotch and British antiquities.[319]

I am, dear Sir,
       Yours with great respect and sincerity,
                          J. B.

I would have wrote to Mr. Barrett, to Mr. Creagh, and others of my friends, but that I have the greatest aversion to letter writing, though nobody wishes his friends better than I do. I find in myself at times a strong disposition to saunter and idle about here; one may do it with profit: the leisure I have from visits is employed in remarks upon and sketching of what I see, so that I hope my friends will be indulgent enough to accept of my good wishes, which, whether I write or not, is always sure to attend them.

Paris [*c*.11 February 1766]

Dear Sirs,

Doubtless Mr. Richard Burke has got home by this time, he must have had a disagreeable journey of it, for the weather has been much colder since his setting out on the road than it was since I came to France. The Seine was frozen over in about two days, for the second time this winter.[320] The academies are all shut up on account of the extreme cold, and probably I shall be shut out for some time from copying at the palais-royal for the same reason, as they won't permit it till the weather is a little warm, so as to do without fire.[321] Though I know you all to be very busy at this time, about important

---

318 Varnished paper was sometimes used for small oil sketches. Barry had asked Richard Burke to see if Edmund Burke could find it in London; then Barry and Richard found some in Paris.

319 David Malcolm, *An Essay on the Antiquities of Great Britain and Ireland* (Edinburgh: T. and W. Ruddimans, 1738).

320 It was not unusual for the River Seine running through Paris to freeze over; such was the severe weather in Paris this February that the magistrates arranged that 'two pounds of bread were daily distributed to every poor person' (*Gentleman's Magazine*, February 1766, 97).

321 The cold spell meant Barry could not yet start work on his copy for Burke of the picture by Eustache Le Sueur in the Palais Royal.

matters, yet I shall not insult you so far as to think of making an apology for mentioning small ones. I am conscious there are heads in the world pregnant with everything that is deep and weighty, and yet find no distraction by an attention to trifles, and it is enough for me that I know whom I write to. After this proem[322] I shall begin by telling you that I don't like an academy; it is a thing which, wherever it is founded will, I think, bring the arts into contempt, and consequently to destruction.[323] We have two of them here, the academy of St. Luke and the Royal Academy: there are such mobs of blackguards go every night to acquire a trade there, as is enough to shock any one who has the least regard for the art. People send their children to make them painters and statuaries[324] (without learning, genius, or indeed any thing else) only because it is less expensive than making them perukiers or shoemakers. I need not observe to you how much these fellows must befoul every thing they lay their hands upon, and how much more than probable it is, that the contempt they must naturally bring upon the art, will be succeeded by the destruction and annihilation of it. To be sure it is very true, that drawing and modelling after nature in the academy, with the assistance of a master, is not likely to mislead any one, and must be useful to a man of real genius, who has all the requisites which are so essential in art, the most complex of all things; but how unlikely is it, when after some time these locusts are spread far and near over every thing, that any man will apply to an art, or rather that any man will be at the expense and pains of acquiring such essentials in an art, that is not only without reputation (the great stimulus) but that is sunk into contempt and nothingness. It is with great pleasure that I recollect your dislike to the founding of an academy in England. The truth of a remark of yours was not as evident to me then as it is now, how that without an academy the English were making great strides after perfection, whilst others, with one, were every day more and more losing sight of it, that our people will go on still farther I have no doubt, and that it will be without an academy, I wish most ardently. There are many advantages here, which the coldness of the season will not suffer me to enjoy, in the mean time I have hired out some busts and casts of the antique, which I study in my own room. Mr. Richard Burke will be

---

322 'A preface, preamble' (OED).
323 Discussions about establishing an academy of art in England had started in earnest in 1756 and were now reaching a crucial stage. The Burkes would have kept Barry aware of developments. By the time the Royal Academy in London had been established by George III on 10 December 1768, Barry still had reservations; he told Burke in January 1769, 'I am not over and above pleased with the founding of an Academy in England' (Barry to Burke, 10 January 1769).
324 Sculptors of statues.

angry with me when I tell him, I have not been to make any of the visits he recommended to me since his departure.

I am, dear sirs,
>Yours always,
>>J. B.

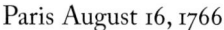

Paris August 16, 1766.

Dear Sirs,

I have finished and brought home the copy last Wednesday, and only wish for a safe opportunity of sending it to you.[325] Mr. Macleane was to have been here before this time, and it was my intention to have left it with him; if he does not arrive before I go, I shall entrust it to the care of Mr. Crammond or Mr. Wilkes.[326] Of the merit or demerit of the copy, I shall say nothing, but there have been no pains or inclination wanting on my side to make it as exactly like, and to preserve as much the spirit of the original as I could—this was my sole object from the beginning; and those artists who have seen them together, think that I have not been unsuccessful in it. I believe I mentioned to you before my opinion of the manliness and gravity which reign throughout the original, in the characters and dispositions of the figures, the colouring, and masterly style of drapery. The taste of Le Sueur must have been of a very different texture from the glitter and puerility, which is so much admired in some of our rising young people in England. In Le Sueur the essentials are studied with the last degree of nobleness and precision, whilst the most inferior things are not neglected. The others are hunting after peacocks' feathers, and gewgaws to lick up and trim the outside with, never considering whether the kernel, body, or soul of the matter be there or not; for it is absolutely impossible for the mind that is little enough to relish such things, ever to have any thing like a thought about the others.[327] Comparing these people together, I think

---

325 Barry had finished the painting during the warmer weather (See n. 321). He was now concerned as to how to have it transported to London.

326 Crammond is not identified; possibly a member of the British embassy staff in Paris. John Wilkes (1727–97) had fled to Paris in 1763 after his paper *North Briton*, no. 45 had been declared a seditious libel. Although Wilkes was an MP, his parliamentary privilege did not protect him from being charged; after an unsuccessful visit to London in May, when he hoped to negotiate a pardon, he returned to Paris in July. Barry had probably met Wilkes in Paris through either Burke's brother Richard or Lauchlin Macleane.

327 A commonplace criticism, especially of English portrait painting. Barry was to write later: 'Being attached to little things, we came naturally to admire and to over-rate the little men who succeeded in them; one admirer builds upon the admiration of another,

one may see that the corruption and decline of art arises from an over attention to the ornamental parts. Those who best understood oratory and poetry ascribe their fall to this cause.[328] The warmest advocates for modern music (I mean, as it is distinguished and separated from poetry, such as Sonatas, &c.) have nothing to shew us but unisons, harmony, and what not; they must confess its powers and impressions to reach no farther than the nerves, whilst they leave to other arts the understanding and the passions.[329] It only concerns painting to be divested of all kind of scheme and story, and reduced to a mere harmonical assemblage of blue, green, red, and yellow colours, and it may be made as tickling and agreeable to the eye, as the other is to the ear: it has been more than once attempted, and with the same success, but such contemptible tricks are beneath censure. The vestiges of antiquity have been the inlet and guide in other arts; unhappily nothing of this kind remained for the musicians to form themselves upon,[330] so that I cannot say positively, if it is not the single circumstance of its being of modern Gothic[331] invention, that has turned me so much against it. I may venture to say as much as this without knowing either the geometrical musical proportions, or the management of any instrument. Whether or not, I will affirm with confidence, that in the arts which I know any thing of, it is evidently the case: the French architecture is entirely daubed over with the beautiful things of art, from Versailles and the Thuilleries to the

---

    until this mole-hill grows up into a mountain and bounds our prospect' ('An Inquiry into the Real and Imaginary Obstructions to the Acquisition of the Arts in England' (1774), *Works of James Barry*, ii, 246).

328 Johann Wincklemann, citing Quintillian — the Roman writer on education — makes the same point: 'corruption has at all times crept into the style of writing, and thus music, renouncing its manly tones, degenerated like art into the effeminate. The actual excellence in any production is frequently lost by the very care with which it is elaborated' (Johann Joachim Winckelmann, *History of Ancient Art*, 3 vols, translated by G. Henry Lodge (1880; Bristol: Thoemmes, 2001), iii, 144).

329 Notable among theorists of harmony was the French musician Jean-Philippe Rameau (1683–1764) who wrote extensively on the subject, and was translated into English. Barry voices a widely held view that eighteeth-century music, unaccompanied by words, was of limited value; such music provided sensuous pleasure but was powerless on its own to achieve the ultimate purpose of the arts — to move the passions: 'A great part of our fashionable music seems intended rather to tickle and astonish the hearers, than to inspire them with any permanent emotions' (James Beattie, *Essay on Poetry and Music, as They Affect the Mind*, 3rd edition (London: Dilly, 1779), 150).

330 Charles Burney remarked of ancient Greek writers on music, 'we have nothing left but the names' (*A General History of Music, from the Earliest Ages to the Present Period*, 2nd edition (London: Burney, 1789), iii).

331 'Barbarous, rude, uncouth, unpolished, in bad taste' (OED).

palace of Louis XV.[332] Indeed it must be granted that their painters are far from being luxuriant or excessive in point of colouring; on the contrary, (this is only what we promise) they are in the other slovenly, dirty extreme, Their affectation lies in the extravagance of expression and attitude, in over-doing the adventitious and decorative parts; Pierre and Boucher will be, whilst they are known, striking instances of the grimace of expression, and the outrè and maniere of attitude.[333] A retrospect on the periods of improvement of art would still more considerably enforce and elucidate this. The first artists went no farther than the mere inanimate man, horse, &c.. The succeeding race made this man, &c. doing something; action, story, and expression were added.[334] Posterity were busied in the establishing, adding strength to the expression, beauty to the colouring, and ornament and decoration to the subordinate parts. People who were very able to determine whether this was like a man, horse, &c. or whether this seemed to speak, that to hear, were no longer masters of correct opinions, when matters became more complex, when profusion, ornament, and glitter were poured out before them. If truth and nature are plainly laid down before ordinary capacities, no one is at any loss about it; but it is too true that folly or extravagance of every kind may be so trimmed up, so varnished over, as to establish itself in the most popular manner, to the exclusion of every thing else. On recollection, it were better, I believe, I had not wandered so far in matters I am so likely to be mistaken in; but I am easy, as my errors will be far from having any weight in your judgment, whilst they furnish your good nature and indulgence to me with an opportunity of exerting itself. You will probably repent your having let me know that you like the little remarks I have hitherto made, as it will, when I have any leisure, incline me to tire you with them. I shall

---

332 Versailles, the magificent royal palace outside Paris, built for Louis XIV at the end of the seventeenth century; the Tuileries Palace, in the centre of Paris, constructed for Catherine de Medicis (1519–89), widow of Henry II of France (1519–59), in the sixteenth century; the Place Louis XV, renamed Place de la Concorde after the French Revolution. This part of Paris was developed in the mid-eighteenth century as part of the plan 'pour célébrer le culte monarchique au coeur de la cité' (Jean Chagniot, *Nouvelle Histoire de Paris: Paris aux XVIIIe siècle* (Paris: Hachette, 1988), 154).

333 French painter Jean-Baptiste Marie Pierre (1713–89) had recently succeeded the artist and designer Francois Boucher (1703–70) as director of painting at Les Gobelins in Paris. 'Outré': 'eccentric, unorthodox' (OED); 'maniere', or 'maniéré': 'affected, precious'. Barry echoes Diderot's criticism of Boucher whom he called 'maniéré': 'je dis maniéré, et ce mot s'étend au dessin, à la couleur et à toutes les parties de la peinture' (*Correspondance littéraire*, ii (2), July 1758, 340).

334 Cf. Winckelmann: 'In the course of time, increasing knowledge taught the Etruscans and Greek artists how to forsake the stiff and motionless conformations of their earliest essays… and enabled them to express different actions in their figures' *(History of Ancient Art*, ii, 141).

think of setting out for Italy about the next week, with a heart full of spirits and alacrity, and thank God with excellent health. I have remaining eight louis d'ors, and as I shall want some few shirts and a coat, I shall I believe, apply to Mr. Panshaw, for seven or eight more.[335] I have been here a good part of my time, in a most unfixed, idle manner, which made my expenses more than I hope they will be hereafter when I get to Rome.

You will make me the happiest man in the world, in contriving to send my chest off to Rome, as soon as possible, as I shan't know how to do without some things in it. Farewell, and God bless you my dear sirs, I shall, wherever I am, remain most sincerely,

Your obliged humble servant,

J.B.

My best respects to my dear friend the doctor, to Mrs. Burke, Mr. Nugent, Mr. Ozier, and all friends. My compliments to Mr. Reynolds, Mr. Barrett, Mr Hamilton, &c.[336]

Turin, Sept. 24, 1766.

My Dear Sirs,

I left Paris the 7th of this month, and had, thank God! a most agreeable journey. The weather being extremely fine, the country of Burgundy, and the other southern parts of France, made a most delicious appearance, being at that time teeming over with all the riches and abundance of autumn. We may in England talk as much as we please of cultivation and plenty, but I must honestly confess, that I never before saw any thing but the faint glimmerings of it, compared with this country, where nature seems ambitious of doing every thing herself. The people, who are extremely numerous, are (or seemed to me to be) for the most part, very amply employed in the gathering and storing up of fruits. Methinks without any great poetical amplification, it is

---

335 Panshaw was probably a banker or agent in Paris; the Burkes were financing Barry and he could draw money as he needed on their London agents, Nugent and Netterville. The 'louis d'or' was the gold coin introduced by Louis XIII (1601–43), and in use until the French Revolution, bearing the head of the king; its value varied.

336 John ('Jack') Nugent (1737–1813), brother of Mrs Burke, a surveyor of Customs in London; Ozier not identified; Hugh Douglas Hamilton (1736–1808), Irish painter from Dublin who came to work in London in 1764, and then moved to Italy where he made a name for himself painting portraits of British and Irish travellers on the Grand Tour; a friend also of George Barret.

somewhat probable, when Bacchus[337] made his rounds of the earth, that his head quarters must have been in one of the vallies of Burgundy, where on every side mountain peeps over mountain, and appears cloathed in all the variegated hues of the vine, interspersed with sheep, corn, and I may say, with every thing. This, and the crouds of busy contented people, which cover (as one may say) the whole face of the country, make a strong, but melancholy contrast to a miserable—which I cannot help thinking of sometimes.—You will not be at any loss to know that I mean Ireland; and that I glance at the extensive, unpeopled wastes where only now and then one is to see some meagre, scared fellow, who has almost a day's journey to drive cattle to a habitation, where his ill-fated family perhaps may make a Christmas dinner upon the offals of these very cattle; very little of which falls to his share out of the market that is made of them for other countries,—but hang them all, I have long since given them up,[338] and will go on to give you such accounts of the Alps as I can, though I should repeat, as I often do, what you know already, and have much better informations of than I can possibly give you.

From the confines of France over mount Cenis,[339] to within about thirty miles of Turin, we have been in one continued ascent, though strictly speaking it was all the way through Savoy, up and down the horrid ridges of the mountains, and sometimes in the most gloomy vales between them, which would have made it almost impossible to say whether we were upon the rise or fall in general, if it was not for a great river,[340] by the side of which our road lay, and which takes its rise near mount Cenis, and tumbles and cascades all the way through rocks and precipices, into France. You may conceive how high its source must be by this observation (which I think is pretty just) that in every hundred yards taken one with another, it cascades near twenty feet at

---

337 Mythological god of agriculture in the ancient world and, in this context, associated with wine.
338 Ireland exported much of its beef and butter to England, the Continent and the colonies through Barry's home city of Cork; French ships 'were accorded by French law the quite exceptional permission of calling to Irish ports to load beef directly for the colonies' (L. M. Cullen, *An Economic History of Ireland Since 1660* (London: Batsford, 1972), 55). Barry's hostility to Ireland was later replaced by sympathy: see for example his 'Account of a Series of Pictures' (1783), *Works of Barry*, ii, 458–61. His Commonplace Book shows he had read Geoffrey Keating's *Foras Feasa ar Éirinn* (The Basis of Knowledge concerning Ireland) (c.1632) and Sylvester O'Halloran's *General History of Ireland*, 2 vols (London: Hamilton, 1778); he was also an admirer of Irish patriot writers Jonathan Swift (1667–1745) and William Molyneux (1656–98).
339 The passage over the Alps by the Mont Cenis pass (c.2,000 metres) was described with varying degrees of alarm by several travellers.
340 The river Arc, which rises in the Mont Levanna glaciers, then joins the Isère and flows into France.

least; then taking in the length of the way, you will believe me much nearer heaven upon mount Cenis than I was before, or shall probably be again for some time. We passed this mountain on Sunday last, and about seven in the morning were near the top of the road over it, on both sides of which the mountain rises to a very great height, yet so high were we in the valley between them (where there is a fine and large lake) that the moon, which was above the horizon of the mountains, appeared at least five times as big as usual, and much more distinctly marked than I ever saw it through some very good telescopes. The mountains, seas, &c. were so evident, their lines of separation so traceable, that I would actually have stopped the mule to have made a drawing of them, if I had not been in some apprehensions of a troop of Savoyard soldiers, who were at that time passing, and would doubtless have taken me up as a spy and a dangerous person.[341] I was more than once cautioned how I let any of these people see me drawing, at which I was constantly employed all the way. My friend Barret was exceedingly out in his notions of Savoy and the Alpine country. The drawings he saw of them might be, as he said, bird's eye views—but had he been here himself, he would have made a very different work of it; he would have seen, as I did, for above five days together, the most awful and horridly grand, romantic, and picturesque scenes, that it is possible to conceive; he would say every thing else was but bauble and boys play compared with them. All this tract down to Grenoble, one sees was the country Salvator Rosa formed himself upon: nobody esteems Salvator more than I do, yet I must say he has not made half the use of it he might have done; the wild forms of his trees, rocks, &c.[342] (for which he is condemned, as frantic, by some cold spiritless artists, whose notions reach no further than the artificial regular productions of their own climes,) are infinitely short of the noble phrenzy in which nature wantons all over these mountains; great pines, of the most inconceivable diversity of forms, some straight as arrows, others crooked as a horn, some the roots uppermost, are hanging over frightful rocks and caves, and torrents of water rolling amongst them.

But I should lose myself in attempting to speak of them, and shall reserve for the colours and canvass the observations I have made. Though in the best

---

341   The Savoyard soldiery presumed themselves guardians of the Alpine passes; their reputed suspicion, even hostility to travellers, dated back to wars between the Savoyards and Louis XIV of France, who threatened their capital, Turin.

342   Salvator Rosa (1615–73), prolific Italian painter independent in style, flamboyant in personality; his landscape paintings are characterised by 'wild forms of trees, rocks &c'. Barry's enthusiasm was not unusual: the poet James Thomson (1700–48) had called him 'savage Rosa' in *The Castle of Indolence* (I, xxxviii), and Reynolds said his paintings had 'that sort of dignity which belongs to savage and uncultivated nature' (*Seven Discourses Delivered in the Royal Academy by the President* (London: T. Cadell, 1778), 175).

hands any of these views painted singly must fail in its effect in comparison of the reality, where the continued succession of them leads on and advances the operation. One thing by the way, the people are just the species of figures for such a landscape; though I believe they may be honest as they are said to be, yet every countenance has that ferocity and assassin look, which Salvator Rosa has so truly, and so agreeably to the costume, introduced into his pictures. Lest you may be tired with the length of this letter, I shall keep the king's collection at Turin,[343] and other things, for the next, and I am, my dear sir, your's and the family's,

With great respect and sincerity,

J. B.

Two days before my departure from Paris I left your picture with Mr. Crammond, who is either to give it to Mr. Macleane, or to forward it by some opportunity.

Rome, November 2, 1766.

Dear Sir,

The receipt of your two letters, the day before yesterday, made me extremely happy, as I will do myself the justice to say, that I feel as I ought to do every thing that concerns and is interesting to the few friends God has blessed me with. I am now almost ashamed to write to Mr. Macleane, lest it may be thought that the desire of honouring myself with the acquaintance and connexion of the Secretary is more prevalent with me than any love for his person or sense of the favours he has conferred upon me.[344] There is all the apparent reason in the world to be shocked at my baseness and ingratitude in never writing to him, even after he desired it; but as I have no thought of concealing any part of my conduct from you, I shall out with the truth, though I may suffer by it in your opinion.

---

343 Charles Emmanuel III, (1701–73), King of Sardinia, great-grandson of Charles I of England, lived in Turin where he built up a collection of artefacts, frequently visited by Tourists; James Boswell noted that the King's museum had 'a very curious collection of antiquities and natural curiosities' (*Boswell on the Grand Tour: Germany and Switzerland 1763–1764*, 30).

344 Barry is writing to William Burke, whose recent letters told him Macleane (see n. 308) had been appointed Undersecretary to William Petty, 2nd Earl of Shelburne (1737–1805), Secretary of State in Lord Chatham's administration; he had facilitated Barry's letter of introduction from Lord Shelburne to the British envoy in Florence, Sir Horace Mann (1706–86). Barry was to deliver the letter personally to Mann; it would ease his entry to museums and private galleries.

Mr. Macleane, with his usual warmth and good nature, has been often interrogating me upon my allowance,[345] and insisting upon adding to it annually. He used every different mode of friendly persuasion, telling me how much it would be obliging him to have an opportunity of being serviceable to any body you interested yourselves about, and I avoided writing to him, merely to take away any opportunity of his doing what in my opinion I ought not to have accepted of. There is no longer any reason for this disagreeable conduct in me, now that I find I shall be able, with God's help, to live very happily upon about forty pounds a year, whilst in my studies; though for the present year my voyage and the buying of furniture and other necessaries, will unavoidably make it more. I am exceedingly distressed to know what to do about Lord Shelburne's letter. It is five or six weeks since I have left Florence, and did not know any thing of this letter till the day before yesterday: if you tell me by the return of the post, that it is necessary to go back to Florence and deliver it, I shall do it directly, or in a month, or two months, just as you think it may be proper. A good part of my time may be excellently employed at Florence after the antique and other things there, and it is but 150 miles off: the journey will not be very expensive,[346] and I shall set off the very instant you appoint for it. You will be so kind as to let me know about this by the return of the post, as I perfectly agree with you in thinking that such a letter ought to be minutely attended to.

I am, dear sir,
    Yours,
        J. B.

Rome [July 1767].

Dear Sirs,

We subscribe for the newspapers here, so that once a week, as changes were talked of, I had long since hopes of hearing something agreeable.[347] Though I do not wish to give you often the trouble of writing, yet I should be glad to hear that all the family are well, that Mr. Richard is well recovered, and whatever else you please. I have more than once suspected that your silence was owing to your disapprobation of my conduct in having any disputes with the people here; but it was a thing, that, though I never sought for, I could not well have avoided, as I was at that time ignorant of the kind of conduct necessary for this

---

345 Edmund and William Burke gave Barry an allowance of about £40 a year while he was studying on the Continent.

346 The journey from Rome to Florence cost 3/6d per stage, and 3/6d for lodging per night (Thomas Nugent, *The Grand Tour* (London: A. Miller, 1749), iii, 39–40).

347 The air of impending change in English politics had also been noted by Caroline Lennox in January 1767 (see p. 244); the Chatham administration collapsed in 1768.

place; but our bickerings have subsided a good while, and we live together very agreeably, and are likely to continue so.

I found upon a little consideration, that any copies after Raffael in the Vatican,[348] would have answered no purpose to you, as the whole composition of any pictures would be too large, and any particular part and group would come indifferently enough by itself, deprived of its relation to the other parts and story of the pictures. There are single figures of the virtues, &c. painted in many parts of the stanzas,[349] but I believe you would as little relish copies of them as I should the being employed about them; the only thing, that I could discover, where I believe we shall be both satisfied, is the history of Cupid and Psyche, which is painted in the angles, (or compartments) of the little Farnese.[350] There are a good many of them, consisting of two, three, or four figures each, and designed in the highest gusto of Raffael. You will see prints of them at Mr. Reynolds's. The figures are as large as life; but I mean to copy them nearly in the Poussin size, as the more convenient for you.[351] As I am thoroughly satisfied of the entire superiority of about seven or eight antique statues, I thought studying those a little would enable me to succeed in copying Raffael. Accordingly I have obtained a licence for six months, and have been at work in the Capitol after the statues for some time past, and I shall be ready to go to the little Farnese about the latter end of February next, please God. There are also some things in the Capella Sistina,[352] which will answer our purpose. I confess I have a difficulty more than ordinary in studying here, as my stay is not a little expensive to you. I shall after three or four months spent on the antique, endeavour to contrive it so, as that what I shall do may answer the end of pictures for you, whilst they will be studies to me, as I do not find much relish for any thing here except the antique, Raffael, and Michael Angelo.[353] About three years will complete what I mean to do. I have hitherto waved speaking out my whole opinion about Michael Angelo and Raffael, for a reason which should still incline me to be silent—they so often come near perfection, and so often depart from it in the same particulars, that I believe it

---

348 Barry had offered to copy a work by Raphael (1483–1520) for Burke in the papal rooms in the Vatican. Raphael's frescoes covering the ceilings of the rooms are often referred to as the Loggia di Raffaello.
349 Stanza: 'In Italy, an apartment, chamber, room… applied to certain rooms in the Vatican' (OED).
350 Raphael's frescoes of the story of the mythical figures Cupid and Psyche were in the Villa Farnesina belonging to the Roman banker Agostino Chigi (c.1465–1520).
351 A painting of Cupid and Psyche by Nicolas Poussin (1594–1665) measured 76.7 cm × 56.6 cm; Poussin had studied Raphael's work in the Farnese.
352 The Sistine Chapel.
353 Michel Angelo Buonarroti (1475–1564), distinguished Italian sculptor and painter.

impossible almost to draw up a general character of them,—I mean in those particulars where we may set up the antique as the standard. I see in no part of Raffael's works, any figure that I may call truly and correctly beautiful, like the Antinous or the Venus de Medicis; or any that is truly grand, like the bust of the Alexander; or sublime like the Apollo:[354] as to the Torso,[355] the Laocoon,[356] and such like characters, he appears not at all qualified to succeed in them. The Angels which I shall copy at the little Farnese, appear to be the utmost stretch of his capacity in point of beauty and character; and upon a comparison with similar figures and characters of the antique, those of Raffael seem to be much wanting in a correct idea of the detail, and in an equality of proportion and correctness in the same figures. As to his cartoons, and his pictures in the Vatican, they may be more expressive of the passions, and may be more correct in a mediocrity of character—a little more than that, which comes into any of these works, or even into his Transfiguration.[357] In short, there is neither figure nor character in Raffael which is standard in its way. Michael Angelo appears still less near the standard than Raffael; the few pictures that remain of him, and certain severities of manner, as well as a choice of subject, in some measure out of the way of beauty, make one inclined to rate him not so highly as he ought. He is infinitely above Raffael in point of knowledge and correctness, yet his ostentation and shew of this, and Raffael's art of concealing, with choice of subject and pleasing well wrought draperies, his want of it, bring them nearly to a level, at least with the bulk of mankind—yet I rather believe fewer people have attained Michael Angelo's merits than Raffael's, though no one has come

---

354 The Antinous, a sculpture in the Belvedere of the handsome young favourite of the emperor Hadrian (76–138) who drowned in the Nile while accompanying the emperor; classical Greek sculpture in marble of Venus, in the Uffizi gallery; the bust of Alexander the Great in the Capitoline Museum, Rome; marble statue of Apollo, the mythological god associated with the sun and light, in the Belvedere gallery, the Vatican.

355 The Belvedere Torso, a fragment, probably of a statue of Hercules, by a Greek sculptor, was displayed in the courtyard of the Belevedere in Rome. Joseph Addison (1672–1719) wrote of it: 'Among the many famous Pieces of Antiquity which are still to be seen at Rome, there is the Trunc of a Statue which has lost the Arms, Legs and Head, but discovers such an exquisite Workmanship in what remains of it, that Michael Angelo declared he had learned his whole Art from it' (*The Spectator*, no. 229). The Torso features in the right-hand background of Barry's *Self-portrait* (1767).

356 *Laocoön and his Sons* (second century BC) a group in marble of the Trojan priest Laocoön, and his two sons, strangled by serpents (cf. Virgil, *Aeneid*, ii, 199–231); Laocoön had warned the Trojans in vain against the Greeks' wooden horse.

357 Raphael's *The Transfiguration* (410 cm × 279 cm) in the Vatican was painted on wood (*c.*1519–20), the subject taken from the gospel of Luke 9: 28–36.

near Raffael upon the whole. Michael Angelo's Moses,[358] and many other things of his, are rather extravagant, though accompanied with such proofs of knowledge and capacity as will for ever make his name sacred among artists. Now, I have prevailed with myself to say almost all the ill that may be said of those two fathers of painting, you will, I hope, do me the justice to remember, that I have the highest and justest sense of the beauty, elegance, and propriety of Raffael; though I believe them rather, perhaps, diffused amongst his works, than to be found in any particular one; and I hope to give you some, though a faint idea of Michael Angelo's grandeur, knowledge, and even elegance and beauty in some of his figures and stories in the compartments of the ceiling of the Systine Chapel.

There is a great bustle here at fitting up of palaces and preparing operas against the coming of the Emperor, which will be in the latter end of the year. He is to lodge, it is said, at the Villa Medici,[359] just near my quarters, so that I shall have an opportunity of spinning out a letter or two with a description of his person.

There was a very melancholy accident happened here two days ago. The daughter of one D'Auprat, (a wine merchant in the place D'Espagne,[360] and well known to all the English who come here,) really a very fine girl, as to her person, and still more remarkable for her knowledge and practice in drawing, music, and languages, living and dead.—This girl was in love with a person whose affairs some time since obliged him to leave Rome. The father, in order to wean his daughter from a match he did not approve of, forged a letter, giving an account of the marriage of his daughter's lover. Shortly after which the daughter took the first opportunity of stealing out and throwing herself into the Tyber. Whilst she was in the water some people reached out things by which she might have saved herself, but she refused all assistance, and with a melancholy firmness plunged out into the depths of the river. Amongst the various reasonings here on this unhappy accident, some ascribe it to a contagion she might get from the English,[361] who used to lodge at her father's; but the generality believe it was occasioned by her reading books, and making those compacts with the devil, which is usual with such as are deep learned. Since as much learning and knowledge is in your family, as there is good nature, if it be

---

358 Michael Angelo's statue of Moses for the tomb of Pope Julius II in the Church of St Peter in Chains, Rome.
359 Joseph II (1765–90) of Austria, Holy Roman Emperor, was expected to visit Rome this summer and to stay in the villa built by the Medici family, next to the Borghese gardens, renowned for its collection of sculptures.
360 Near the Trevi fountain in the heart of Rome. Barry collected his mail from the English coffee house there.
361 Perhaps a coded reference to venereal disease or unwanted pregnancy.

proportioned with its quantity of diabolical influence, Dr. Nugent and three or four more of the family are very deep in it. You will please to remember me to them all, to Mr. Macleane, Mr. Reynolds, Mr. Barrett, and Messrs. Hamilton, English,[362] and whoever else you please.

———◆◇◆———

Rome, February 26, 1768.

My dear Will,[363]

I waited ever since the receipt of your letter to no purpose, in expectation of being able to send you this by hand.

It was unlucky our not meeting in Paris, but you had not advised me of the time I should expect to see you there. My stay in Rome will be for two years and a half longer, and then I shall set out, God willing, for Florence and Venice, where I shall stay half a year, or so,—then on through Flanders to England, where I hope to be at farthest in about four years hence. The vast collections here of statues by the old Greeks and Romans, and pictures of the Italians in Julius II. and Leo X.'s times, are the masters I attach myself to.[364] The art being almost dwindled away to nothing amongst the present race of Italians, of whom, without fear of saying too much, it may be affirmed safer and better to avoid, than to imitate.

Arts follow in the train of Minerva,[365] or, to be less figurative, arts generally, if not always, accompany knowledge and power, and are surely not to be found existing amongst the people who have little either of the one or the other. This is one reason why we should be the less surprised to see the descendants of naked Picts, and savage islanders,[366] rising in the arts of elegance and refinement in nearly the same proportion that Greece, and other nations,

---

362 Thomas English (c.1725–98), had assisted Edmund Burke on the *Annual Register*.
363 The letter was addressed to William O'Brien, brother of Charles O'Brien, Barry's boyhood friend in Cork who was travelling in France.
364 Julius II (1443–1513), Pope from 1503, commissioned many of the major works by Raphael and Michael Angelo; he was succeeded by Pope Leo X (1475–1521), a notable patron of Raphael.
365 Minerva, Roman goddess of the arts, particularly of painting, in Barry's view: 'the employment for which Minerva is peculiarly distinguished from all the celestial personages, is her skill in the labours of the loom… she was sovereignly skilful in the art of painting in tapestry, and could employ that universal language of forms, both actual and possible, to all the grand, ethical purposes of information, persuasion, and instruction' ('Letter to the Dilettanti Society', (1798), *Works of James Barry*, ii, 585). Barry imaged Minerva in several of his works, for example *The Birth of Pandora*.
366 The Picts were tribes of Scotland dating from pre-Christian times. Burke discussed them and early Britain in his (unfinished) *Abridgment of English History*; Barry may be

have been sinking and falling from them,—but enough of this, or I shall run into a history of the ancients and moderns, and the migration of the sciences, and what not, which however would be less criminal than beginning again to advise, and as I now do, to recommend a certain course of reading to you.

I know of nothing, my dear Will, that can excuse these liberties that I take so frequently, if you do not ascribe it to a friendship evidently warm and sincere, though perhaps very little to the purpose. Agreeably to the practice of most men of study you probably have a bye course of reading,[367] which you prosecute in your moments of leisure and retirement from your profession and main object.—Now, considering how much the acquisition of taste and elegance of thinking in all the fashionable arts, is thought to depend on our knowledge of the ancients, and particularly the Greeks, I would recommend to you the reading often, if not translations of a few of the principal Greek writers, at least, compilations from them, such as the ancient history of Rollin,[368] &c. and you may easily run through Plato, Zenophon, Pindar,[369] and the few others. French translations may be had in abundance, as well as English; if you can resist this temptation, you may very well content yourself with Rollin. It is a very agreeable piece of entertainment to trace step after step, the different periods of improvement in knowledge and arts; and though this makes but an under part, and is generally overlooked as such, yet— —but I will here check myself again, as I cannot conceive how the devil I come to turn adviser and director, especially to one who is in so little need of it as you are. Perhaps it is because I have so little to inform you of concerning myself; two or three words being sufficient for that, viz. that I am incessantly studying old statues, heads, and legs, &c. &c. Besides, I can say nothing of the place or its curiosities that would not appear worn out to you; who must have read every thing that can be said upon these matters in the books of travels and descriptions. The conveniencies to be had here in matters of study, make my time pass away very agreeably. It is perhaps the greatest satisfaction most of us enjoy here. We are

---

    alluding to such writers on the early Britons as Caesar, *De Bello Gallico*, v, 14, Tacitus, *Agricola*, and Dio Cassius lxxvii, 12–13.

367 A bye course: 'The opposite of main—of secondary importance, casual or incidental' (OED).

368 The French historian Charles Rollin (1661–1741) produced two major works on ancient history, *Histoire ancienne des Egyptiens, des Carthaginois, des Assyriens, des Babyloniens, des Medes et des Perses, des Macédoniens, des Grecs* (Paris: Estienne, 1730–7), and *Histoire romaine, depuis la fondation de Rome, jusqu'à la bataille d'Actium* (Paris: Estienne, 1741); these were translated into English as *Ancient History* and *Roman History* and appeared in many forms during the eighteenth century.

369 Plato (427–347 BC) celebrated Greek philosopher, author of *The Republic*; Zenophon (435–354 BC), writer on history, economics and philosophy; Pindar (*c.*522–443 BC), famous Greek lyric poet.

in number about thirty students, English, Scotch, and Irish; and as there is in our art every thing to set the passions of men afloat, all desiring consequence and superiority; it is no wonder if distrust, concealed hatred, and ungenerous attempts, are perhaps oftener experienced, than friendship, dignity of mind, or open square[370] conduct.

If you have heard any thing lately from Cork, insert it in your next, as it is now a year good[371] since I received any letter from that place. I am almost tempted to think there is something the matter in my family, which may be the occasion of this silence. Mr. Brabant,[372] the Dane, has last week set out for Naples; as I am uncertain whether you will receive this, I have no inclination to spin it out to any greater length.

You should have mentioned how long you intended staying in Thoulouse, whether you purposed fixing there, or returning to Paris; to no one of such questions could I receive the least satisfying answer in your letter, as you only speak of taking a trip to Thoulouse next month. This is all you say on that article. I am obliged to you for the mention you make of your brother's success—you do me but justice to think I am interested in whatever concerns you. Your next will, I hope, bring better news of your health. Thank God, I can complain of nothing.—My health, vigour, and spirits, suffer no alloy, and my pension is just sufficient to make the two ends meet together. Direct your letter to Monsieur Wm.[373] Barry, gentilhomme, Anglois, à au Caffe Anglois à Rome. Never mind postage,[374] let me have a letter from you directly, and fill it with what you please, so you fill it.

Rome, September 30, 1768.

Dear Sirs,

I am so much out of humour with myself for not answering sooner your very kind letter of July last, that I believe you will be easier satisfied with my old apology of application to study than I shall be myself. There is a particular in your letter I do not understand, you say, 'I am glad of Hamilton's opinion, it cannot fail of being serviceable to you some way or other.'[375] What this alludes

---

370   'Honest or straightforward' (OED).
371   Inversion for 'a good year'.
372   Unidentified.
373   'Wm.' may be an error for 'Js' (James) which was how Barry often wrote his initial.
374   Postal charges could be paid by the recipient of the letter.
375   Burke to Barry, 19 July 1768. (Sir) William Hamilton (1730–1803), British Minister at Naples and noted patron of the arts; he greatly admired the painting of Adam and Eve that Barry was working on.

to I know not. Another particular in your letter also has altered the plan I laid down to myself, of making copies of my studies here; your house is full,[376] and though there is likely to be many English travellers here this winter, I surely have not the least expectation of disposing of any thing, and have long since given up all thoughts of either friendship or profit in any person that I am likely to be shewn to here.

You will probably call to mind from a piece of vanity that dropt from me in a former letter, that I do not think thus of my situation from any feebleness that I believe is discoverable in me on a comparison with others; but Mr. Hamilton, our envoy, excepted, every one else that I have seen, has been entangled in the wiles and mediums laid for them by one or other of two or three clear-sighted, knowing men, who are extremely well calculated for the prosecution of the business they have in hand.

I am heartily sensible of your goodness and friendship in so frequently enjoining me to be upon good terms with the people here; but I believe if you saw how agreeably we kill the time when we get together (which is not seldom) how we laugh, how we drink, how we sing, how we tell stories and talk *nonsense*, you would be satisfied there was enough in all conscience to answer the purposes of relaxation and social intercourse; some of us, to be sure, know this to be nothing more than outside and false fire, yet that does not hinder our making the best use of it; and though there be amongst us one or two discontented, recluse men, yet of the many English, Italian, and French that know me, there is not even one, but has often taken notice that I was farthest from that character of any Englishman at Rome.[377]

You are accustomed to have a partiality for me, and notwithstanding that I have not allowed myself to dilate and explain matters (which will be better reserved for our entertainment and conversation hereafter, of which I could fill volumes) yet I hope I have hinted just enough to keep my place still in your good opinion. My two copies after Raffael,[378] together with many studies of things I liked at the little Farnese being finished some time, I have been ever since at work at the palais Borghese,[379] and am far advanced in entire copies of two of the most capital Titians I ever saw; one is called the three graces,

---

376 Burke's house, Gregories, near Beaconsfield, was already full of pictures.
377 Although Barry was Irish, Continentals assumed that any native speaker of English was an Englishman.
378 Studies after two Raphael paintings in the Vatican, *The Holy Family under the Oak* and the *Transfiguration*.
379 The Borghese Palace was built by the Medici family, next to the Borghese gardens in Rome; it was renowned for its collection of sculptures. The Farnese Palace, built in the sixteenth century for the Farnese family in Rome, noted for its art collection and classical sculptures.

the other an adoration of the shepherds.[380] Notwithstanding my enthusiasm for Raffael and Michael Angelo, (to whom I shall return when these copies are finished, for the short time of my stay here) I so far agree with the world as to think that Titian possesses as large a share of the art as any of them, and has conducted himself with as much, or even more strength of observation and judgement in this his inferior mechanical part. I have nothing now to say of him; his character is truly drawn by most writers—bad contour,[381] limbs disproportioned, no expression or character in any thing above ordinary nature; but my ideas (I was going to say human ideas) of a beautiful, true, and sound colouring cannot possibly rise above the performances of Titian; whilst I cannot help affirming, that some great and industrious genius might, with allowing himself proper time and study so avail himself of the beauty, character, just symmetry, and elevated idea of the antique as to carry the excellencies of Raffael and Michael Angelo very much beyond the point of perfection they have fixed them at. But to return to Titian and colouring, if it was not taking too much upon myself, I would now venture to affirm, that all pretension to secrets and Magilphs[382] is to be met with only amongst knaves and fools: the former for reasons sufficiently obvious, may find it their interest to circulate such a notion, whilst there will never be wanting of the latter, who not knowing what to do with the common materials, are ready enough to imagine the fault does not lie in them, and desperately run adrift in the search of a terra incognita. It is certain that there is some little cleanliness required in the choice, preparation, and management of colours; this allowed, Titian would paint just the same with my pallet as with his own. There is nothing in his pictures whiter, bluer, or yellower—but they may be made now as much and even more so, if the merit consisted in that. But the judicious application and mixing together of things is what puzzles in Titian, for he hardly ever laid on a colour simple, pure, and in its full force. Bassano, Rubens, Vandyke, and Paul Veronese,[383] are all good colourists, though all different; with a little displacing of the favourite tints, less blue, less red, purple, or yellow, put on here, the other there, and you may change each of them into the other with respect to colouring, and you may transform any or all of them into Titian in the same manner. A few changes in

---

380 Titian's *Venus Blindfolding Cupid* or *The Three Graces* and *The Holy Family with a Shepherd in a Landscape*.
381 Outline, or physical shape (Italian 'contorno').
382 Usually spelt 'megilp'; a mixture of linseed oil and turpentine or mastic varnish used to coat oil paintings.
383 Jacopo Bassano (c.1515–92), Italian painter, more often of secular than religious subjects; Sir Peter Paul Rubens (1577–1640), major Flemish painter and designer; Sir Anthony van Dyck (1599–1641), regarded as the greatest Flemish portrait painter; Paulo Veronese (?1528–1588), trained in Verona and then worked mainly in Venice.

the placing and force of the tints will convert an ill coloured French or Italian picture of Pierre, Boucher, or Battoni,[384] into the colouring of Reynolds, of the Venetians, Flemings, and of nature.

Then in this just distribution, strengthening, or weakening of tints, consists visibly the whole art of colouring; the whole Venetian and Flemish schools worked upon the same principles as their founders, but with different degrees of verity in the application of them, and have continued in a sort of succession to this day: some colour animals well, some bread, fruit, and still life: others do well in the painting of carnations and the nude; and in short, every man of parts and genius amongst them succeeded more or less in representing whatever part of nature, long study and diligent observation gave him a thorough and sufficient knowledge of: so that we find the success in practice has been always in proportion to the diligence and truth of the painter in laying on and ranging the colours, half colours, weakenings, strengthenings, &c. in the same manner, and in the same individual places of his picture, that they are seen to occupy in his natural archetype. We ought therefore to have little hesitation about pronouncing that the whole arcana[385] of fluids do not afford any one medium that will, in the hands of a man wanting in the fore-mentioned requisites, produce that propriety of colouring in all the different objects of nature, so variegated in itself, and so distinct in the one object from the other. So much your condemnation of Magilphs has encouraged me to say on the subject.

The greater number of our people here have been laid up with sickness of one kind or other, occasioned by the extraordinary heats of the last summer. They are all now, thank God, either up or out of danger, whilst without ailment or complaint, God Almighty has preserved me through one continued and uninterrupted course of labour, which has not allowed me the time to see Tivoli, Frascati, Albano,[386] or even to go three miles out of Rome ever since my arrival, though I have been pressed to it very warmly by parties of Italian, French, and English, who were desirous of taking a little mirth and good humour along with them; for you cannot think what a pleasant fellow I am ever since my coming abroad, as I have been under no apprehensions either of getting into debt or of wanting my dinner.

---

384 Pompeo Batoni (1708–87), Italian painter and draughtsman, famous for his portraits, not least of foreign Tourists on the Grand Tour: 'for travellers to Italy on the Grand Tour, sitting—or more often standing—for a portrait by Pompeo Batoni was an essential rite of passage' (Jonathan Keates, 'Eleven madonnas for my children', *TLS*, no. 5,484 (9 May 2008), 13).
385 Mysteries or secrets.
386 Tivoli, ancient town some 30 kilometres from Rome; Frascati, famous for its Roman villa, 20 kilometres south-east of Rome; Albano, about 16 kilometres from Rome on the Appian Way, said to have been founded by Ascanius, son of the Trojan leader Aeneas.

You may see by this, which is really the truth, how little reason there was for your dreading my becoming recluse and unsociable. I did not even know myself that I was master of so much ease and tranquillity of mind, or had such a fund of natural gaiety, until I was put to the trial. But all that they could do and may do, I can assure you, never gave me any other real uneasiness than that as they put it out of my power to contribute in any wise to the defraying of my expenses here, (by the sale of any thing I have done or might do) I found myself under the necessity of being burdensome to you for it.

Two nights ago, while we were chatting together at our coffeehouse, I happened, out of mere wantonness of talking, to say, that you and Mr. William were to be here this winter. The confusion I observed in some people upon it, occasioned my immediately improving the hint, and joining two others to it; four of you all coming out to see Italy together. They were very much embarrassed about it, as they foresaw it would in great measure put it out of their power to act agreeably to their intentions this winter, which is, they know, the last I am to stay here.[387] If this trick of mine does me no good, I believe it will do me no harm. God bless you, sirs, my best respects wait on you, Mrs. Burke, and the whole family.

My worthy and dear friend Dr. Nugent made me very happy by his kind letter; he will, I hope, do me the justice to believe that it is neither through want of love or respect that he has not my acknowledgement in a sheet of paper directed particularly to him—the same, I hope of Mr. William, and Mr. Richard. I am fatigued, and am besides arrived at the end of my paper, but what need of my foolish apology, when the dear sirs at the top of my letter cannot be explained otherwise than by *their* being understood in it.

Rome Nov. 29.th 1768

Sir[388]

Not to make the liberty I take in writing to you too intollerable by keeping you in Suspense with apologies & excuses for it, I shall just beg to accquaint you that Lord Fitzwilliam and Mr Crofts[389] in a conversation they had on their return home with Mr Burke (a freind of mine) said many civil good natur'd

---

387 Barry spent one further winter in Rome before he left in April 1770.
388 The text is taken from the Barry manuscript in MS Autograph Letters Collection, National Library of Ireland, Dublin; an edited version is printed in Fryer, *Works of Barry*, i, 168–9; no attempt has been made to correct spelling, punctuation, or capitalisation. Barry is writing to the British Minister in Naples, William Hamilton.
389 William Wentworth (1748–1833), 2nd Earl Fitzwilliam, accompanied on the Grand Tour by his tutor Thomas Crofts, had met William Burke in Paris in October 1768.

things of my picture of Adam & Eve – & my other little Studies[390] all of which they quoted you for. The Satisfaction my freind had in hearing that any thing of mine was honor'd with your favourable notice (whose character as a man of Taste I find he is no stranger to) is a thing that very much affects my concerns as I am supported during my Stay abroad by that gentleman & another of the same name.

Indeed were it not for this Single account my freinds in England had of me 'tis more than probable they must have imagined that I had done nothing & Slept away my time here, as care has been industriously taken that I should be kept out of the way of accquiring here either freinds, character or any thing that may be useful or agreeable in the carrying of a man thro' through life. Except yourself, who I heard had set out with the resolution of seeing all the Artists in Rome, & Lord Fitzwilliam & Mr Crofts who came with your name in their mouths I have never been shewn to any other of the many travellers & people of distinction who have been about amongst the Artists here: however a man whose mind is occupied with Studying the Antique & the people of the Sixteenth Century,[391] may bring himself to that pass as to be content for a time to give up the profits of his profession, although the profits in this as well as in most other professions are inseparably linked to & followed by reputation & character which we all have a hankering after.

Sir you will I hope forgive the liberty I have taken in writing to you, as I don't believe 'twill be in my power to have the honour of waiting upon you at Naples & gratitude would not Suffer me to think of leaving Italy (which I shall do in about half a year[392]) without returning you my most Sincere thanks for the obligation you have conferred upon me.

  I am Sir
  with the greatest respect
  your most Obedient Humble servt
  James Barry

---

390 Apart from the painting Barry was working on, *The Temptation of Adam*, he had done a number of studies, including one after Michael Angelo's Adam in *The Creation of Adam*; he had also done several drawings on classical subjects (see William L. Pressly, *The Life and Art of James Barry* (London: Yale University Press, 1981), 242–6).
391 Barry often uses the term 'antique' to refer to classical Greek sculpture and architecture; the sixteenth century was the era of major paintings in Renaissance art.
392 Barry did not leave Italy until January 1771.

Rome, November 8, 1769.

My Dear Father and Mother,[393]

Can I believe that my poor brother Jack should die amongst you, and no one of you think of making me acquainted with it. The satisfaction and hopes you have had from his sober careful conduct and application, which I so often joyed to find in your letters, interested me ten thousand times more about him than his being my brother. Poor Jack! he was the last of the family that I parted from,[394] and amongst the last of those I would part with, and his death has blasted almost all the hopes I had of being useful to the family, as the business he was bred up to, and his sober conduct, gave me great expectations of his being able to put in practice some matters of architecture which my residence in Italy gave me opportunities of taking notice of; but this is all over, and it seems you have another son remaining with you who is of a very different cast; can this be Patrick, and is it possible that his own future prospect in life, the death of his poor brother, and the situation of his parents in their decline, can work no other effects upon him?[395] But this is not all, my father thinks of making his will; what can occasion this? For God's sake let such of you as are living, my father, mother, my two brothers, (since I have only two) my sister and my uncle John,[396] write their names at least, to a letter directed for me at the English coffee house in Rome, by the return of the post. I leave Rome in the latter end of January, and shall make but a very short stay at Venice of a fortnight or three weeks, so that if my father writes to me on the receipt of this, I shall either receive it at Rome, or a friend of mine who is here will send it after me to Venice. My mind has some little ease in seeing that excellent man Dr. Sleigh, interest himself about my father and family. Good God ! in how many singular and unthought of ways, has the goodness of that gentleman exerted itself towards me. He first put me upon Mr. Burke, who has been under God all in all to me; next he had desires of strengthening my connexion with Mr. Stewart, which is the only construction I could make of the friendly letter which I received from him in London, and afterwards he is for administering comfort to my poor parents. I shall with the blessing of God be in England

---

393 Barry was the eldest child of John Barry and Juliana Reardon; his brothers were Patrick, Redmond and John ('Jack'); his sister was Mary Ann. Barry's father had worked in the building trade, in shipping, and as a publican in Cork.
394 Since John intended to become an architect, he may have been studying architecture or the building trade in London when Barry left for Paris in October 1765.
395 These remarks suggest Patrick was unreliable; he enlisted in the navy in 1771, but deserted. Pressly writes, 'Patrick died in the Indies, and Redmond, as a blind, disabled seaman, turned up only after the artist's death' (Pressly, *Life and Art*, 198, and Pressly, 'James Barry', (ODNB).
396 Probably John Reardon, brother of Barry's mother.

about May next; and I hope there is no need for me to mention to one, of my father's experience in the world, how necessary it is to be armed with patience, and resignation against those unavoidable strokes of mortality, to which all the world is subject. As we advance in life, we must quit our hold of one thing after another, and since we cannot help it, and that it is a necessary condition of our existence, that ourselves and every thing connected with us, shall be swallowed up in the mass of changes and renovations, which we see every day in the world, let us endeavour not to embitter the little of life that is before us, with a too frequent calling to mind of past troubles and misfortunes; and if ever God Almighty is pleased to crown my very severe and intense application to my studies, with any degree of success in the world, I am sure the greatest pleasure that will arise to me from it, will be the consolation it will give my dear father, mother, and friends.

Your affectionate son,

J. B.

Mr. Burke was so kind as to send me Dr. Sleigh's letter, containing the account of the death of my brother. I had three brothers, and he does not say which it was, but by the good character he has given of him, it must be poor John.

Rome, Nov. 8, 1769

Dear Sirs,

If you just take the trouble to look over the two enclosed letters to Dr. Sleigh, and to my father, you will see all I have to say on the melancholy occasion of Dr. Sleigh's letter.

I have about a week ago finished my studies after the statues of the Belvedere and other places,[397] and have nothing to detain me here at present, except a collection of antique heads, which I intend making studies of, and by about the latter end of January next, shall set out for Florence and Venice, where I hope to compleat my little scheme of art, and be with you, God willing, in May next.

When I was at the Laocoon, I had an opportunity of seeing into the absurdity of a modern remark and practice. There was in the time of Poussin and Fiamingo, at the villa Ludovisi, a picture of naked children painted by

---

397   Barry had often admired the sculptures in the Belvedere, a gallery and courtyard in the Vatican: J. J. Lalande called it, 'perhaps the most remarkable place for art in all Italy, or perhaps in the whole universe' (*Voyage d'un francais en Italie fait dans les anneés 1765 & 1766, 1769*, iii, 184, cited in *Boswell on the Grand Tour*, 67, n. 8).

Titian, which Poussin and Fiamingo formed themselves upon, according to the opinion of several writers, and which I believe to be true, as there is in my neighbourhood, a very careful drawing of it by Poussin, and which agrees excessively well with the style of the boys, modelled by Fiamingo:[398] the reputation of the boys of Fiamingo came in a little time to be so fixed in the world, that he became a standard for boys with all succeeding sculptors; these boys, though they may be acknowledged a good imitation of children about a year old, cannot therefore in reason be a good model for boys in a more advanced age, and yet the writers and people who find fault with the sons of the Laocoon, calling them little men, will find their criticism grounded on the above absurdity; for upon examination I never saw so happy a system of character and proportion for boys of sixteen and seventeen years old, as in the two sons of the Laocoon. And besides one thing which you will observe as a remarkable propriety in this, is the character and age of the father, which seems better to accord with sons of that number of years; as well as the consideration that these boys according to custom might attend at a sacrifice, where a child of a year old would be useless. The Meleager (commonly called the Antinous of the Belvedere) I often, as well as many others, thought had a little caricatura in the sway of the attitude.[399] Upon a very narrow inspection, I see it was occasioned by the restoring and putting of the figure together. It grows late, and I shall refer any more to another opportunity. I am, dear sirs, with my whole heart, your obedient humble servant,

J. B.

Bologna [October 1770].

Dear Sirs,

I am still in Bologna, and I am afraid, as the season is far advanced, if I shall be obliged to stay here much longer, that it will be hardly in my power to get out of Italy before the beginning of spring, as the winter is exceedingly severe in

---

398 *The Worship of Venus* (1516–18), oil on canvas, by Titian (*c.*1485–1576), was in the Villa Ludovisi until 1638 (Hans Tietze, *Titian, the Paintings and Drawings* (London: Phaidon, 1950), 381). Nicolas Poussin arrived in Rome in 1624 and lived there most of his life; the Flemish painter François Duquesnoy (1597–1643), who often signed himself 'Fiamingo', shared a house with Poussin for a time. The villa Ludovisi, recognised as one of the most beautiful villas in Rome, was owned by Cardinal Ludovico Ludovisi (1595–1632), a patron of the arts.

399 Sculpture of Meleager, a hero in Greek mythology, in the Vatican Museum; 'caricatura' suggests slightly ludicrous exaggeration. The Antinous in the Belvedere was a different sculpture.

those parts. My picture of Philoctetes is finished,[400] and those artists who have seen it and my other things, have been more favourable in their opinions of that and of me, than I could have well expected; the figure is larger than the life. I did it as well as I could, and as to the point of time, &c. in the story, I followed closely the Greek epigram upon Parrhasius's picture of the same subject, and I found the Philoctetes of Sophocles, an useful comment upon it.[401] I have not as yet sent it to the institute,[402] as I am without money, and if I should be much longer so, I must think of pawning it with some painter, if I can. It is a little unlucky that it is not some saint, or miracle of a saint, and then perhaps as much might be raised upon it as would have paid my lodgings; but I doubt even, as the Italians are all full of the idea of selling pictures to the English, who are full of money, and the richest, and consequently, the most respected people in the world, but that the idea of an Englishman's expecting to get money from *them* for pictures, would be thought a most extravagant solecism. As you desired my staying some time at Bologna, when I had finished at Venice,[403] I came back to Bologna, as it was not losing ground in my journey, and would, I well knew, be more agreeable to my plan of study. The post after you received my last letter, Messrs. Netterville and Nugent received a bill for thirty pounds,[404] which I foresaw, from my stay in these places, would be necessary to carry me home. It is almost a month since Signer Vergani (to whom I gave the bill) came to my lodging to tell me the bill was refused payment. The letter which he read to the people, at whose house I lodge, made me a little uneasy, as I love to live in harmony and friendship with all people, particularly with the Italians, for whom I have the greatest esteem; and I then foresaw that the doubts it gave them of my morals and probity, were in no wise favourable to those impressions I hope to leave on all people, with whom I live: however, I

---

400 *Philoctetes on the Island of Lemnos*; it measured 90 × 62 inches. Philoctetes, son of King Poeas of Meliboea in Thessaly, a famed archer who fought for the Greeks in the Trojan War, was stranded for a time on the island of Lemnos.
401 Parrhasius (*fl.* fifth century BC), Greek painter of Philoctetes; the mythological Greek hero featured in ancient Greek plays, notably by Sophocles (*c.*496–405 BC). Cf. Ovid, *Metamorphoses* xiii, 51–54: Philoctetes, stranded on the isle of Lemnos, 'broken by illness and hunger, is clothed and fed by the birds, and in looking for birds he uses those arrows which were meant by fate for Troy'.
402 The Institute of Science and the Arts (1714) which incorporated the Academy of Science and the Academy of Arts, known as the Accademia Clementina. Barry painted this picture for the Accademia when he was awarded a diploma there.
403 Edmund Burke had written, 'I think it right to see Florence and Bologna; and that you cannot do better than to take that route to Venice' (Burke to Barry, 16 September 1769).
404 Burke used these merchants in London to handle Barry's finances while he was in Italy. The bill of exchange was given to Vergani, a banker in Bolgna.

endeavoured to content myself the best I could with the accident. Vergani has heard nothing further about it since, so that about the latter end of this week, I shall be obliged to pawn the watch, which was given me in Paris by Mr. Richard Burke,[405] as I have nothing else, upon which I could raise any thing; studies of the antique, of Michael Angelo, of Raffael and Titian, carrying no value with them amongst pawn-brokers.

    I am very fond of Guercino; his two pictures at St. Gregorio, and at the Carthusians are excellent.[406] I have seen no picture of him any where equal to that at St. Gregorio: Agostino Carrache is admirable in his Assumption of the Virgin.[407] There are in no work of art in Bologna, stronger examples of sound merit and real knowledge, taste, and drawing, than in some heads, hands, and arms, &c. of this picture; Guido has a little figure of a Christ,[408] in the same church, which is also admirable: as to Ludovico, and Annibal Carrache,[409] I never wanted a high opinion of them, and I am never likely to want it, as it encreases daily, the more I see of them. Some pictures of Cavedone also deserve the reputation they have.[410] I have at present but little gusto to write any more. I wish to get upon my journey, to send you some account of Corregio.[411] My love and best respects wait upon the family, upon Sir Joshua Reynolds, and all friends.

    I am, dear sirs,
        Yours whilst I exist,
            J. B.

Bologna, Nov. 17, 1770.
Dear Sir,[412]
I hope you will excuse the liberty I take in troubling you with the care of this letter, for Messrs. Burke, which I beg you will send to them speedily into the

---

405 Burke's brother Richard had visited Barry in Paris in December 1765.
406 Giovani Francesco Barbieri, known as Guercino (1591–1666), major painter from Bologna. One of the pictures was *Circumcision of Christ* which Barry discusses in 'Observations' (*Works of Barry*, ii, 29).
407 Agostino Carrache (1557–1602); his *Assumption of the Virgin* (c.1590) was the altarpiece for the church of San Salvatore, Bologna.
408 Guido Reni (1575–1642); possibly his *Resurrection* (69 × 63 centimetres) in the Basilica of San Dominico, Bologna.
409 Painters from Bologna; Ludovico Carrache (1555–1619) was a cousin of Annibal Carrache (1560–1609).
410 Giacomo Cavedone (1577–1660), celebrated for his *Virgin and Child* in Bologna.
411 Antonio Allegri (c.1490–1534) called Correggio after the town where he was born and died.
412 Barry is writing to Sir Joshua Reynolds.

country, if they be there, as I have some reason to think they are, by my receiving no answer to the three last letters I sent them. To one of which at least an answer was exceedingly necessary for me, as it was upon a money affair; but to be sure these letters have never reached them.

As both you and Mr. Burke advised my staying some time in Bologna, I am extremely sorry that so much of my attention was left to my own taste and discernment. I could have wished to have known how the old Bolognese painters stood in the judgment of my friends; and when your name was mentioned in Mr. William Burke's letter, I really hoped that some advice would have followed it, regarding the particular manners and differences that are found in the good pictures here of Ludovico, Annibal, Agostino Carrache, Guercino, Guido, and Dominichino:[413] I remember one day at your house a very just and useful remark you made upon the solemn low tone of colouring of Ludovico. Guercino has also much of this manner in his fine picture at St. Gregorio, with this difference, that I observe in this picture of Guercino more mellowing and fuoco[414] in the colouring. Many of Ludovico's pictures have been cleaned and retouched a few years ago, as I have been informed, and are much the worse for it. It is a great pity that Guercino did not paint all his pictures in the grave majestic tone of this at St. Gregorio. He has in the general run of his work too much white among his colours.

There is hardly any thing that could be more welcome to me than a letter from you, in which I could wish above all things, that you would speak your opinion plainly upon whatever advantages you think I might derive from Correggio's works at Parma,[415] or other works of art which lie in my way home, and which I have not yet seen.

By letters from Rome, I am informed of the arrival of my things in England, so that before this time you will have seen my picture of Adam and Eve,[416] by which you will be enabled to point out to me whatever remedies, you think may be necessary to correct my deficiencies. It is what I expect from your candour and the obliging friendly dispositions which were manifested in the letter you favoured me with in Rome; I wish ardently you was to do it, as it is much my interest and desire to fortify myself as well as I can in my profession, before my arrival in England. Messrs. Netterville and Nugent, merchants in the city, will inform you by penny post, whether the bill I drew upon them is paid; if so, and that you think of favouring me with a letter, direct to me at the post

---

413 Like the other painters named Dominichino (1581–1641) was from Bologna; they are all discussed in Barry's 'Observations' (*Works of Barry*, ii, 29–33).
414 Italian for fire; here perhaps meaning warmth of colouring.
415 Correggio worked for most of his life in Parma where Barry intended visiting next.
416 Barry's painting, which he hoped to show in the next exhibition of the Royal Academy in 1771; it had been sent to London and was to be a present for Burke.

in Parma; but if the bill is not answered, direct to me at Bologna, where your letter must infallibly find me. I am, dear sir, with great affection and respect, your most obedient humble servant,

J. B.

In consequence of the compliment made me by the Bolognese artists of receiving me into their body, I have painted a picture of Philoctetes for the Institute; the figure is larger than the life.

Bologna [17 November 1770]

Dear Sir,
I wrote you by the last post, but as I am afraid that some accident, miscarriage, or your being in the country, or in Ireland, or I do not know what has happened, which has occasioned my confusion, I now write to you through the hands of Sir Joshua Reynolds, who I know will forward it speedily wherever you are; as I foresaw after my arrival in Bologna, that I should in some time want money to carry me home, I gave Vergani, the banker here, a bill, which he was to forward to Messrs. Netterville and Nugent. I asked nothing from him till the bill was paid; above a month ago his correspondent wrote to him that the bill was refused payment, but that Messrs. Netterville retained it in their hands, in expectation that another friend would come, who they believed would answer the bill, of which Vergani's correspondent was to inform him by the succeeding post. More than a month is now past, and Vergani has heard nothing further about it. He tells me he is afraid that the letter is lost, or he does not know what has happened, and I am a small matter in debt in my lodging, which is daily increasing, the people full of doubts and disquiet about me. Not able to go out of the house for want of a winter coat, my mind is so uneasy that I am not master enough of myself to be able to paint, so that if the bill of Vergani should not have been paid, or I do not hear from you by the return of the post, I must be obliged to take a walk some morning out of my lodging, which I am very unfit for, leave all my little studies behind me, and go, where God knows, for I do not. I am yours and the family's.

J. B.

As to the pictures of the old masters here, it was my opinion that it was better for me to visit them often, than to copy them, as I had already formed my stile of drawing, colouring, and composition, by copying much at Rome and Venice of the antique, Michael Angelo, Raffael, and Titian, so that I began and finished that picture of the Philoctetes to put up in the Institute, as it would, in case it merited the attention of travellers, be seen by every one who came to Bologna, through which all pass.

Bologna [20 November 1770]

My Dear Sirs,
Yesterday Signor Vergani came to my lodging with an account of the bill's having been paid : it has delivered me from much shame, and from ten thousand distresses which you cannot conceive, and which it would answer no purpose at present for me to describe to you. From the letters I wrote to you without receiving any answer, and from the accident that has happened regarding that bill, I had argued myself firmly into the persuasion that both you and Mr. William were in the country some where or other, or were come abroad to see Italy, as you often mentioned: which of these was matter of doubt and speculation, the only thing certain with me was that my letters had not reached you. In the confusion I was in, many schemes offered themselves to me, one was to forward a letter to you through the hands of your friend Sir Joshua Reynolds which I did last post. However this would have answered no purpose, as I could not have been able to stay in Bologna until even the arrival of the answer. Another scheme was the running naked out of my lodging and turning friar, when I imagined that by the means of my art I should meet with a sort of reception—but this was a remedy that I thought much worse than the disease. What I had at last agreed upon was, by the means of pawning what I had with some body or other, to raise as much money as would carry me to Turin, where I intended applying to Mr. Coke,[417] your friend. But I am delivered from the disorder occasioned by the delay of the bill, without the application of any of those caustics, by the same hands through which all my emollients[418] come.

It is now the 20th of November, and as I have not as yet seen Parma, it is a matter of doubt with me, whether I shall be able to get out of Italy this winter, however this will depend entirely upon the letter I hope to receive from you at Parma.

The great and essential parts of the art are not to be learned at Bologna, as the three Carraches, who are the noblest characters that this place ever produced, are in the leading articles of design and colouring, far short of the degree of perfection we find in Michael Angelo, Raffael, and Titian. The

---

417   Not identified.
418   The term 'caustics', literally, refers to a substance that burns away human tissue; used figuratively here of remedies for Barry's anxieties. 'emollients' meant relief.

Carraches are not to be disesteemed for this, as there is a happy aggregate of all the parts of the art, which is not to be found in the others; and though a man might not make the Carraches, Guercino, &c. his model in great matters, yet there is much of the art to be learned from them, and if I do not profit myself exceedingly from what I have seen of theirs, it is more my fault than theirs. It is a matter of doubt perhaps, whether some of their pictures, taken in the lump and balancing one thing with another, are not of the first class of pictures. I am here tempted to say something upon the different characters of merit of the three Carraches, of Guercino, Guido, &c. but I find it a little puzzling; as Annibal is a Proteus,[419] and admirable in all shapes, Ludovico is different in his styles, and always proper and adapted to his subject, and Agostino has left but few pictures behind him, in which are some particulars even superior to the capacity of either Ludovico or Annibal; though upon the whole, Agostino seems the least formed in the practice of a picture of the three, and yet he seems to have had an amazing and graceful practice in his drawing.

Dear sirs,
I am and ever shall be,
    Yours and the family's,
        J. B.

If Parma does not answer my expectation, and that the weather permits, and that I have no orders from you to the contrary, I shall go on directly for England.

[Lyons, February 1771]

Dear Sirs,
In order to divert my attention from disagreeable reflections upon the fatigues and extraordinary expenses of travelling in this time of the year, as I have also an idle day upon my hands in waiting for the diligence, and as there is nothing worth looking after here in Lyons, except trade and manufacture, in which I have neither knowledge nor taste, so I shall turn to my old resource of more pleasing memorial.[420]

I shall say nothing of Corregio's ceilings in the Duomo, and in S. Giovanni at Parma: they are, I will allow, what might be expected from the great abilities of such a man; but as I do not like this kind of painting where macchia[421] and effect is more consulted than expression, beauty, form, and character, so I shall

---

419   Proteus, sea god in Greek mythology, capable of changing his shape at will.
420   Remembrance, recollection (OED); an unusually late usage of the word in this sense.
421   A quick sketch.; also, stain, smear, blotch (Italian).

leave for others to say about it whatever they please. Corregio's fragment of the Annunciation[422] is excellent, full of grace and beauty. His Madonna della scudella[423] is admirably well coloured in all the parts, and in the whole together, but the drawing is bad and much wanting in the proportion, &c. This picture is a convincing testimony, that he was ignorant of drawing (very ignorant) and yet some part of his other picture of S. Girolamo, at the academy,[424] proves as convincingly that he drew well, and very well, and in excellent, proper, and variegated proportions. To reconcile this might be more difficult and troublesome than useful, and therefore, I will only suppose either that this Madonna della scudella was an early work of Corregio's, or that sometimes he made light of the drawing of his figures, or that sometimes he succeeded in his drawing more from pains, and a habit of mere imitation, than from principles and knowledge. There are other pictures by him in S. Giovanni,[425] in which there is much to praise, and something to dispraise. In the palace of S. Vitale is a little Madonna and Child by him, which is very excellent, and much like Titian's manner of colouring, which is very different from the general style of Corregio. In the same palace is also a most beautiful precious little picture of S. Cecilia, and two angels by Parmegianino:[426] it is admirable in every respect, for most elegant true drawing, good colouring, most gracefully invented, and cleanly and well finished; the landscape and foliage are full of taste, spirit, and beauty. There is also a collection of drawings, several by Parmegianino, which are now engraving by Signor Bosse, a man of merit both as a *stuccatore* of fruit, &c. in which he is very able, as in engravings in *aqua-fortis*.[427] There are also two studies, done with a pen by Michael Angelo, for figures in his Last Judgement. There is also a picture, with Leonardo da Vinci's name wrote upon it;[428] there is much of a painful, laboured merit in some parts of it, but as it is totally devoid of taste, it cannot surely be his, so that the name must have been forged.

The famous Volta in Piacenza,[429] by Guercino, merits all the praise which is generally given to it. It is his best and most *gustoso* manner of colouring, with

---

422 The fresco designed for the church of San Francesco, Parma, was badly damaged, but Correggio's drawing for it survives.
423 The Madonna is seated and has a bowl (scudella) in her hand.
424 San Girolamo in the Academy of Fine Arts in Parma.
425 The church of San Giovanni Evangelista, Parma, where Correggio painted frescoes, notably *The Vision of St John the Evangelist at Patmos*.
426 The picture by Parmegianino (1503–40) has not been identified.
427 Begnino Bossi (1727–92), court stuccatore at Parma; he was working at the time on a book of engravings of Parmegianino which was published in Parma in 1772. (We are grateful to Esther Chadwick for the information.)
428 Leonardo da Vinci (1452–1519), the great Florentine artist, scientist and thinker.
429 Fresco by Guercino in the cupola of Piacenza cathedral.

a *chiaro scuro*, broad, and as the Italians say, *piazzato*.⁴³⁰ The style of design, and the naked, are infinitely more noble, and more in the historical character, than he generally has them. Of all the works I have seen of Guercino, this is what does most honour to his character.

The two bronze equestrian figures of Alexander, and Ranusio Farnese,⁴³¹ are very good, and also the bronze *basso relievos*⁴³² on the pedestal shew much taste of design, invention, or composition. There are some singularities in the manner of working those *basso relievos*, which we will reserve for conversation, as I want to come to matters of more importance.

In the academy of Milan is Raffael's Cartoon (in oiled charcoal, or black chalk) for the school of Athens:⁴³³ there are parts of it not finished, others only in the *contorno*, some few parts of it different from the picture. The head of Diogenes is rather a placid, general sort of a head, without that acute, critical character of face, which he has given to him in the picture. As this cartoon has merit enough to pretend to be original, the above particulars incline me to think that it is undoubtedly so.

There is a piece of an admirable cartoon by Julio Romano of a battle.⁴³⁴ Also a drawing of Michael Angelo, for the angle of the Capella Sistina, of the brazen serpent. It is outlined with a pen, and washed with bistre and white.⁴³⁵ Angelo's powers in the naked all are agreed upon; but there is besides in this drawing, an admirable conduct in the grouping and composing the figures; and a general effect, and broad *piazzato* manner of *chiaro scuro*, which I could hardly have believed, had I not seen this drawing, notwithstanding I had seen the picture.

---

430   Italian: 'gustoso', tastefully; 'chiaro scuro', 'The treatment or disposition of the light and shade, or brighter and darker masses, in a picture' (OED); 'piazzato': painted in a sweeping manner.
431   Two bronze equestrian statues of Ranuccio (1589–1622) and his father Alexander Farnese (1545–92), Prince of Parma, in the Piazza dei Cavalli, Piacenza.
432   Bas-reliefs, 'sculpture or carved work in which the figures project less than one half of their true proportions from the surface on which they are carved'. (OED).
433   *The School of Athens* by Raphael was in the Vatican. Cartoons were drawings or paintings on paper, usually of the same size as the proposed work.
434   Giulio Romano (1499–1546), Italian architect and designer; his *The Battle of Milvian Bridge* is in the Vatican. Shakespeare describes him as 'that rare Italian master' (*The Winter's Tale*, V, ii, 96).
435   A preparatory drawing for the biblical scene with the brazen or brass serpent which would feature in the decoration of the Sistine Chapel in the Vatican, which Barry often visited. Michael Angelo worked from Numbers, 21: 8–9 where Moses 'made a serpent of brass, and put it upon a pole', as instructed by God, to protect the Israelites. Bistre: 'A colour made of chimney-soot boiled, and afterwards diluted with water' (Chambers Cyclopedia).

There is here[436] also a holy family, &c. by Bernardo Lovino, in which the pleasing sweetness in the heads of the Christ, the Virgin, and the S. Anna, deserve every commendation,[437] and is not inferior to Leonardo da Vinci himself, whose scholar he was. As to Da Vinci, there is here of him, a half figure of S. John Baptist, a bust of Christ, and a portrait of the Duchess Beatrice.[438] In the sacristy of S. Celso, is the S. Anna, Madonna, &c. of Da Vinci: it is a copy by Salaio;[439] the great sweetness of character, the roundness, and great *relievo*, breadth of effect, deep thinking and *gusto*, in those pictures, verify what Vasari says, that Leonardo was the pillar and foundation of the perfection that was given to art in the *cinque cento*.[440] Giorgione might well have drawn from this source his strength of *relieve* and shadowing, and Raffael his pleasing sweetness, expression, precision, and truth of nature; and though all those perfections do not exist together in any single work, yet they might be well collected from his works in general.

As to his picture of the Last Supper,[441] which has made such a noise in the world, the account I have to give you about it is as follows; when I came into the Reffettorio, I found a scaffold erected, which on ascending, I saw one half of the picture covered by a great cloth; on examining the other part that was uncovered, I found the skin of colour, which composed the picture, to be all cracked into little squares of about the eighteenth of an inch over, which were for the most part in their edges loosened from the wall and curling up—however nothing was materially lost. I saw that the picture had been formerly repaired in some few places; yet as this was not much, and as the other parts were untouched, there was nothing to complain of. The wonderful truth and variety of the expressions, so well described by Vasari and Rubens,[442] and the admirable finesse of finish and relievo taken notice of by Armenini

---

436 Although Barry is writing on his way to, or in Paris, he is talking about what he saw in the Academy of Milan.
437 Bernardino Lovino, or Luini (?1480–?1540), a follower of Leonardo da Vinci.
438 Beatrice d'Este (1475–97), Duchess of Milan; Da Vinci presented her with this portrait as a wedding gift.
439 Many years later, in a lecture 'On Design', Barry is less certain that this is a copy by Jacop del Salaio (1442–93) of the picture in the church of St Celso, Milan (Lecture III, *Works of Barry*, i, 426).
440 See Vasari, 'Life of Leonardo da Vinci', *Lives of the Most Eminent Painters Sculptors and Architects*, translated by Gaston Du C. de Vere, 3 vols (New York: Abrams, 1979), ii, 778–94.
441 Da Vinci's wall painting of the Last Supper in the monastery of San Maria delle Grazie, Milan.
442 Vasari, *Lives of the Most Eminent Painters*, ii, 784–5; the Rubens allusion has not been found.

were still remaining.⁴⁴³ Whilst I was examining this part of the picture, two gentlemen came up the scaffold and drew aside the cloth which covered the other half, which to my great horror and astonishment was repainted. One of those men seemed to be at great pains to shew the vast improvements the picture was receiving by this repainting: but the repainting and the discourse so kindled my indignation, that I was no longer master of myself: What, Sir, said I, is it possible that you do not perceive how this painter, if I can call him a painter, has destroyed the picture in every part on which he has laid his stupid hands? Do not you see that this head is distorted and out of drawing, that there is no longer significance or expression in it, that all his colouring is crude and wants accord? Do, Sir, open your eyes and compare it with the other half of the picture which he has not as yet buried under his cursed colours. He answered me that this was only a dead colour,⁴⁴⁴ and the painter was to go over it a second time. O confusion, said I, so much the worse; if he has thus lost his way whilst he was immediately going over the lines and colours of Leonardo's work, what will become of him when he has no longer any guide, and is left blind and abandoned to his own ignorance: and turning myself to two friars of the convent who stood by, fathers, said I, this picture and the painter of it has suffered much by the ignorance of your order. It was whitewashed over some years ago, it has been again hurt in washing off the white, and now you have got a beast to paint another picture upon it, who knows no more of the matter than you do yourselves; there was no occasion for thus covering it over with new colours; it might be easily secured in those parts that are loosening from the wall, and it would stand probably as long as your order will. The friar told me that he did not understand those matters, and that he spoke but very little Italian, that he was Irish, and that it was by the order of the Count de Firmian,⁴⁴⁵ who was secretary of state, that this picture was repainted, and that the convent had no authority and had given no order for it. Indeed then countryman said I, the world will be very little obliged to Count Fermian; it were to be wished, and it will be for the interest and honour of your convent, if you can prevail upon the count to spare at least what is remaining of the picture and take down the scaffold immediately.

There is in this church of the Dominicans the Christ crowned with thorns by Titian; it is certainly in the number of his very best pictures. All that is admirable in Titian's character is to be found in this picture, and it is in excellent preservation.

---

443 Giovanni Battista Armenini (c.1525–1609) wrote *De veri precetti della pittura* ('The true way of painting') (1587).
444 The first coat, or laying-in of the paint.
445 Count Karl Joseph von Firmian (?1712–72), Governor General of Lombardy.

In S. Celso there is a good picture of Paris Bordone,[446] the tone of colouring in the landscape and figures is as usual very Titianesque. There is in the Reffettorio of the church, a large picture of Abraham, Melchisadeck, &c. by Paolo Lomazzo,[447] a man famous for his writings upon art. One sees in it that he knew every thing and imitated every thing; there is Raffael, Da Vinci, Titian, and every body to be found in it, and yet it is good for little: it is a mere hateful *caput mortuum*[448] without perfection or worth of any one kind.

In Turin I saw the royal collection of pictures, but, except a picture or two of Guido, which I did not like,[449] all the rest are Flemish and Dutch, Rubens's, Vandyke's, Tenier's, Rembrandt, Scalken, &c.[450] They are without the pales of my church,[451] and though I will not condemn them, yet I must hold no intercourse with them. God help you, Barry, said I, where is the use of your hair-breadth niceties, your antiques, and your, &c.? — Behold the hand-writing upon the wall against you; in the country to which you are going, pictures of lemon peels, oysters, and tricks of colour, and other baubles, are in as much request, as they are here.

I am now in Paris, and expect with the blessing of God to be over with you on the heels of my letter. I will just look over the things here, and will bring you accounts about them in my pocket. I say nothing to you of Savoy and the Alps; the country was no longer to be found, all was snow, and sleet, and misery. My head was disturbed and clogged with the drams and the wine with which I was obliged to fill myself in order to thaw the blood of my veins. I am, dear sirs, whilst I live, as I should be,

Yours and the family's,

James Barry.

---

446 Paris Bordone (1500–71), pupil of Titian who painted mainly in Venice. The picture is unidentified, but possibly *Holy Family with St John the Baptist* in an extensive landscape, or another painting on the same theme; Francis Palgrave noted in the church of San Celso, Milan, 'one fine, and some small pictures, by Paris Bordone' (*Hand-Book for Travellers in Northern Italy*, 3rd edition (London: John Murray, 1847), 162).

447 Giovanni Paulo Lomazzo (1538–1600), who, when he went blind at 33, turned to writing two major works, *Trattato dell'arte de la pittura, scoltura, et architettura* ('Treatise on the art of painting, sculpture, and architecture') (1584) and *Idea del tempio della pittura* ('The ideal temple of painting') (1590); the picture has not been identified.

448 Latin: 'Death's head', i.e. the painting has no life.

449 Barry had visited the collection in the Royal Palace in Turin on his way to Rome in the autumn of 1766.

450 David Teniers the younger (1610–90), Flemish painter ; Rembrandt (1606–69), the foremost of Dutch painters; Godfried Schalken (1643–1706), Dutch painter who did a portrait of the English king, *William III by Candlelight*.

451 Pale: 'A stake, fence, or boundary' (OED); the term was used in Ireland to define the boundary of English jurisdiction: 'beyond the pale' were the supposedly wild, uncivilized Catholic Irish. Barry was a Catholic.

Lady Holland (Caroline Lennox); Allan Ramsay. Oil on canvas, 1766

Caroline Lennox (1723–74): Letters (1766–7)

> I love vastly to see places where such and such people have been, and where great Events have hap'ned. And that pleasure is great in Italy, the more so as the things hap'ned so long ago, and that just now I'm more read in Antient than modern History... The ruins and remains of the Roman Empire really amuse [i.e astonish] me. [19 December 1766]

IN WORDS which could have been used by perhaps the majority of travellers on the Grand Tour, Caroline Lennox wrote from Naples to her sister Emily, Marchioness of Kildare (from November 1766, Duchess of Leinster). Her social position made the ambition she describes one that could be realised. Her father, Charles Lennox (1701–50), prominent in the English Court, succeeded to the title of Duke of Richmond in the year of her birth; her mother, Lady Sarah Cadogan (1706–51), born at The Hague, was accustomed all her life to living in the Dutch Court where Caroline's grandfather, Earl Cadogan, had been British Envoy, and then Ambassador. It is therefore not surprising that Caroline was used to Continental travel and was encouraged by education (partly in French) to pursue interests beyond the borders of her native country. There seem to have been few or no constraints on her visits to France: no paternal warnings about expenditure such as dogged George Lyttelton, no paternal directions as to where or how often she should travel such as suffered by James Boswell. But she had her own difficulties. Her parents strongly disapproved of her marriage in 1744 to the politician, Henry Fox (1705–74). He appeared to have a promising parliamentary career ahead of him: he had been a member of the Cabinet, was appointed Privy Councillor in 1746 and Leader of the Commons in 1755, but two years later fell from favour into political oblivion. His elevation as 1st Baron Holland in 1763 did little to assuage his bitterness.

It was in the years following his retirement from active politics that Caroline (now Baroness Holland in her own right) undertook her Grand Tours — three of them. We are concerned only with the first (in 1766–7) and the letters written to her sister Emily during that period. Her earlier experiences of visiting France probably explain the confidence and seemingly reckless speed with which she travelled from Kingsgate on the south coast of England, to

Calais, and thence to Lyon, where a family group of travellers assembled. The entries in her notebook allow us to appreciate her determination and remarkable energy. For example:

> Tuesday the 23ᵈ of Sep. Set sail from Kingsgate at 6 O Clock in the morning landed at Calais at three the same day
> Wednesday the 24 Set out in the afternoon and arrived at St Omers that Night
> Thursday 25 left St Omers early in the morning dined at Bethune came in the Evening to Arras
> Friday 26 left Arras

And so on. Within a week she arrived in St Dizier; in less than a fortnight she had reached Lyon.

Caroline used the right-hand half of her paper to record the facts of her journey—such as those quoted above—dates, where she stayed, dined and slept; the left-hand part was reserved for more descriptive commentary. For instance, the 'facts' of her journey from St Dizier to Lyon are recorded as follows:

> October ye 1ˢᵗ Wednesday left St Dizier dined at Vignerai [Vignory] came in the Evening to Chaumont
> Thursday 2ᵈ Breakfasted at Langres dinned at Tille came in the Evening to Dijon
> Friday 3ᵈ left Dijon dined at Bea[u]ne
> Saturday 4ᵗʰ Lay at Chalon sur Saone
>   Left Chalon dined at Tournus and lay at Macon
> Sunday the 5ᵗʰ dined at Villefranche came early in the Evening to Lyons

Opposite this factual record she wrote:

> the road from Dijon to Lyons thro' the most beautiful Country I ever saw, the Inn at Bea[u]ne the neatest? quietest Inn I ever was at, we travelled in the time of Vendange [grape harvest] which made our journey charming we had but one rainy day between Calais and Lyons, all the rest fine, at Tournus and thereabout the peasant women in the House wear a white Muslin hand ker chief pinned like a Veil on their heads which they call Couvre chef it is odd and becomming, persons all thro burgundy better looking people not so poor as those I had seen in the rest of France

Comparison between this passage and the letter Caroline wrote to her sister from Lyon on Monday 6 October suggests that the one may have provided a kind of *aide mémoire* for the other. She did not invariably transmit every recorded detail to her sister. For example, while the information in her notebook that, on 10 October, 'Mr Churchill and L[ad]y Mary dined with us went all to the play *La Chasse d'Henri quatre*' was passed on in the letter of 18 October, Caroline did not tell Emily that she went a second time to the theatre on the 11th. However, perhaps reminded by her notebook entries on the 14th and 16th, she remembered to mention that her husband, Lord Holland, went twice to the theatre, the second time to see *Les Femmes Savantes* which she had herself seen in Paris in May 1763.

The group of travellers who met in Lyon comprised: Caroline and her husband (invariably referred to even in her private notebooks as 'Lord Holland'); her eldest son Stephen ('Ste') and his wife of six months, Lady Mary Fitzpatrick; her younger sons, Charles James and Henry ('Harry'), 17 and 11 years old respectively; her nephew William Robert Fitzgerald (Emily's second son) with his tutor, Bolle; and Clotworthy Upton (created 1st Baron Templetown in 1776). They decided to split into two groups, one going south to Marseilles and by sea to Naples, the other proceeding eastwards to cross the Alps at Mont Cenis, thence to Turin and Florence, and finally via Rome to Naples, then perhaps the most important city in Italy. Caroline was in the second group together with her younger son Harry and Upton.

Her route to Mont Cenis took her to Chambéry where she 'came at night' on 24 October and 'found Ste and Lady Mary' there. She dined at Montmélian and stayed overnight at St Michel; she dined at Modana on the 26th and slept at Lanslebourg 'at the foot of Mont Cenis.' It is manifest that, though the overall experience of crossing the Alps may have been 'most delightful' in retrospect, Caroline was terrified by the actual business of getting to and over the pass. Her letter to Emily of 29 October, together with the jotting in her notebook—'the crossing Mont Cenis… is terrible'—make that abundantly clear. To recover from the nervous ordeal, she and her companions rested for three days in Turin which they approached by way of Susa. Leaving Turin on Sunday, 2 November, they spent a night in an 'excellent Inn' at Vercelli and arrived in Milan the next day. They devoted only a morning to Milan and then, in the afternoon, set off on the short journey to Lodi. By the 5th they were in Parma; they dined in Modena on the 6th and that night they 'lay at Bologna'. Though Caroline described Bologna as 'a beautiful town' it was not allowed to detain them; they left it the next day. They crossed the Appenines and on Saturday 8 November arrived 'at Florence at 3 O Clock in the afternoon'. They remained there till 13 November.

The warmer climate, in contrast to the extreme cold of the Alpine region, was obviously welcome to Caroline: she records it in her notebook as well as telling her sister about it by letter. She attended a *conversatione* at the residence of the English Minister at the Court of Tuscany, Sir Horace Mann, and was appalled (as was her daughter-in-law, Lady Mary) at the 'vulgar' women who were also present. Except for the Medici Gallery which had 'a few beautiful things [but] much trash', other Florentine riches were ignored. However, at least the environs were considered 'delightful' deserving 'the most poetical descriptions'; 'the Villas round about quite enchanting.'

Then followed four exhausting days en route for Rome via Siena and Viterbo. The speed of their progress is vividly revealed in a remark from Caroline's letter to Emily on 18 November: 'The only principal town we came thro' was Luna, by moon light it appear'd well built, but we came into it between ten and eleven at night and left it by six the day following.' Accommodation varied in quality: the inn at Siena was 'very good', and in the larger towns was usually satisfactory, but, generally speaking, Caroline found 'the Inns so bad and alltogether the travelling is very bad indeed for Women.'

Rome's vast resources took her by surprise: as she recorded in her notebook, 'the great profusion of fine things in the Villas churches and palaces quite exceeded my expectations.' She and her companions spent a week in what she described for her sister (quoting Addison's *Cato*) as '*the heart of Empire, Nurse of Heroes and delight of Gods.*' Caroline was kept indoors for two and a half days suffering from (presumably) neuralgia in her face; nevertheless the city satisfied an abundance of interests in compensation: as she told her sister on 2 December, 'the things that are to be seen there, which would really employ a month even to those not particularly curious to seeing everything.' In sharp contrast with the inexhaustible delights of Rome, Villetri—the first overnight stop on the way to Naples—was dismissed as 'a vile place.' But her spirits recovered during a brief stay in a private house at Malla di Gaeta, described in her Notebook as 'a most lovely place very fine air, situated on the Mediterranean Sea full of Orange and Myrtle trees all about it.' And the next day the party arrived in Naples: 'Ld Holland and Charles came to meet us 2 Miles out of the town.' After a journey of five weeks, her relief and pleasure are obvious.

That was Thursday 27 November 1766. The next entry in Caroline's notebook is dated 1767, 'March ye 16'; it reads: 'left Naples with Charles and Harry.' For the intervening four months her letters, often written on folio sheets, provide a valuable source of information and insights. Inevitably, since Caroline was writing privately to a much-loved sister, she felt free to mention matters of a particularly personal kind, even if in a coded fashion. Emily would understand her allusion to irregular periods—'I have been out of order at a week, ten days, and a fortnight's end, never get beyond three weeks'—and her apprehension at early signs of the menopause—'I am now past forty-three, something of that kind may be beginning.' And she conveyed to her sister her disapproval of Italian women openly talking about 'having a certain distemper... most of the women have it', presumably referring to some kind of venereal disease. But the femininity apparent in the letters is not limited to such personal matters: frequently there is evidence of a distinctively feminine intelligence which points to differences between Caroline's observations and those of her male companions.

She considers it important, for example, precisely to describe the headgear worn by French agricultural workers: 'a little kind of a black high-crown'd hat'; then she pauses to make the description more accurate: '(but not peaked crownd like the old English ones).' To make the point even sharper she adds a description of a girl at Margate who sells eggs and cucumbers: she is 'dressed in a blonde fly cap, as they call it, and silk gown.' Caroline obviously derived great pleasure as well as enlightenment from her powers of observation: 'It is extremely entertaining to drive about the streets to see how very unlike everything is to what we see at home.' Little seems to have escaped her attention. Few men would have considered it sufficiently important to record—perhaps even to notice—that among Neapolitan women 'none of them make you a curtsey but a bow, and take hold of your hand', or that there was 'no such thing as women shop-keepers.' It is perhaps unsurprising that Caroline revealed her distaste for the dress of female guests at Sir Horace Mann's *conversatione* reminding her of London prostitutes 'showing such a quantity of neck, vastly laced up, no covering either on the head or neck.' But then there is the additional observation about the vulgar women: though each of them had a male companion, there was 'no conversation seeming to pass between them.' That is the startling detail which unifies the parts into a *tableau vivant*.

The letters also prove invaluable to an understanding of how the wealthy aristocratic Tourists spent their time when not actually travelling. We learn, for example, the daily routine: 'We generally air in the morning and dine at three o'clock, which is late here... We sup always en famille at ten exactly and keep good hours.' There were, however, many social activities and duties to accommodate. Caroline found it 'proper and convenient... to have a conversatione... once a week'; a new acquaintance, Princess de Trankavilla, was 'at home every night; one goes about nine, plays at cards and sups if one chooses it'; Mrs Hamilton, wife of the British Envoy at Naples, was 'at home with a concert and assembly once a week, and the Imperial Envoys Wife once a week.' Caroline admitted to a great love of the card game, loo; fortunately it was a fashionable pastime. She and Countess Mahony 'have a loo party made up with Gentlemen' three or four times a week. Then there was the 'Opera which is an assembly'; Caroline had been 'twice to the Opera' in her first fortnight in Naples and intended to go 'once a week or once a fortnight' in future. She also received visits from 'numbers of Italian ladies' but, after an initial visit, they did not come again; Caroline did not find this behaviour offensive since she regarded Italian women as 'Ordinary, Noisy and Underbred, debauchd to a degree.' With so much socialising, gossip flourished. One catches the tone of resulting conversation in such remarks as: 'there is a Sir Thomas and Lady Betty Worsley, mighty good but deadly dull, and... their son, rather pert'; or, Countess Mahony 'daughter of fat Lady Newburgh'; or again, Italian women 'are taught no one thing in their convents, not even to work.' She is acerbic about 'the great people'; they are 'made up of ignorance, pride, debauchery and show... they live all the year round on a little Macaroni and greens, in order to keep Equipages and Servants.' Nevertheless, Caroline felt it necessary to follow the example of ladies who have 'two or four footmen behind their coach, two running footmen to go before, and two pages': 'I have been obliged to hire two running footmen.' The cost of such ostentation is not a matter of comment or complaint; indeed monetary considerations are never mentioned.

Caroline's activities were not limited to the social round; she found Naples unsurpassed in antiquities: 'for those nothing beats this place.' She visited 'the King's Museum at Portici, which is built over Herculanium' and gives Emily a full account of what she saw. Similarly her visit to Pompeii prompts another detailed description and discussion. On the homeward journey (except for Geneva, following the outward route) her letters and notebook entries give further evidence of her cultural interests. She recounts her pleasure in Guido's painting, *Aurora*, in Rome; she records her appreciation of Guercino's painting of the Crucifixion in Bologna and Correggio's *Mystic Marriage of St Catherine* in Parma. When in Geneva she ordered for her sister 'four new Volumes of Voltaire's Works printed last week'; she also went to the theatre to see his tragedy *Les Scythes* and his *petite pièce*, the comedy *La Femme qui a Raison*. She shared her sister's enthusiasm for the letters of Mme de Sévigné; she was clearly conversant with the writings of Pascal; and she quotes affectionately (even if slightly inaccurately) from Goldsmith's poem *The Traveller* published only two years before.

Her Grand Tour reached its conclusion when she, her husband and young sons 'came to Calais' on 23 May 1767; they embarked on the 25th and left Calais 'at Nine O Clock in the morning landed at Kingsgate Nine at Night'. Her final notebook entry reads:

> Here ends my long journey, the end of which is answerd by Ld Holland being restored to a better State of health than when we left England Sep ye 23 1766.

For permission to publish Caroline Lennox's letters from her MSS the editors wish to thank the Board of the National Library of Ireland.

For permission to publish extracts from Caroline Lennox's notebook (Add MSS 51445) the editors wish to thank the British Library. To illustrate the relationship between Caroline's notebook and her letters to Emily, extracts from the former (prefaced by *MS*) will occasionally be included among annotation to the latter.

Letters of Caroline Lennox

Kingsgate
Sunday ye 21 of Sep [1766]

I allways forget my dearest sister[452] to inform you where to direct to me, during my *Sejour* in foreign parts, the best way will be to send them to me in Picadilly, and my porter has orders to send them to us, this is probably the last letter I shall write this side the water, Tuesday next we embark from this door; the weather at present is heavenly. I hope you injoy it. I can injoy nothing with the thoughts of crossing this odious Sea. I fear I shall scarcely hear of you my sweet sister till I arrive at Naples which will not be till December probably, unless you write time enough for me to receive your letter at Lyons, where I hope we shall be till the middle of October. I have appointed William[453] to be with us the 8th of that Month there in case we should be hurry'd away, as it's thought better to cross the Alps before the rainy season comes on. Lord Holland[454] continues delightfully well. I shall write a line from Calais, my love to dear Louisa[455] tell her to send her letters to Picadilly also. Adieu, my dear siss. Charles[456] left us yesterday; he takes Paris in his route to Lyons; we do not; we shall go thro' Champaigne and Burgundy. I hope we shall be in the *Vendange* season.[457] Once more adieu; you comprehend the fidget and feel I have I'm sure. What a great part of one's life is passed in preparation for the future and how little the present is injoy'd in quiet, which is [a] state I believe not intended for us this side the Grave. I frequently wish it all over; perhaps, tho', that's as well as other journeys I might aprehend when it drew near.

---

452 When Caroline Lennox wrote the early letters to her sister Emilia (invariably known as Emily) which follow, Emily was Marchioness of Kildare by virtue of her husband James Fitzgerald (1722–73) having succeeded his father as Earl of Kildare in 1744. On the occasion of their marriage in 1747 he was created Viscount Leinster in the Peerage of Ireland; in 1761 he was created Marquess of Kildare and Earl of Offaly also in that Peerage. He was created Duke of Leinster in November 1766; during the time of these letters, therefore, Emily became Duchess of Leinster.
453 William Robert Fitzgerald (1749–1804), later 2nd Duke of Leinster; Emily's second son.
454 Henry Fox (1705–74), Caroline's husband; created 1st Baron Holland in 1763.
455 Louisa Augusta Lennox (1743–1805), Caroline's youngest sister; married Thomas Conolly in 1758.
456 Charles James Fox (1749–1806), Caroline's second son, later a prominent Whig politician.
457 grape harvesting

Arras
the 25 of September [1766]

I take every opportunity of writing to my dearest sister tho I have nothing to say to her but to answer her obliging letter of the 13. which I received at St Omers where we lay yesterday, and to tell her how well Ld Holland bears his journey. We are at present in a nasty Inn waiting for Horses till Eleven O'Clock, Arras is the Capital of Artois. St Omers where we lay last Night is a fine town full of Irish Papists, the route we now pursue thro Flanders is a part of that beautiful Country I had never seen but I find it allmost equally beautifull with the Brussels road, the Towns are so fine and the fortifications make them appear so pretty, I shall however be more amused when we get out of Flanders as the people and Country and look of every thing will be more new to me. Ld Bristol[458] to be sure never can outlive a Winter at Dublin. Ld John Cavendish not only govern'd my Brother but Ld Rockingham; he and the Duke of Newcastle were most undoubtedly the cause of this last Change.[459] Ld Frederick[460] is not I believe in such vast favour as he was, the D[uche]ss at least has got another flirt whom she don't own to love as well as Ld Frederick but whom it is suspected she does, Mr Beauclair,[461] the most self sufficient Coxcomb, in my opinion I ever saw, he has the rage of being fine and his following her is only because she is a D[uche]ss. L[ad]y Bolingbroke is his passion, if he has any passion but for himself which is doubted. The D[uche]ss laughs about it and says 'who wd *thought* I should ever flirt with a Macaroni?'[462] I can easily account for my partiality to the French; it was early taken, you know my father had it strongly, we went when I was quite a Child to Holland and France; the servants and Children of consequence hated Holland and the

---

458 George Hervey (1721–75), 2nd Earl of Bristol; he was appointed Lord Lieutenant of Ireland in 1766, but never visited the country.
459 Lord John Cavendish (1734–83), youngest son of William Cavendish, 3rd Duke of Devonshire. He acted as tutor or 'governor' to Caroline's brother Charles and to Charles Watson-Wentworth (1730–82), 2nd Marquess of Rockingham who had, in July 1766, resigned after a year in office as Prime Minister; he was succeeded—in 'this last Change'—by the Earl of Chatham. Thomas Pelham-Holles (1693–1768), 1st Duke of Newcastle-upon-Tyne, a very influential politician (he had served twice as Prime Minister).
460 Lord Frederick Cavendish (1729–1803), younger son of the 3rd Duke of Devonshire.
461 Topham Beauclerk (pronounced 'Bo-clare') (1739–80). He had an adulterous relationship with Lady Diana, wife of the 2nd Viscount Bolingbroke (1732–87) resulting in her being divorced in 1768. She and Beauclerk then married.
462 A dandy of the kind which arose in England *c.*1760 consisting of young men who had travelled in Europe and affected the manners and fashions prevalent in Continental society. The earliest use recorded in OED is in 1764.

Dutch, and were violently fond of the D[uche]ss of Portsmouth;[463] it seems foolish but those early impressions do remain with one. Set your heart at rest tho and be satisfied with their liking Louisa and me the rest will do nothing to retrieve their good name and will I fear make little Sal[464] forfeit hers in the short stay she will make at Paris with them and the Fitzroys who are now there to complete the Cotterie.

I hear from so many people that Ld Barrymore[465] is a mauvais sujet that I do not at all regret his not staying for your Emily.[466] I wish to God Sal cd make Carlisle[467] marry her a Year or t[w]o hence. Tis a sweet pretty boy he is Sally's Cicisbeo,[468] he comes to Italy. I hope to see your dear William at Lyons. We have heavenly Weather I am vastly well thank God. Ld Holland as I before told you is surprisingly so.

Yrs C. Holland

All the Country I have now passed thro belongd to those Dukes of Burgundy: what a fine appanage[469] situated so between England and France.

Lyons
the 6th of October Monday [1766]

Here we are my sweet siss all well I thank God after our tedious long journey which alltogether has been pleasant: weather, roads, every thing in our favour. Ld Holland has at times been fatigued, but in the main bore it surprisingly well: he has rather gain'd flesh, I flatter myself. We arrived here last Night; when I found a letter from you; dated the 15 of October: I received another from you since I left England, which I thank'd you for in one I wrote from Arras, pray while I am abroad allways mention the letters you receive from me; their dates and the place they are dated from; that I may know you

---

463 Louise de Kéroualle, Duchess of Portsmouth was the mistress of Charles Lennox, 1st Duke of Richmond and mother of Charles Lennox (1701–50), the 2nd Duke, who was in turn Caroline Lennox's father.
464 Caroline's sister, Sarah Lennox (1745–1826). In the 1760s she had several affairs which became public knowledge and the stuff of scandal.
465 Richard, 6th Earl of Barrymore (1745–73).
466 Lady Emily Mary Fitzgerald (1752–1818), Emily's second daughter.
467 Frederick Howard, 5th Earl of Carlisle (1748–1825).
468 The name given in eighteenth-century Italy to the recognised gallant or *cavalier servente* of a married woman. OED quotes Lady Mary Wortley Montagu writing in 1718: 'The custom of cecisbeos… I know not whether you have ever heard of such animals.' See p. 254.
469 A grant of land by a monarch.

receive them, we expect Ste and Ly Mary[470] here to morrow, so we do William and Charles—we must be here a week to prepare for our journey over the Alps, I will give you some account of our journey hitherto, for Im sure you like to follow us as we go: I wrote from Arras, which is the Capital of Artois in Flanders but belongs to the French. We got again into Picardy then into Champagne. We staid half a day at Rheims the Capital of that province, 'tis a fine old town, but the French towns are not so fine as the Flemish ones. There is in it the finest old Gothick Church I ever saw, the Country about it is open and Ugly like Wiltshire, when we came more south in the same province the road was very beautifull from a view of the River Marne in the valley, and high hills coverd with Vines, Parks and Woods; a very Romantick pretty prospect all the Way. But when we came into Burgundy the chearfulness, gaiety, richness and beauty of the Country is not to be described; Dijon the Capital of it, is a most agreeable town, and the road from thence here which is all thro the same province, is really heavenly, the feel of the Air is so pure so soft and so charming. The river Sonne [Saone] which runs thro it, and meets the Rhone here, is as fine as the Thames, the Valley thro which it runs full of Meadows, Corn, Flax and every kind of Culture, the Hills of each side coverd with wood, Vines, Villages, Hamlets, Gentlemen's Houses Churches, Convents, make alltogether the most delightful prospect:[471] and is more worth seeing than any thing I ever saw; without exaggeration you drive Miles together with a View of much such a prospect only far exceeding it, as you see from Richmond Hill;[472] the Vineyards in some places close to the road, where one stops and for sixpence eat as many delicious grapes as you please and very delicious they are, it is now Vendange time, the Country is vastly peopled and the peasants look more comfortable than in any other part of France I have seen. The womens dress is comical and pretty, like some old pictures I have seen, the peasants I mean; other people are dressed the same all thro France; at one town the Common people had what they call couvre-chefs,[473] a square Muslin handkerchief pin[n]ed like a Veil on their heads, I have a notion they wear the same in some county in Ireland; it looks neat and pretty. Those in the fields wear a little kind of black high-crownd hat (but not peaked crownd like the old English ones), I do think it both neat and decent that the Common people should have a particular dress and not as it is in England all alike, at

---

470 Caroline's elder son, Stephen Fox (1745–74) and his wife Lady Mary Fitzpatrick; they had married on 20 April 1766.
471 'The hills… delightful prospect': *MS 3* 'Lyons a disagreeable situation subject to foggs the environs of it pretty, beautiful prospects from the Villas and Country on the adjacent Hills, which are full of them'.
472 Richmond Hill afforded extensive views over the city of London.
473 A covering for the head.

Margate[474] there is a Girl comes to sell Eggs and Cucumbers, dressed in a blonde-fly cap, as they call it and silk gown. We are now in the Lyon[n]ais, if I don't send this letter to day you shall have some account of this place. If I do send it now it will be because some English people are going to England from hence, and if I hear they go immediately I will send my letter by them, if not, I'll keep it till your Boy arrives and give you some account of him; the people are not going immediately to England so I will not close my letter yet, but say adieu for the present.

Ld Ophaly[475] is arrived with Charles from Paris looking very well and is grown Genteel; he will write himself to you; he has seen more French than you imagine — at the Camp he lived chiefly with them; both he and Charles confirm all I heard of the Richmonds, Mrs Greville[476] writes word the same but all say that those few who know my Brother George like him and that he likes them but dare not live with them for fear of the rest. Adieu my dearest sister before I leave Lyons I hope to write again to you but will now finish this letter having several to write within these two or three days believe me —

Yrs C Holland

[Lord Holland adds postscript]

Your Sister's kindness is Proof against long journeys that she hates. No man was ever so happy as I am in my Family. I feel infinitely oblig'd to them and particularly Dear Caroline. Adieu, Dear Lady Kildare. I am *trop attendri*[477] to say any more now. But I believe, dear Mad^m, I shall see you again. Adieu!

Lyons
the 18 of October [1766]

I promised to write before I left Lyons my dearest sister, and I have the pleasure to inform you I really think Ld Holland much mended; he eats, sleeps and is so cheerfull as to have gone twice to the play here, the Theatre is a very pretty one, the Actors tollerable. There is a petite piece much in fashion here

---

474 Seaport and market town in Kent, a short distance from Kingsgate where Caroline lived.
475 Following the death of Emily's eldest son, George Fitzgerald in 1765, aged 18, her second son William Robert Fitzgerald was styled Earl of Offaly.
476 Fanny Greville (née M'Cartney), celebrated wit and beauty; Flora in *Maxims, Characters and Reflections, Critical, Satirical, and Moral* (London: Tonson, 1756).
477 Feeling too tender.

called La Chasse d'Henri quatre, taken from our Miller of Mansfield,[478] tis prettily wrote and exceedingly interesting because one can suppose Henri quatre in such circumstances so much better than any other King. We have been to see some antiquitys, remains of old Roman walls Baths etc which I don't care a pin for but the driving up the Mountains is charming; the prospects are so beautifull; the situation of this Town low and damp but warm. I am quite glad it was not the place for us to settle in for it really don't agree with me; we are detain'd here on account of some springs being put to the Carriage necessary for our Italian Journey. We have not attempted making accquaintance here as we were only passengers; but I'm told the society is agreeable. I see at the play very genteel, fine sort of people, tis the most populous town I ever saw. Monday or Tuesday next I hope to leave it, Ld Holland who has by the Italian post Book calculated my journey tells me that stopping two days at Turin, three at Florence, seven at Rome without travelling long journeys I may be at Naples the 21st of November. We had the Churchills in this Town 4 or 5 days travelling for amusement only or rather restlessness; for they told me they had a comfortable House at Nanci which is they say and I have allways heard is an agreeable place. Ly Mary[479] is grown old her affectation wore off, you know she cd allways be agreeable when she pleased. Ste and Ly Mary meet Harry Mr Upton[480] and I at Turin, they were here a week, they are now gone to Geneva; she among other very aimiable qualitys has that delightfull one belonging to Youth, of being pleased and liking every thing she sees. We were both much diverted with a Fête the Common people have here about a league from the town, where they dance eat and junket in the open air; tis impossible to describe the kind of thing to you, but its vastly pretty. I went to see the silk Manufactory here which is really curious. William is very good humoured and agreeable and seems to like us all. Voltaire has wrote two more Books not such as you or I shall read, in the stile of his Dictionnaire Philosophique.[481] It's really quite shocking my dear sister that such an old wretch, loaded with infirmitys, just going out of the world should take the trouble to disturb those who are so happy as to enjoy the only thing that makes life comfortable in it. I have quite

---

478   Robert Dodsley, *The King and the Miller of Mansfield. A Dramatic Tale* (London: Dodsley, 1737); Dodsley (1703–64) was born in Mansfield; later he became a leading London publisher.
479   Colonel Charles Churchill (?1720–1812), married Lady Mary Walpole in 1746; they were both in Lyon in October 1766. Lady Mary was Sir Robert Walpole's natural daughter. The Churchills dined with Caroline on 12 October (*MS 3*).
480   Henry (Harry) Edward Fox (1755–1811), Caroline's third son; Clotworthy Upton (1721–85) probably acting as Harry's 'governor'.
481   François-Marie Arouet (1694–1778), wrote under the name Voltaire. His *Dictionnaire Philosophique* was published in 1764.

a horror for him, but I comfort myself, he is little qualifyed to convince peoples understanding, tho he has in my opinion more talents to divert their fancy than any author I ever read; I shall scarcely, my dear Sister write till I get to Naples, unless I should find time from Rome; be assured I shall miss no opportunitys of letting you hear of me. William who will be with Ld Holland will let you know how he does. Adieu my love to your Girls. Will Ld K[ildare] take Ld Hollands advice and claim the promise of his Dukedom?

Yrs C. Holland

Pray inform me if my letters come safe to your hand, it seems such a long way, and pray dont forget to mention the dates of them in your answer.

———⋙•⋘———

Lyons
Sunday the 19 of October [1766]

I wrote very lately to my dearest sister but having received your kind letter of the 30th to day I cant help writing again to thank you for it before I leave Lyons which I hope will be the day after to morrow, not but that I'm comfortable enough now we have dry clear Weather but I'm impatient to get over the Alps while this Weather lasts as I believe that journey being very pleasant, or very much other ways, depends entirely on the Weather. When once we are t'other side the mountains it is not so material.

We went yesterday to see a Country House just out of the town, upon the Hill indeed I was tempted to break the tenth commandment, for so enchanting a place I never saw 'tis a fine old Chateau in which Henri trois was born;[482] I saw a bed in it where Henri quatre had lain; the House is one of those old fashion'd comfortable houses I love; and it appears to be comfortably inhabited. A large Gallery of 170 feet long with a large Salle de Compagnie adjoining to it above stairs for the Summer apartment; the Autumn apartment below stairs op'ning to a little garden full South overlooking a most heavenly prospect. The House is on a Hill, a fine long natural terrasse to the South, with a view of the same prospect, which is really not to be described. You see from it the rivers Sonne [Soane] and Rhône winding in a rich cultivated valley; the Town of Lyons, which makes a beautifull object; the Hills rising on the other side, coverd with Houses and Vineyards, and full of fine objects, behind the House and terrasse a charming oak wood on a rising ground to the North. Can you

---

482 'We went yesterday... born': *MS 3* 'the Chateau de Mad^{me} la presidente de Navare the most beautiful situation I ever saw, the Chateau a fine old House with a Gallery of 170 feet long in it, Harry 3^{d} of France born there'. Henri III (1551–89) was born at Fontainebleau, not in the chateau.

imagine any thing more lovely? It was one of those fine October days described by Mme de Sevigné,[483] ces beaux jours de crystal d'octobre; so much the finer in those South climates as the sun has more power; the orange trees and greenhouse plants are still out of doors.

How happy I am when I can think of passing again some Months with my dearest sister tho I don't foresee the time, for should Ld Holland pass as we flatter ourselves he will, a more comfortable Winter out of England than he has for Years passed in it, he is much more inclined to come Abroad again another Winter, but not so far from home as we now do, that would really be almost impossible, and very, very uncomfortable to come over again every Winter. But all those are distant thoughts not to dwell upon now, why should not my dearest sister come next spring to England? I suppose all the English at Naples are accquainted and of course we shall become so with the family you mention; how much we may be so you know depends entirely on accidents and chance. However, one is allways more inclined to cultivate an accquaintance with those one knows something of, than with intire Strangers and I am obliged to you for your information. Swift's Letters I own entertaind me of all things, Miss Vanhomrigh's less than the others, a love story one can feel interested about is dull; I love Mrs Johnson vastly, don't you? I did like Ld Hydes letter very much.[484] You will in my last see how we jump in a thought frequently, my dear

---

483 Marie de Rabutin-Chantal (1626–96), married Henri, Marquis de Sévigné, in 1644; celebrated letter writer. 'Ce sont des beaux jours de crystal de l'automne, qui ne sont plus chauds, qui ne sont pas froids' [These are the beautiful crystal days of autumn which are no longer hot, and not cold].

484 Jonathan Swift (1667–1745), prominent satirist, political pamphleteer and poet. Caroline appears to have had access to Volume III of *Letters Written by the late Jonathan Swift, D.D., Dean of St Patrick's, Dublin, and Several of His Friends*, edited by John Hawkesworth (London: Davies and Dodsley, 1766). It contained letters from Swift to Esther Vanhomrigh (1688–1723), known as 'Vanessa', his intimate and correspondent for 17 years, and to 'Stella', Esther Johnson (1681–1728) who took her place in Swift's affection. It also contained a single letter from Henry Hyde (1710–53), close friend of Henry St John Bolingbroke, who dedicated his *Letters on the Study and Use of History* (London: Millar, 1752) to him; he succeeded to the title 5th Baron Hyde in 1750. Hyde's letter, dated 7 March 1752, was to the poet and miscellaneous writer, David Mallet (1705–65) whose reply is also included in the Hawkesworth volume. Mallet had been entrusted by Bolingbroke (who died on 12 December 1751) with his MSS, and all writings that had been prepared for publication; these included *Letters on the Study and Use of History* which Bolingbroke had circulated among his friends (including Hyde) on the understanding that they would not be published. Hyde urged Mallet not to publish Bolingbroke's sceptical views on revealed religion and his attack on the established church. In reply, Mallet insisted that he would not 'omit or alter any thing in those works, which… Bolingbroke had deliberately prepared for the press, and I will publish no other.' He published Bolingbroke's collected works in five volumes in 1754.

siss. Not all Voltaire's lively entertaining writing can reconcile me to him, nor to his continuing to publish Books by which he intends to disturb the peace of peoples minds. I am mighty glad to have seen so much of les *beaux Esprits* and les esprits fort[485] as I did at Paris, because they entertain me, and I had an opportunity of seeing how frivolous they are, indeed they do all the mischief their petit Esprit[486] are capable of, and are the most contemptuous set of people in the World; they will change and spoil the character of the sweet nature, which I think an aimiable one; several of the old fashioned French people complain sadly, and are of my opinion, they say they have allready at Paris changed that delightful gayety the French naturally have, and tis true the young people all affect to be grave; an old French lady of my acquaintance says *nous avons bien perdu au change un esprit qui vaut bien un esprit fort.*[487] I agree with her.

William I believe writes to you himself; he is a dear good boy as ever lived, vastly obliging and attentive. He goes every morning to the riding house here, which is I believe very good for him; he takes long walks and seems desirous of not growing fat. I wish my Ste would take the same method, but tis too late with him I fear now, his size is so enormous.

Dont abuse me for not putting a case[488] to my letter; as it is, it will cost you a sum of money. Ld Holland continues pure well. We don't go till Wednesday; our nasty carriage won't be ready.

Turin
Wednesday the 29 of October [1766]

We arrived here safe and well my dearest sister yesterday afternoon, and I am quite impatient to tell you so, as you wd be to hear so, did you know or cd you have any Idea of what it is to pass Mount Cenis. I will not attempt to describe it, but refer you to some of your Men accquaintances who have done it. Let it suffice you to know that one goes in open Chairs for six hours together, carry'd by Men up and down rocks that it seems quite impossible for any thing but Goats to walk upon, that one is often carryd within a hair's breadth of the most frightfull precipices, and yet they assure one there is no danger; the Weather was so cold going up the Mountain twas scarcely bearable; on the top and coming down rain and fog, so that fear of cold and the fright I was in,

---

485 Men of wit and free-thinkers.
486 Limited intelligence.
487 'With the change we have certainly lost a lightness of wit that is just as valuable as free thinking.'
488 A cover; an envelope.

scarcely permitted me for some time to put my Nose out to look about me.[489] I at last tho took Courage and considerd I was under the same protection on the top of the Mountain as I was in [my] own room, and when I did get the better of my fears the sight was indeed glorious, tho the fog prevented seeing all the beauty of it, only think sweet siss I was unluckily out of order just the day I passed Mount Cenis, exposed to all the Cold and wet, poor Ly Mary just recovered [from] a tooth ache her face still swell'd, and Mrs Hobson[490] with a pain in her face and sore throat, and yet we are all well. No new cold got, nor none increas'd God be thankd. The journey thro Savoy which is the journey thro the Alps, till you come to the foot of Mount Cenis is really charming, the weather was lovely, we went so slow in our carriages that I often walked three or four Miles a day. The greatness, solemnity, and singularity of the views exceed all one can imagine: Hills far above the clouds, immense falls of Water rapid torrents, great rivers, vast groves of spruce, fir, Scotch fir, Larix's[491] and Birch-wood, tis really immense and not possible to be imagined till you see it. Nor is it to be imagined the horrid hovels for Inns one cant call them, that one eats, and sleeps at. I had a bed of my own. What a number of reflexions such a journey makes one make on the great and wonderful Works of the Creator and also how the love of gain causes us to break thro all difficulties: one wd imagine no human beings wd ever have thought of passing the bounds Nature seems there to have placed between France and Savoy; but the Silk trade carryd on between this place and Lyons has conquerd those difficulties and Mules loaded with that Commodity and others continually pass and repass. After having passed Mount Cenis we came to a town called Suza the first in Piedmont, about 30 Miles from this, of Turin, which appears to be a regular well built town; the approach to it fine, for above six Miles a delightful Avenue of high fine trees. We feel so happy to be in a House again. This is a good comfortable Inn; and as I before told you since we left Lyons, the Inns are dreadfull; thank God here we are well and safe, and here we intend to rest two or three days. The poor people in Savoy are wretchedly poor and the most honest creatures in the World, poor wretches cultivate up the top of those great Mountains and are sadly oppressd by the Government; the Piedmontese are reck'ned quite the reverse all cheating and sharp. This is not reck'ned a fine Climate but I see the orange trees still out of doors, so it must be hotter than ours, the Weather is

---

489 'We arrived here... look about me': *MS 4* 'the whole journey crossing the Alps most delightfull except the wretched horse and the crossing Mont Cenis which is *terrible*. The views are beyond all description fine Solemn and Great particularly the two day journey of the 25 and 26 [October]. The cold and rain prevented my seeing much of the beautys of Mont Cenis as I kept coverd up in my Chair and seldom looked out'.
490 Unidentified; possibly Lady Mary's companion.
491 Larch

coldish, but pleasant just now. I'm told we shall be five days going from hence to Florence our next resting place, not all the buildings, palaces pictures and curiositys I shall see will please me half so much, I'm sure as what I saw in Savoy three of our days journey particularly and even the crossing Mount Cenis in a fine day I can imagine pleasant, tho allways dreadfull if one can get the better of ones fears.

Ly Mary admires the womens head dress here—I mean those we meet in the Street, who are smart looking people: I suppose Bourgeoises and trades people. They wear a black lace or black Gauze hood covering half over their face like a veil—it really looks pretty. I hope and believe Ld Holland and our two boys[492] saild yesterday from Marseilles; this is fine weather for them. Whether I can hear of them till I come to Naples where I do suppose I shall find them; God knows! We met Ste and Ly Mary in our second days journey from Lyons, at Chambery, in Savoy. Adieu my dear sister. I shall send this fro hence before I go, should I have any thing to add to it I will – for the present adieu.

I have seen Madame St Gille[493] the famous Italian Lady all our Men are so fond of. She don't strike me as so inchanting I must confess: twas very civil in her to come and see us, tho. We went airing and saw several of the fine Ladies, there seems to be much beauty among them and they have a great advantage over my friends the French Ladies which is not wearing that detestable rouge, tho they do not appear to me to have that ease and Gentility the french women have, but when I have seen more I'll tell you more about them. The Environs of this town are charming and what I did not expect so far south the verdure most beautifull. The town itself built quite regular which has a very pretty Effect, as has also the great number of Country Houses all about the town.

Thursday the 30th

The post goes to morrow and Saturday we go so adieu sweet Siss I shall not be sorry to get to my journeys end. Thank God I bear it as well as I do

Friday the 1st of Nov^r [494]

One of our servants illness has detaind us here till now but to morrow I hope we shall go. We have been at an opera which tired me to death but to Ly Mary Musick is a great treat. Italy will be very amusing to her on that account she also understands drawing and painting and has much taste for it. We allso went to Madame St Gilles assembly very like an English Assembly of the moderate kind not a rout, beginning and ending at the same hours ours

---

492 Harry (Caroline's son) and William (Emily's).
493 Unidentified.
494 Friday was 31 October.

do. One Essential difference tho there is I don't think there were above a dozen women and above 30 Men. I dare say the Womens manner, dress, and appearance is in the Stile of common Women, and I quite understand why our Men like Italy – the Women pay them such court and if a woman cant contribute to an English Mans pleasure as she wishes, she does it in another way either by being convenient with regard to some other woman or to his play. Now God knows the French Women some of them are Abandon'd enough, but they will have court paid them which *John*[495] don't like, besides Galantry is not the sole business of a French [illegible] life who is ever so bad. Here it is all they think of, they have no education at all, I'm sure by the little I have seen and all I hear from a very sensible Man here, who comes often to us I shall not like the ways and manners and shall stick to my old Women; the French are the only people who understand all the ease of Society and the number of little agremens[496] that make it pleasant. This letter is long enough, I hope.

Yrs C. H.

Florence
the 9th of Nov^r. [1766]

Here we are My dear Sister since yesterday (after a tedious fatiguing journey of seven days) in the *sweets of Arno's Vale la belle Italia centre des beaux Arts et du gout*.[497] I wrote to you from Turin and will proceed with my journal for my letters to you are at present journals. We passed thro Lombardy soon after we left Turin. We came thro several very fine towns such as Milan, Placenzia, Parma, and Modena but in my opinion thro the ugliest Country one can see, excessively rich, and deep, all flat, every now and then a river and some pretty Villas, even the farm houses and barns in good Architecture. We then came to Bologna by much the finest built town I ever saw, most of the Streets with fine Colonades all along the Houses of fine Corinthian and Dorick pillars which has a Noble Effect. When we left Bologna which is a day and a half from this town, we began to cross the Appenines and the scene all along is beautiful: numbers of Villas and beautiful buildings with Groves of Cypress trees and falls of Water;[498] the verdure as in England up close to the Houses and very

---

495   John Bull, a typical Englishman.
496   pleasures
497   'the beauties of the valley of the Arno, beautiful Italy, the centre of art and taste' (Florence stands on the river Arno)
498   'We then came… falls of water': *MS 5* 'Bologna a beautiful town the Country from Bologna to Florence charming, full of Villas and pretty Scenes, with Cypress Groves, falls of water etc'.

fine indeed. In short it is a continual picture from Bologna to Florence. The Appenines tho high Mountains, after the Alps appear nothing; at Bologna we met the Provost of Dublin who complains heavily that in the midst of Vineyards he can't get a good glass of Wine.[499] The variety of dress among the peasants in Italy is entertaining. Mr Upton and Ly Mary find them out to be mighty pretty and pictoresque, Ste and I think they look like what we used to call *Cousin Bettys*[500] with their dirty greasy hair hanging about without Caps. They allso find out much more beauty in the Italians than we do, tho to be sure the Common people are not ugly like the French, but not near so pretty as our English paysannes. Ly Mary says its well Mr Upton is with us to stand by her about Musick, to be sure at one place there came a ballad-singing Girl who made a noise that appear'd to Ste, Harry, and I, like the screaming of Catts, which they assured us was mighty pretty. Ste and I divert ourselves with finding out French Chimney pieces or some imitation of French in allmost every town of Italy, for Mr Upton is a most violent prejudiced Italian, he really admires all he sees here, tis the tenth time he has crossed the Alps. Ste has one great fault to find which is the eating is so horrid here; I don't care about it as I find starving is the only way to keep well on so long and tedious a journey. Tho I have at last got one of my uncomfortable bad colds, we have still warm weather; but within these two days rain. I have seen many more Gloomy days than I expected when I left England to see. The situation of this Inn is charming looking on the river and seeing two beautiful bridges. The Environs of this town vastly fine, the town itself, less so, than most other Italian towns but alltogether tis reckned a sweet place. Tis four days journey from hence to Rome; in three days after that we hope to arrive at Naples, that is in three after we leave Rome for there we shall stay a few days. I heard of Ld Holland and his Young Companions being well at Marseilles the 31st of October, and being to embark the next day. I shall indeed dearest sister be very glad to get to Naples; tis a most tedious and most uncomfortable journey for a woman to take and tho I meet with great amusement at times it dont repay the trouble, pray look in the map and see what a way we are come. I do flatter myself from the great mildness of the Climate that our journey may have the desired effect for Ld Holland. I travel as you may suppose in very pleasant company. Ste except his deafness is well and in good spirits, and I rather think he is less deaf. Ly Mary grows more aimiable every day the more one knows her, and Mr Upton has more spirit and more good humour than any body ever had,

---

499 Francis Andrews, Provost of University of Dublin (d.1774); 'he was fond of, and indulged in the pleasures of the table', *Annual Register*, 1811, 36. (See Ingamells, *Dictionary*, for a fuller account.)

500 prostitutes

minds no difficulties, bustles about and does every thing for us. Harry is as happy as can be except when he don't meet with a good horse.

Adieu Yrs ever my dear sister, you see I neglect no oportunity of writing. Yrs
C Holland

Rome
the 18th of November [1766]

I left Florence with regret my dear Sister; the environs of it and the Country about it are so enchanting they quite answer the most poetical descriptions. Orange Groves, Catalonian jasmine hedges growing out in the gardens and all the Hills and sides of the Hills coverd with Villas, Cypresses, firs, and the most beautiful buildings.[501] The Climate also answers my expectations, tho I had a bad cold when I first came to Florence caught on the road, the weather was so mild the most part of the time we were at Florence, tho showery that we sat with open Windows and no fire. Our Inn looked upon the River and from it a charming prospect, indeed I cd not have imagined any thing in the Stile of the Country about Florence, it really resembles what one reads in story books and fairy tales. The *Traveller* justly observes of Italy '*Man is the only thing that dwindles there*',[502] perhaps I don't say it right but some thing to that purpose. I went to see the fine Galery and Collections made by the Medici familly, which allso exactly answer'd my expectations, as all Collections do – a very few fine things and a vast deal of tiresome stuff.[503] I shall never grow *virtu*.[504] I was at a conversatione at Sr Horace Mann,[505] an English assembly with the addition of a Concert only think how horrid! Ly Mary and I agreed we never saw such a set of vulgar stupid looking women dress'd like our women of the town, showing such a quantity of Neck, vastly laced up, no covering either on the head or Neck, few of them talking any thing but Italian, all with a Man by her side but

---

501 'I left Florence... beautiful buildings.' *MS 6* 'The environs of Florence most delightful, answers the most poetical descriptions, orange Grove Cypress sweet jesamins, the Villas round quite enchanting'.
502 Oliver Goldsmith's recently published poem, *The Traveller, or A Prospect of Society* (London: Newbery, 1764), line 126 ['Man seems the only growth...'].
503 'The weather... stuff.' *MS 5–6* 'The Inn at Florence well situated my apartment looking to the river, the weather so warm during our stay at Florence we did not have a fire and generally with our Window open, but Gloomy and rainy. We went to a *conservatione* at S^r H Manns, a Stupid assembly with the addition of a Concert, we went to see the Galery of pictures [ ] busts etc where we saw a few beautiful things much trash'.
504 Become a virtuoso.
505 Sir Horace Mann (1701–86), British Minister in Florence, 1740–86.

no conversation seeming to pass between them. I really feel the grandmother of the Company when I go into Company here—you don't see a middle-aged woman at least any who from either dress or manner chuse to appear so, all are young. Those who can speak French don't speak a word to one, nor did I see any of them talk to one another, the way of life is unsociable to a degree; no people eat together—they live at the Spectacle or these odious conversationes without any conversation together except a Man and a Woman. To be sure a Cicisbi must be the most tiresome of all animals. Milan is the only town in Italy [where] people dine or sup together and I own I am so French as to think there is no Society without it, you get more accquainted with people at table. The road from Florence here is four most fatiguing days' journey, some part of it a beautifull Country very Mountainous which makes it tedious to a degree.[506] The only principal town we came thro was Lina [Luna], by moon light it appeard well built but we came into it between 10 and 11 at night and left it by six the day following. After 4 of those fatiguing days last Night we arrived here, in this famous place near *the heart of Empire Nurse of Heroes and delight of Gods*.[507] The approach to it is fine. I am resting myself this morning and am afterwards to see a vast deal. The weather is charming, a bright sun shine; three of our days journey was the same and last Night we enter'd this town by moon light near ten O'Clock with our Landau open. I do wish you cd see a villa by Florence. I'm quite wild about the Air, the Country and the prospects. The Villas are not comfortable Houses but the being white, beautifull architecture and full of Arcades Colonnades etc, have the most pleasing Effect with the Orange trees etc. I'm sure this place with all the Virtu[508] here wont afford me the same pleasure, tho there is some pleasure in the consideration of being in this same spot one has read of so much. Ste and Ly Mary are delighted. I found a letter from Ld Holland here which tells me they landed the 11th at Naples and were all well. Adieu my dear Sister. Should I have time to add any thing to my letter while I stay here I will but I dont think I shall. At Naples I will give you some account of Rome, in the mean time adieu. I do assure [you] the Idea of amusing you with an account of my journey adds greatly to the pleasure I have in what I see. I know so exactly what wd strike you and what wd not, as fine; tis pitty the journey is so long and the Inns so bad alltogether the travelling is very bad indeed for Women. At these great towns tho one is comfortably lodged which is a great relief. I shall stay here five days.

Yrs C Holland

---

506 'The road from… degree.' *MS 6* 'The road from Florence to Rome very tedious full of mountains, some very beautiful'
507 Joseph Addison, *Cato: A Tragedy* (London: Tonson, 1713), IV, iv.
508 Curios; objets d'art.

Naples
Friday December ye 19th 1766

I have only wrote you a short letter since my arrival here dearest Sister to wish you and the Duke of Leinster joy, which I again repeat and do from my heart. I have three of your letters to answer but I wrote you so many on the road I was resolved to let you rest a little, particularly as Ld Kildare[509] cd give you an account of our health. I love him dearly both on his own and your account. I never knew a more obliging good natured attentive disposition than his; he is not the least shy with regard to making acquaintance for he knows all Naples—but he is diffident which I like him the better for. He improves in his person and takes proper pains not to grow fat by fencing, walking and riding at the Riding House; indeed my sweet Siss he goes on just as you would both wish him to do. This letter wont go these three days, but as it rains I will take the opportunity of answering your three letters regularly, and begin with that of the 22nd of October; you are mistaken and so was I when I thought that except England Ireland and Flanders, there was no verdure; in Burgundy it is as fine as any I ever saw, so it is in the Lyonnais; and in allmost all the parts of Italy I have come thro, indeed I have seen prospects that beat any I ever saw before. Your Observation of the uncomfortable distance between us is very true; I do feel it greatly, ones correspondence is not half so pleasant. I hope never to be again this side these same Alps. I have seen no plants but what we have in England, all the difference is that what we keep in Green houses grow common here, and how they are lost upon these stupid people who, either do or fancy they do faint away at the smell of any perfume; one must not have the least hungary or Lavender Water on ones handkerchief, or the least Scent in ones powder or pomatum.

The rest of your letter of October the 12th was about the method of claiming the Dukedom, which now requires no answer. I mistake for I have been answering yours of Novr the 3d all this time, now for that of October the 12th. I agree with you I love vastly to see places where such and such people have been, and where great Events have hap'ned. And that pleasure is great in Italy, the more so as the things hap'ned so long ago, and that just now I'm more read in Antient than modern History. 'tis some years since I have read in the French memoirs, and you know those things strike one just according to [the] situation of ones mind at the time. The ruins and remains of the Roman Empire really amuse me. Only think tho of there being now a marshy desert

---

509 Caroline and Lord Holland wrote a joint letter on 2 December to congratulate Emily's husband on his being created Duke of Leinster. Emily's second son, William, became Marquis of Kildare on his father's elevation to the dukedom.

place between this and Rome when once there stood 24 great Cities, now only some ruins here and there. Baia a famous place where the Romans had Villas is near here; Formium about half way between this and Naples, but I have a notion you don't love the Roman History, if so you'll not care a fig about it all. I like your account of yourself mightily dear Siss: God send you your health. The D[uche]ss is much changed, at least last Winter she seemed to dress and go about more than any body. She certainly likes admiration, and is much impressed by it, she is very agreeable and sociable allways with me, and I have a great regard for her, tho we see little of one another lately. I wont wish your Emily[510] married in England since you are angry at it, indeed nobody has fewer Schemes for futurity than I have, building Castles in the air I have quite done with; I fear tis a sign of stupidity and old age but so it is. A quiet Mind is all my ambition in this World, and to injoy the present as chearfully as I can, when that same hurry of spirits you mention will permit me so to do. Indeed my dear Siss I can but too well understand what you mean by it, for that is what I mean by low spirits. Gloomy splenetick ones I thank God I never have but that dreadful hurry and flutter I suffer much from. Lately to[o] I have been in a way that increases that disorder vastly. I suppose tis owing to the journey, but I have been out of order at a Week, ten days, and a fortnights end, never get beyond three weeks, scarcely. I own I dread disorders of that kind, particularly as I am now past forty three, something of that kind may be beginning. There is one most terrible circumstance here to me, we live up 80 pair of Steps, some people I visit are 90 and a 100 up; it's a shocking fashion and I cant resolve to be carryd up as you may suppose Ld Holland is. Sal you know by this time has been ill and is well—both she and Louisa flatter me she is quite cured. I think Ld K[ildare] has done well to take the Halls.[511] I will be as civil to them as I can, when in England but I don't propose to embarrass myself much with those young ladies, having no Girls at home, tis out of my way you know; it looks as if Ld K had no intention of marrying.

Your letter of the 10th of Novr I received tother day only. I knew Lady Clanbrazil[512] at Bath; she was ill and not in spirits then but I thought her exceedingly agreeable, but talking much of oneself is really a great fault, my dear Siss, except to people nearly connected for after all *qu'importe ce qu'on pense*[513] to the generality of the World, tis a common fault tho, I don't particularly remember her having it. You again mention your poor head as you call it. I do

---

510 Lady Emily Maria Fitzgerald (1751–1818).
511 Unidentified (but see Ingamells, *Dictionary*, under 'Hall').
512 Lady Clanbrassil, friend of Caroline's sisters Emily and Louisa; she lived at Templeogue, four miles from Dublin.
513 'what does it matter what one thinks'

pity you for those feels,[514] particularly as I'm sure you imagine as I do often that young people about you think it affectation and fancy. Ld Holland has not that feel but within these last six or seven months he owns too many people tire and overcome him; indeed I saw it last Winter but he wd not believe it himself tho have seen him so low with it he cd hardly speak. He is not so well again these last four or five days, he has no complaint, for his asthma he has been quit of since our four or five days journey from Calais, but at times he seems so low and languid he has scarcely voice or spirits to speak. Perhaps before I send away my letter he may be better again, but its melancholy to see him so. I think William is in love with Ly Mary: tis an aimiable Girl indeed, her behaviour to every body is so very proper, and her affection and attention to Ste so very natural and agreeable. Poor boy he is as deaf as ever, it has quite alterd his Caracter. I don't wonder at it but he is so shy; he is miserable at seeing strangers or any people he is not very intimate with; should it continue he will live intirely out of the World, and all I fear from that is, that as it is not his natural disposition so to do, he will repent it. I have now answerd all your letters and will another day before the post goes out give you some account of my Life and conversations here. At present adieu.

Sunday, the 21st.

I will begin by telling you what English are here. In the first place there is our Envoy and his wife, Mr and Mrs William Hamilton;[515] he is very agreeable, she is as Affected and Stupid as possible but they are both exceedingly polite and obliging and consequently of use to one as they are much liked here. There is a Sr Thomas and Ly Betty Worsly,[516] mighty good but deadly dull, and a Master Worsly their son rather pert; she is a daughter of Ld Corks. Ly Oxford[517] whom you know by fame resides here on account of the health of a Certain Chevalier, a Florentine who she keeps; she is lively and agreeable. Those, with

---

514   Feelings or sensations, mental or physical.
515   William Hamilton (afterwards Sir) (1730–1803), antiquarian and archaeologist, British Envoy to Naples, 1764–1800; married Catherine Barlow in 1758; died in 1782. (His second wife, Emma, whom he married in 1791, became Nelson's mistress.)
516   Sir Thomas Worsley, 6th Baronet (1728–68), married Lady Elizabeth Boyle, daughter of John Boyle, 5th Earl of Cork, in 1749. The 'rather pert' son was Richard (1751–1805), later 7th Baronet. He went on his own Grand Tour in 1769; at the end of it Gibbon (a family friend) saw 'many alterations and little improvement', adding that Worsley 'spoke in short sentences, quotes Montaigne, seldom smiles, never laughs, drinks only Water, professes to command his passions, and intends to marry in five Months.' (Ingamells, *Dictionary*)
517   Susannah Archer; married Edward Harley, 4th Earl of Oxford (1726–90), in 1751; died in 1804.

Ld Tylney,[518] an insupportable Nephew of his and quiet young Mr Osborne[519] who is rich, make up the number of our English acquaintances. Now for the people of the Country. There is the Countess Mahony a near relation of ours, daughter of fat Ly Newburgh and sister of Ly Fanny Clifford;[520] she is a Widow and has been settled here 26 years, speaks English French and Italian very well, is clever and entertaining; your son and Charles are mighty fond of her and she of them. Ly Mary who dislikes her because she tells some queer story of Ld Ossory, when he was here, says she puts her in mind of Mrs Fortescue.[521] There is a French Lady married here to a Count de Gaetani,[522] she is a Cousin of Madame Guerchy and is a pretty-looking gentle lively little woman as can be, gives herself no airs, is very conversable and reasonable, not very happy I believe at being settled here. Indeed I don't see how its possible for a French Woman to be comfortable out of her own Country; their Stile of Life is so different. Numbers of Italian Ladys have been to see me. There are many pretty looking women among them, some handsome, but all Ordinary, Noisy and Underbred, debauchd to a degree; they talk of having a certain distemper here as freely as we do of any other Illness, and most of the Women have it. Madame Gaetani tells me their Education is abominable, they are taught no one thing in their convents, not even to work, no musick which is the chief amusement here. There is a sweet Woman here that Charles admires, whom I'm sure in another Country wd turn out well, a princess Belmonto, the prince of Brunswick was in love with her while he was here.[523] She is a beauty of mine, very like Mrs John Pitt[524] when she was in her beauty, only with a tall fine figure, which cd she know how to dance or walk wd be a charming one. The Ladies here dont plague one with visits for, except the first visit – except any body is ill or lying in—they never go to one another, unless to the assemblies. I find it proper and convenient for me to have a conversatione as they call it once a Week; they will like it vastly, and I own whether I like the people or not, I cant bear not returning civilitys in a foreign Country; but were I to stay here ages I should never get acquainted with any of the Women. The Men in

---

518 John Tylney, 2nd Earl Tylney (1712–84).
519 Unidentified.
520 Charlotte Maria, Countess of Newburgh (1694–1755); by her first husband, Thomas Clifford (1687–1719) she had two daughters—Frances ('Fanny') and Anne. Anne married Count John Joseph Mahony.
521 John, 1st Lord Ossory (b.1745); Mrs Fortescue is unidentified.
522 Claude-François-Louis de Régnier, Comte de Gaetani (1715–67), French ambassador in London from 1763; married Gabrielle-Lydie d'Harcourt in 1740.
523 Possibly Ferdinand, Prince of Brunswick-Luneburg (1721–92), distinguished general. The Princess was probably Donna Anna Fransesca Belmonte.
524 Marcia Morgan, wife of John Pitt (1706–87), MP.

general are as Ignorant and as Vulgar as the Women. No Italians give to eat except at one House, the Princess de Trankavilla's[525] who has more the manners and Air of the World than the rest of them. She is at home every Night; one goes about Nine, plays at Cards and Sups if one chooses it. Mrs Hamilton is at home with a Concert and Assembly once a Week and the Imperial Envoys Wife once a Week;[526] this with the Opera which is an Assembly is all that is to be done; quite enough it is for me. When I'm at home Madame Mahony, any of the English or Madame Gaetani call on me. There is a Danish Envoy to a friend of Sr George Macartneys[527] who speaks English, that sometimes comes, and a Mr Temino, an old accquaintance of Ld Hollands who is Consul here,[528] so that we have company enough with our own familly. We generally Air in the morning and dine at three O'Clock which is late here but otherwise we should have no morning, and sometimes the weather is so charming that one should grudge losing it. I have been twice at the Opera since I came, and I believe I shall go once a week or once a fortnight if I'm well so one hears no Musick at it. The drives about this town are delightfull. We sup allways en famille at ten exactly and keep good hours. I hear nothing of the Southwell family here.

Ld Holland is much as he has been in my opinion this long while, sometimes better, sometimes worse, to-day seems a good day, to-morrow may be a bad one. Upon the whole if I'm well which is not at present the case, I shall pass my time more agreeably here than in London, except the disagreeable Idea of being so distant. This town is excessively populous; there are numbers who live in the street, one sees them settled there all day. The scene is odd and curious, the infinite variety of dresses pretty; the common people are less handsome here than in the rest of Italy, yet one sees many pretty faces, that is, as pretty as they can be with unhealthy sallow complexions, which is the case here. The Women have beautiful hair, and one sees it in full perfection, their great occupation being to louse one another in the Street all day long in the sun, and one sees such beautifull quantity of hair tis amusing. It is extremely entertaining to drive about the streets to see how very unlike every thing is to what we see at home. They are the most lazy set of people in the world, no industry among them, consequently no honesty. The government is weak and oppressive, there is no kind of police, nor justice; murder they don't look upon as a great Crime, at least not in the same light we do. The great people are made up of Ignorance, pride, debauchery and show. They live all the Year round on a

---

525 This might be a misspelling for 'Francavilla', in which case the Princess would probably be a member of the Belgian aristocracy.
526 The Envoy was probably Prince Wenzel Anton Kaunitz (1711–94).
527 Sir George Macartney (1737–1806), friend of Stephen Fox; envoy extraordinary to Russia in 1764; created Earl Macartney, 1792.
528 Unidentified.

little Macaroni and greens, in order to keep Equipages and Servants. No lady here stirs out, without two or four footmen behind their Coach, two running footmen to go before, and two pages as they call it to wait on them at the Opera and at home. They wont come up to make you a visit till a servant out of livery which they call a page comes down with a lighted torch to conduct them up. I have been obliged to hire two running footmen. Au reste[529] I will do them the justice to say, that Strangers may go their own way in Italy, and you're not told *ceci ne se fait pas*[530] as you are at Paris, which to me was no objection as I liked the Paris ways, but to many English it is disagreeable. Here they love the English because they love our money and that interested motive weighs with the great as well as the little folks; the Ladies like our English Men on that account and the Men get by selling Antiquitys etc, and imposing on our *Virtu taste*. This letter is of an enormous length my dear Siss; I really grudge for you the money it will cost you. You will find it as unintelligible as Ld Kildares I fancy. I'm sorry he writes so bad, as I'm sure he takes great pains to improve himself in every thing, and I'm sure you'd like to hear that every minute of his time from seven in the morning is imployd either in diverting himself or in learning something. I tell you this because I know the Duke of Leinster and you both hate a lounging life (by the by I don't know how to spell the Word) for young people and you are in the right; this what the Youth at present give sadly into, but I do assure you William *n'est pas dans ce cas là*;[531] he has more to do than he has time yet he allmost allways comes home to supper at ten with us, or we know where he sups when he don't. I make no excuses for saying so much on so interesting a subject to you. Adieu my dearest Sister. I will write regularly henceforwards to you and not such immense letters.

Yrs C. Holland
Monday 22^d

A Merry Xmas and happy New Year to all the fire-side at Carton.[532]

Naples
New Year's day [1767]

A Merry Xmas and a happy New Year to my dearest Sister and all her fire-side; we have no fire-side, but the sun so hot in the middle of the day we

---

529 'Nevertheless'
530 'that isn't done'
531 'isn't guilty of that'
532 Carton House, Maynooth, west of Dublin, a large mansion designed by Richard Cassells and built for Robert Fitzgerald, Earl of Kildare, in 1739.

sit with our windows open, only think of that at this time of the Year. I have a little fire to get up and go to bed by but Lord Holland sees none; he wrote last night to the Duke of Leinster, and gave a pretty exact account of his own health I think, in which I don't find any material alteration either for better or worse, since I came here, but great alterations from one Week or one day to another. I have no letters of yours to answer and one should imagine after the immense long letter I sent from hence last Tuesday seven'ight I should have no more to say, and yet I dare say I shall arrive at the end of this folio sheet before next Tuesday. I wd not be longer than a fortnight without writing, because such long letters as my last tire me to write and I'm sure must tire you to read. I had a great many people at my Assembly which I began last Thursday. Indeed there are a number of handsome looking Women here and tho this place is the least famous for beauty of all Italy tis amazing the number of pretty girls one meets driving about the environs of this town, which you'll imagine I do very much as you know my taste for airing in fine weather. There is a vast variety both in the countenances and dresses, one sees, tis very entertaining. Then Hollydays there is a great mixture of the antient and the Eastern dress here, some very like those of the Greek Islands in the cent estampes.[533] They wear very singular kind of white Veils; the Hair of those you see without Veils is drawn back and breaded with bodkins or plaited as you see the hair of the Antient busts exactly. The body dress seems very Eastern, no stays but close waistcoats laced with Gold lacing, loose jackets of black velvet, scarlet Cloth, and various other colours richly laced, some of them with Gold, gold Chains about their necks and Gold earrings; some one sees in milk white Waistcoats, white Veils and a white petty coat with a border embroiderd in worsteds of divers colors. The people of fashion dress in the French and English stile, better than the latter not so well as the former, except that they dont wear that odious rouge. The middling sort of people are sad tawdry figures; French, English and their own dress all mixt together, make a very ugly appearance. I'm told in one of the Islands here about there is exactly the greek dress among all sorts of people. This part of the World was you know formerly comprehended under the name of Greece, and a glorious place it must have been when tollerably governd, from Climate and Situation. The remains of Antiquity here are more curious than any where I'm told. Adieu, I will leave of[f] here; breakfast is ready and I will leave room on my paper (hoping the morrow's post may bring me some letters from you, that I may answer them.)

---

533 'Receuil de cent estampes' was a well-known collection of prints (1707–8) by Jean-Baptiste Vanmour showing different nations of the Levant.

Jany ye 3^d

Yesterdays post brought me dearest Siss a letter from you dated Novr ye 23^d an answer to my Turin letter, and the first I have had signed by the Dutchess of Leinster. I should have wishd to have stay'd some more days at Turin, but for the reason you mention: I thought Ld Holland wd be lonely and want us. Mrs Mim you mention is I suppose Mrs Close, Ly Mary's Housekeeper, injoying herself quietly at Winterslow [534] without the perils and dangers of a long journey. I should certainly, had we had a fine day, not have dreaded *Mont Cenis* so much, but I don't like being carryd in those same Chairs. There is certainly no manner of danger in that terrible Rhone described by Madame Sévigné: I love you for calling her dear Madame Sévigné. I'm quite glad to think I shall have forgot her letters enough to read them over again.[535] I'm quite angry with Charles and Mr Upton who say they are very affected. The French Women have I believe a great deal of Coquetry and little passion about them; the Italians are the contrary, have much *temperament* by all accounts and little Coquetry. One must allow for Climate and consequently pity them but yet *cela revolte*; its nasty, and not to be called passion. Then that Coqueterie d'Esprit[536] that most French Women have gives that universal desire to please, that makes them mighty agreeable; some of them are to be sure abandon'd enough, as one is told at least, and yet was you to sit and talk an hour or two with even some of those you wd never guess it, but think them so sensible, so proper and so agreeable you wd be charm'd. I have just had an account of the death of the French Woman I loved best, poor Madame de Bouzoles;[537] Sal writes me word of it. She was perfectly good in every sense of the Word; sensible, cheerful, polite, gentle and truly pious, with as little prejudice as cd be expected from a Roman Catholick bred up at St Germain. I really loved her. Ld Kildare is not in love; he seems a general flirt and loved by all. Since I began my letter we have had cold bad weather, and as they have no precautions against Cold in this Country one feels it indeed very much. The accident of the Ships is dreadful and must have shock'd you vastly. The poor Woman you mention cd not have a better preparation for death than the care you tell me she had of the poor people in Ireland. How much more good is done in a private Walk of life sometimes! Adieu.

Yrs C. Holland

---

534 A tiny village six miles north-east of Salisbury, Wiltshire. Winterslow House was the home of Stephen Fox and his wife, Lady Mary; it was destroyed by fire in January 1774, less than a year before Stephen's death.
535 Over 1,300 of her letters had already been published.
536 'that disgusts me… flirtatious spirit'.
537 Laure-Anne (1713–66), who married Louis de Montagu-Beaune, Marquis de Bouzoles; her father was the Duke of Berwick (1670–1734), natural son of James II.

Naples
Monday January the 12th [1767]

Ld Kildare my dear Siss will write you word probably that I have been ill. I wd not therefore omit writing myself that you might not be alarmd. I went to bed last Wednesday with St Anthonys fire[538] in my Cheek and the side of my face, attended with some fever as that disorder allways is but which went off sooner with me than it does with most people thanks to my *wretched* Stomach which, whenever I have any other disorder, grows so bad that I can keep nothing upon it. I had had the Erysipelas coming some days before without knowing what it was, but thank God this same starving, lying in bed and sweating with bleeding have carryd off both fever and that, at least there is very little remaining. My plague here is physick which teases my poor Stomach which had not recoverd nor my spirits which are bad, and the weather is so bad I don't know when I shall be able to get out of a morning. I have been particular about myself because I know at such a distance one takes panicks about ones friends and the Erysipelas disorder has frequently provd dangerous when people have got Cold. How one misses somebody to Nurse one and read to one in those illnesses. You have a great Comfort with your dear Girls about you in that respect dear Siss, indeed at home I have Mrs Fannen,[539] and Sal if she is in the way here. I wanted one sadly for tho dear Ly Mary is obliging and attentive as possible you know that cant be the same thing, besides she is so *occuppée de son Mari*.[540] Only think how lucky that boy has been to get such a Girl. I only fear that from his unhappy deafness, and a little humorsomeness in his disposition, he will use himself never to bear her out of his sight or even from his side. Charles teazes them both finely you may suppose about it. I only fear her growing tired, for she has really every talent and accomplishment for publick as well as private life and tis impossible to be so totally free from vanity in that case as not to chuse to be known more than in the narrow circle he will live in should his present disposition continue. Lord Holland continues as he was. Tis now *grande Fete* here; the King is to day of Age.[541] I don't find it produces any more diversion than the Opera for three Nights more lighted up than usual. We have really Abominable weather but it gives Ld Holland no asthma thank God. Adieu dear Siss. I have nothing more to add by this post but that I am

Yrs Sincerely C. Holland

---

538   Ergotism or erysipelas.
539   Mr and Mrs Fannen were, respectively, Caroline's steward and housekeeper at Holland House.
540   'preoccupied with her husband'
541   'great celebration' for the birthday of Ferdinand IV (1751–1825), King of Naples and Sicily.

This letter is so queerly wrote you'll scarcely make it out, but here ends this first letter, tother side is a continuation of the loose sheet added.

Tuesday ye 13th

Last night I was favour sweet Siss with your kind letter of the 10th of December, an answer to my Florence letter. By the long one you receivd from Rome you'll find I did see the great Galery, that at Rome I was in better Spirits and began to taste *Virtu*;[542] by the time I return to England (as we propose to pass at least a fortnight at Rome on our return) I may give myself *Airs*. Rome in that way exceeds all that can be seen or imagined. Some Antiquitys I have seen here, for those nothing beats this place and I taste them more than Virtu, but there are many still to be seen here which I shall see, but you know every body is apt to put off what they can see every day, and we are alike about that here. I know we shall be hurryd to death at last. I assure you my dear Siss I have given you the true Idea of Paris. I know it better than any other English Woman does except L[ad]y Hervey[543] and she is too much prejudiced about it, and as you know a little affected about all things. Perhaps one of the reasons I like it is the partiallity shown me. Sal writes word the D[uche]ss of Northumberland[544] is not pleased at all with it. Sal will [be] as much as she pleases I'm sure with those I introduced her to before, but Ld Fitzwilliam, Ld Carlisle who are there, and Sr Charles will prevent her living much among them, you may be sure, as that will make an agreeable Cotterie of their own, with Selwin who is there.[545] He indeed lives very much among the French but I'm very sure Sr Charles is the worst person in the World to be at Paris—why they went God knows. But I'm in no pain about Sal there; her manner is so very civil and ingaging and she will do all that's proper by Madame Geoffrin[546] and those who are so very particularly civil to us. In Italy they are civil to all the English but make no distinctions, *cela ne flatte point l'amour propre*[547] you know. I agree with you intirely about Italian buildings – beautifull to look at, detestable to live in. A little Cards in long Evenings is a resource. I love loo

---

542   'develop a refined aesthetic judgment'
543   Mary Lepell (1706–68); married John Hervey (1696–1743), 2nd Baron Hervey of Ickworth, in 1720. Her eldest son was George William Hervey, 2nd Earl of Bristol.
544   Lady Elizabeth Seymour (1716–76), daughter of Algernon Seymour, Duke of Somerset; in 1740 she married Hugh Percy (1714–86), created Duke of Northumberland, 1766.
545   William Wentworth-Fitzwilliam (1748–1833), 2nd Earl Fitzwilliam; Frederick Howard (1748–1825), 5th Earl of Carlisle; Sir Charles is unidentified; George Selwyn (1719–91), friend of Thomas Gray, Horace Walpole, Charles James Fox.
546   Marie-Thérèse Rodet (1699–1777), married Pierre-Francois Geoffrin in 1713; Caroline was an habitué of her Parisian salon in rue Saint-Honoré, one of the most celebrated in the eighteenth century.
547   'that doesn't at all gratify one's self-esteem'

very well, its very fashionable here. They love deep play and Ld Kildare, who seldom plays himself, and Mrs Hamilton have taught them loo. Ld K and his cousin Mahony are very *great indeed*; she is wonderfully fond of him, she must be 50 Years old, but a very well looking Woman of her Age, *de l'Embonpoint de la fraicheur*.[548] She is really drole and intertaining, very like Mrs Fortescue, Ly Mary says. I'm glad Ld B[ristol][549] and the Duke of Leinster will be on good terms. I love peace and quiet; besides I like so many things Ld Chatham[550] has done, I wish his Ministry may go on. You know I wish well to Ld Bute,[551] the more so as this last year I have been a good deal conected with the Women of his familly, where I find more worth and good sense than one generally meets with. They have sought my acquaintance which is flattering, as politicks on both sides is out of the question with us. Adieu. This is the continuation of the loose sheet of paper and don't belong to the letter.

Naples
the 1st of Feb. 1767

I begin of course upon a foglio sheet dear Siss tho I don't know what I have to say to fill it with. I have at present no letter of yours to answer, perhaps I may before Tuesday, this is Sunday and to-morrow is the English post. Tis a good while since I wrote to you. I should [have written by the] last post but that I wrote to Louisa which I reckon much the same thing. I have been vastly well and in good spirits since my disorder, most people I find pay a little tribute of that kind to the Climate; living on this *Volcano* must make a vast difference in our constitutions, and I think we don't enough attend to the necessity of altering our diet. I find the less meat I eat, and the more ice water I drink, the better I am. Charles has had a little fever and impostume[552] in his Ear, but is pretty well again. Ly Mary has a little feverish disorder to[o], but I hope it will be very slight. Ld Holland is undoubtedly mended in the main, yet for some days past he has been as low and bad as ever; perhaps before I seal up this letter, he may be well again. We had a Month bad Weather, within this Week; fine again; and fine Weather here is so much finer than fine Weather *chez nous*, tis quite heavenly and I have injoy'd it. I have seen since I wrote to you the Kings Museum at Portici, which is built over Herculanium, and all the

---

548 'plump and radiant', or, 'with a fresh countenance'
549 George William Hervey, 2nd Earl of Bristol; see n. 543.
550 William Pitt (1708–78), 1st Earl of Chatham; his second ministry, formed in 1766, collapsed in 1768.
551 John Stuart, 3rd Earl of Bute (1713–92), Prime Minister 1762–3.
552 an abscess

Antiquitys found in the latter are placed there. Tis very curious indeed, to see things so well preserved; all the bronzes and Utensils for their Sacrifices are most beautifull. There is an intire set of Kitchen furniture, very like our Modern ones, and several things very like what we now have, there are allmost of every sort. I should be most curious about the books but there are as yet scarcely any transcribed, nothing but some Musick found. Tis impossible to describe, what kind of things the books are, unless you saw them, and I dont quite understand how they are, tho I saw them. They had some Idea of printing or stamping, which makes it wonderfull they did not make any progress in that art, which in my opinion has made a more total change in this world than any other thing.

We have a new acquisition here of a very agreeable Woman, Ly Glenorchy; she is Scotch, sister to a pretty Ly Sutherland who died last Year with her Husband and Child at Bath whom you must have heard of.[553] Was I to stay long here I should be very glad of an agreeable *Compatriote* for all the English here are very bad indeed. Mr Hamilton is well enough, but I'm prejudiced against him by Charles Hamilton: his Wife whom I must see a great deal of is a tiresome affected silly Woman as ever I met with, and not good-natured. Luckily she loves loo exceedingly so that three or four times a week the Countess Mahony, she and I have a loo party made up with Gentlemen; it comes without trouble to me, and I love loo so it does very well and is a resource. We have fine fun about Ld Kildare and his old Cousin who is wonderfully fond of him, and we are in hopes particularly Upton and I, that she will bring it [MS torn] some day when she carries him [ ] lying-in Ladies, in the Coach with [ ] she is really very entertaining [ ] well bred, but she has not that [ ] comfortable kind of conversation [ ]. Madame Gaetani the French Lady, is by much the most agreeable conversable Woman here, and a friend of hers, the Comtesse Kaunitz the Imperial Ministers Wife is agreeable enough. Unluckily our foolish Mrs Hamilton hates her, and one lives in dread of some tracasserie,[554] if one attempts to go any where or be presented any where by those Ladies, not but that the quarrels and *tracasseries* divert one to[o], tho one dont chuse to be a party concern'd. We begin to think of moving; when our journey is settled you shall know all about it.

Feb the 3rd

No letters from England or Ireland yesterday. I must again mention the weather, it is so very fine; what a glorious sun now in the month of Feby, but

---

553 Willielma Maxwell (1742–86); in 1761 she married John Campbell, Lord Glenorchy (1738–71). In the same year, her sister Mary Maxwell (1740–66), married William Gordon, the 18th Earl of Sutherland (1735–66); they died from a 'putrid fever' contracted while visiting the Spa at Bath.
554 mischief making.

how terrible must it be in summer. There is no shade at all about this place, that is no shady walks for there are trees enough about but no walks about but by the Sea and up hills—they are delightfull now. Its amazing how many Eastern customs are preferred here; except some few of the Women who have conversed with strangers, they none of them make you a Curtsey but a bow and take hold of your hand. The old Italian Icabus custom subsists a good deal among the bourgeois, for you never see any Women of that rank out, but to go to Church on Sundays. The quality and the peasants are all one sees about; no such thing as Women shop-keepers; indeed any shops are very rare, nothing to be had but by bespeaking. I allready told you how pretty the peasants dresses were and what an Infinite variety there was. Adieu. I have come to the end of my paper, I find.

Ld Holland has an indigestion and purging which causes his present lowness.

Naples
the 20th of February 1767

Tis an age dearest Sister since I had a letter from you; perhaps to-Nights post may bring me one. We have indeed fine Weather now, I'm obliged to take my Airing and Walk so as to return home soon after ten when the Sun begins to be too hot to bear it. Only think of that at this Season; but the Weather being contrary to my expectations as changeable here as with us, I shall hope for some cooler Weather to travel in. We intend setting out the 14 of March. Ld Holland goes by land with us; the same journey we came except that instead of going from Turin to Lyons we shall go from Turin to Geneva which is rather a shorter journey than the other, over the Alps equally. I shall not be sorry to see those horrid beautifull Alps again. I have a sweet pretty Airing here that you wd doat on, to a place called *Grotto del Cani* where there is a Cavern in which they put a poor dog to show one how the Vapour throws it into convulsions, a ceremony I never wd see. But the spot is beautifull, a large lake inclosed all round with Hills coverd with wood, the sides of the lake green turf, and the most delightfull walking imaginable. This place is about 2 little Miles from Naples and my usual drive. One goes out of the town that way thro a long dismal Grotto or Cavern of half a Mile long, I believe, which is not pleasant, and seems a strange approach to such a town as Naples. I was last week to see Pompeii, or the ruins of an old roman town so called, which was first destroyed in the year 66 by an Earthquake, rebuilt and destroyed 16 Years afterwards by showers of pumice stones that came down from Mount Vesuvius; it has been found but within these two or three Years that they have begun to dig. We saw the remains of a small temple, of what is supposed to have been soldiers Barracks, a street, and one place supposed to have been a private House. But the simpletons throw the earth back again and don't go on when they come to what they imagine was a private House, which is provoking as one should have infinite more curiosity to see that, than any public building. We saw a great deal of pretty Grotesque painting. The situation thereabouts is most charming indeed. That and some of the environs of Naples were famous places where the Romans had Villas in formerly. Tis really a most extraordinary Country, it seems to be all fire and Volcano and gives matter of great speculation to the Naturalists and Philosophers. This same Globe of ours seems to have undergone strange changes and revolutions for some good end no doubt, but the more one reflects on those things, sweet Siss, and the more discoverys are daily made the more in my opinion one is convinced how very little we do know, and how little we are intended to know. I think as Monsr Pascal[555] does, all things lye hidden among the secrets of Providence which we ought to reverence and adore but not attempt to trace or penetrate.

Ste and Ly Mary leave us next week; they intend to see Venice, Genoa, Leghorn, and all they have not allready seen in their way. She is very glad to go; he is heartily tired of Naples and has a longing to be at Winterslow his own house which he is exceeding fond of, and which is very natural as he is doing a good deal to it, and that it is the first House he ever had of his own. Ld Kildare stays some time longer than us at Naples. Charles goes to Florence where we part with him; he proposed to stay some time longer in Italy but has not yet determined on his own motions. Mr Upton and Harry return with us. I begin to aprehend the long journey again, it really disagrees so much with me. I shall be glad to see Holland House[556] again and very glad indeed should I find you in England, sweet Siss, which is not I hope quite unlikely. When I have been well I have passed my time agreeably enough here, but the effect I feel from the sun now makes me imagine the hot weather wd be quite insupportable to me in this place. This Country and indeed all Italy is a most curious Country to see, and I'm glad I have seen it, but shall hope Ld Hollands complaints will not oblige him to come so far South again. Staying in England a Winter I fear we must not attempt. He is certainly mended tho his Nerves are still very weak, and he dont get any Strength, but asthma he is quite free from. Adieu, dear Sister. I leave a little room in case I should have a letter by tonights post to thank you for.
                                                                                                            C. Holland

---

555 Blaise Pascal (1623–62), celebrated French philosopher, theologian and mathematician; famous for his *Les Provinciales* (1657) and *Pensées* (1670).
556 Holland House, built in 1605 in Kensington, London; acquired by Caroline's husband, Henry Fox; he entertained notable literary and political figures there, a practice continued in the nineteenth century by 3rd Baron Holland.

21st

Last Nights post brought me a letter from Ciss:[557] how form'd her hand and stile and manner of writing is since I last received a letter from her which is I believe near a year ago. I'm vastly sorry your poor Eye is bad again but I hope as there is no inflammation it will soon go off. I shall answer Cecilia's letter so adieu.

Only think dear Sister H[olland] House had like to have been burnt down; as it hap'ned no damage was done. It really makes my blood run Cold to think of it, and I hate to think how much concern it wd have given me.

Tuesday the 10th of March [1767]

I had seald up my letter to Cecilia yesterday—indeed it was wrote so full that I cd not have added a word, when last night I received another from her dated the 8th of February, which I will answer now by this post to you my dear Sister, as I shall I hope leave Naples before this day seven'ight when the post goes out again. I'm glad to hear the Duke of Leinster is so well and wish your poor Eyes wd get well. Ld Holland will, I flatter myself be tollerably chearfull but his Nerves are weak, easily ruffled, and you must not expect the chearfullness you once remember. Upon the road I write when I can which often obliged me to write longer letters than I intended as I know you like to have every thing described as particularly as possible. I will now answer all your questions. I mean by braiding or plaitting the hair, is the same I believe. The peasants and common people do it up strait, then plait it and twist it round a bodkin as you have seen in pictures very frequently, in a kind of bunch or Crown on the top of their head; they drag away their hair from their foreheads sadly, in general. The Ladies never braid their hair but do it up in a loose ugly Chignon I think. Madame Sevigné carryd her love to her daughter to excess as one sees it made her Miserable; as for the expression of fondness to those who have corresponded with the french must know, its their way of writing. I have had several *billets* and letters from french people exactly like love letters; tis their way and I write so to them again. I'm sorry dear Sal says I imposed on her *un fagot des jeunes français*[558] because it makes me fear she has been flirting with some of them, and as I am not mistaken about them I should be sorry for it. I know how self-sufficient vain and coxcomical they are, thinking every Woman in love with them; at least this is their general character both from their own people and Strangers. To be sure there are some exceptions to

---

557   Caroline's youngest sister, Lady Cecilia Margaret Lennox, then aged 16.
558   'a host of young Frenchmen'

all those things you know, and I hope those Sal likes are some of them. She has been vastly liked and much the fashion *comme de saison*.[559] You need not fear her having offended by neglecting visits, the french are too reasonable about those things to be angry with her, at her age, in Carnival time when all *la jeunesse de Paris est folle*[560] with diversions to omit visiting regularly. She has fallen into the set of Company I imagined she would naturally, and the most likely to contribute to her diversion; it was a set too *répandue*,[561] as they call it, for me, their dreadfull late hours wd have killed me. Ly Holderness[562] who lived a good deal with them did not recover [from?] the Carnival she spent at Paris till she came to bathe in the sea last summer. But what I like so much in Paris is that all ages and all dispositions may find houses and society to suit them. They found out soon *que Miladi Holland n'aimait pas le grand monde*[563] so I was invited by those who lived more quiet. Madame Boufflers and Madame Mirpoix, who Sal lives much with are very agreeable, indeed the latter has a very superior understanding, but there is a Madame Luxembourg[564] with them whom I dreaded getting acquainted with. She is a clever old Woman but capricious and ill-natured, they all tell you, and if people dont happen to please her says the most brutal things to them, even to her friend Madame Boufflers; Ly Holderness tells me she says things so shocking at times she is amazed she ever sets her feet in her House. Now I make it a rule never to make acquaintance with those kind of people, and declined being introduced to her House which you'll not wonder at. The Fitzjames[565] were not people for Sal to be with much; in Winter Madame Bouzoles familly broke up. The D[uche]ss of Fitzjames does not keep House at Paris; she is passionately fond of her Country House and divides her time chiefly between that and Court where she must often be. When I was at Paris she gave up her time intirely when she was there to an old father and allways lives in her own familly; she is by no means stupid tho', for she is excessively lively. All that familly are a little devot[566] but

---

559 'and fits in well'
560 'the young people of Paris are crazy'
561 'far-fetched'
562 Mary (née Doublet); married Robert D'Arcy, 4th Earl of Holderness (1718–78), in 1744.
563 'that Lady Holland isn't fond of high society'
564 Madeleine Angélique de Neufville Villeroy (1707–87), married Charles François II, Duc de Montmorency-Luxembourg, in 1750. Presumably her friend Madame Boufflers was a relative of her first husband, Duc de Boufflers (d.1747). Madame Mirpoix is not identified; Caroline may have intended 'Mirepoix', a lady well known in courtly circles.
565 Victoire Louise Josephe (née Gouyon); married Charles, Duc de Fitzjames (1712–87), in 1741.
566 devout

the different Societys and Houses and the different kind of life people live in those different Societys at Paris is very great; some never dine, others never sup. Several people are allways at home. Young people may divert themselves very well in London or at Paris, Middle Aged and old people infinitely better at the latter in my opinion, but certain it is few English people like it. Tis certainly but few tho who get enough into french Company to know whether they do or no. So much for france which between Sals and my letters you'll be perfectly acquainted with. I long to kiss pretty MacAlison,[567] who is he like? Its very odd but when I do set down to write *cela ne finit point.*[568]

Adieu Yrs dear Siss C. Holland

[Postscript by Lord Holland]

I suppose I am told what *MacAlison* means, that I may call you Dutchess MacAlison. Well, as long as my conscience will give me Leave, so I will. You'll follow the Princess *del Monte Rotondo's* example, I dare say, and be Dutchess *del Ventre Rotondo* again very soon notwithstanding what you say. Della Dutchessa MacAlison, Chumilliss (?). Schiave. La Vecchia Donna.[569]

Holland

Are you wise to let that great Girl Cecilia call you Mama, still? Why you'll be a Grandmother in a trice, and Granum *MacAlison* won't sound well.

Rome
the 19th of March [1767]

I have but little to say to you dearest Sister but will write whenever I have an oportunity as I imagine you'll be anxious to know how Ld Holland bears his journey. He was a good deal fatigued but has recoverd [from?] that and is much as he has been these last six weeks. Thank God the worst part of the journey is over, for it is impossible to conceive there can be such roads between two such Towns as Rome and Naples. Florence is our next *Gite*.[570] We shall I believe leave Rome next Saturday the 28th.[571] I shall write from thence. The

---

567   A long-established nickname in the Fitzgerald family; its use here is unclear.
568   'there is never an end to it'
569   The postscript presumably depends on family 'in-jokes'. In 'Princess del Monte' there is perhaps a play on 'princess Belmonto'; similarly in 'Donna' there may be a reference to Donna Anna Francesca Belmonte (see n. 523).
570   resting place
571   The date is confirmed by an entry in the Notebook for 28 March: 'Ld Holland Mr Upton Harry and I left Rome.'.

Weather is charming, fresh sharp mornings and a fine sun all day; it agrees with me vastly. I am better than I have generally been this Winter. Ld Kildare we expect to day, but I imagine he informs you regularly of his motions. We were all sorry he wd not come with the Countess Mahony and the Prince and Princess Justiniani[572] who proposed it to him and who are coming to Rome where the Justinianis live. They are of a very old Roman family descended they pretend from the Emperor Justinian. She is the Countess Mahonys daughter, consequently our Cousin, and the best bred agreeable Italian I have seen; has no Cisisbeo and is attached to her Husband and Children of which she has seven. I understand she is much loved and respected here. I believe the Roman Ladies are rather better educated than the Neapolitans as Madame Mahony, who is a sensible Woman, sent her daughter to a convent here preferable to keeping her at Naples. I believe it must be a disagreeable place to live in, tho the pride and Etiquette which is tiresome among all Italians is more here than any where, I understand. Since I wrote thus far Ld Kildare is arrived very well. All the english Gentlemen are come from Naples here just now which by no means makes the place more agreeable. I have been to see some fine things since I came, there is indeed great profusion of them in this town. The fine Guido's Aurora of which you have so frequently seen prints and Coppys, is indeed charming, tho it is painted on a Ceiling which makes it less agreeable to look at, than if it was on the side of a Wall.[573] Fine Villas are numerous. In short there is I believe more to be seen in this single town than in all the World besides. It has a triste melancholy look, tho, and the Country about it is not fine.

So I find the Duke of Buccleuch marries pretty Ly Betty Montagu;[574] tis a pity Ciss had not her chance of him. One says these things of course, and for a moment thinks them, but a little reflexion after all makes one see the Idleness of such thoughts, and how very little one knows what is best or worst to happen, except for the present minute. Matches put me in mind of poor Ly Emily Stanhopes being so queerly put off.[575] I pitty the Girl, tis a most disagreeable situation to be in; what do you hear about it from Ly Barrymore?

---

572   Cecilia Carlotta (1740–89), daughter of Count John Mahony and Anne Clifford (see n. 520); married 5th Prince Benedetto Justiniani in 1757.
573   Guido Reni (1575–1642), Italian Baroque painter; his ceiling fresco, *Aurora* (1613) was commissioned by Cardinal Scipione Borghese.
574   Henry Scott, 3rd Duke of Buccleuch (1746–1812); married Lady Elizabeth Montagu (1743–1827) on 2 May 1767.
575   Lady Amelia (Emily) Stanhope (1749–80); married Richard Barry (1745–73), 6th Earl of Barrymore, on 16 April 1767. According to London newspapers the wedding had been delayed; it had been expected to take place when Barry came of age in October 1766. Lady Barrymore was the widow of the 5th Earl.

I forgot tho that before I receive your answer to this, I shall probably be in England. Adieu dearest Sister.

Yrs C. Holland

Florence
the 13 of April [1767]

 I must say a word to my dearest Sister before I leave this pretty place where I have spent a very agreeable fortnight. Nothing can be prettier than the environs of this place so riant and gay; the climate is far inferior tho to Naples and we have had cold East winds *comme chez nous*.[576] Now it is charming tho, Spring much advanced and such quantitys of sweet flowers its delightfull. There is a sweet pretty promenade called the Costines which I have frequented very much. I have been very well the whole time, so has Ld Holland except that lowness of spirits at times which I fear will never be quite cured. I think his spirits are to the full as well if not better, when we travel than when we are quiet; it is amazing how he bore the fatigue of the journey here. The rest of our journey will not be near so fatiguing except *Mont Cenis* which I begin to dread again. It is in our power to make it quite easy. We shall be at Turin our slow way of travelling the 22 of this month, and at Geneva I hope the 2nd or 3rd of May. We have received here the melancholy account of poor Ld Tavistocks death.[577] How I pity them all. Tis indeed a most cruel stroke, and I fear will go hard with poor Ly Tavistock. Ly Mary is much shockd. Charles goes on to Turin with us, where he leaves us to meet Ld Fitzwilliam at Genoa. Ste and Ly Mary set out to morrow I believe for Leghorn, and propose making part of their journey by sea, but have not yet settled their route; they will however be in England before us. We have been at Court here, which neither Ly Mary or I liked to do, but the grand D[uche]ss expressd a desire to see us so we cd not help it. She is the King of Naples sister, the grand Duke is one of the Archdukes brother to the Emperor;[578] they are lately settled here and mighty fond of having people presented to them; they are both mighty Young. The Minister is a German, a Comte de Rossemberg who was in England when you were married.[579] He says

---

576 'riant... *nous*': 'cheerful... the same as at home'
577 Francis, Marquess of Tavistock (1739–67), son of the 4th Duke of Bedford, who was killed on 22 March by falling from his horse while hunting, aged 27. He married Lady Elizabeth Keppel (daughter of the 2nd Earl of Albemarle), in 1764.
578 Leopold I (1747–92), Grand Duke of Tuscany (later Emperor of the Holy Roman Empire, 1790–92); married Maria Louisa (1745–92), daughter of Charles VII of Naples, who became Charles III of Spain.
579 Perhaps Francois, Comte Orsini de Rosenberg (1723–96).

he has been in many Countrys since but never yet saw any thing so beautifull as Ly Emily Lennox (Ld Holland says this paragraph will make you drunk with Vanity). He is really a mighty good sort of man and has showd me great civility here. The people are rather more civilized as well as the Country more cultivated than at Naples. I met another old acquaintance, the Grand D[uche]ss *Grande Maitresse* is one of those little Mlle *Rinshacks* you may remember at the Hague; she is an odious woman tho. The french Envoy here is a very agreeable Man, quite a french Man to be sure; but very sensible and pleasing.

I have been with all those people at some agreeable dinners, for our Minister here, Sir Horace Mann is the most obliging polite man that ever livd, has a charming House, shows away and lives most elegantly. The mixture of Germans and other Strangers makes this place better than Rome or Naples for Society, for among Italians I find more and more every day there is no such thing. The two Ladies I have seen any thing of except at Sr Horace Mann *conversatione* , where I saw many, are his Ly to whom he is *Cavaliere Servante*, an Italian, and a very agreeable little pretty Irish German woman whose name is Butler. The women here are not near so handsome as at Naples. I have wrote to Louisa and to Ly Emily since I came here. I will write to some of you when I can. At present adieu.

Yours most sincerely C. H.

We are setting off this afternoon. There are two pairs of Gold scissors bought here for Ciss and Ly Emily.

Turin
ye 24 of April [1767]

I found here letters from Ciss and Ly Emily, the former dated the 26th of March the latter without a date. They both tell me you have again a bad Eye my sweet Siss, and also another piece of bad news, viz that we are not likely soon to see you in England. Alas, when shall we meet again? But il faut prendre patience[580] and I will comfort my self with the thoughts of your being easy and quiet at home; a situation I perhaps think the more enviable as I am little likely to enjoy it at a place I love as well as you do Carton, Kingsgate,[581] which I like too, and going abroad which I dont like, will interfere so much with all pleasant schemes of being comfortably settled there. After all we are but travellers in this World, when and where our rest will be, God knows. We staid three days

---

580 we must be patient
581 The Lennoxes' family home was at Kingsgate on the North Foreland, east Kent.

at Milan; by the little I saw of it, it appears to be by much the most Sociable and what I call civilized place in Italy.[582] The Town is old and Ugly, so is the Country about it, a dead flat, very rich. There is a Comte Firmian (?)[583] there, the Austrian Minister who is one of the best bred, best natured, polite, good looking Men I ever saw; I dined with him. He lives in a magnificent Stile. Two Milan Ladies dined there both speaking french, and both civil to one, not often to be met with in Italy; tho their not being so is not from meaning to be rude, but as *Madame Gaetani* used to say *elles n'ont rien à dire*[584] nor do they trouble their head about one. The Verdure of this place at this spring season is charming. We shall stay here only a few days. Ld Holland bears his journey vastly well indeed, and is better, to be sure infinitely better, has no dangerous illness at present certainly, but so changed from what you have seen him, sweet Siss, it wd surprise you. I have a sad horror of this same Mont Cenis now the time of crossing it draws near and I am really in very bad spirits so will write no more at present. I wrote to Emily from Florence, so I did to you. I will write to Ciss from Geneva. I have had a letter from dear William to inquire after us which tells me the Duke of Leinster and you wish him to return to Naples, which I fear will now be very dull to him tho he generally continues to divert himself. I think him as safe as most young men as I dont think him apt to be in love; but dear Sister dont leave him too long in Italy; except *Virtu*[585] nothing is to be learnt in it. The Women are dangerous in every respect, nothing to be learnt from them, Vice and illness frequently got by them and if once a Young Man becomes a real cicisbeo tis a lounging idle life which when once got into is difficult to get out of. There is Ld Cooper[586] has been 8 Years now abroad, and has not the heart to go home. I do assure you I should have great uneasiness at leaving Charles but that he wont be long in any of the places, and that I think his love of politicks and desire of making a figure at home will allways call him back; besides I don't see any disposition towards the ladies of Italy in him. But now William will be all alone at Naples, no English there and what makes me afraid is seeing Mr Upton at his time of life so ridiculously in love with an impudent looking Woman at Naples, as to propose returning in the summer again to Italy. Adieu. My advice wd be to let William run thro Italy,

---

582 'by the little… in Italy'. *MS 9* 'Milan seems to be more sociable than any other place in Italy by the little I saw of it'.
583 See n. 445.
584 'they have nothing to say'.
585 a love of the fine arts
586 George Nassau Clavering Cowper (1738–89) had succeeded his father as 3rd Earl Cowper (pronounced 'Cooper') in 1764, and had (as Caroline Lennox implies) arrived in Italy in 1759; he stayed for 30 years. In his exhaustive account, Ingamells says that Cowper was 'seduced by an elegant lifestyle and the exercise of patronage', *Dictionary*.

see whats to be seen, then as he is Military and that his father likes he should be so, send him to Germany. Vienna is much commended by many people. I have given you my thoughts, sweet Siss. I may judge wrong, but it is my real opinion. I don't like the thought of leaving a Young Man defenceless(?) and alone a long time at Naples, where they have other English company, tho that may be subject to some objections, I think the others are stronger.

I have not yet heard of Ly Mary and Ste being got to England. Did I tell you, she was breeding? If I did I told it no one else as she very naturally did not wish to have it talkd of so early as people may frequently be mistaken, but her femme de chamber Mlle Petit, has not been so silent I find, as all my English letters mention it. I'm very anxious to know how she does after her journey, as she is so delicate a little creature. They were to sail from Havre to Southampton, which last is but twenty miles from their own Country House. I heard from them from Lyons, but not since; I do hope she will go on well; both Ste and she will be so happy. Some of you shall hear of us all when I land. God send that may be to morrow—how I dread the Nasty Sea.

[Postscript from Lord Holland]

Harry is wrong'd. He speaks both Italian and French, very well.

Geneva
the 8th of May [1767]

My dear Sister you will probably not hear from me again before I arrive in England which I hope to do before the end of this Month. I wrote to your daughter Emily since I came to this place; she is a delightfull correspondent, her stile quite formd. I have given her some account of Voltaire. I have desired the Banker here to send you four new Vols of Voltaires Works printed last week; they are *mélanges*, plays etc. I am to go see one of his plays performd Sunday. Monday we set out. This is quite a new scene of life to me. I was a little discomposed on my arrival and so was Ld Holland, to find we were to be in our Bankers House, and worn to death as we thought with their civilitys; but tout au contraire they are such honest, easy good-humoured people its no constraint at all. He is generally out on Business and Madame Gaussin his wife is a jolly merry frank Scotch Woman with whom I am as much at my ease as I should be with Mrs Liegois or Mrs Calcot. Tis all bourgeois in this place, one sees every where industry, comfort and excessive cleanliness very different from *La Bella Italia*; so is the Climate for we have had a cold East Wind ever since we came. There are no Beggars here, no stealing. No Murders or disorders happen, every one is imployd, every one obliged to keep in their own station, a particular dress for the Maid servant which is neat and tidy, and which they must not transgress on any account. The Environs of Geneva are full of Country Houses, Vineyards, fields and all look so chearful and so cultivated it gives one spirit to see them. The prospects of the Mountains and the Lake are beautiful except the prospects which are great as well as chearful, *tout est en petit*[587]—Houses, Gardens, way of life, I dare say in time I should get to like it, but one accustoms oneself *au grand* too easily, particularly with regard to Houses. I own I am grown to dislike small ones which you'll say is no misfortune for a person who has H[olland] House, now its my own too. The people in this Country were too happy and have quarreled among themselves, the people and the Magistrates. The french have medelled in their quarrels as Mediators and they much fear their little republick will be ruined by it; such is the fate of all in this *Bas Monde*,[588] neither liberty or plenty can secure happiness, and I doubt whether the poor Neapolitan lounging himself in the sun who lives on Chestnuts don't enjoy as much happiness as the rich Bourgeois of London or Geneva.

> How small a part of what the human heart indures
> Is it in Kings or Laws to cause or cure![589]

I don't write the lines as they are in that sweet poem the *Traveller* but you who have read and admired it will know what I mean. Ld Holland is as much mended in his journey as he was with his *sejour*[590] at Naples.

Adieu my dear Siss. I hope sweet Ly Mary is breeding.[591]

Yours ever C. Holland

I have a great deal of Ld Hollands poetry to send you; have I sent you any allready; I forget. I believe W[illia]m did; if so I have still one coppy of Verses more to send you.

Calais
the 24 of May [1767] Sunday

We came here yesterday my dear Sister where I found your kind letter of the 26 of April which I thank you for and rejoice to hear your Eyes are well again. I cant say we are Wind bound here for we cd have set out this morning

---

587 'everything is on a small scale'
588 'nether world'
589 Goldsmith, *The Traveller*, ll, 429–30 ['How small, of all that human hearts endure, That part which laws or kings can cause or cure!'].
590 'sojourn'
591 She gave birth to her daughter, Caroline Fox (1767–1845), later in the year.

but cd not have got into Kingsgate without two tides which wd have obliged us to anchor, a dreadfull thing to sick people, and the Captain gave us no hopes of being less than 16 or 17 hours aboard a ship; we therefore determind to stay here to day. I wont call this a good Inn; it really is an exceeding fine pleasant Gentlemans House, a fine appartment below opening to a large Garden, and all within clean and Comfortable easy Chairs and in short all kind of conveniencys. We had bad Weather the last few days of our journey and bad roads, but here we are thank God very well, and happy to have performd our long and tedious journey so agreeably, and without accidents. Here my narrations will end. I will therefore take leave by giving you some account of my journey from Geneva. We went the first days journey thro the Pais de Vaud all by the Lake of Geneva. The day was fine, the roads good, the Inns excellent so that it was all together delightfull; nothing can be more lovely than that Lake. The pais de Vaud is in the Canton of Bern, and as far as injoying Liberty and all the Comforts of life can contribute to make people happy in this life, those people possess it. They have no taxes, no standing Army, no monks no priests to mollest them; great industry among them—affluence without Luxury and Religion without Superstition. To be sure the Swiss may be reck'ned the happiest people on this spot of ours. Their Laws and regulations prevent Luxury, which is generally the ruin of people at ease; before these troubles at Geneva in which the French interfere, they were also very happy. I am glad I have seen them, I own, and I think after all were I obliged to live out of my own Country I wd fix somewhere among the Swiss; tho perhaps in some respects Paris wd amuse me more, yet I think a Country House in the environs of Geneva or in the pais de Vaud wd be a more rational thing. My travels sweet Siss, make me see the Misery caused by a superstitious religion and a great standing Army in a light I never before saw it; to be sure priests and soldiers are the bane of human kind. I was at Church at Geneva and was much pleased with the Sermon, and all the form of it, as for *la preche* so much talked of as lasting so long, I did not find it. I was not above an hour in the Church with the psalms, Chapters prayers and all.

Now for answering your questions. Pray ask as many as you please. I really do see a great improvement in Cecilia. I dare say she is a charming Girl and now her understanding begins to form I'm sure she will make a great progress. Some young people are childish infinitely longer than others and I have been used to see early understanding. I'm sure I see the contrary now for nothing ever was so childish as Harry, but as he is sensible I hope it will go off; yet it quite disturbs me. Ly Betty Montagu[592] is five and twenty years old I believe. I have given you an account of Charles' Schemes in many letters. He is now at Venice with Ld Fitzwilliam. I hope none will keep him long from me; he is the

---

592 See n. 574.

great joy and Comfort of my life, a more valuable boy never lived. Ld Carlisle is not gone to Italy; he will I dare say go to Spa where Sally is imediately going with Sr Charles who is ill of a disorder in his Stomach. William did speak Italian but not well I believe. I never learnt any; what surprises me most is Ly Mary learning none, tho she had a Master. Charles learnt it very well, and intends to be a perfect Master of it. Harry learnt a little Neapolitan, but not much; *voila le progress de nos etudes*[593]. You'll say we were all stupid. To be sure Ly Mary, William and Harry should have known it perfectly, but alas between 40 and 50 sweet Siss one don't learn any thing. Ste determined he wd not learn it. I cant say I tryd, thinking it in vain. The little I did understand of it made me find out that I had no great desire of hearing any Italian conversation, which is generally confined to two people, or some kind of noisy buffoonery, which I should not understand did I know the language. The *very, very* few conversable Italians I met with had travelld, and talkd french.

I don't know whether Sidney Bidulph[594] is finishd or no, if it is I will imediately on my arrival send it you. I have just room in my paper to tell you I was at Voltaires play, which entertaind me of all things, tho he did not act. The play was *Les Scythes*, a play of his own, and the *petite piece, la Femme qui a raison*, his own also.[595] They were really well acted, but the best part of the show was his eagerness and commendations both of the play and the performance. Ld Holland continues well thank God. I hope we shall go tomorrow.

C. Holland

Kingsgate
the 26 of May [1767]

We landed here yesterday my dear Sister after a Voyage of eleven hours. I was not very sick but enough to be very uncomfortable. I feel happy and very thankfull to have ended our tedious peregrination so well. Ld Holland was as well yesterday as he has been at all, and I hope in God he may continue so. He will stay here a few days. To morrow I hope to see pretty H[olland] House, which I dare say I shall think to the full as pretty as ever, notwithstanding all I have seen.[596] We are come to a busy scene in the political world I find; the

---

593 'such is the progress of our studies'
594 *Memoirs of Miss Sidney Biddulph, Extracted From Her Own Journal*, 3 vols (London: Dodsley, 1761); novel by Frances Sheridan (1724–66), mother of playwright Richard Brinsley Sheridan.
595 Voltaire's tragedy, *Les Scythes*, published in 1766; *La femme qui a raison*, his comedy, 1748.
596 'To morrow... have seen'. *MS 12* 'May ye 27 1767 came to Holland House with Harry in the Evening. Left Ld. H at Kingsgate found Ste and Ly Mary at H House.'.

Ministers all divided, the great Man,[597] tis reported not right in his head. The vulgar report is that Ld H[olland] was sent for to England to advise, but there is not the least truth in it; the great indifference and the little concern all those things give me will easily convince you. Ld Holland will have nothing to do with politicks. If he was in the way of having the least share of them I should dread going near London; as it is it only diverts me, except poor Ld Chathams illness, which I am really very sorry for, as it is the greatest calamity human Nature can be subject to. I pitty his Wife and Children exceedingly if it is true and feel quite angry at a pamphlet come out about it. Adieu sweet Siss.

Yrs C. Holland

I thank you for the poplin—what do I owe you?

---

[597] William Pitt (1708–78), created Earl of Chatham in 1766; the mental disease from which he suffered—bordering on insanity—drove him to resign as Lord Privy Seal in 1768.

APPENDIX A

The Hazards of Collecting Art on the Grand Tour

Collecting Art on the Grand Tour

THE REASONS for collecting classical and Renaissance works of art in eighteenth-century Britain are many and complex.[598] One could argue that the trend had been set by King Charles I, who started by purchasing 'the entire cabinet of the Duke of Mantua, consisting of eighty-two pictures, and esteemed the most valuable in Europe, for which he paid £20,000'.[599] Not far below the surface of the burgeoning interest was an awareness that British achievements in painting and sculpture did not yet rival those of France or Italy. The Reformation had been a major factor in explaining the decline of art in Britain and distinguishing it from art in Continental Europe. The 1688 Revolution marked the turning point, after which Britain gradually acquired a more confident outward-looking identity. As one critic puts it, the new 'Great Britain' was based 'on a Protestant culture, which was seen as providing the basis for free enquiry and commercial success'.[600] Commerce brought considerable prosperity to the upper classes, along with a desire for improvement. Hence, the Grand Tour was not just an opportunity for the traveller's self-improvement, but part of a larger trend to re-establish links with certain aspects of European culture.

There were various ways in which this became apparent, but for our purposes three interlinking factors are of particular interest.

---

598   See for example Andrew W. Moore, *Norfolk & the Grand Tour: Eighteenth-Century Travellers Abroad and their Souvenirs* (Norfolk: Norfolk Museums Service, 1985). Also: <http://www.artsandcollections.com/index.php?/article/grand_eighteenth_century_tourists_228>

599   William Hayley Mason, *Goodwood, its House, Park and Grounds with a Catalogue Raisonné of the Pictures in the Gallery of His Grace the Duke of Richmond, K.G.* (London: Smith and Elder, 1839), 23. The purchase included paintings by Titian and Corregio.

600   William Vaughan, *British Painting: The Golden Age from Hogarth to Turner* (London: Thames and Hudson, 1999), 11.

First, there had been a gradual change of attitude towards Renaissance art during the seventeenth century. Rather than emphasise its religious aspect, British painters and intellectuals generally now emphasised its rich aesthetic achievements. Painters from Jonathan Richardson (1665–1745) to Reynolds argued that British painters should develop their gifts by 'conversing with the Works of the best Masters of Painting', especially Michelangelo, Raphael and Rubens.[601] British art would develop, as Reynolds kept repeating in his annual lectures to the Royal Academy, only if students would go back to the masters of the Renaissance. They needed to study and copy, as he had done, in Rome. That is what great painters like Raphael had done:

> Raffaelle, it is true, had not the advantage of studying in an Academy; but all Rome, and the works of Michael Angelo in particular, were to him an Academy. On the sight of the Capella Sistina, he immediately from a dry, Gothick, and even insipid manner, which attends to the minute accidental discriminations of particular and individual objects, assumed that grand style of painting, which improves partial representation by the general and invariable ideas of nature.[602]

A second feature of Britain's engagement with European art was the growing number of major art collections in the houses of the nobility. Aristocratic families consolidated their collections of fine art from the Continent, and some opened them to public viewing. For example, the Dukes of Northumberland had acquired an outstanding collection of paintings at Northumberland House in London. Gentlemen too acquired collections. William Lloyd, from whom Edmund Burke bought his house 'Gregories', had collected over £20,000 worth of paintings and sculptures from Rome. Hester Thrale (1741–1821) said, on a visit to the Burkes in 1774, that the collection 'would not have disgraced the City of Paris itself'.[603] Later in the century, Sir Richard Worsley (1751–1805), after returning from the Grand Tour in 1772, displayed dozens of Greek marbles and recently acquired paintings at his home, Appuldurcombe House, on the Isle of Wight, in what he called his Museum Worsleyanum. He produced a two-volume catalogue for visitors. Writing to his nephew from Rome, Sir Richard Lyttelton remarked, 'What a figure my fine room will cut

---

601 Jonathan Richardson, *An Essay on the Theory of Painting: By Mr. Richardson* (London: John Churchill, 1715), 14–15, 225, 132.
602 Reynolds, 'Discourse I', *The works of Sir Joshua Reynolds, Knight;... containing his Discourses, Idlers, A Journey to Flanders and Holland, and His Commentary on Du Fresnoy's Art of Painting...* edited by Edmond Malone, 3 vols (London: Gadell and Davies, 1798), i, 9.
603 Cited by Elizabeth Lambert, *Edmund Burke of Beaconsfield*, (London: Associated University Presses, 2003), 55. For a list of Burke's collection, see Carl B. Cone, 'Edmund Burke's Art Collection', *Art Bulletin 29* (1947), 126–31.

when it is adorned with all the fine pictures I am collecting'.⁶⁰⁴ The acquisition of pictures, sculptures and other classical artefacts was a reflection of a gentleman's standing.

A third way in which links with European culture were revived was the Grand Tour. This adventure enabled travellers to witness the remains of that classical world and see for themselves those works of Renaissance culture which had so influenced the development of their own thought and tastes. The Tour was regarded by many as their main chance to collect artworks that would both remind them of their experience, and reflect that appreciation for antiquities and for Renaissance painting expected of a well-educated, well-travelled British aristocrat.

A striking feature about the Tourists in this collection is that they show little or no inclination to participate in this aspect of the Tour. Whatever their reasons, they kept their distance from what had developed into a thriving trade. It could be argued that Lyttelton was too young to get involved, that neither Spence nor Boswell had the money to start collecting, and that Lennox had no pressing need to since the family home in London, Holland House, was sufficiently supplied. Barry is the exception in that he did collect a number of sculpture casts to take back to England so that he could work from them at the Royal Academy. Even so, it is curious these Tourists pay so little attention to what so many others regarded as an important part of their Tour.

What to Collect

So what did people collect? For those who had the means, a prime purchase would be a painting by one of the acknowledged masters of the Renaissance. Failing that, a copy done by one of the resident painters in Paris or Rome. Prints were in demand, as were sculptures — statues, busts — as well as more portable items such as coins and medals.⁶⁰⁵ Ceramics and glass became fashionable to collect later in the century, a trend highlighted by the acquisition of the Roman cameo glass vase, known as the Barberini, in 1778, by Sir William Hamilton, British Ambassador to Naples.⁶⁰⁶ In addition, if they had money

---

604 Cited by 'The National Gallery': <www.nationalgallery.org.uk/the-grand-tour/*/viewPage/3)>
605 One of the finest collections of coins in Europe, assembled by William Hunter (1718–83), Scottish physician and Professor of Anatomy in the Royal Academy, was on display at his house in Great Windmill Street, London. His extensive library and museum were open to anyone who wished to visit them.
606 Hamilton brought it back to England and sold it in 1784 to Margaret Bentinck (1715–85), Duchess of Portland, a noted collector. The vase, known as the Portland Vase,

enough, they could have their portrait painted by one of the resident artists in Rome.[607] These included English, Scots and Irish students, Barry among them, who supported themselves by such commissions. They were also available to do copies of major works in the galleries of Rome or Naples as part of their apprenticeship. While in Paris, Barry did a copy of Le Sueur's 'La maladie d'Alexandre' as a gift for Edmund Burke.

There were also intangible things to be collected. Tourists collected ideas, new ways of thinking about history, civilisation, aesthetics, and particularly architecture. Visits to classical monuments, to Rome's Forum, to the villa Ludovizi, one of the most beautiful in Rome, or a perusal through the engravings of Rome by the Italian architect Giovanni Battista Piranesi (1720–78),[608] gave the Tourist new ideas about architecture and the use of space to take back and adapt to their houses and gardens. The style of Venetian architect Andrea Palladio (1508–80) became fashionable in England, evident for instance in Chiswick House in London. A passage such as this description of the area outside St Peter's gives a suggestion of totally new ways of envisaging design and space:

> There is a magnificent area encompassed with a piazza of a circular form. This piazza consists of four rows of fine marble columns, adorned with a prodigious number of statues, with a stately obelisk in the middle, and a large fountain on each side.[609]

One result of the Tour was that classical marble columns, statues, obelisks, and fountains gradually found their way into British architecture and landscapes from the late seventeenth century onwards.

How Did They Collect?

THE PRINCIPAL ways of collecting art were by commissioning an agent, or by doing the purchase oneself on the Tour. Nobility often worked through an intermediary in Paris or Rome. When, in 1765, Boswell visited his friend in

---

was loaned to the ceramic artist, Josiah Wedgewood (1730–95), and greatly influenced his work. For more on Hamilton and collecting art in Naples, see David D. Nolta, 'The Body of the Collector and the Collected Body in William Hamilton's Naples', *Eighteenth-Century Studies*, 31 (1997), 110–114.

607 Records indicate that the Italian painter Pompeo Batoni (1708–87) did some 200 portraits of British Tourists in Rome.
608 Piranesi's *Vedute di Roma* (Views of Rome), a collection of 135 engravings, was greatly sought after by Tourists.
609 Nugent, *The Grand Tour*, iii, 325.

Rome, the Scottish painter Gavin Hamilton (1723–98) he found him working on a picture commissioned by the Duke of Bedford: 'Achilles dragging the Body of Hector at his Chariot Wheels'.[610] In similar vein, Horace Walpole (1717–97) wrote to Horace Mann (1706–86) with a general remit to collect 'medals, antiquities, or pictures for the King'.[611] To do this effectively, one needed to have the right contacts. On the other hand, people making the Tour could avail themselves of the well-established network on the ground which would quickly introduce them to the market.

On their way to or from Italy, Tourists might pause in Paris to see what collectibles were on offer, and make a purchase. Dealers were ready to advise, and auctions were frequent. If the Tourist was interested in prints from engravings — which were a brisk business in Paris — it was important to be aware that there were shady merchants; the key was to find a reputable one.[612] A print of Titian's 'Les Pèlerins d'Emmaus' by the French engraver Antoine Masson (1636–1700) was sold for 200 livres; but others could be purchased for much less.[613] Some dealers pretended an engraving was older than it was in order to increase its price; others sold the engraving in a frame which concealed imperfections. To purchase original paintings by acknowledged Masters was an expensive business in Paris. Carl Vanloo's 'Le Mariage de la Vierge' went for 6,000 livres, and his 'Adoration des Bergers' fetched 4,800 livres; Rubens, 'L'Adoration des Rois' sold for 10,000 livres.[614]

But the principal marketplace for British Tourists was Italy — notably Rome. As Barry's letter to Burke, discussed below, tells us, a network of agents, connoisseurs, 'cicerones', and dealers was at work to facilitate and often dupe unsuspecting patrons into the purchase of sculptures and paintings. Local guides were on hand — among them English and Scots — to explain items of antiquarian, archaeological, historical, or artistic interest, to show the traveller to the studios of painters, and to arrange viewings. French Tourists had the added benefit of L'Académie de France in Rome where they could meet the students and engage one of them to show them around the city: 'il se font

---

610 Frederick A. Pottle, *James Boswell, the Early Years, 1740–69* (London: McGraw-Hill, 1966), 219. Gavin Hamilton had moved to Rome in 1748; he became well known as a picture dealer (see David Irwin, 'Gavin Hamilton: Archaeologist, Painter and Dealer', *The Art Bulletin*, June 1962, 87–102).
611 *Letters of Horace Walpole to Horace Mann* , 14 Nov 1760, I, 11.
612 François Charles Joullain, *Réflexions sur la peinture et la gravure, accompagnées d'une courte dissertation sur le commerce de la curiosité et les ventes en général* (Metz: C. Lamort, 1786), 146–7.
613 Joullain, *Réflexions sur la peinture*, 207.
614 Joullain, *Réflexions sur la peinture*, 185, 166.

ensuite un plaisir de vous conduire partout, et vous épargnent bien de temps dans l'examen des curiosités'.[615]

However, as Barry shows in his letter to Burke, not all guides were trustworthy. A French traveller summed up the feelings of many when he warned his readers against the 'cicerones': 'Il est bon cependant de prévenir les curieux de ne point donner une confiance trop aveugle à ce qu'on leur dira de plusieurs de ces tableaux que l'on met un peu légèrement sous le nom de très grands maîtres qui n'y ont jamais travaillé'.[616] The broad procedure was that the guide would take the Tourist to various studios to view the works on offer or in progress. The next best thing to an Old Master was a copy done by a painter resident in Rome. Once an item was selected, and the price negotiated, the dealer would arrange for permission to export from the Papal Commissioner for Antiquities.[617] That done, the items were shipped back to England in crates. On arrival there, customs officials would require payment for the imported goods. Duty on paintings was calculated according to the size of the canvas.[618]

Notable among the dealers in Rome were English and Scots: James Byres (1733–1817), a Scot from a family of Jacobite sympathisers, who lived in Rome from 1758 to 1790 before going back to Scotland; Thomas Jenkins (1722–98), who specialised in Roman sculpture and antiquities; [619] the antiquarian, Colin Morison (1732–1810); and Barry's friend, the Scot Gavin Hamilton, painter and antiquarian, who moved to Rome in 1748.

---

615 Charles Duclos, cited by Charlotte Guichard, *Les Amateurs d'Art à Paris au XVIIIe Siècle* (Seyssel: Champ Vallon, 2008), 194. (It is then a pleasure to take you everywhere, and save you much time in looking at things that interest you.)
616 J. D. Cassini, *Journal du voyage fait en Italie, en mil Sept cent SoixanteQuinze*, cited by Gilles Bertrand, *Le Grand Tour Revisité* (Rome: École Française de Rome, 2008), 419, n. 72. (It is good to warn the curious not to put too blind a confidence in what is told them of several of the paintings which are casually suggested as the work of great masters who never worked on them.)
617 Setmour Howard, 'An Antiquarian Handlist and Beginnings of the Pio-Clementino', *Eighteenth-Century Studies*, 7 (1973), 40.
618 Holger Hoock, *The King's Artists: The Royal Academy of Arts and the Politics of Culture, 1760–1840* (Oxford: Oxford University Press, 2003), 240–42.
619 See 'James Byres: Principal Antiquarian for the English Visitors to Rome', *Apollo*, XCIX, June 1974, 446–61, and 'Thomas Jenkins: Banker, Dealer and Unofficial English Agent', *Apollo*, XCIX, June 1974, 416–25; for more on the practice of dealers like Byres, see Jules David Prown, 'A Course of Antiquities at Rome, 1764', *Eighteenth-Century Studies*, 31 (1997), 90–100.

Barry's Letter to Burke, 23 May 1767

An unusual insight on the way some dealers in Rome went about their business is given in a long letter from Barry to Burke not long after he had settled in Rome.[620] He spends some time on his first impressions of various works of art he has seen, but the brunt of the letter is about his reaction to Rome's art dealers.[621] From the opening remarks it is clear that he is very sensitive that his opinions might be taken poorly, or give offence, in some quarters.

At the head of the letter is a cautionary note: 'don't read this Letter to any strangers'. That said, Barry starts calmly by discussing some of the sculptures he has seen, their anatomical skill, his admiration for Michelangelo's work in the Sistine Chapel, his 'freedom & greatness of style', and Raphael's manner with facial expressions. He has some reservations about certain aspects of these artists, well aware that it is unusual to say so — but he adds this is strictly his 'private view'. The mention of Raphael reminds him of a recent unpleasant conversation he had had in the company of other painters and one of the dealers. He writes:

> I was some time agoe at a Conversation here where were some Artists & English & other Gentlemen, amongst other talk Minx's copy after Rafael (which is at Northumberland house) [622] came on the Tapis[623] & it was observed by one present (who from the nature of his business & situation is courted exceedingly by such artists as desire to make either money or friends here as he & one or two more of the same interest & opinion are the only channels through which the acquaintance of English Gentlemen come) it was observed by him as I said Minx's copy was not well relish'd at first by the people at home, which was not to be wonder'd at as it required some time to form the Taste of a Nation & that he was sorry that Minx was not in England to teach &c I begged him to excuse

---

620   The full text is available at <www.texte.ie/barry/index.html>; the source is Fitzwilliam MS, Wentworth Woodhouse Manuscripts, Sheffield City Council, Libraries, Archives and Information. The transcription follows the manuscript, and makes no alteration to spelling, punctuation, or capital letters.

621   For more on the art trade in Rome, see Christopher M. S. Johns, 'The Entrepôt of Europe: Rome in the Eighteenth Century', *Art in Rome in the Eighteenth Century*, edited by Edgar Peters Boron and Joseph J. Rise (London: Merrell, 2000), 39–40; stringent laws made it difficult for Tourists to export works of any great value.

622   The German painter, Anton Raphael Mengs (1728–79); the gallery in Northumberland House had copies by him of paintings by Raphael — for example, 'School of Athens', 'Assembly of the Gods', and of the 'Marriage of Cupid and Psyche' (Edward Walford, 'Northumberland House and its Associations', *Old and New London*, vol 3 (London: Cassell, Petter & Galpin, 1878), 135–141).

623   'On the table-cloth, under discussion or consideration' (OED). The ensuing argument may have been with Thomas Jenkins or James Byres (see Pressly, *The Life and Art of James Barry*, 10–11).

me If I took the Liberty to observe that it looked a little oddly to expect the introduction of Good Taste from a copy after Rafael by Minx, if the Cartoons the best work of Rafael [...] which were in England ever since the time of Charles 1st. [...] were not able to effect it.[624]

Barry began to think the dealer an unscrupulous charlatan, ready to dupe British Tourists and descry British painters for the sake of financial profit:

> As he is a man of great civility I never would have thought of observing this or any thing else in contradiction to what he said if I had not seen clearly into the drift & tendency of his frequent hints of the incapacity of the people at home, & that a nod from him would set his dependents to tear up & trample upon every thing we held sacred, Reynolds could not draw, his coloring was white, was blue, was [...] red, was every thing that could damn him, he stole what he had & he mangled what he stole. Barrett[625] was nothing, could be nothing, the mushroom of a day whose pictures whenever people came to have any taste would be hung up at Rag fair,[626] in short Gainsborough's Landscapes were nosegays, & west[627] who according to their Letters was so much the fashion afforded a convincing proof that drawing was not sought after & that a true Idea of Art was wanting as nothing would go down but magilps[628] & mysteries.

Barry, holding his peace for the moment, responds with a more positive view of the artists mentioned, only to meet open hostility:

> in the beginning I took it but for the effects of envy, jealousy & what not, which sometimes infect the minds of Artists, & thought it ought not to break any sociable ties between us, but I had no sooner attempted to excuse our people at home from the Aspersions thrown upon them & from the prepossessions which our Travellers here were likely to get against them but I was immediately pointed out as a person who not coinciding with the designs of the dealers might be dangerous in the company of English Cavaliers...

Barry, bitter at this rebuff, tells Burke his utter scorn for the dealer and his like, who find it necessary:

---

624 Charles I of England (1600–49), while still Prince of Wales, bought Raphael's cartoons for the Royal Collection in 1623.
625 George Barret (c.1728–84), Irish painter, and friend of Barry.
626 'A market for the sale of old clothes, held at Houndsditch in London' (OED).
627 Thomas Gainsborough (1727–88), English portrait and landscape painter; a founder member of the Royal Academy in 1768. Benjamin West (1738–1820), history and portrait painter, born in Pennsylvania; a founding member, and later President, of the Royal Academy; appointed by King George III as historical painter to the Court in 1772.
628 A mixture of linseed oil and turpentine or mastic varnish used to coat oil paintings; usually spelt 'megilp', but there are many variations.

every now & then to run out into the praises of an indifferent antique head with a modern body & legs cobbled to it, or of an old picture which they Christened in the name of this or that master & which has seldom other merit than that as nothing is visible in it so nothing can be objected to.

Dealers are able to function in this way, partly because there are so many antique pieces of sculpture about, many of them without merit:

> It requires no proof that there are great numbers of Antient Statues & Basso Relievo's little worthy of notice for any skill in the workmanship & [...] designing they have been only preserv'd because of some custom that they may serve to explain some manner of dress or some opinion of the ancients which they may elucidate: this may be when they are entire or in great part so, but there are legs & thighs & feet & heads brought out of old houses, gardens & other places where they have mostly lain unheeded ever since the 15 Century when they were thrown away as soon as they were found being wanting in every thing that could entitle them to a place in a repository.

An additional help to the dealers was that British Tourists seemed to have had more money than sense.[629] None of the Tourists in this collection would be exempt from many a dealer's wry perception of them:

> As the English have much money to lay out in Vertue[630] & have perhaps a greater passion for the ancients than they have (generally speaking) judgment to distinguish amongst them. Those into whose hands they fall here & to whom their commissions are sent take care to provide heads with bodies & legs & vice versa, fragments of Gods & Senators are jumbled into the same figure of furies & Graces, 'till it comes out a monster like that which rose from the hide the three deities pissed into.[631] There are instances to be sure of some one or two good things going over, but the multitude of those that are exceeding bad, [...] (much below the work of any tolerable french or other modern artist) make us the amazement & ridicule of all indifferent people. Tis pity to see our Gentlemen who come out of England with the best intentions, & with a national spirit so dup'd & made even instruments of dissension twixt the Artists here. The Antiquary & dealer are each provided with his set of puffers, & in return whatever Gentleman falls into his hands is taught to believe that next to the old pictures & statues which they deal in these are the only people here or at home & a Job of some trifling matter is suffer'd to fall now & then in their way. The rest if they are heard of tis to their disadvantage but care is taken that they shall be never seen.

---

629 Lennox makes the telling point that the Italians 'love our money'; Smollett remarked that the English seem 'to have more money to throw away; and therefore a greater number of snares are laid for them' (Smollett, cited in *The Fatal Gift of Beauty*, edited by Manfred Pfister (Amsterdam: Rodopi, 1966), 85).
630 'A love of, or taste for, works of art or curios' (OED).
631 The allusion has not been found.

These vituperative remarks against 'mercenary' dealers stem not least from Barry's deep commitment to the seriousness of his profession as a painter:

> I have wearied you & myself, but you will excuse it as these things seemed to me to affect the very vitals of Art: I would further add that tho for the most part intrigue & mercenary ways may be prevalent here as the truth is never without a witness [...] there are a few who follow Art for its own sake, these are as easily distinguish'd by their Abilities as the others may be by their want of them.

Having told Burke his frank opinions, he returns to the anxiety and fear he expressed at the head of the letter:

> I am almost afraid even to send what I have wrote as I always dread the resentment of base spirited people incapable as I know of an open Generous revenge. There are two sorts of people they are desirous of gaining over, such who are likely to be known to or recommended to the Gentlemen who come hither, & others whose understanding & conversation may be usefully employed to their purposes & from the compliments paid me in the beginning it should appear they judg'd me in some measure proper for them, a very little time shew'd the contrary [...] for on speaking civilly of the works of Reynolds Barrett, Hamilton here & Nevi[632] twas whispered that I spoke too much for a young man & resolved from that time that I should have for the future but few opportunities of speaking in the company of English Cavaliers to whom it was necessary to convey opinions of another tendency. as we know each other we are very quiet & as sociable as I can when we meet together which is the course I shall take whilst I stay here. You will I believe think it prudent to keep this letter to yourself as should it be known that I laid such matters open these people would soon be advised of it & perhaps assassination may be the consequence of it.

The letter ends with news of the work he has been doing, his money problems (the Burke family was supporting him), and family matters.

Collecting was a key element of the Tour, but not for everyone by any means. Barry's personal account of how some dealers operated, informed as it is from inside Rome's art world, leave us little room to wonder why some Tourists, like those in this collection, steered clear of them.

---

632 James Nevay, (1755–1811), minor painter from Scotland whom Barry admired.

APPENDIX B

Advice to Travellers on the Grand Tour

THE FOLLOWING passages are examples of the kind of advice available to travellers in guidebooks and in the accounts of people who had already made the Tour.

Preparing for the Grand Tour

THERE IS certainly no Place in the World where a Man may Travel with greater Pleasure and Advantage than in Italy. One finds something more particular in the Face of the Country, and more astonishing in the Works of Nature, than can be met with in any other Part of Europe. It is the great School of Musick and Painting, and contains in it all the noblest Productions of Statuary and Architecture both Ancient and Modern. It abounds with Cabinets of Curiosities, and vast Collections of all Kinds of Antiquities. No other Country in the World has such a Variety of Governments, that are so different in their Constitutions, and so refined in their Politicks, There is scarce any Part of the Nation that is not Famous in History, nor so much as a Mountain or River that has not been the Scene of some extraordinary Action.

As there are few Men that have Talents or Opportunities for examining so copious a Subject, one may observe among those who have written on Italy, that different Authors have succeded best on different sorts of Curiosities. Some have been more particular in their Accounts of Pictures, Statues and Buildings; some have search'd into Libraries, Cabinets of Rarities, and Collections of Medals, as others have been wholly taken up with Inscriptions, Ruins and Antiquities. Among the Authors of our own Country, we are obliged to the Bishop of Salisbury, for his masterly and uncommon Observations on the Religion and Governments of Italy: Lassels may be useful in giving us the Names of such Writers as have treated of the several States through which he pass'd : Mr. Ray is to be valued for his Observations on the Natural Productions of the Place. Monsieur Misson has wrote a more correct Account of Italy in general than any before him, as he particularly Excels in the Plan of the Country, which he has given us in true and lively Colours.

There are still several of these Topicks that are far from being exhausted, as there are many new Subjects that a Traveller may find to employ himself upon. For my own part, as I have taken Notice of several Places and Antiquities that no Body else has spoken of, so, I think, I have mentioned but few Things in common with others, that are not either set in a new Light, or accompany'd with different Reflections. I have taken care particularly to consider the several Passages of the Ancient Poets, which have any Relation to the Places or Curiosities that I met with: For before I entered on my Voyage I took care to refresh my Memory among the Classic Authors, and to make such Collections out of them as I might afterwards have Occasion for. I must confess it was not one of the least Entertainments that I met with in Travelling, to examine these several Descriptions, as it were, upon the Spot and to compare the Natural Face of the Country with the Landskips that the Poets have given us of it.
[Joseph Addison, Preface, *Remarks on Several Parts of Italy, &c. in the Years 1701, 1702, 1703* (London: J. Tonson, 1718, n.p.)]

What to Take

INTO A small trunk I would have you put a dozen of shirts; they ought to be much coarser than the English in general wear them; otherwise, their slovenly manner of washing (which is by beating them with a board against a stone in cold water) will soon oblige you to buy others; half a dozen pair of shoes; a pair of boots, and buckskin breeches, would be requisite; as the French leather is not proof against water: your stockings, should be silk, which is the fashion of France, even among the meanest mechanics; these, with the cloaths on your back, and the hat on your head, with the best French dictionary and grammar, are all the luggage you ought to take; for at the first town you propose to reside at, you should fit out *à la mode de France*, and continue so as long as you stay in that country:… as an English dress, is a sufficient object for French knavery: I had almost forgot two necessary articles called a knife and fork; which if you neglect taking with you, you'll often run the hazard of losing your dinner; it being the custom of those very polite people (women, as well as men) to lug out their great sharp-pointed knives when going to their meals; as there are seldom any laid on the table, except called for.
[*The Gentleman's Guide in his Tour through France. Wrote by an Officer* (London: Kearsly, 1770), 9–10.]

Crossing the Channel

THE PASSAGE in the packet from Dover to Calais, is only half-a-guinea each person; the distance being no more than twenty-one miles: the hire of a whole vessel to yourself, is precisely the same from Dover to Boulogne as from Dover to Calais, five guineas; and by going to Boulogne, instead of Calais, you will save the expence of travelling twenty-four miles by land.

Most of the Dover packet-boats are the property of one man, or one set of men; by which means they endeavour to keep up the price to five guineas: however, there are one or two bye-boats that will carry you over for three guineas; but these cannot always be procured.

When a gentleman hires a packet-boat from Dover to Calais, let him insist upon being carried into the harbour in the ship, without paying the least regard to the representations of the master; when he tells you it is low water, or the wind is in your teeth, say, you will stay on board till it is high water, or the wind comes favourable; and if he sees you resolute, he will find means to bring the ship into the harbour, or at least to convince you, that it absolutely is not in his power. I mention this, because nothing is so great a deception to people unused to objects from the sea, as the distance it is to high land; and the boatmen will demand almost as much for rowing you to shore as you gave for your whole passage.

[*The Gentleman's Guide in his Tour through France*, 15–16.]

Travel Prices

TRAVELLING IS no where more convenient than in *France*, with respect as well to carriages as accommodations on the road. Where there is conveniency of rivers, they have water-carriages, which are large boats drawn by horses. Their land carriages are of four sorts, *viz.* post chaises, the *carosse* or stage-coach, the *coche*, and the diligence or flying-coach. Their post-chaises are made much in the same manner as ours, and are to be had at a minute's warning all over the kingdom. The price of a post-chaise is at the rate of 30 sols each post.[633] Travelling by post-horses, you save the expence of the chaise, but it is not so pleasant, nor can you carry so much baggage. In most towns they have a little book, which determines the price of post-horses, either with or without a chaise, and the number of stages you pay for, to prevent travellers

---

633 There were approximately 20 'sol' to a 'livre', and 24 'livre' to a gold piece called a 'pistole' or 'Louis d'or'. This was worth a little less than a British pound at the time. A 'julio' or 'giulio' in Italy was worth about eight 'sol'.

from being imposed upon by the postilion. The common price of riding post used to be only two livres or forty sols a post, that is twenty sols for each horse, and ten sols to the postilion; but it is now raised to sixty sols a post, *viz.* thirty sols for each horse. The postilion by authority can demand no more than five sols a post for himself; yet custom has increased it to ten sols; and not content with this, by his importunity and impertinence he frequently exacts four or five sols more. The distance of each post is about six miles. All those posts that lead from *Paris*, or from any place where the king actually resides, are called royal-posts, and the charge of riding them is double the others, with regard to the horses, but not to the postilion. Besides, it is an established custom to require fifteen sols for coming into *Paris*, The post-stages are seldom above one post and a half, or two posts long, and then you change both horses and postilion. The horses are none of the best, being frequently apt to stumble; for which reason the postilions are generally provided with jack-boots made of very hard leather, that if the horse should fall upon them, they may slip their leg out of the boot, while it is under the beast, without injury. This precaution may be recommended to gentlemen that travel with post-horses; and 'tis also adviseable when the horse proves dull, as is often the case, to make the postilion go behind, and drive the beast before him, for they are generally provided with better horses, and have a peculiar knack of spurring them on.
[Thomas Nugent, *The Grand Tour. Containing an Exact Description of most of the Cities, Towns, and Remarkable Places of Europe*, 4 vols (London: A. Millar, 1749), iv, 39–40.]

Staying in Paris

There are a great many fine inns at *Paris*, where travellers may be extremely well accommodated, in proportion to the figure and expence they intend to make. The principal of these are, the *Hotel Imperial*, in the street *Dauphin*, and suburb of *S. Germains*; and over-against it the *Hotel d'Anjou*; the *Hotel d'Hambourg*, the *Hotel d'Orleans*, and the *Hotel de Piccardie*, in the street *Mazarin*; the *Hotel d' Espagne*, in the street *de Seine*; the *Hotel Imperial*, in the *Rue de Fou*; the *Doge of Venice*, in the street *de Boucherie*; the grand *Hotel de Luine*, and the little *Hotel de Luine*, on the *Quay des Augustins*; the *Croix de Fer*, the *Croix Blanche*, and the *Croix Dorée*, in the street of *S. Denis*, besides several others too tedious to mention. Those who intend to stay some time at *Paris*, and do not chuse to be at the expence of living in these Hotels, may hire a furnished lodging, and dine at the public ordinaries, of which there are a great number at very reasonable prices. Or else they may board with a private family, where they can be furnished with a neat room, a hot dinner and supper (breakfast they find themselves) with a pint of wine at each meal for the sum of sixty livres, which is two pounds twelve shillings and six-pence *English* money a month; though some will have more, according to the goodness of the apartment, or the variety and elegance of the entertainment.

[Thomas Nugent, *The Grand Tour*, iv, 89.]

On the Road — Carriages, Baggage, and Refreshments

THE *carosse* is not unlike our stage-coach, containing room for six passengers, but does not move so quick, and is more embarrassed with goods and baggage. The *coche* is a large heavy machine, which serves the use both of waggon and coach; it is long shaped, and provided with windows at the sides, containing generally sixteen passengers, *viz.* twelve in the body of the coach, sitting two a breast, and two on each side at the door of the entrance, a seat being provided there for that purpose. It is furnished with two large conveniencies, one before and another behind, which are made of basket wicker, and are therefore called baskets. Into these baskets they put large quantities of goods, which makes it very heavy in drawing. Sometimes both the baskets are filled with goods, and sometimes the fore one is left empty for passengers, in which the fare is less than in the coach, and they have a covering over-head to preserve them from the injury of the weather. Its motion is but slow, seldom exceeding that of a brisk walk, and as the roads are generally paved with large stone, this kind of vehicle is generally very jumbling and disagreeable. The expence of travelling with the *carosse* or stage-coach is less than half the sum of riding-post, but then you are to make an allowance for being longer upon the road. As for the particular fares of stage coaches, we shall mention them in each journey; only we are to observe here that the expence of baggage is paid apart, and is generally three sols for every pound above fourteen or fifteen pound weight, which is free. As to victuals, your safest way of travelling post is to know the price of every thing before you order it; but with the stage-coach, your meals are generally regulated at fixed prices, as with us; your entertainment is exceeding good, and the whole expence seldom exceeds five or six livres a day. 'Tis customary after meals to give a couple of sols to the servants. The Diligence is a kind of stage coach so called from its expedition, and differs from the carosse or ordinary stage-coach, in little else but in moving with greater velocity. It is used chiefly in travelling from *Paris* to *Lyons*, and from *Paris* to *Brussells*, and has its fixt prices, which we shall give in its proper place, as also the days that this as well as the ordinary stage-coaches set out from Paris to most parts of France.

[Thomas Nugent, *The Grand Tour*, iv, 40–41.]

Routes

Paris to Italy

Those that intend to travel from *Paris* to *Italy* must set out for *Lyons*, to which city there are three different routes, *viz*, two post-roads, and a third used by the *Diligence*. Again, there are four different routes from *Lyons* to *Italy*; the first, and pleasantest, but *longest* about, is by *Marseilles* and *Toulon*, at either of which places there are daily opportunities of vessels going to *Genoa*; but if you don't like the sea, you may proceed by the post-route from *Aix* to *Nice*, and thence by land to *Genoa*, or any other part of *Italy*: the second somewhat shorter, by *Geneva* and *Switzerland*: the third still shorter, by *Grenoble* and *Brianson*: and the fourth as short as the preceding, by *Pont Beauvoisin*. The Diligence from *Paris* to *Lyons* sets out every other day from the *Hotel de Sens*, near the *Ave Maria*; the price to each passenger seventy-five livres. For your baggage you pay five sols a-pound, except twenty-five pounds, which you have free. There are likewise coaches at the same place that set out every third day at four in the morning, and winter and summer go through *Burgundy*. You have also water carriages from *Paris* to *Lyons*; the fare to each passenger is thirty-five livres, and you are ten days upon the road.
[Thomas Nugent, *The Grand Tour*, iv, 113–14.]

To Italy via Nice

Rome is betwixt four and five hundred miles distant from Nice, and one half of the way I was resolved to travel by water. Indeed there is no other way of going from hence to Genoa, unless you take a mule, and clamber along the mountains at the rate of two miles an hour, and at the risque of breaking your neck every minute. The Appenine mountains, which are no other than a continuation of the maritime Alps, form an almost continued precipice from Villefranche to Lerici, which is almost forty-five miles on the other side of Genoa; and as they are generally washed by the sea, there is no beach or shore, consequently the road is carried along the face of the rocks, except at certain small intervals, which are occupied by towns and villages. But, as there is a road for mules and foot passengers, it might certainly be enlarged and improved so as to render it practicable by chaises and other wheel-carriages, and a toll might be exacted, which in a little time would defray the expence: for certainly no person who travels to Italy, from England, Holland, France, or Spain, would make a troublesome circuit to pass the Alps by the way of Savoy and Piedmont, if he could have the convenience of going post by the way of

Aix, Antibes, and Nice, along the side of the Mediterranean, and through the Riviera of Genoa, which from the sea affords the most agreeable and amazing prospect I ever beheld.
[Smollett, Letter XXV, 1 January 1765, *Travels through France and Italy*, 2nd edn, 2 vols (London: Baldwin, 1766), ii, 3–4.]

Handling Money

A TRAVELLER SHOULD be very cautious of pulling out money or valuable things before strange company on the road or in public inns; for almost all the robberies and murders that are committed on passengers, are occasioned by such imprudences. If this be a salutary advice in all countries, 'tis especially so in *Italy*, where though the public roads are not much infested with highwaymen, yet there are a great many villains who are ready to murder or assassinate a stranger in private houses, when they happen to have a prospect of some considerable prey. For this reason a traveller should always be furnished with some iron machine to shut his door on the inside, which may be easily contrived, and made of several sorts; for it frequently happens that the doors of the lodging-rooms have neither locks nor bolts, and *opportunity*, according to the old proverb, *makes the thief*. 'Tis proper also to travel with arms, such as a sword and pair of pistols, and likewise with a tinder-box in order to strike a fire in case of any accident in the night.
[Thomas Nugent, *The Grand Tour*, iii, 61–62.]

On Learning the Language in Italy

ALMOST EVERY province has a particular dialect, such as the *Tuscan*, the *Roman*, the *Venetian*, the *Neapolitan*, the *Calabrese*, the *Genoese*, the *Milanese*, the *Parmesan*, the *Piementese*, the *Bergamasco*, with several others. The reason of this is, as I apprehend, the multiplicity of states and governments in that country, whose laws being different, a diversity also arises in their language. But the principal *Italian* dialect is the *Tuscan* for elegance and purity, and the *Roman* for accent and pronunciation, pursuant to the old *Italian* proverb, *Lingua Toscana in Bocca Romana. The Tuscan language in a Roman mouth.* Those who design to make some stay in *Italy*, in order to learn the language, are advised to chuse *Sienna* for their place of residence; because the *Florentine* pronunciation is accompanied with a harshness that offends the ear, and is troublesome to the throat; and at *Rome* they are confounded by the multitude of strangers, with whom they are daily obliged to converse. But at *Sienna* one may find retirement together with the *Tuscan* language and *Roman* mouth.
[Thomas Nugent, *The Grand Tour*, iii, 47.]

When in Rome

When a traveller comes to *Rome* he is immediately surrounded by a multitude of lacqueys who come to offer their service; but he should be cautious how he trusts them, for they are generally sad fellows. 'Tis most adviseable in case of necessity to take those who belong to the town, or at least to the country, because they give security to perform their duty, and are best acquainted with the people and customs of the place. The ordinary allowance of those *stassieri*, as they call them, is two and a half or three julios a day, when they are at board wages. For ten or twelve pistoles a month a gentleman may have a handsome coach and a pair of horses, except at *Lent* or about *Easter*, when there is a great concourse of strangers at *Rome*, and then they will ask fourteen pistoles a month for a coach and a pair of horses.

'Tis requisite to have a skilful antiquarian at *Rome*, which saves a person a great deal of trouble by directing him to the several remains of antiquity that are particularly worthy of a traveller's notice. These antiquarians are ridiculously distinguished by the name of *Ciceroni*, and may he retained for three or four pistoles a month, Those who do not chuse to be at that expence, may hire them at so much a day. 'Tis adviseable for every one to take a particular view of things themselves, without trusting to other people's relations; on which occasion 'tis better to be in company with other gentlemen, because by that means one improves by their different opinions. 'Tis proper also to be provided with maps, measures, prospective glasses, a mariner's compass and quadrant, and to be able to take the dimensions of things. A *Roman* palm, or a span and a half, makes thirteen inches *English* measure; the *Roman* foot is shorter by six lines than the *English*, and eight *Roman* feet make a cane. A brasse of *Florence* is 22 inches and a half *English*. A complete set of prints of all the antiquities and remarkable things that are to be found in *Rome*, may be bought there for about 100 pistoles, which may seem indeed a large sum to a great many people; but gentlemen should take care not to be too parsimonious in their travels, for otherwise they must expect to meet with trouble and vexation instead of pleasure. A liberal hand gains admission into all places and companies, and is attended with several considerable advantages; whereas a penurious management renders a person contemptible wherever he comes, and since 'tis but once in his life, he had much better appear generous and genteel, in order to gain the public esteem, and to facilitate the means of his own improvement.

[Thomas Nugent, *The Grand Tour*, iii, 64–66]

Bibliography

No attempt has been made to name all the innumerable publications about the Grand Tour. The most extensive, easily accessible list is to be found in Jeremy Black, *The British Abroad: The Grand Tour in the Eighteenth Century* (Stroud: Sutton, 1992), 366–80.

Unless indicated otherwise, the place of publication is London.

A: Primary Sources

James Barry

The letters are printed from the text of Barry's correspondence by T. O. McLoughlin at <www.texte.ie/barry> (2010).

James Boswell

By kind permission of Gordon Turnbull, General Editor, and the Editorial Committee of the Yale Editions of the Private Papers of James Boswell, the text of the letters printed here derives from Ralph Walker's edition of the *Correspondence of James Boswell and John Johnston of Grange* (Heinemann, 1966).

Caroline Lennox

The letters are published from MSS by kind permission of the Board of the National Library of Ireland.

Extracts from the Notebook (Add MSS 51445) are published by kind permission of the British Library.

George Lyttelton

The letters are published from MSS by kind permission of the 12th Viscount Cobham.

Joseph Spence

The letters are published from Egerton MSS 2234 by kind permission of the British Library.

B: Secondary Sources

Addison, J., *Remarks on Several Parts of Italy, 1701–1703* (J. Tonson, 1718)
Baretti, G., *A Journey from London to Genoa, through England, Portugal, Spain, and France* , 2 vols (Davies, 1770)
Barry, J., *The Works of James Barry, Esq: Historical Painter*, edited by E. Fryer, 2 vols (Cadell and Davies, 1809)
Bertrand, G., *Le grand tour revisité* (Rome: École française de Rome, 2008)
Bignamini, I., and Hornsby, C., *Digging and Dealing in Eighteenth-Century Rome* (New Haven: Yale University Press, 2010)
Black, J., *The British Abroad: The Grand Tour in the Eighteenth Century* (Stroud: Sutton, 1992)
Black, J., *The British and the Grand Tour* (Routledge, 1985)
Black, J., *Italy and the Grand Tour* (New Haven: Yale University Press, 2003)
Boswell, J., *Account of Corsica, The Journal of a Tour to That Island, and Memoirs of Pascal Paoli*, edited by James T. Boulton and T. O. McLoughlin (New York: Oxford University Press, 2006)
Boswell, J., *Boswell on the Grand Tour: Italy, Corsica, and France 1765–1766*, edited by F. Brady and F. A. Pottle (Heinemann, 1955)
Boswell, J., *Correspondence of James Boswell and John Johnston of Grange*, edited by Ralph S. Walker (Heinemann, 1966)
Boswell, J., *Life of Johnson*, edited by G. B. Hill and L. F. Powell (Oxford: Oxford University Press, 1934)
Bowron, E. P. and Rishel, J. J., editors, *Art in Rome in the Eighteenth Century* (Merrell, 2000)
Bromley, W., *Remarks in the Grand Tour of France and Italy. Perform'd by a Person of Quality, in the Year 1691*, 2nd edition (John Nutt, 1705)
Burke, E., *A Philosophical Enquiry into the Origin of Our Ideas of the Sublime and Beautiful* (1757), edited by James T. Boulton (Routledge, 1958, 2008)
Chard, C., *Pleasure and Guilt on the Grand Tour: Travel Writing and Imaginative Geography* (Manchester: Manchester University Press, 1999)
Chard, C., and Langton, H., editors, *Transports: Travel, Pleasure, and Imaginative Geography, 1660–1830*, Studies in British Art 3 (New Haven: Yale University Press, 1996)
Cone, Carl B., 'Edmund Burke's Art Collection,' *Art Bulletin 29* (1947), 126–31.
Davis, R. M., *The Good Lord Lyttelton* (Bethlehem, PA: Times, 1939)
Dolan, B., *Ladies of the Grand Tour* (Harper Collins, 2001)

Dunne, Tom, *James Barry 1741–1806: 'The Great Historical Painter'* (Kinsale: Crawford Art Gallery, 2005)
Earl of Ilchester, *Henry Fox, first Lord Holland, his family and relations*, 2 vols (John Murray, 1920)
Fitzgerald, B, editor, *The Correspondence of Emily, Duchess of Leinster* (Dublin: Irish Manuscripts Commission, 1949–57)
Ford, B., 'The Blathwayt Brothers of Durham in Italy on the Grand Tour', *National Trust Yearbook* (National Trust, 1975–76)
The Gentleman's Guide in His Tour Through France: Wrote by an Officer, 4th edition (Kearsly, 1770)
Gerrard, C., 'Lyttelton, George, first Baron Lyttelton (1709–1773)', *Oxford Dictionary of National Biography* (Oxford University Press, 2004) <http://www.oxforddnb.com/view/article/17306>
Gibbon, E., *Autobiography of Edward Gibbon* (New York: Turner and Hayden, 1846)
Gibbon, Edward, *Miscellaneous Works* (including *Memoirs*), edited by John, Lord Sheffield (A. Strahan, T. Cadell Jun. and W. Davies, 1796)
Hibbert, C., *The Grand Tour* (Methuen, 1987)
Hill, R., 'Gentlemen Did Not Dig', *London Review of Books*, 24 June 2010
Hoock, H., *The King's Artists: The Royal Academy of Arts and the Politics of Culture, 1760–1840* (Oxford: Oxford University Press, 2003)
Hulme, P., and Youngs, T., editors, *The Cambridge Companion to Travel Writing* (Cambridge: Cambridge University Press, 2002)
Ingamells, J., *A Dictionary of British and Irish Travellers in Italy, 1701–1800* (New Haven: Yale University Press, 1997)
Ingamells, J., 'Discovering Italy: British Travellers in the Eighteenth Century', in *Grand Tour: The Lure of Italy in the Eighteenth Century*, edited by A. Wilton and I. Bignamini (Tate Gallery, 1996)
John, Lord Hervey, *Some Materials Towards Memoirs of the Reign of King George II*, edited by R. Sedgwick, 3 vols (Eyre & Spottiswoode, 1931)
Jones, T., 'Memoirs' (National Library of Wales MS 23812D)
Joullain, F., C., *Réflexions sur la peinture et la gravure, accompagnées d'une courte dissertation sur le commerce de la curiosité et les ventes en général* (Metz: C. Lamort, 1786)
Laird, M., *The Flowering of the Landscape Garden: English Pleasure Grounds, 1720–1800* (Philadelphia: University of Pennsylvania Press, 1999)
Lambert, E., *Edmund Burke of Beaconsfield* (Associated University Presses, 2003)
Lambert, R. S., *Grand Tour: A Journey in the Tracks of the Age of Aristocracy* (Faber and Faber, 1935)
Lassels, R., *The Voyage of Italy, or A Compleat Journey through Italy* (John Starkey, 1670)
Luff, P., 'Fox, (Georgiana) Caroline [Lady (Georgiana) Caroline Lennox], suo jure Baroness Holland of Holland (1723–1774)', *Oxford Dictionary of National Biography* (Oxford University Press, 2004) <http://www.oxforddnb.com/view/article/48888>
Lyttelton, G., *Works* (Ayscough, 1774)
Mączak, A. (translated by Ursula Phillips), *Travel in Early Modern Europe* (Cambridge: Cambridge University Press, 1995)
Malcolm, D., *An Essay on the Antiquities of Great Britain and Ireland* (Edinburgh: T. and W. Ruddimans, 1738)
Mead, W. E., *The Grand Tour in the Eighteenth Century* (1914; Ayer, 1975)
Moore, A. W., *Norfolk & the Grand Tour: Eighteenth-Century Travellers Abroad and their Souvenirs* (Norfolk: Norfolk Museums Service, 1985)

National Gallery, <www.nationalgallery.org.uk/the-grand-tour/*/viewPage/3)>
Nolta, David D., 'The Body of the Collector and the Collected Body in William Hamilton's Naples', *Eighteenth-Century Studies*, 31 (1997), 110–114.
Nugent, T., *The Grand Tour, Containing an Exact Description of Most of the Cities, Towns, and Remarkable Places in Europe*, 4 vols (A. Millar, 1749)
Pasquin, A. [John Williams], *The Royal Academicians* (Denew and Grant, 1786)
Pfister, M., editor, *The Fatal Gift of Beauty* (Amsterdam: Rodopi, 1966)
Phillimore, R., editor, *Memoirs and Correspondence of George, Lord Lyttelton, from 1734 to 1773*, 2 vols (James Ridgway, 1845)
Pottle, F. A., *James Boswell, the Early Years, 1740–69* (McGraw-Hill, 1966)
Pressly, W. L., 'Barry, James (1741–1806)', *Oxford Dictionary of National Biography*, (Oxford University Press, 2004) <http://www.oxforddnb.com/view/article/1562>
Pressly, W. L., *James Barry, the Artist as Hero* (Tate Gallery Exhibition Catalogue, 1983)
Pressly, W. L., *The Life and Art of James Barry* (Yale University Press, 1981)
Prown, J. D., 'A Course of Antiquities at Rome, 1764', *Eighteenth-Century Studies*, 31 (1997), 90–100
Redford, B., *Venice & the Grand Tour* (Yale University Press, 1996)
Reynolds, Sir J., *Discourses*, edited by Pat Rogers (Penguin, 1992)
Richardson J., *An Essay on the Theory of Painting: By Mr. Richardson* (John Churchill, 1715)
Sambrook, J., 'Spence, Joseph (1699–1768)', *Oxford Dictionary of National Biography*, (Oxford University Press, 2004) <http://www.oxforddnb.com/view/article/26111>
Scott, J., *The Pleasures of Antiquity: British Collectors of Greece and Rome* (New Haven: Yale University Press, 2003)
Shackleton R., 'The Grand Tour in the Eighteenth Century,' *Studies in Eighteenth-Century Culture*, 1 (1971), 127–142.
Sharp, S., *Letters from Italy, Describing the Customs and Manners of that Country in the Years 1765 and 1766* (R. Cave, 1766)
Smollett, T., *Travels through France and Italy*, 2 vols (Baldwin, 1766)
Soros, S.W., editor, *James 'Athenian' Stuart, 1713–1788: The Rediscovery of Antiquity* (New Haven: Yale University Press, 2006)
Spence, J., *Joseph Spence: Letters from the Grand Tour*, edited by Slava Klima (Montreal: McGill-Queen's University Press, 1975)
Spence, J., *Observations, Anecdotes, and Characters of Books and Men*, edited by J. M. Osborn, 2 vols (Oxford: Oxford University Press, 1966)
Spence, J., *A Guide to Classical Learning: or, Polymetis abridged*, by N. Tindal (Dodsley and Horsfield, 1764)
Tillyard, S., *Aristocrats: Caroline, Emily, Louisa and Sarah Lennox, 1740–1832* (Chatto and Windus, 1994)
Vaughan, W., *British Painting: The Golden Age from Hogarth to Turner* (Thames and Hudson, 1999)
Walpole, H., *Letters of Horace Walpole to Horace Mann*, 2 vols (Philadelphia: Lea and Blanchard, 1844)
Wilton, A., and Bignamini, I., editors, *Grand Tour: The Lure of Italy in the Eighteenth Century* (Tate Gallery, 1996)
Woodfine, P., 'Poyntz, Stephen (*bap.* 1685, d.1750)', *Oxford Dictionary of National Biography*, (Oxford University Press, 2004) <http://www.oxforddnb.com/view/article/22694>
Wright, A., *Joseph Spence: A critical biography* (Chicago: University of Chicago Press, 1950)

Index

Note: The principal travellers are referred to by their initials: GL, JS, JB, CL; Boswell is Bos because his initials are the same as Barry's.

academies
    Académie de France in Rome 264–65
    at Berlin a riding school 136
    fees to be paid despite absence 45
    at Lunéville 11, 31
    'mighty good' at Sienna 41
    quite costly 36
    of St Luke in Paris 170, 178
    variety of 11
Adam, James 9
Adam, Robert 9
Addison, Joseph 10
    Cato 216
    Remarks on Several Parts of Italy &c 12–13, 108, 112, 131, 143, 146, 157
Albano 195
Alexander (sculpture) 188
Alexander, Mr 75
Allegri, Antonio 202, 203, 206, 207
Alps 68, 102, 113, 145, 184, 219, 225, 246
Alves, James 155
Andrews, Francis 231
Annual Register 9, 175, 231
Antinous (sculpture) 188, 200
Antiquities of Athens Measured and Delineated 6
Apollo (sculpture) 188
aqueduct, discovery of 98, 147–48
Arbuthnot, Robert 40, 59, 60, 75
Armenini, Giovanni Battista 209–10
art dealers 264–65, 266–69
Athanasius, St. 163
Auchinleck 137, 150, 157

Auchinleck, Lord (Bos's father)
    opposes Bos's European tour 129, 130; relents 144
Ausonius 133, 146
Avignon 132, 164
Ayscough, Francis (son) 35, 74, 78
Ayscough, George Edward (father) 35

Bacchus 183
Baden-Baden 130, 142
Baden-Durlach, Margrave of 140–41
bankers *see* Alexander, Arbuthnot, Netterville, Panshaw, Ray, Vergani
Barbieri, Giovani Francesco 202, 203, 206, 208
Barret, George 170, 175, 177, 182, 184, 190, 267, 269
Barry, James
    'affectation' of French artists 180–81
    on artists
        Corregio 207
        da Vinci's *Last Supper* 209–10
        Raphael and Michael Angelo 186–88, 194, 206
        Titian 170, 194
    attitude to the Tour 170
    copying Le Sueur's *La Maladie d'Alexandre* 170, 176, 177, 179
    crossing Mt. Cenis 183
    death of his brother 'Jack' 198–99
    delighted by Burgundy 182–83
    early career 169
    fellow students in Rome 192, 195, 196

hand-writing 16
'misery' of return journey in winter 211
money problems 172, 187, 196, 201–2, 204, 205
paintings
  Temptation of Adam 197
  Philoctetes on the Island of Lemnos 201, 205
  Progress of Human Culture 173
  in Paris 170, 174–75
  and Reynolds 170–71, 203
  scorn for art dealers in Rome 267–68
  self-portrait 168
  sketches and studies by 174, 193, 197
  suggests a course in reading 191
Barry, John ('Jack', JB's brother) 171, 198–99
Barry, John and Juliana (JB's parents) 169, 198–99
Barry, Patrick (JB's brother) 198
Barrymore, Richard, Earl 221, 251
Barrymore, Lady 251
Basle 142
Bassano, Jacopo 194
Batoni, Pompeo 195
Beauclerk, Topham 220
Beckford, William 1
  Dreams, Waking Thoughts and Incidents 1
Belloni, Jean Angelo 75
Belle 105
Belmonte, Princess Donna Anna 237, 250
Belson, Miss 89, 91
Belvedere gallery 199
Belvedere Torso (sculpture) 188
Berlin, 'the Court very dull' 135
Bernacchi, Antonio 106
Blacklock, Thomas 82
Blathwayt, John (son) 11
Blathwayt, William (father) 11
Blathwayt, William (son) 11
Bolingbroke, Lord 83, 220
Bolingbroke, Lady Diana 220
Bologna 76, 111, 131, 149, 215, 230–31
Bolonia 152
Bordeaux 25, 41
Bordone, Paris 211
Borghese Palace 193

Bosse, Abraham 207
Boswell, David (Bos's brother) 134, 137, 149, 152, 156
Boswell, James
  attends 'Course in Antiquities and Arts' 131, 150
  delights in Midnight Mass in Avignon 132, 164
  enthusiast for antiquities 132
  fantasises as soldier 157–58
  fascinated by Italy 130
  goes to prostitutes 155
  his 'romantic stile' 152
  laments loss of a language 156–57
  letters intended for oral delivery 133
  lively imagination of 133
  pleased by religious processions 163
  self-assessment 136, 138, 139–40, 150–51, 164, 165
  self-mockery 133–34
  venereal disease 132, 155
  visits Corsica and General Paoli 132
  visits villa of 'Divine Horace' 131
  writes verse 139–40
Boswell, John (Bos's brother) 152
Boswell, Thomas (no relation of Bos) 155
Boucher, Francois 181, 195
Boufflers, Madame 249
Bourbon, Louis-Henri, Duke of 88, 114
Bourbon, Duchess of 126
Bouzoles, Madame 249
Brescia 157
Britain, the 'moral yardstick' for travellers 3
Bromley, William 4, 32, 34
  Remarks in the Grand Tour 4
Bruno, St 158
Brunswick 135, 147
Brutus, Marcus Junius 119
Burgundy, Dukes of 221
Burke, Edmund 4, 17, 20, 169, 170, 196, 198, 199, 203, 261, 263
  Sublime and Beautiful 27
Burke, Jane (Mrs) 175, 177, 182, 196
Burke, Richard (Edmund's brother) 175, 176, 177, 178, 186, 196, 202
Burke, Richard (Edmund's son) 175
Burke, William (friend of Edmund) 17, 18, 169, 171, 196, 203, 205

Bute, Lord *see* Stuart, John
Butler, James, Duke of Ormonde 44
Byres, James 11, 12, 265

Cadogan, William, Earl (CL's grandfather) 213
Caesar, Julius 3, 119
Calais 83, 86, 214, 218, 256
Calcot, Mrs 255
Calvin, John 145
Calzona 71
Camoëns, Luis e 28
　Lusiads 28
Carlisle, Lord *see* Howard, Frederick
Carracche, Agostino 202, 203, 206
Carrache, Annibal 202, 203, 206
Carrache, Ludovico 202, 203, 206
Carton House 239, 253
Cascade of Terni 113
Cavedone, Giacomo 202
Cavendish, Lord John 220
Cavendish, Lord Frederick 220
Cervantes (*Don Quixote*) 63, 64
Chapelle, Claude-François de la 163
Charles I, King of England 260
Charles V, Emperor 159
Charles-Emmanuel III, of Sardinia 146
Chartreuse, La Grande 62, 64
Chartreux, College of 91
Cheyney, Mr 107
Cholmondeley, Sir George, Viscount
　Malpas 30
Cholmondeley, Robert 175
Churchill, Charles and Lady Mary 214, 224
Cicero, Marcus Tulius 5
ciceroni 264, 277
cicisbeo 221, 233, 251, 254
Cincinnatus 118–19
Clanbrassil, Lady 235
Clarence, Earl of 123
Clement XIII, Pope 152
Clent 33
Clinton, Henry Fiennes 82
Cobham, Lord *see* Temple, Richard
Cobham, Lady *see* Temple, Anne
Cochin, Charles-Nicolas 13
coffee-houses 18, 153, 198

Coke, Mr 205
Collier, Mary 83
Colquhon, Katharine 152
connoisseur 12, 175, 264
Conolly, Thomas 219
conversatione 215, 217, 232, 233, 237, 253
Cooper *see* Cowper
Cope, Sir John 147
Corrandini, Gertrude 150
Corregio *see* Allegri, Antonio
Corsica 162
Coryat, Thomas (*Crudities*) 4
Costines (Florence) 252
Cotheret, M. 89
Cowper, George Nassau Clavering, Earl
　Cowper 254
Craftsman, The 49
Crammond, Mr 179, 185
Creagh, Mr 175, 177
Crofts, Thomas 36, 196–97
Currie 137

Dance, George 11
Dansell (GL's servant) 33, 45, 47, 65, 66
Dante 9
D'Arcy, Mary, Lady Holderness 249
Darius 138
dating, Old and New Styles ix
Dauphin, Louis of France 54
da Vinci, Leonardo 207, 209–10, 211
de Bouzoles, Laure-Anne 241, 249
de Craon, Prince Marc 30, 33, 47
de Geismar, Mlle 133, 142
de Kéroualle, Louise, Duchess of
　Portsmouth 221
de Sévigné, Mme 218, 226, 241, 248
Deleyre, Alexandre 155
de Neufville Villeroy, Madeleine Angelique,
　Lady Luxembourg 249
Denny, William 94
de Régnier, Claude-Francois-Louis, Comte
　de Gaetani 237
de Régnier, Madame de Gaetani 245, 254
de Rosenberg, Francis, Comte 252–53
Dessau 136
Devonshire, Earl of 4
de Zuylen, Isabella Agneta Elisabeth 152
Dijon 16, 41, 83, 86, 87, 94, 214, 222

Dilettanti Society 6
Dodsley, Robert 224
Dominichino 203
Don Carlos 50, 57, 70
Douglas, Henry (son of Duke of Queensborough) 107
Dresden 136, 139
dress 10, 83, 107, 120–21, 124, 153, 217, 222, 223, 229, 230, 231, 232, 235, 240
    clerical 126, 152
    country women 90, 95, 96, 104, 246, 256
Drumgold, John 174, 177
Dryden, John 83
Duck, Stephen 82
Dudley, Sir Robert, Earl of Warwick 121
Duquesnoy, Francois 199–200
Dutch parliament 57–58

Edinburgh 143, 153
Edmonstone, Colonel James 154
English, Thomas 175, 190
English tourists 37, 41, 42, 121, 189, 193, 195, 223, 230, 243, 251, 254, 255
    English Assembly 229, 232
    'full of money' 201
    'ignorant' 33
    'Lorded abroad' 103
    at Naples 226, 236–37
    spendthrifts 144
    students in Rome 171, 192, 251
    'they love the English because they love our money' 239
    'very bad' 245
    well-dressed 36
    'worthless fellows' 38
entertainments (concerts, theatre, opera) 88, 140, 153, 157, 159–60, 223, 255, 258
Ernest-Leopold, Prince 114
Erskine, Andrew 153
Exeter, Earl of 11–12
expenses 15–16, 33, 43, 58, 59, 68–69, 71–72, 73, 77, 156, 182, 185, 201–2, 203, 204, 205, 274, 277
    clothes 35–6, 47, 58, 182
    meals, at an Ordinary 31, 92, 140–41
    transport 68, 185
    wine 93

Eyles, Sir Joseph 69, 75

Fannen, Mrs 242
Farinelli 71
Farnese Gallery 188, 193
Farnese, Elizabeth of Parma 57
Faustina *see* Hasse, F. B.
Ferdinand, Prince of Brunswick-Luxembourg 237
Fergusson, Mr 137
Ferney 131
Ferrara 111
Festivals and sights 95
    Carnival, Venice 107–8, 109–10
    Carnival, Florence 123–24
    Christmas Mass, Avignon 164
    Fair, Leipsic 138
    Grande fête, Naples 242
    Lyon 224
    Procession, Nice 163
Fiamingo *see* Duquesnoy, Francois
Fielding, Henry 24
Firmian, Count Karl Joseph von 210, 254
Fitzgerald, Emily Mary, Lady (Emily Lennox's daughter) 253, 254
Fitzgerald, William Robert (Emily Lennox's son) 215, 219, 221, 223, 224, 225, 227, 236, 239, 254, 256, 258
Fitzjames family 249
Fitzwilliam. Richard 36
Fleury, Cardinal de 55
    absolute power of 61–62
Florence 76, 118, 120, 122–23, 147, 152, 161, 215, 230, 231, 232, 250
    Medici Gallery 215, 250
Florence, Duke of 85
Fontainebleau 49, 225
food *see* meals
Fortescue, Mrs 244
Fox, Charles James (CL's third son) 215, 216, 219, 222, 223, 237, 241, 242, 244, 247, 252, 254, 257, 258
Fox, Henry ('Harry', CL's fourth son) 215, 224, 231, 247, 255, 257, 258
Fox, Henry, Lord Holland 213, 216, 219, 220, 221, 223, 225, 226, 229, 231, 233, 235, 236, 238, 240, 241, 244, 246, 248, 250, 252, 254, 255, 256, 258, 259

Fox, Lady Mary, née Fitzpatrick (CL's daughter-in-law) 215, 222, 224, 228, 229, 232, 233, 237, 242, 244, 247, 252, 255, 256, 258
Fox, Stephen (CL's eldest son) 215, 222, 224, 227, 229, 231, 233, 236, 247, 255, 258
Francis I 158–59
Frascati 195
Frederick, King of Prussia 52, 53
Frederick, Prince of Wales 27

Gaetani, Claude-François-Louis, Comte de 237
Gainsborough, Thomas 267
Gallatin, Barthelémy 101
Gaussin, Mme 255
Gay, John 83
   Beggar's Opera 39
Geneva 62–63, 83, 101, 130, 136, 149, 255–56
Genoa 41, 67, 147, 152, 252
   corrupt voting system in 68
Geismar, Mlle de 142
Geoffrin, Marie-Therèse 243
Georg, August, Margave of Baden-Baden 142
George II, King of England 48
Gibbon, Edward 3, 8, 10, 236
Gilpin, William 27
Giorgione 209
Goldsmith, Oliver (*The Traveller*) 218, 232, 256
Gosport 48
Graeme, William, of Bucklyvie 154
Grande Chartreuse La 25, 62–64
Graham, Provost 137
Grant, William, Lord Preston Grange 137
Grassi, Serafina, Padre 158
Gray, Thomas 13, 134
   Elegy Written in a Country Churchyard 134, 160–61
Greville, Fanny 223
Grimaldi 67, 68
Grotto del Cani 246
Grotto of Pausilippo 115
Guastalla 160
Guercino *see* Barbieri, Giovani Francesco
guidebooks 4, 5, 12, 13
Guido *see* Reni

Hagley Hall 23, 26, 53, 67
Halifax, Charles, Lord, Addison's poem to 77
Halsey, Edmund 56
Hamilton, Catherine 217, 236, 238, 244, 245
Hamilton, Charles 245
Hamilton, Gavin 264, 265, 269
Hamilton, Hugh Douglas 170, 182, 190
Hamilton, Sir William 192, 193, 196, 236, 245, 262
Hänni, Jacob (Bos's servant) 141
Harrington, William, Lord 39, 70, 74
Hasse, Fustina Bordoni 106
Hay, Mr 137
Hermitage, Lord Henry 33
Hervey, George, Earl of Bristol 220, 244
Hervey, John, Lord 75
Hervey, Lady Mary, née Lepell 243
Hesse-Rheinfels, Caroline 114
Hickman, Dr 103
Hill, Robert 82
Hobbes, Thomas 4
Hobson, Mrs 228
Hogarth, William 10
Holderness *see* D'Arcy
Holdsworth, Edward 113–14
Holland 129, 135
Holland House 247, 248, 256, 258
Holland, Lord *see* Fox, Henry
Holyrood 136
Horace 5, 84, 131
Howard, Frederick, Earl of Carlisle 221, 243, 258
humour 6, 84–85, 88–90, 108, 123, 133–34
Hunt, Mrs 32
Hyde, Henry 226

inns 166, 231, 233, 276
   generally bad 216, 228
   nastiness of 15
   nasty 220
   variety of 14
Irvine, Mr 137
Italian preachers 108

James II, King of England 112
Jardine, Sir Alexander 152
Jenkins, Thomas 12, 265

Jesuits (in Avignon) 164
Johnson, Samuel 9, 20, 130, 158
Johnston, John, Laird of Grange 19, 129, 132, 133, 134
Jones, Henry 83
Jones, Inigo 4, 121
Jones, Thomas 10
Joseph II, Emperor 189
Julius II, Pope 190
Justinian, Emperor 251
Justiani, Prince and Princess 251

Kaunitz, Prince Wenzel Anton 238
Kaunitz, Countess 245
Keats, John 82
Keene, Benjamin 50, 51
Keith, George, Earl Marischal 129, 135, 136
Keith, John, Earl of Kintore 47
Kelly, Mrs George 88, 106
Kéroualle, Louise de, Duchess of Portsmouth 221
Kildare, Lord, 219, 234, 239, 241, 242, 244, 245, 247, 251
King and the Miller of Mansfield, The 224
Kingsgate 213, 218, 219, 223, 253, 257, 258
Kingston, Duke of 103, 105
knowledge of foreign languages
  French 92, 255
  Italian 255, 258
Knox, John 145

Laocoön (sculpture) 188, 199, 200
Lassels, Richard 4, 270
Leghorn 121, 156, 247
Leinster, Duke of (Emily's husband) 234, 239, 240, 244, 248, 254
Leinster, Emily, Duchess of (CL's sister) 213
  her beauty 253
  'sweet siss' 229
Leipsic 138, 147
Lennox, Caroline
  abandons building castles in the air 235
  admires Mme de Sévigné 218, 226, 241, 248
  city and environs of Geneva delightful 256
  confident traveller 213–14
  congratulates sister and brother-in-law on their ennoblement 234
  considers men in Naples as ignorant and vulgar as the women 237–38
  daily routine of 217, 238
  delights in playing loo 217, 243–44
  detests Voltaire 224–45, 227, but gives his Works to sister 255
  dreads 'the Nasty Sea' 255
  envies Swiss people their 'Affluence without Luxury and Religion without Superstition' 257
  feels 'sad horror' towards Mt Cenis 254
  holds Goldsmith's *Traveller* in high regard 256
  laments decline in social eating 233
  Milan the 'most sociable' place in Italy 254
  regards invention of printing as universally important 245
  strong powers of observation 217, 248
  suffers from erysipelas 242
  'thankful to have ended our tedious peregrination so well' 258
  vivid description of Neapolitan society 236–39
  'we are but travellers in this world' 253
Lennox, Charles, Duke of Richmond (CL's father) 213
Lennox, Lady Cecilia Margaret (CL's youngest sister) 248, 250, 251, 253, 254, 257
Lennox, Louisa Augusta (CL's sister) 219, 221, 244, 253
Lennox, Sarah née Cadogan (CL's mother) 213, 221
Leo X, Pope 190
Léopold Joseph, Duke of Lorraine 33
Leopold I, Grand Duke of Tuscany 252
Le Sueur, Eustache *La Maladie d'Alexandre* 170, 179, 263
letters: cost, posting and receiving of 16–18, 91, 227
letters of introduction normally essential for travelling 11, 29–30, 67, 138, 184
Leyden 129
Libertine, The, or *Don John* (Thomas Shadwell) 121

288 INDEX

Liegois, Mrs 255
Lloyd, William 261
Lomazzo, Paolo 211
Lorain 27, 36–37, 43
Loretto, Holy House 111–12, 149
Louis, Dauphin of France, birth of 54
Louis XIV, King of France 61, 180
Louis XV, King of France 26, 60–61, 126
Lovino, Bernardo 209
Lowth, Robert 81
Lumisden, Andrew 155
Luna 216
Lunéville 24, 25, 26, 29, 30, 34
   dearer than Paris 36
   GL disliked because of 'worthless' English there 38, 42
Lunsford, Sir Thomas 81
Luxembourg *see* de Neufville Villeroy
Lyon (Lyons) 25, 41, 60, 83, 94, 98, 100, 166, 214, 221, 225
Lyttelton, Charles (GL's brother) 33
Lyttelton, Christian, 'Chrissy' (GL's sister) 23, 30, 31, 34, 35, 36, 39, 49, 56, 69, 72, 74, 75, 77, 78
Lyttelton, Christian (née Temple (GL's mother) 23, 34, 35, 36, 37, 38, 40, 43, 49, 50, 54, 59, 63, 64, 66, 69, 71, 72, 74, 78
Lyttelton, George
   aware that his purpose was 'Improvement and not Show' but latter necessary for former 45, 58
   delighted to be in 'the Suite of an Ambassador' 47
   encouraged Pope in patriotism 3, 77
   expenses at Lunéville 36
   has access to 'Secret intelligence' 43
   his publications 27–28
   his reaction to 'the Gosport affair' 48–49
   hoped to acquire excellence in spoken French and Italian 40
   impressive knowledge of European politics 26, 51–54
   Lunéville his 'School of Breeding' 42
   makes robust defence of Louis XV of France 60–62
   shared Whig hatred of arbitrary power 26, 62
   suffers from 'Distemper' 58
   unable to keep journal equal to William Bromley 32
   verses addressed to Pope and to Poyntz 23–24, 75, 77
   very conscious of importance of dress 35, 47
   'weary of losing money at cards' 33
   wishes to move to Soissons 34, 38
Lyttelton, Molly (GL's sister) 23, 31, 36, 69, 72
Lyttelton, Sir Richard (GL's uncle) 23, 261
Lyttelton, Richard (GL's brother) 51
Lyttelton, Sir Thomas (GL's father) 15–16, 23, 25, 26
   letter of reprimand to GL 68–70, 129
   Thomas Smith his illegitimate son 49
Lyttelton, Thomas (GL's brother) 33, 44, 49, 51

Macartney, Sir George 238
Macleane, Lauchlin 175, 177, 179, 185, 190
Magliabechi, Antonio 83
Mahony, Anne, Countess 217, 237, 238, 244, 245, 251
Malcolm, David 177
Mallet, David 226
Mallet, Paul-Henri 154
Malpas, Viscount *see* Cholmondeley
Malta 41
Manlius 119
Mann, Sir Horace 11, 17, 215, 217, 232, 253, 264
   conversatione 215, 217, 232–33, 237, 253
Mannheim, 'a very bad court' 130, 136, 140
Mantua 159–60
Mantua, Duke of 260
Marlborough, Duke of 23, 99
Marlborough, Duchess of 23, 27
Margrave of Baden-Durlach 141
Marseilles 76, 77, 215, 229, 231
Massei, Marquis Scipio 19
Masson, Antoine 264
Maxwell, Mary 245
Maxwell, Willielma, Lady Gleorchy 245
meals 93–94, 99
Mengs, Anton Raphael 266
Michael Angelo 5, 9, 170, 187–89, 190, 194, 197, 202, 205, 206, 207, 208, 261, 266

Middlesex, Lord *see* Sackville, Charles
Milan 13, 19, 25, 41, 65, 67, 75, 104, 105, 108, 131, 133, 146, 158, 208, 215, 230, 233, 253–54
   Grand Hospital 104–5
Milton, John 4, 24, 28, 29
Minerva 190
Mirpoix, Mme. 249
Mitchell, Andrew 135, 136
Modena 77, 215, 230
money 68, 276
Montagu, Lady Elizabeth 251, 257
Montagu, Lady Mary Wortley 7
Montagu, Robert, Duke of Manchester 105–6
Montmélian 215
Montpellier 165
monuments
   Rome 119
   Verona (amphitheatre) 157
Morecroft family 89, 107
Morgan, Lady Sydney 7
Morrison, Colin 150, 265
Morrison, Robert 176
Moses (sculpture) 189
Môtiers 130-1, 144
Mount Cenis 13–14, 65, 66, 102–3, 131, 183–84, 215, 227, 228, 229, 241, 252, 254
Murray, James, Earl of Dunbar 164
Murray, Marjorie, Lady Inverness 164
museums
   'Museum Worsleyanum' 261
   Museum Philarmonicum 156
Myrton, Sir Robert 59

Namur 86, 87
Nancy 224
Naples 14, 25, 41, 77, 114, 115, 131, 148, 150, 215, 216, 231, 247, 250
   'disagreeable place to live in' 251
Netterville and Nugent 201, 204
Neufchatel 131, 144, 147
Nevay, James 269
Newburgh, Charlotte Maria, Countess of 237
Nicene Creed 163
Nicholl, Sir Charles Gunter 108
Northumberland, Dukes of 216

Northumberland, Lady, née Seymour 243
Nugent, Dr. Christopher 175, 177, 190, 196
Nugent, John 182
Nugent, Thomas 12

O'Brien, William 171
Offaly, Earl of 223
Orleans 25, 41
Orleans, Duke de 55
Ormond *see* Butler, James
Orr, Mr 137
Osborn, Mr 23
Ossory, John, Lord 237
Otway, Thomas (*Venice Preserved*) 132
Oxford, Lady (Susannah Harley) 236
Ozier, Mr 182

Padua 25, 41, 108, 153
Page, Mrs 92, 113
paintings 156
   Albani, Francesco, *Apollo and the Seasons* 122
   Alves, James, Boswell's miniature 155
   Barry, James, *Adam and Eve* 196–97, 203
   Barry, James, *Philoctetes on the Island of Lemnos* 201, 204, 205
   Barry, James, *Progress of Human Culture* 173
   Carrache, Agostino, *Assumption of the Virgin* 202
   da Vinci, *The Last Supper* 209–10
   Guercino, *Mystic Marriage of St Catherine* 218
   Raphael, fresco of the story of Cupid and Psyche 187
   Reni, Guido, *Aurora* 218, 251
   Reni, Guido, figure of Christ 202
   Rubens, *L'Adoration des Rois* 264
   Titian, *Les Pélerins d'Emmaus* 264
   Vanloo, Carl, *Adoration des Bergers* 264
   Vanloo, Carl, *Le Mariage de la Vierge* 264
Palladio, Andrea 263
Panshaw, Mr 182
Paoli, General 132, 162
Paris 25, 26, 34, 41, 43, 243, 249
   Academy of St Luke 170, 178
   agreeable 126
   expense of 47, 73

opera in 126
quiet of 125
where to stay 273–74
Parrhasius 201
Parma 131, 147, 149, 152, 230
Parthenope 148
Pascal, Blaise 218, 247
Pavia, Battle of 159
Pelham-Holles, Thomas, Duke of
    Newcastle-upon-Tyne 220
Petty, William, Earl of Shelburne 185–86
Philip V, King of Spain 57
Pierre, Jean-Baptiste Marie 181, 195
Pindar 191
Piranesi, Giovanni Battista 263
Pitt, Billy (brother of Thomas) 31
Pitt, Christopher 81, 115
Pitt, Marcia (née Morgan) 237
Pitt, Mrs 116
Pitt, Nanny 51–52
Pitt, Thomas (husband of 'Cissy' Lyttelton)
    23, 31, 36
Pitt, William, Earl of Chatham 134, 161,
    244, 259
Place d'Espagne 171, 189
Placentia 149, 230
Plato 191
Pliny the Elder 13, 156
Plowden, William 72, 75
Pompeii 218, 246–47
Pope, Alexander 3, 24, 77, 81, 86, 143
Potsdam 135
Poussin, Nicolas 12, 170, 187, 199–200
Poyntz, Stephen 37, 38, 39, 44, 45, 47, 55, 58,
    69, 71, 75, 78
    GL in entourage of 26
    GL's admiration for 56, 59
    letter from 46
    ordered to Paris 43
    role model for GL 23
Pretender, Old *see* Stuart, James Francis
    Edward
Pretender, Young *see* Stuart, Charles
    Edward
Priam, King 153
prices *see* expenses
Pringle, Robert, Lord Edgefield 137
Provence 41

Prussia, King of 52, 53

Quadrille, popularity of 6, 33, 38, 44, 136
Quadruple Alliance 57, 70
Queen Caroline 76
Queensborough, Duke of 107

Raphael 5, 187–88, 193, 194, 202, 205, 206,
    208, 209, 211, 261
Ray, Alexander 165
Remarks on Several Parts of Italy (Addison)
    12–13, 270–71
Rembrandt 211
Reni, Guido 202, 203, 206, 211, 218, 251
René, Louis-Charles, Comte de Marboeuf
    162–63
Reynolds, Sir Joshua 3, 20, 170–71, 173, 175,
    176, 182, 187, 190, 195, 202, 203–4, 204,
    205, 261, 267, 269
    Burke on 20
Rheims 222
Rhone valley 100, 222, 225
Richardson, Jonathan 261
Richelieu 61
Richmond Hill 222
Ridley, Glocester 81
Rimini 131
Ripperda, John-William, Duke of Ripperda
    39, 43, 44, 191
Robertson, William 159
Rolle, Edward 87, 89, 93, 114, 126–27
Rome 25, 41, 75, 76, 131, 154, 216, 231, 250
    expensive 77
    Bos desperate to see 136
    'exceeds all that can be seen or imagined'
        243
    advice on visiting 277
    Académie de France 264–65
Romulus 3
Rosa, Salvator 184–85
Ross, Colonel 130
Rousseau, Jean-Jacques 131, 134, 136, 144,
    149, 156
Royal Academy 20, 170, 173
    founding of 178
Rubens, Sir Peter Paul 194, 209, 211, 261

Sackville, Charles 82, 83, 86, 87, 89, 103, 105

St Anthony of Padua 153
St Dizier 214
St Gille, Mme 229
St Omer 29, 214, 220
Sandby, Paul 27
San Ildefonso 57
Santa Cruz, Marquis of 65, 66
Sardinia, King of (Charles Emmanuel III) 67, 101, 145–46, 151 *see also* Turin, King of
Schalken, Godfried 211
Schaw family 137, 154, 155
Scott, Henry, Duke of Buccleuch 251
Scott, Henry, Earl of Delorain, Viscount Hermitage 33
Seckendorf, Frederick Graf von 55
Selwyn, George 243
Senesino 71
Sestof 107
Shakespeare, William 86, 123, 132
  Two Gentlemen of Verona 156
Sharp, Samuel 15
Shirley, Sewallis, 1st Earl Ferrers 106
Shuttleworth, Sir Richard 94
Sidney Biddulph 258
Sienna 25, 41, 120, 121, 276
Sinclair, George, Lord Woodhall 137
Sistine Chapel 187, 188, 266
Skinner, Brinley 122
Sleigh, Dr Fenn 169, 198–99, 199
Smith, Thomas, Lieutenant 48
  Sir George Lyttelton's illegitimate son 49
Sm[yth], Mr 123
Soissons 19, 23, 25, 26, 34, 37–38
Soleure 131, 143
Sophocles 201
Spain, Princess of, Maria Luisa 159
Spence, Joseph
  authority on landscape gardening 84
  Cascine 122
  crossing Mt Cenis 102–3
  description of Cascade of Terni 113
  descriptive skill 86–87, 87–88, 90, 95, 100–1
  devoted to his mother *passim*; he was her 'straggling, wandering, Prodigal Son' 125
  education 81
  'England is the country to live in' 85
  Essay on Pope 81
  fascinated by 'humble poets' 82
  gifted raconteur 19
  humour of 84–85, 88, 90, 95, 123
  ordained and held college livings 82
  Oxford Professor of Poetry 81
  unrivalled as anecdotist 83
  vivid accounts of
    domestic burglary in Rome 113–14
    hospitality from French country gentleman 99
    monastery 91–92
    nunnery 95
    river at Dijon 96–97
    Whitsun procession 95
  wide learning evident in *Polymetis* 82
Spence, Mirabella (mother of JS) 83–84, 86
  expected to follow JS's route by 'the Map [which] lyes at her right hand' 84, 104, 113, 120
  assumed *au fait* with Horace 84, 122
  'I wou'd not tell Fibs to my Mother for all the world' 113
Spence, Richard (JS's brother) 89, 91, 93, 120, 126
Spencer, Robert, Earl of Sunderland 30
Splitzerber and Daum 136
Spoleto 131, 147
Stanhope, William (later Earl of Harrington) 39, 43–44, 57, 68, 70, 74
Stanhope, Lady Amelia ('Emily') 251
Stanislaus, King of Poland 126
Sterne, Laurence 133
Stewart, Margaret 152
Stowe 56
Strange, Robert 155
Stuart, Charles Edward, 'Young Pretender' 147
Stuart, James, 'Old Pretender' 72
Stuart, James 'Athenian' 169, 175, 198
Stuart, John, Viscount Mountstuart 153, 154
Stuart, John, Earl of Bute 154, 161, 244
Susa 215
Sutherland, Lady 245
Swallowfield, manor house 56

Swift, Jonathan 83, 226
  admired GL 24
  Dermot and Sheelah 134, 148
  Gulliver's Travels 5
  Tale of a Tub 123
Switzerland 131, 149
  Swiss people 257

Tavistock, Marquess Francis 252
Temple, Anne, née Halsey, Lady Cobham 43, 76
Temple, Richard, Lord Cobham 43, 60, 74
Temple, William Johnson 166
Teniers, David 211
Terni 131
Theodore, Karl, Elector 139
Thomson, James, GL edited poems of 24
Thrale, Hester 261
Titian 9, 170, 171, 172, 193–94, 199–200, 202, 205, 206, 210, 211
Tivoli 10, 195
Trankavila, Princess de 217, 238
travel
  diligence 14, 166
  gondola (in Venice) 106
  Italian chaise 29, 45
  'Post Waggon' (for luggage) 138
  post-chaise 94
  prices 272–73
  river 97
  road 29, 86, 103, 125, 166, 167, 250, 257, 272–73
  routes 275–76
  sea 29, 86, 111, 272
treaty of
  the Quadruple Alliance 57–58
  Seville 75
  Vienna 58
Trevor, John Morley 82
Trevor, Richard 82
Tully *see* Cicero
Tunbridge Ware (Tunbridge Wells) 92
Turin 18, 25, 41, 65, 105, 131, 149, 215, 227, 229, 252
  King of 65, 66, 185
Turretin, Jean Alphonse 101
Tuscany 25, 41, 156, 161
Tuscany, Grand Duke of, Leopold 159

Tylney, John, Earl 237

Upton, Clotworthy 215, 224, 231, 241, 245, 247, 254
Utrecht 129, 134

Van Dyck, Sir Anthony 194, 211
Vasari, Giorgio 209
Venice 25, 70, 105–6, 109, 147, 152, 247, 257
  carnival 109–10, 123–24
Venus de Medicis (sculpture) 188
Vergani 201–2, 204, 205
Veronese, Paulo 194
Versailles 61, 180
Vesuvius, Mt 83, 115, 116–17, 118, 246
Vienna 254
Villa Ludovisi 199–200, 263
Villa Medici 189
Villars, Duke of 66
Villetri 216
Virgil 5
  tomb of 115–16, 132, 133, 148, 159, 160
virtuoso 150, 159
visits 91–92
  Cascine, Florence 122
  convent and church, Pavia 158
  Grotto del Cani 246
  King's museum, Portici 218, 244–45
  Lyon 224
  Lyon, country house 225
  Medici gallery 232
  Mt Vesuvius 116–17
  Pompeii 218, 246–47
  theatre (Paris) 126, (Lyon) 223–24
  Virgil's tomb 115–16
  wine-making, Florence 123
Viterbo 120, 216
Voltaire 28, 131, 136, 145, 149, 218, 224, 227, 255, 258
von Zinzendorf, Count Nicholas Ludwig 43

Walpole, Edward 73, 74
Walpole, Horatio (later Baron Walpole) 17, 37, 38, 39, 43, 70, 264
Walpole, Sir Robert 30, 31, 47
Watson-Wentworth, Charles, Marquess of Rockingham 220, 252

Wavell, Daniel 88, 89, 91, 93, 107, 108, 112
weather: Lyon 98; Florence 121–22, 252; Milan 75; Mt Cenis 227, 228; Naples 238, 242, 244, 246; Paris 125, 177, 178; Rome 247; Soleure 143; Venice 106
Wentworth, William, Earl Fitzwilliam 196–97, 243, 257
West, Benjamin 267
West, Gilbert 55
Westphalia 147
Wilkes, John 131, 134, 148, 150, 161, 179
William III, King of England 99
Williams, Charles Hanbury 59
Williams-Wynn, Sir Watkin 27
Winchester 107
Windham, William 34
wine 1, 15, 34, 59, 84, 123, 130, 142, 147, 162, 211, 231, 274
Winterslow 241, 247
women: in Florence 253; in France 89–90, 97, 98, 222, 229, 230, 241; in Italy 104, 216, 217–18, 230, 237, 241, 246; in Naples 149, 216, 238, 240, 251; in Paris 126; in Rome 232, 251; in Sienna 120–21; in Turin 145

Worsley, Lady Betty 217
Worsley, Richard, 'the rather pert son' 217, 236
Worsley, Sir Richard, 'his Museum Worsleyanum' 261
Worsley, Sir Thomas 217, 236
Wycherley, William 83
Wyndham (or Windham), Charles 62, 64, 65, 67, 71
Wyndham (or Windham), Sir William 62, 71

Yearsley, Ann 83
Young, Arthur 10, 15
Young, Edward 81

Zenophon 191
Zinzendorf, Count Nicholas 43
Zondadari, Cardinal 76
Zonzandari (?), Cardinal 76
Zuylen, Isabella Agneta de 152